The Two Koreas and their Global Engagements

Andrew David Jackson
Editor

The Two Koreas and their Global Engagements

palgrave
macmillan

Editor
Andrew David Jackson
Monash University
Melbourne, VIC, Australia

ISBN 978-3-030-90760-0   ISBN 978-3-030-90761-7 (eBook)
https://doi.org/10.1007/978-3-030-90761-7

© The Editor(s) (if applicable) and The Author(s), under exclusive license to Springer Nature Switzerland AG 2022
This work is subject to copyright. All rights are solely and exclusively licensed by the Publisher, whether the whole or part of the material is concerned, specifically the rights of translation, reprinting, reuse of illustrations, recitation, broadcasting, reproduction on microfilms or in any other physical way, and transmission or information storage and retrieval, electronic adaptation, computer software, or by similar or dissimilar methodology now known or hereafter developed.
The use of general descriptive names, registered names, trademarks, service marks, etc. in this publication does not imply, even in the absence of a specific statement, that such names are exempt from the relevant protective laws and regulations and therefore free for general use.
The publisher, the authors and the editors are safe to assume that the advice and information in this book are believed to be true and accurate at the date of publication. Neither the publisher nor the authors or the editors give a warranty, expressed or implied, with respect to the material contained herein or for any errors or omissions that may have been made. The publisher remains neutral with regard to jurisdictional claims in published maps and institutional affiliations.

This Palgrave Macmillan imprint is published by the registered company Springer Nature Switzerland AG
The registered company address is: Gewerbestrasse 11, 6330 Cham, Switzerland

*Dedicated to the Memory of
Pamela (Pam) Hibbs CBE, OBE, FRCN (1935–2021),
Healthcare Pioneer*

Acknowledgments

I wish to acknowledge Camille Davies, Manikandan Murthy, and John Justin Thomyyar who provided invaluable support and great patience throughout this project. Thanks also go to Isaac Lee, Ji-yoon An, Perry Iles, Roald Maliangkay, Codruţa Sîntionean, Maria Rost Rublee, and Sonja Häussler, whose feedback and help significantly improved the work. Finally, I thank Sharron Pickering, Kevin Foster, Lucien Brown, Ahn Heekyung, and Bae Wonae for facilitating the research leave that made this work possible.

This work was supported by the Core University Program for Korean Studies through the Ministry of Education of the Republic of Korea and the Korean Studies Promotion Service of the Academy of Korean Studies (AKS-2017-OLU-2250002).

A Note on Romanization

We have used McCune-Reischauer to Romanize Korean, Hepburn for Japanese, and Pinyin (without diacritics) for Chinese, except in the case of commonly accepted alternative spellings of places like Pyongyang and Seoul and other words like taekwondo and Hangul. The names of many authors, film directors, and actors are better known by their Revised Romanization spellings, and in these cases, we have appended the McCune-Reischauer spellings as well. We have used the Korean order of names with surname first and given names hyphenated, as in Ch'oe Nam-sŏn. The exception is in the case of well-known names like Park Chung Hee and Syngman Rhee.

Contents

1 The Two Koreas and Their Global Engagements   1
Andrew David Jackson

Part I   Film

2 The Dictator's Daughter and the Rising Sun: Scars of Colonialism in South Korean Cinema During the Park Geun-hye Era   35
Russell Edwards

3 Fighting "The Man": The Production of Historical Knowledge in Cho Kŭn-hyŏn's *26 Years*   59
Niall McMahon

4 Squaring the Circle: *The Schoolgirl's Diary* and North Korean Film in the Era of Marketization   83
Andrew David Jackson

Part II   Music

5 Singing Through Impossible Modernization: *Sopyonje* and National Cinema in the Era of Globalization   117
Seung-hwan Shin

6   Valorizing the Old: Honoring Aging Practitioners
    of Korean Traditions   141
    Roald Maliangkay

7   The Transmedial Aesthetics of K-Pop Music Videos:
    References to Western Film Cultures   161
    Ute Fendler

Part III   Transformed Language

8   Korean Language, Power, and National Identity   187
    Young-Key Kim-Renaud

9   Swearing Granny Restaurants: An International
    Perspective on Rudeness in Korean   223
    Soyeon Kim and Lucien Brown

Part IV   Society and Space

10 Korean "Multicultural Literature" and Discourses
    About Koreanness   259
    Andreas Schirmer

11 Realizing *Filiality Rights*: The Role of Filial Piety
    in Localizing Human Rights in the Contemporary
    Korean Context   289
    Hong-Jae Park

12 Natural Consequences for Koreans in Japan: The
    Fluid Nature of the Identity Formation of Chongryon
    Koreans   311
    Min Hye Cho

13 North Korea All at Sea: Aspiration, Subterfuge,
    and Engagement in a Global Commons, 2020, Dark
    Fleets and Empty Streets   337
    Robert Winstanley-Chesters

Index   363

NOTES ON CONTRIBUTORS

Lucien Brown is Senior Lecturer of Korean Studies at Monash University. His research focuses on linguistic politeness. He is the author of *Korean Honorifics and Politeness in Second Language Learning* (John Benjamins), co-author of *Korean: A Comprehensive Grammar* (Routledge), and co-editor of *The Handbook of Korean Linguistics* (Wiley Blackwell).

Min Hye Cho is a Lecturer at BNU-HKBU United International College in Zhuhai, China. Her research primarily focuses on the field of the sociolinguistics of minority group's language education. Her interests center around Korean and English language education, various minority groups' cultural and linguistic identities, and their multilingual abilities.

Russell Edwards film critic, filmmaker, and Ph.D. candidate, teaches Asian Cinemas at Melbourne's RMIT University. A former President of the Film Critics Circle of Australia, Russell spent a decade reviewing films from the Asian film festival circuit for international trade publication *Variety* and has been a long-time adviser to the Busan International Film Festival.

Ute Fendler is chair of Romance, Literary, and Comparative Studies at the University of Bayreuth (Germany). Her research interests include comparative romance literary and film studies (Caribbean, West Africa, Indian Ocean, South America), iconographies, transmediality, popular culture.

Andrew David Jackson is currently an Associate Professor of Korean Studies at Monash University, Melbourne, where he has worked since 2017. Prior to this, he taught Korean Studies at the University of Copenhagen, Denmark. He obtained his Ph.D. in Korean history from the School of Oriental and African Studies, the University of London, in 2011.

Soyeon Kim is a Ph.D. candidate at Monash University researching family language policy for cross-cultural families in Australia and South Korea. Her educational background includes an M.Ed. from the University of Queensland, and she has been in the teaching field since she acquired a B.Ed. in 2004. She also currently enjoys teaching Korean language to students at Monash University. Her research interest is not only limited to Korean language education in an Australian context but also looks at the language from various socio-linguistics perspectives.

Young-Key Kim-Renaud is Professor Emeritus of Korean Language and Culture and International Affairs and Senior Advisor to the Institute for Korean Studies at the George Washington University. She is a former President of the International Circle of Korean Linguistics (ICKL, 1990–1992) and previous Editor-in-Chief of its journal, *Korean Linguistics* (2002–2014).

Roald Maliangkay is Associate Professor in Korean Studies at the Australian National University. Fascinated by the mechanics of cultural policy and the convergence of major cultural phenomena, Maliangkay analyzes cultural industries and consumption in Korea from the early twentieth century to the present. He is the author of *Broken Voices: Postcolonial Entanglements and the Preservation of Korea's Central Folksong Traditions* (University of Hawai'i Press, 2017) and co-editor of *K-pop: The International Rise of the Korean Music Industry* (Routledge, 2015).

Niall McMahon is a Korea Foundation Postdoctoral Fellow and Early Career Researcher in Perth, Western Australia. His main research interests are South Korean cinema, the historical film genre, and the war film genre, with a specific focus on films that depict the Japanese colonial period and the Korean War.

Hong-Jae Park is a Senior Lecturer with the School of Social Sciences, Western Sydney University, Australia. He is a native of the Republic of Korea who has maintained a long-standing interest in future-oriented filial piety (intergenerational solidarity) and has conducted research projects on later-life migration, elder abuse, and social isolation among older migrants.

Andreas Schirmer is Head of the Korean section at the Department of Asian Studies at Palacký University Olomouc. He coordinates a Korean Studies network in Central and Eastern Europe, overseeing exchanges between sixteen institutions in ten countries. His current research relates to Translation Studies or the literary representation of contested issues.

Seung-hwan Shin lectures in the Department of East Asian Languages and Literatures at the University of Pittsburgh. He specializes in Korean cinema and popular culture. He is currently working on a book project on the film renaissance of South Korea in the 1990s and 2000s.

Robert Winstanley-Chesters is a geographer, Lecturer at the University of Leeds and Bath Spa University, and Member of Wolfson College, Oxford, formerly of Birkbeck, University of London, Australian National University, and Cambridge University. He is the author of *Environment, Politics, and Ideology in North Korea* (Lexington, 2014), *Vibrant Matters(s): Fish, Fishing and Community in North Korea and Neighbours* (Springer, 2019), and *New Goddess of Mt Paektu: Myth and Transformation in North Korean Landscape* (Black Halo/Amazon KDP, 2020). Robert is currently researching North Korean necro-mobilities and other difficult or unwelcome bodies and materials in Korean/East Asian historical geography.

ABBREVIATIONS

c.   Circa
C.   Chinese
CE   Common Era
cf.   Latin "confer" (compare to)
J.   Japanese
K.   Korean
lit. Literally
n   Footnote
n.d. Not Dated

CHRONOLOGY

This chronology includes the kingdoms, dynasties, and leaders featured in this book.

Historical Chronology of Korea

Unified Silla	668–935 CE
Koryŏ	918–1392
Chosŏn	1392–1910
Japanese colonial period	1910–1945

South Korean Presidents (And Dates in Office)

1948–1960	Syngman Rhee (Yi Sŭng-man; born: 1875 died: 1965)
1960–1961	Yun Po-sun (Yun Po-sŏn; 1897–1990)
1961–1979	Park Chung Hee (Pak Chŏng-hŭi; 1917–1979)
1980–1988	Chun Doo Hwan (Chŏn Tu-hwan; 1931–2021)
1988–1993	Roh Tae Woo (No T'ae-u; 1932–2021)
1993–1998	Kim Young Sam (Kim Yŏng-sam; 1927–2015)
1998–2003	Kim Dae Jung (Kim Tae-jung; 1924–2009)
2003–2008	Roh Moo-hyun (No Mu-hyŏn; 1946–2009)
2008–2013	Lee Myung-bak (Yi Myŏng-bak; 1941)
2013–2017	Park Geun-hye (Pak Kŭn-hye; 1952)
2017–Present	Moon Jae-in (Mun Chae-in; 1953)

North Korean Rulers

1948–1994	Kim Il Sung (Kim Il-sŏng) (1912–1994)
1994–2011	Kim Jong Il (Kim Chŏng-il) (1947–2011)
2011–Present	Kim Jong Un (Kim Chŏng-ŭn) (1982)

List of Figures

Fig. 2.1	Yi removes his *Hinomaru* facepaint in *The Tooth and the Nail*	48
Fig. 2.2	The scar of colonialism is still present after "Japan" is removed	49
Fig. 2.3	Ok-bun reveals her scars and tattoos to the US House of Representatives in *I Can Speak*	50
Fig. 4.1	Opening of *The Schoolgirl's Diary*, Su-ryŏn returning from school	98
Fig. 4.2	Su-ryŏn waits in vain for her father to come to her school's open day	99
Fig. 4.3	Su-ryŏn waiting at school dissolves to an older Su-ryŏn returning from school	100
Fig. 4.4	Su-ryŏn hides from her teacher who visits her home	101
Fig. 9.1	Halmŏni does not meet Trickid-z gaze (Screen capture used with permission from CKOONY)	234
Fig. 9.2	The telop at the bottom reads "even though he is being sworn at, he is too happy" (Screen capture used with permission from CKOONY)	236
Fig. 9.3	Halmŏni and Trickid-z are all smiles at the end of the visit (Screen capture used with permission from CKOONY)	237
Fig. 9.4	*Kaejiral* is censored in the telops and followed by laughter marks (Screen capture used with permission from CKOONY)	238
Fig. 9.5	Nonverbal behaviors produced by Morris (Screen captures used with permission from Heechulism)	241

Fig. 11.1 The gap in poverty rate (between 18–65-year-olds and 66-year-olds or over; figure by author) (Source of information: OECD Social and Welfare Statistics [Income distribution]: Poverty rate [2018]) 299

LIST OF TABLES

Table 9.1   Taxonomy of impoliteness strategies (Culpeper 1996)   232
Table 9.2   Viewer opinions on Yangp'yŏng Tofu video   239
Table 9.3   Viewer opinions on The Wiener's Circle video   244

CHAPTER 1

The Two Koreas and Their Global Engagements

Andrew David Jackson

From the early 1990s, globalization—or the integration of national economies into international flows of trade, investment, capital, information, and people—was widely accepted as the driving force behind the new post-global Cold War order (Kim 2000a, 15–16; Vaish 2010, 2; Potter 2009, xv).[1] I am writing this chapter in the aftermath of the global COVID-19 pandemic, during which one cornerstone of globalization—the free movement of peoples around the globe—was severely restricted. At the height of the pandemic in 2020, even the most basic and necessary reasons for movement—to visit the sick, elderly and weak or to attend funerals—were frequently restricted. Governments sealed borders and closed off avenues of compassion, and the bulwark of global connectivity became a source of widespread fear. How far this global pandemic marks an end or a partial end to the wave of international integration that started in the 1990s remains to be seen. Still, the

A. D. Jackson (✉)
Monash University, Melbourne, VIC, Australia
e-mail: andrew.david.jackson@monash.edu

© The Author(s), under exclusive license to Springer Nature Switzerland AG 2022
A. D. Jackson (ed.), *The Two Koreas and their Global Engagements*,
https://Doi.org/10.1007/978-3-030-90761-7_1

pandemic will undoubtedly lead to a rethink on the interconnectedness of a world shaped by globalization.

Three central factors helped create the greater global integration that emerged in the 1990s. The collapse of the former Soviet Union and its satellite states brought an end to the global Cold War politics that had fragmented international affairs for almost half a century. Globalization was also significantly enhanced by the 1995 formation of the World Trade Organization (WTO), which helped liberalize the international movement of goods and services. Finally, a communications revolution facilitated the global spread of digitalized information (Kim 2000a, 13). Of course, as many researchers have observed, globalization in the form of trading networks and the establishment of flows of information has been a feature of human societies for millennia (Potter 2009, xv). However, the 1990s brought a more specific wave of globalization, distinguished from prior waves by the substantially larger flow of international trade and the integration of developing countries, especially those in East Asia, within the interlinked chains of finance, capital, production, and the information economy (Kim 2000a, 15–16). These new communication tools, markets, actors, rules, and institutions combined to intensify the flows of capital, people, and information across state borders that were becoming increasingly porous (Kim 2000a, 16). And yet, this was not just an economic or political process. Globalization also encouraged the spread of social and cultural practices worldwide; these were flows driven by the internet and the development of new digital technologies (Kim 2000a, 16).

The social and cultural impact of globalization has provoked some of the most sustained criticisms. Some feared and still fear that globalization threatens distinctive local cultural traits, destroys traditional social orders, and destabilizes the unique identities of individual communities and countries (Baker 2009, 171; Chang 2009, 2). Others criticize globalization for taking representative and responsible decision-making about important cultural or political issues away from people at local levels and passing power to the vagaries of the market (Kim 2000a, 7). Far from being a level playing field leading to more significant interactions between economies, societies, and cultures, globalization in some quarters is seen as a process that maintains the greater economic and political advantages of Western countries (in particular, the USA) over the rest of the world (Vaish 2010, 9). At the same time, the defenders of globalization have celebrated it as the start of a new world that had been liberated from Global Cold War-era tyranny, a world that embraced free markets, free trade, and free ideas (Potter 2009, xv). Some theorists confidently predicted the gradual withering away of the state in the face of a "juggernaut" of greater international integration fostered by globalization (Vaish 2010, 1; Kim 2000a, 5). However, the 2020 Global Pandemic—which was partly fueled by unrestricted international travel—has shown these predictions to have been premature, as states installed barriers to the free movement of people.

Chang Yun-shik observes that a large amount of research into globalization focuses on the processes through which the world is becoming a more uniform, integrated system, but the studies that are most pertinent to this volume are those that analyze the individual experiences of nations and regions under globalization (Chang 2009, 1). These include the significant number of general studies about South Korea's political and economic development under globalization by Samuel Kim (2000b), Lewis and Sesay (2002), Kim et al. (2008), and Chang et al. (2009). Most of the focus in this research has been on the South Korean economy, understandably because of the global impact of economic crises that have occurred roughly once every decade (in 1996–1997, 2008, and 2020). Another group of scholars has emphasized the impact of globalization upon specific areas of national or regional societies, economies, and cultures.[2] Darrell William Davis and Emily Yueh-yu Yeh (2008), SooJeong Ahn (2011), Chua Beng Huat (2012), and Michael Fuhr (2016), for example, have investigated how globalization has combined with greater regional integration to help the rapid domestic and international expansion of South Korean cultural industries, in particular cinema and popular music. Viniti Vaish's 2010 investigation of the effect of globalization processes upon language in Asia also includes a discussion of the international spread of Korean and the increasing predominance of English use in South Korea.

This current volume builds on the work of the latter group of scholars by focusing on the impact of globalization upon Korean culture, society, and language. The twenty-five years since the promulgation of Kim Young Sam's *segyehwa* policy have seen a significant rise in the perceived value placed upon the internationalization of Korean culture. The global promotion of Korean culture has continued to be a central and defining part of South Korean government policy, demonstrating its value as a soft power tool for the national interest (as we see below). This book also includes a feature that is absent from other globalization studies in the Korean context, which focus exclusively on South Korea (The Republic of Korea, ROK). Any discussion of the impact of internationalizing forces upon the Korean Peninsula should include some consideration of North Korea (the Democratic People's Republic of Korea or DPRK), which along with its southern neighbor and competitor, also claims to be the sole, legitimate representative of the Korean *minjok* (ethnic nation). Of course, there is an issue with including the DPRK in the discussion, as has been pointed out in several studies of globalization that begin with the premise that what is peculiar about globalization and the Korean experience is the North and South are opposites. Samuel Kim (2000a, 3) claims the DPRK is an "island of autocentric and self-reliant development in the sea of the capitalist world system," while Chang Yun-shik (2009, 3) argues that the ROK "accepted globalization as key to development while the DPRK chose a self-reliant or autarkic approach." North Korea does pose a particular problem of categorization for researchers. The DPRK is not integrated into the world economy in terms of technology, global trade, unrestricted movements of people, ideas, or information to the same degree as the ROK. So how can we describe the DPRK's interactions with its geographical neighbors and with other countries globally? We can't call the North's interactions "globalization," and Pitman B. Potter (2009, xv) distinguishes between this latter term and "internationalization which presupposes cooperation and interaction among autonomous nation-states."

It is partly the difficulty of characterizing the two Koreas' very different experiences in terms of their international interactions under a single unifying term like "globalization" that explains the title of this book: *The Two Koreas and Their Global Engagements*. Samuel Kim considers South Korea one of the most globalized states (Kim 2000a, 2) and North Korea one of the least. However, the DPRK is not quite as cut off as Samuel Kim and Chang Yun-shik have suggested because their assertions only partially account for the history and reality of the North's relationship with the world around it. Global developments have continuously influenced the DPRK. Evidence of this can be seen in the strict economic sanctions enforced from 2016 onwards, the precise function of which was to isolate and even provoke the collapse of the DPRK in retaliation for its missile and nuclear development programs. The title of this volume also reflects the understanding of many scholars that the phenomenon of globalization should not be understood as "ideal end[s]" so much as an ongoing process of transformation (Kim 2000a, 8; see also Lewis 2002, 3; Vaish 2010, 1; Chang 2009, 1). In their international interchanges, neither the South nor the North remains static. Both countries constantly formulate policies in response to rapidly shifting global circumstances—a salient example is the 2020 global pandemic.

Rather than dismiss North Korea as being isolated, it would perhaps be more insightful to describe the country's experience of interactions with the outside world in terms of the differences and similarities with its significantly more globally integrated southern neighbor and competitor. The rest of this essay will contextualize the following chapters by describing and analyzing three characteristic features of South Korea's globalization and North Korea's encounters with the world beyond its borders. The first section concerns the state-centered globalization focus of successive South Korean administrations, which has had a transformative impact on the country's cultural industries. The second section shifts its attention to the DPRK's encounters with the international community. This part considers the distinction between North Koreans' official and unofficial interactions with the world beyond its borders. The final section treats the history of competition and rivalry that has dominated the two Koreas' international affairs. The analyses of these commonalities and differences help us better understand the distinctive history of Korea's encounters with the global over the past seventy years and situate the essays that follow.

Globalization in South Korea: Keeping the State In

Samuel Kim argues about South Korea's development that: "No state in the post-Cold War world cast its lot with globalization as decisively or as publically as Korea did under Kim Young Sam" (2000a, 2). However, one crucial and consistent feature of South Korea's globalization is that it carried out this ambitious project in a distinctive way compared to other countries by providing a vital leadership role for the state. This top-down rather than purely market-driven planning has gone on to shape the internationalization of South Korea's cultural institutions and industries.

Kim Young Sam fervently and openly embraced globalization partly because his administration saw it as the most effective method of bringing the ROK up to the ranks of what it perceived as "world-class" and "advanced" countries in North America, Western Europe and beyond (Kim 2000a, 2). South Korea would be able to take advantage of an integrated global market (Chang Yun-shik 2009, 7). Another reason for Kim's globalization drive derived from South Korea's phenomenal export-driven expansion, which meant there were increasing external (as well as domestic) pressures to open up and globalize its economy (Chang Yun-shik 2009, 7). But for South Koreans, globalization did not just mean economic liberalization, embracing the free market and minimizing state intervention as advocated by many proponents in the West. Instead, it was a top-down strategic plan with a clear government role (Kim 2000a, 3). This difference, as Samuel Kim points out, is reflected in the deliberate selection of the term *"segyehwa"* (internationalization) instead of a romanized version of "globalization" (Kim 2000a, 2).[3] The important place for the government at the heart of this process was not just a feature of South Korean *segyehwa* but also a trait that was shared by other states in Asia as part of the globalization process. The state-guided globalization model adopted by countries like Singapore, Taiwan, South Korea, and Hong Kong was criticized by Western media commentators as responsible for the 1997–1998 Asian Financial Crisis. Some neoliberal economists contended that the neo-Confucian patriarchal ideology and "crony capitalism" of East Asian countries effectively distorted Western structures of globalization, resulting in inevitable economic problems (Vaish 2010, 5–8). However, as Viniti Vaish (2010, 8) argues, formerly derided East Asian style protectionist policies began to look more sensible in the aftermath of the 2008 global financial crisis. East Asian countries like South Korea regarded national economies as too important to be left to unbridled capitalism.

Government institutions also helped engineer the international expansion of the South Korean cultural industries in the two decades following the Asian Financial Crisis. The background to this reflects what Chua Beng Huat argues was a trend in "global capitalism" from the late 1990s onwards, which saw the rise of cultural industries based on the "mass commodification of culture" (Chua 2012, 12). Starting with Kim Young Sam, South Korean administrations clearly understood the financial and diplomatic potential offered by the cultural industries, and they elevated the economic status of popular culture to that of an export industry. They did this by designating governmental institutions like the Korea Creative Content Agency (KOCCA) and the Korean Film Council (KOFIC) to help create policy and coordinate cultural exports (Fuhr 2016, 15). One result of this coordinated policy has been a phenomenal spread of *hallyu* or the Korean Wave of film, pop music, television dramas, variety shows, online gaming, and more recently, webtoons, lifestyles, and Korean-style cosmetic surgery around East Asia and beyond (Davis and Yeh 2008, 5; Parc 2017, 619). The domestic cultural content market continued to expand, and by 2014, South Korea had become one of the world's top ten media and entertainment markets (Fuhr 2016, 7–10). As well as the immediate national economic benefits derived from the export of cultural commodities (Chua 2012, 12), Michael Fuhr argues the South Korean government is also motivated by a strong desire for the continued international expansion of the K-Pop industry, to be a "global player" and to be acknowledged internationally as a producer of culture for the global market (Fuhr 2016, 15). However, there are also important domestic and national goals for the state-led support and direction of cultural industries, which can be seen most clearly in the rise of the South Korean cinematic industry.

For many years, South Korean domestic cinema was highly regulated, and foreign film imports were strictly controlled. From the 1960s until agreements were reached in the 1980s, the US film industry's lobbying group, the Motion Picture Association of America (MPAA), targeted South Korean cinema for economic opening, believing it was a potentially lucrative market (Yecies 2007, 1–5). The Chun Doo Hwan administration traded the opening of South Korea's cinema sector for rights to export Korean-made cars to the lucrative US market (Paquet 2009, 50).[4] Chun allowed Hollywood distributors direct access to the South Korean market, and within a few years of these rights being granted, many South Korean commentators were arguing that the domestic film industry was on the verge of collapse. Cinema, because of its star power, its prominence in the global cultural imaginary, and its industrial-scale production, is perhaps the most prestigious of all cultural industries, and the South Korean government was keen to avoid the collapse of the domestic film market that had occurred in Mexico and Taiwan when their domestic markets were opened to direct Hollywood competition by the MPAA (Yecies 2007, 2). The Chun administration defended South Korean productions through the screen quota system, which guaranteed a minimum number of days when exhibitors had to show domestically produced movies. But these measures weren't enough. By 1993, only 16% of films shown at the domestic box office were locally made, and cinema attendance had dropped to catastrophically low rates (Choi 2010, 206; Yecies 2007, 1). The governments of Kim Young Sam and Kim Dae Jung promoted a coordination role for state agencies such as KOFIC to ensure the survival and expansion of the industry. By 2001, when audience numbers had increased dramatically, South Korean-produced films were regularly capturing 50% or more of domestic box office revenues, South Korean directors began to win prestigious awards in international film festivals on a more regular basis, culminating in the 2019 victory of Bong Joon-ho's film *Kisaengchung* (*Parasite*, 2019, ROK) at both the 72nd Cannes Film Festival and the 92nd Academy Awards. According to Kyung Hyun Kim, South Korea is "the only nation during the post-Vietnam War era that has regained its domestic audience after losing it to Hollywood movies" (2004, 270).

KOFIC's coordination and direction have brought more than just cultural and economic benefits to South Korea. Chris Berry notes that the South Korean film industry is remarkable because it is one of only a handful of industries in the world that has developed what he calls a "full service cinema" consisting of a full range of modes of production, including documentary, commercial, art, and independent film as well as support for film festivals and archives (2002, 7). Berry argues that other cinematic industries placed all their eggs in one basket by targeting one form of production like festival-oriented film (Taiwan) and ended up collapsing. However, KOFIC helped to create a more diversified South Korean cinema featuring full modes of production and consumption, and as a result, the industry prospered phenomenally. So what is it about a more diversified movie industry that helps it thrive?

On the one hand, as Chris Howard has noted, the regulation of cinema according to a "national conjunction" of "film text, industry strategy and mode of consumption" has allowed Korean film to serve national interests in several areas (Howard 2008, 89). In any given year, the South Korean film industry can point to various potential modes of success—critical recognition in international film festivals or record-breaking domestic commercial box office successes. These results not only depict a thriving cultural industry but also justify government support for the sector. However, as well as serving national interests, the diversified film industry is strong for other reasons. There is considerable evidence of crossover of personnel and expertise between different modes of production—for example, independent film directors successfully moving into commercial genre filmmaking (and vice versa). This has helped keep all sectors functioning at a high level of creativity (Kim Young-jin 2019, 11–12). Finally, a diversified cinematic industry has equally helped serve the needs and desires of small but significant groups of consumers and producers in South Korea. The numerous international film festivals organized in South Korea since the late 1990s—such as the Korea Queer Film Festival, Persons with Disabilities Film Festival, the Seoul Human Rights Film Festival, and the Seoul International Women's Film Festival, among many others—are supported by the government and provide an important space for the discussion and development of identity politics (Kim 2005, 82). In addition, support for output targeted at niche markets like independent and art film sectors also serve influential communities. This is particularly true of the generation of political and independent filmmaking activists who led the 1980s anti-dictatorship movement and who subsequently became influential in government institutions under the reformist presidencies of former political dissident Kim Dae Jung and Roh Moo-hyun (Park 2015, 163; Chang Yun-shik 2009, 13). Maintaining a diverse cinematic industry helps meet the various needs of different constituencies within South Korean society.

The ongoing strategy of successive South Korean governments to satisfy the different needs of these communities is evidence of the importance it accords to the cultural sphere. The government saw high prestige cultural industries as too important to be left to unpredictable market forces. State-directed internationalization was seen as a vital way of defending against the homogenizing aspects of globalization and as a means of shaping institutional structures that serve the specific needs of diverse communities within the country. Therefore, this state intervention is a significant part of South Korea's globalization processes, especially in developing its now global cultural industries.

THE DPRK'S OFFICIAL AND UNOFFICIAL INTERNATIONAL DEALINGS

One distinguishing feature of the DPRK's international relationships is a clear demarcation between the official and unofficial interactions of North Koreans with the world beyond the peninsula. When analysts think of the DPRK's overseas engagement, more often than not, they consider the official, state-led relations of Pyongyang with the international community. The North is perhaps best known for its belligerence, particularly its nuclear tests, rocket firings, threats to South Korea, Japan, and most famously, the United States. These provocations represent one method of engaging with the international community—of ensuring that the world remembers the continued presence of the DPRK and pays attention to it (instead of the common policy of "strategic patience" or ignoring it until it collapses; see Lankov 2013, 211). Another observation frequently made of the North Korean state's dealings with the outside world is that it is less than cooperative, if not downright awkward to handle (Smith 2015, 1). The North likes to describe its ruling ideology as *uri sik sahoejuŭi* (socialism of our style), a term that provides insight into its involvement with the outside world. At the state level, international relations appear to be conducted in North Korea's own "style." According to Barry Gills (1996, 260), for example, the DPRK was initially able to achieve a far higher degree of national political autonomy than the South by accepting large-scale external assistance from fraternal socialist countries during the early post-Korean War (1950–1953) reconstruction of the country.[5] The DPRK developed an extremely nationalistic socialism alongside this receipt of overseas largesse, and Gills argues that the North Koreans "manipulated external assistance" because their overall aim was the establishment of political and economic autonomy rather than international solidarity (Gills 1996, 260–261).

During the height of the Sino-Soviet split, the DPRK continued to tread this independent path in which they could obtain considerable economic, political, and security assistance simultaneously from the People's Republic of China (PRC) and the Soviets without ever fully committing to one side (Armstrong 2013, 4).[6] The DPRK's strategy of rejecting US supremacy while limiting the political influence of the communist superpowers was successful in that it had a positive impact upon the North's international standing between the 1960s and late 1970s (Gills 1996, 260). This strategy allowed the DPRK for a time to aspire to leadership of Non-aligned countries and to serve as an inspiration for anti-colonial Third World movements (Young 2021) and even appeal to researchers in the 1970s as a model for development (Gills 1996, 261).[7] Of course, as the 1990s economic collapse and famine has shown, the DPRK did not offer any credible or sustainable model for development, but the regime's ability to survive despite economic collapse and a precarious geopolitical position is in some ways due to an official foreign policy that is able to extract maximum concessions from allies and even enemies (Armstrong 2013, 5). Charles Armstrong argues that the DPRK's twenty-first-century dealings with the global community have followed the basic patterns established during the period of global Cold War politics (2013, 2). There are then two significant points to take away from the history of the DPRK state's official engagements with the global community and these are the official desire to chart an autonomous path and the significant degree of continuity in negotiating behavior over the seventy years of its existence.

While considering this overall history of the DPRK's state-level global interactions, it is sometimes easy to overlook the fact that more recently, a considerable number of North Koreans have commenced nominally proscribed international contacts. The DPRK authorities effectively sealed off the country's population from the outside world until the 1990s economic collapse. But since the calamitous famine, cross-border interactions of ordinary North Koreans have proceeded without official approval and according to local needs. For almost two decades following the start of the famine, the DPRK has become far more integrated into the Sino-Korean borderland economy than many people realize, and this has implications for the movement of goods, ideas, and people into and out of the North. How this situation occurred requires some explanation.

The period from 1993 to 1998 witnessed a massive shift in the DPRK that had ramifications for borderland communities and the connections between ordinary North Koreans and the outside world. 1993 saw the death of Kim Il Sung and the culmination of an economic crisis that had been many years in the making. The end of Soviet-era friendship fuel prices, the lack of spare parts to service outdated agricultural machinery, soil erosion resulting from inefficient farming methods, and a series of disastrous floods led to the collapse of the agrarian economy supplying the North Korean Public Distribution System (PDS). The PDS was the principal supply of food for the majority of the population, and its collapse resulted in widespread famine between 1996 and 1999. With the state incapable of feeding its own population, ordinary North Koreans began to take matters into their own hands and created *changmadang* or black markets throughout the country. As part of their survival strategies, North Koreans—women in particular—established cottage industries, farmers sold surpluses at markets, people began selling their labor or transport services. In addition, private citizens began crossing the border with the PRC in increasing numbers, smuggling goods to trade on the black market (Lankov 2013, 85). Andrei Lankov (2013, 92) describes this as the "near collapse of control over the Sino-North Korean border." Smugglers paid bribes to border officials to ensure the safe passage of people or goods (Lankov 2013, 92). Unable to control the smuggling situation, and in need of income itself, the authorities relaxed their previously hostile attitudes toward border crossing and overseas travel.[8]

This widespread "marketization from below" led to a sudden increase in the circulation of contraband goods and forbidden ideas from the outside world (Smith 2015).[9] The overall social and political impact of marketization has been significant. Research by Smith (2015, 221), Hassig and Oh (2015, 68–69), and Choi (2017, 791) indicates that North Koreans developed an unprecedented level of economic independence from the state. This is especially true of women who are largely responsible for market activities and therefore developed remarkable economic agency.[10] The combination of this economic independence and ideas coming in from the outside has had a knock-on effect upon the attitude of North Koreans toward their ruling elites. Smith argues that North Koreans are more aware than ever before of their absolute poverty in comparison to their regional neighbors (2015, 224), and as a result, increasingly question the official principle of self-sacrifice for the greater good from a state incapable of providing for its population (Smith 2015, 231). Ordinary people pay lip service to official pronouncements and treat officials with barely concealed contempt (Hassig and Oh 2015, 231). The marketization presented the regime with a dilemma: how could it deal with the increasing amount of illegal goods and ideas coming in from abroad and still retain control over its population? This is not one that it was ever able to resolve by suppression and therefore, it unofficially accepted the reality of marketization and illegal border crossing (Abrahimian 2018, 57; Lankov 2017, 1).[11]

Although markets continued to provide an important means of subsistence for many North Koreans, the situation has been radically altered since 2016 by attempts to seal off the DPRK's borders. Initially, in response to North Korea's belligerent behavior, successive US administrations imposed stringent sanctions aimed at isolating the Kim Jong Un regime economically and politically. In 2020, the DPRK authorities sealed off their own borders to prevent the spread of COVID-19 into the country to prevent the pandemic from potentially overwhelming its inadequate health system. From the standpoint of 2021, the impact of these restrictive measures upon marketization processes, food supply, and the ultimate fate of the country is unclear. Analysts continue to strongly disagree about the impact of sanctions on the DPRK, partly because of unofficial cross-border exchanges by marketeers and partly because of the unwillingness of the PRC to seal off economic lifelines that might cause the collapse of its nominal ally and destabilize northern areas of

China (see Noland 2009). There is ongoing disagreement among political analysts about the DPRK's stability (see Kim and Choi 2021). What is certain is that the robustness of the food supply, society, and ultimately the state itself depends in part not just upon state-led but also on unofficial, people-initiated interactions of North Koreans with the world beyond the Peninsula.

What is significant about the advent of this period of greater interactions over the Sino-Korean border is that it is roughly synchronous with both the era of greater global integration and South Korea's *segyehwa* project, suggesting close links between the demise of the global Cold War order and the pathways of the two Koreas. The end of South Korea's military dictatorship in 1987 and the start of democratization, the 1989–1991 collapse of European communism, the end of Soviet-era friendship prices, and the 1993 death of Kim Il Sung led to the unraveling of previously dominant internal political, economic, social, and cultural structures of both the ROK and the DPRK. This is an illustration that it is not just the ROK that is tied to international geopolitical shifts; the DPRK is as well.

One other important aspect of North Korea's overseas contacts is its competitive and antagonistic relationship with its southern neighbor; this inter-Korea rivalry has deeply impacted the recent history of the relationship between the Peninsula and the outside world; this will be discussed in the next section.

HISTORICAL PARALLELS IN ATTEMPTS AT GREATER GLOBAL INTEGRATION

One problem with the frequent and simplistic characterization of the DPRK as autarkic, hermit-like, or isolated (see Kim 2000a, 3; Chang 2009, 3) is that it omits the history of some significant parallels between the North and South Koreans' interactions with the world beyond the Peninsula. The ROK and DPRK have not formulated international policy in total isolation from one another, but often, it appears, with a firm eye on how each could outdo the other (Choe 2018). The fact of the division of the Peninsula into two Koreas is often ignored in the context of globalization (except by Lewis 2002, 1), but this separation of competing states is not irrelevant to the true story of Korean global integration. In fact, this constant game of one-upmanship represents an important part of the story. Korea is different from many other territories and countries in the world because of the specificity of its division, which influences the dealings of the two states with both the region and the rest of the world. Previous attempts at greater global integration have been two-pronged, in that both the North and South have not just been concerned with trade and commerce but also with foreign recognition. Barry Gills (1996) argues that since their division, the two Koreas have engaged in a competition for global attention in terms of which of the rival states has the right to lead the 80 million Koreans worldwide. Gills continues that:

> A state becomes a state because it establishes control over territory and people; or a state becomes a state because it is recognized as such by other states. Both the DPRK and ROK fulfilled the criteria of the first theory, but the international community [historically] failed to arrive at a sufficient consensus concerning recognition. (Gills 1996, xix)

Arguably, the struggle between the two Koreas reached its peak at the height of the 1970s–1980s Cold War struggles over memberships of global organizations and over their comparative "international standing" (Gills 1996, xix). Historically, this inter-Korean rivalry often resulted in curious competition between the two countries in their quest for global recognition; some of the activities of the South appeared to be copied or inspired by the North, and vice versa. This can be seen in two historical attempts at more significant global interaction—the 1988 Seoul Olympics and the first Korean Wave—both of which had (and arguably still have) significant ramifications for social, cultural, and even political change in their respective countries.

Sports One-Upmanship: The 1988 Olympics and the 13th World Festival of Youth and Students

In 1981, the International Olympic Committee decided to award the 1988 Olympic Games to Seoul, a decision that signaled an important symbolic shift in the balance of power on the Peninsula. According to Barry Gills (1996), North Korea initially had the upper hand over its southern rival in the struggle for international recognition, due in part to its rapid economic development. Gradually, however, Seoul's greater adaptability and flexibility in its global economic approach saw a shift in the balance of power by the 1980s (Gills 1996, 18–19). 1988 was the year in which Seoul's ascendancy in this fraternal struggle for global acceptance was confirmed. As Charles Armstrong states: "More than any other single event, the 1988 Olympics demonstrated South Korea's eclipse of the North in international prestige" (Armstrong 2013, 259). The IOC's decision to award the Games to Seoul also helped to create rifts between Pyongyang and its major allies. The North Koreans initially attempted to persuade Seoul into co-hosting the Games with Pyongyang, and when this failed, the DPRK tried but were unable to persuade allies to withdraw from participation (Armstrong 2013, 259). Instead, Pyongyang decided to host its own competing event the year following the Olympics, when it held the 13th World Festival of Youth and Students, an international event organized by the World Federation of Democratic Youth. This saw the participation of 22,000 young people from 177 different countries who gathered in Pyongyang in July 1989 to take part in sporting, social, cultural, and political events.

Most of the previous World Festivals of Youth and Students had been held in former Eastern Bloc countries, bankrolled by the Soviet Union and attended by pro-Moscow or other leftist organizations from around the globe (Lankov 2013, 222).[12] The DPRK attempted to deflect attention from South Korea's successful organization of the historic 1988 Olympics, which had seen the participation of both the USA and the USSR for the first time since 1976. However, North Korea failed in its aims on several levels. First, the World Festival of Youth and Students was a minor event that lacked the prestige of the Olympics; the world's media largely shunned it, and the press attention it did garner was for all the wrong reasons (see below). Second, the estimated US$4 billion the DPRK authorities spent on the project virtually bankrupted the country, contributing directly to the economic collapse of the 1990s (Armstrong 2013, 265). The event was supposed to celebrate North Korea's greater standing in the international community to its population, but it was a public relations disaster for Pyongyang.

The 13th World Festival of Youth and Students was held just a month after the bloody suppression of the Tiananmen Square pro-democracy protests by armed forces of the PRC. Although the Kim Il Sung regime had attempted to block news about the unrest in the capital city of its major ally, foreign participation at the Pyongyang events led to news of the massacre leaking out. Left-wing Nordic student delegations launched protests calling for democratic reforms in the PRC and the DPRK in the main stadium at one event, leading to clashes with security forces. This disruption was recorded by the international press attending the events. Upon witnessing the protests, Kim Il Sung allegedly left the stadium in disgust. This was not the only disruption in Pyongyang caused by the wave of protests that spread throughout the communist world that year. Earlier that summer, rumors about the Tiananmen Square crackdown filtered back from North Korean students studying in Eastern Europe to the Kim Il Sung University in Pyongyang, resulting in short-lived and rapidly suppressed pro-democracy demonstrations (Myrseth 2016, 5; Macias 2014).

Another attempt by the North Korean authorities to demonstrate the international support for their regime backfired spectacularly. The North Korean authorities thought they had achieved a public relations coup in the visit of Im Su-gyŏng, a Hankuk University of Foreign Studies French major and political activist based in Seoul. It was strictly forbidden for South Koreans like Im to visit the North, but she had made the trip to show the support of a left-leaning student organization for the Festival and the DPRK. The authorities beamed images of Im meeting North Korean dignitaries on domestic national television, believing it demonstrated international support for the regime. However, North Korean defector testimony indicates that ordinary people showed little interest in Im's vocal support for Pyongyang. Instead, people were intrigued by Im's glamorous appearance and her treatment by the South Korean authorities when she returned to Seoul. Defectors reveal that they had previously been taught that the ROK was a fascistic regime in which their southern compatriots lived in abject poverty. They believed Im would be executed upon her return to the South and her family and relatives thrown into jail. Yet, the televised coverage of her demeanor and the freely given media interviews with her parents, together with the fact of her release from prison after three years all indicated to the population in the North that the South was considerably wealthier and freer than they had been led to believe (Lankov 2013, 222–225). Andrei Lankov argues that the televised coverage of Im during the Festival was one of the earliest breaches in a strictly controlled media blockade enforced upon the DPRK population and one that helped impact subsequent social changes within the North (Lankov 2013, 225).

Although it was a public relations and economic disaster, the hosting of the World Festival of Youth and Students also brought some small but not insignificant cultural changes to North Korean society. Testimony from overseas students of Korean, who acted as interpreters at the Festival, indicate some changes on the part of the regime toward traditional Korean culture around this time (Häussler 2015, 2016). An example of this is the revival at the Festival of the well-known *Arirang* folksong. This is perhaps the most famous piece of Korean music and one which is played frequently in South Korea to represent the quintessence of Korean culture. Foreign interpreters who had studied as language students in North Korea reported hearing *Arirang* performed for the first time at the Festival (Häussler 2015, 2016). The aim was evidently to show traditional aspects of Korean culture to the assembled foreign guests. However, the DPRK authorities had not always embraced aspects of its traditional culture so openly. Balázs Szalontai (2009, 155) argues that official attitudes toward its cultural patrimony were marked by inconsistency, ranging from periodic "anti-traditionalist" campaigns to public celebrations of Korean heritage. Attitudes shifted according to the perceived use-value and function of Korea's cultural revival. For many years, Korean folk music had been regarded officially as the "music of slaves, serfs, landlords, and drunkards, which is unsuitable for instilling enthusiasm in the workers" (Szalontai 2009, 155). However, the reported revival of *Arirang* for the festival was likely an attempt to impress the foreign delegations and reach out to the South Korean population by celebrating a symbol of common Korean culture.[13] North Korea's attempt to compete with the South by hosting its own version of the Olympics and demonstrating its international integration succeeded in bringing unintended consequences in ways the regime would never have imagined—by provoking some small but still significant social and cultural shifts in North Korea.

An interesting postscript to the history of the 13th World Festival of Youth and Students is the fact that this wasn't the only time that Pyongyang attempted to overshadow the international attention fostered upon its rival by hosting its own spectacular event. Another important "upstaging" effort came in 1995 with the largest ever professional wrestling show in the history of the sport. This event was held in Pyongyang, opened by none other than Muhammad Ali, and featured Ali's one-time adversary, the legendary Japanese wrestler Antonio Inoki (Kanji Inoki).[14] Officially, it was called the "Pyongyang International Sports and Culture Festival for Peace" and unofficially known as "Collision in Korea," and organizers and international journalists reported crowds of between 150,000 and 165,000 people in attendance. It was co-promoted by the Japanese New Japan Pro-Wrestling (NJPW) and—perhaps crucially, the USA's World Championship Wrestling (WCW) (Hall 2020).[15] The event was an attempt to help thaw relationships between three adversaries: the DPRK, the US, and Japan. Pyongyang was also keen to generate as much positive publicity as possible, but following poor pay-per-view sales, there was never any follow-up to the event.

Another opportunity for sports diplomacy on an epic scale came a few years later, and the resulting event—the Mass Games—provided a longer-lasting legacy for Pyongyang to showcase its organizational prowess. In the late 1990s, South Korea was awarded the right to co-host the 2002 World Cup with Japan. This was the largest and most prestigious event in the calendar of the world's most popular spectator sport. Seoul had been in fierce competition with its rival in Tokyo to gain the sole rights to host the event, but in the end, FIFA awarded it to both countries. By awarding Seoul the joint rights to host one of the world's biggest sporting festivals, South Korea gained considerable international recognition and prestige over the North. Pyongyang responded by hosting the "Grand Mass Gymnastics and Artistic Performance Arirang" or "Arirang Mass Games" to coincide with the World Cup and rival South Korea's event. The games were named after the folk song, which was reportedly revived to coincide with the 1989 World Festival of Youth and Students. These games are examples of highly choreographed mass gymnastics performed by thousands of men, women, and children. Such practices were developed initially in communist Eastern Europe but were expanded to a new and more spectacular level in the DPRK. While only a handful of foreign tourists visited the event in 2002, the event has continued intermittently ever since and represents a prime way of drawing foreign tourists into the country. According to Udo Merkel, the Games have an important domestic socialization and ideological function but also appeal to the South Korean public since *Arirang* connects to a common Korean ethnic identity. In addition, the event has a vital foreign policy dimension, showing itself as a rival event to "commodified and globally controlled mega sports events" like the World Cup (Merkel 2013, 1256). The Games present the DPRK with what it believes is an appealing image: as a bulwark resisting US global hegemony, rather than as a leftover from Stalinism.

The First Korean Wave of Culture

Another small but vital cultural shift that occurred in the North in the 1980s was based on the country's attempts toward greater integration with the international community during a period of significant economic downturn for the regime. Balázs Szalontai (2009, 163) observes that Pyongyang "took part in relatively sophisticated cultural diplomacy throughout the post-Korean War decades." The North Korean authorities realized from early in the country's history the importance of "mobilizing the 'soft power' of culture against domestic and South Korean opponents, and they utilized it vis-à-vis their communist allies, most notably the Soviet Union" (Szalontai 2009, 163). Szalontai maintains that smaller-scale cultural campaigns, like the revival of traditional folk music, were often employed to secure economic cooperation from fraternal socialist allies during the long economic decline the North experienced from the 1960s onwards.[16] As well as securing financial aid, the DPRK was equally keen to demonstrate common cultural bonds to South Koreans during the occasional periods of détente between the two Koreas (see Kim 2015). However, the DPRK also launched one larger-scale attempt at cultural diplomacy in the mid-1980s that was aimed at securing greater international recognition and possibly economic benefits during the North's slow period of decline. This 1980s internationalization campaign would help provoke significant shifts in the country's cinematic output and encourage attitudinal shifts toward official ideology among the population.

Many people identify *hallyu* or the Korean Wave of popular culture as a South Korean phenomenon that began with the popularity of the K-pop group H.O.T. in China in the late 1990s. However, there was an earlier and briefer Korean Wave of popular culture in the early to mid-1980s that was led by the DPRK. This wave was initiated by Kim Jong Il with the help of two South Koreans: film-maker Shin Sang-ok and noted actress Ch'oe Ŭn-hŭi. Kim Jong Il personally instructed the pair to take over responsibility for North Korea's moribund filmmaking industry and elevate it to international standards (Chung 2014, 177–179; Armstrong 2013, 237–238). Under their guidance, North Korean cinema was transformed. Shin and Ch'oe made seven pictures, including *Toraoji anŭn milsa* (*The Secret Emissary*, 1984, DPRK), *Sogŭm* (*Salt*, 1985, DPRK), and *Pulgasari* (1985, DPRK). The pair brought North Korean cinema the international attention that Kim Jong Il had desired. Ch'oe Ŭn-hŭi won prizes for direction at the 1984 Karlovy Vary Film Festival for *The Secret Emissary* and for her performance in *Salt* at the 1985 Moscow Film Festival (Chung 2014, 177).[17] Shin also innovated widely, helping to popularize DPRK films both domestically and internationally. Shin introduced fantasy movies, foreign locations, amorous content, and martial arts action into North Korean cinema. Overt propaganda content was reduced heavily, and DPRK films generally became popular with local audiences, perhaps for the first time. Up to this point, only 10% of movie audiences saw films in theaters, and most people viewed them on television if they lived in Pyongyang[18] and on collective farms and factories if they lived outside. Many of the films served what Kyung Hyun Kim describes as an "explicit social function" of state management by popular consensus (Kim 1996, 90). With the innovations introduced by Shin, North Korean film was revolutionized, and movie theaters saw ticket scalpers for the first time in DPRK history (Chung 2014, 177–179). The pair escaped back to South Korea in 1986, but after their re-defection, their influence on DPRK film continued. Martial arts, adventure, and period films like *Hong Kil Dong* (dir: Kim Kil-in, 1986, DPRK) among many others proved particularly popular with domestic and international audiences alike. As with Hong Kong films of the 1970s and 1980s, North Korean films developed a reputation as action-packed martial arts spectaculars among audiences in the former Eastern Bloc.[19]

Shin and Ch'oe's influence had elevated North Korea's reputation in terms of international filmmaking, and Kim Jong Il's strategy showed that the country's cinematic industry could compete on a par with other fraternal socialist nations (Chung 2014, 179; Schönherr 2012, 75). However, this attempt at spreading a Korean Wave of culture across the socialist world of the 1980s was costly, and this approach to cultural diplomacy was abandoned after a few years. Despite the reversion to normal standards of ideological content in DPRK film from the late 1980s onwards (see Schönherr 2012), the experiment in international cultural engagement had other unintended consequences for the regime. DPRK defector testimony indicates that viewing films aimed at mass entertainment permanently altered ordinary North Koreans' views of cinema and leisure:

> In the 1980s, we just watched our films...And accepted them the way they were... But after the Shin Sang-ok era, we had new eyes. Then we could judge which movies are interesting and which are not...Through his

films we could see the life of people in other countries, including South Korea – and we could see that they live better than we did in North Korea. (Quoted in Schönherr 2012, 191–192)

Films up to that point had not reflected the lives of ordinary people in the DPRK, but genre cinema produced according to the principles of classical Hollywood continuity editing that bound the spectators into the narrative and offered viewers an encounter with an alternative reality, gave many North Koreans a self-reflexivity that had been largely absent before. This represented the social significance of this encounter by North Koreans with a different view of the world, and it was an inadvertent and unintended consequence of the DPRK regime's attempt at international cultural engagement.

While it would be an exaggeration to suggest that the earlier North Korean wave of culture inspired the later South Korean *hallyu* Wave, it is noteworthy that the DPRK predates the ROK's cultural expansion policy by over a decade. The DPRK, like the South following the initiation of Kim Young Sam's *segyehwa* policy, aimed to use soft power to bring economic and political benefits to the country. The outcomes of the North's cultural campaigns were not as successful as *hallyu*; however, they did encourage some small changes in attitude among the North Korean population. The Cold War has never ended on the Korean Peninsula, and as a result, this struggle is ongoing. The dealings of both Koreas with the international community still contain an element of this historical tussle for recognition.

These then are some salient points about the relationships of the two Koreas to the world beyond the Peninsula. South Korea has successfully globalized according to its own terms—by providing a vanguard role for the state in the coordination of national cultural policy. North Korea has never been cut off but has engaged with the outside world, also in its own particular way, often to extract resources from stronger powers and construct its own vision of autonomy and independence. The attempt by the DPRK to stage-manage and steer international relationships has always been taken with half an eye on the success of its southern neighbor and has often resulted in unintended consequences for the regime. The manner in which the state has pursued resource extraction reveals a degree of continuity between the pre-Soviet collapse period and the twenty-first century. One development in the DPRK case has been the post-famine period of *unofficial* cross-border interactions of ordinary North Koreans, leading to significant social change.

Many of these issues: the official and unofficial interactions, autonomy, and independence mentioned above are revisited in the essays that follow in this collection. The overall consistent focus of the chapters is on the impact of overseas connections on the society, culture, and language of the two Koreas.[20] Contributors take two general approaches to the examination of Korea's encounters with the global in their studies. First, several authors take broader historical perspectives and investigate the long-term impact of the international influences on Korea to contextualize more recent developments.[21] A second focus is on specific Korean cultural, linguistic, and social changes since the 1990s demise of the global Cold War and greater international integration. The bulk of the chapters included here analyze the transformed culture, language, and society that has emerged during the *segyehwa* era. These are arguably the most prominent and noteworthy changes to have impacted either of the two Koreas.[22] That being said, the inclusion of three chapters focusing specifically on the results of North Korea's contacts with the outside world in terms of culture, education, and economy since the 1990s is further evidence of the importance of the DPRK's interactions with other countries.

The book starts with two sections on culture, beginning with a discussion of attempts by South and North Korean filmmakers to create appealing products within two very different cinematic contexts: one a globalized industry and the other with virtually no international profile. The second section of the book also treats culture, focusing on music. The chapters, on the one hand, deal with the musical traditions that many Koreans believe have been lost in the drive to modernize, and on the other hand, the essays analyze the K-pop phenomenon that has helped globalize Korean culture. The third part on language investigates some of the linguistic transformations in twentieth-century Korea, which has seen shifting geopolitical influences, declining Chinese power, Japanese colonial rule, Cold War division, and increased overseas interest in Korean popular culture. All these shifts have impacted the Korean language that both native and non-native speakers learn and use. The fourth and final part of the book deals first with the results of increased globalization affecting South Korean society and culture, and second the DPRK's interactions with the wider region and how these links have led to significant changes in North Korea's domestic and diasporic communities.

I dedicate my closing remarks to the inspiration for this book, which came from a Korean Studies conference held in August 2018 at Monash University, jointly organized by David Hundt and Jay Song from Deakin and Melbourne Universities. The conference title was: "Reimagining Korean Identity Through Wars, Money, Ideas, and Exchanges: 70 years' Identity Transformation." The conference aimed to discuss the social and cultural transformations on the Peninsula since the establishment of separate states in 1948. Its organization was motivated by a belief that Korean Studies should include the investigation of all facets of Korean civilization, including the study of the culture, society, language, and history of South, North, and premodern Korea, and the large diaspora. Like the conference, this book is multi-disciplinary and brings together areas that include linguistics, diasporas, education, film, music, sociology, and literature—subjects not commonly treated together. The idea is that discussing these diverse areas is vitally important to enable a more comprehensive understanding of the transformed and transforming cultures and societies on the Korean Peninsula.

Notes

1. Charles Armstrong distinguishes between three Cold Wars, the Global Cold War between the US, its allies, and the Soviet bloc; the Sino-Soviet rivalry and the inter-Korean conflict (Armstrong 2013, 2–3).
2. Another example of this latter type includes Kevin Gray's (2007) study of the impact of globalization on the South Korean labor market.
3. The use of *segyehwa* is a rare case of when Korean policy makers deliberately avoided using the Romanized version in order to make a point about national autonomy as Kim implies (2000a, 2).
4. Chun's government also struck a deal after threats by the US of trading sanctions for what the MPAA argued was unfair Korean competitive practices (Paquet 2009, 50).
5. The country was flattened by US bombing during the Korean War and the rebuilding effort was only achieved thanks to the foreign assistance of socialist countries between 1953 and 1960. The biggest donors were the USSR and the People's Republic of China (PRC), which provided roughly two thirds of the total aid received, while other fraternal socialist countries including Mongolia and

North Vietnam supplied the remainder. East Germany helped with the reconstruction of Hamhŭng, North Korea's second largest city and a vitally important industrial center (Armstrong 2013, 56–57).
6. The Soviets and the PRC also supplied vital technical and logistical support to facilitate the modernization of the North Korean industrial economy. The aid provided by foreign powers was essential in making the North Korean economy the most advanced in continental East Asia (Lankov 2013, 19).
7. See Foster-Carter (1977) and Brun and Hersh (1976) for examples of work that acknowledged the lead that the North had over the South in terms of economic and even social progress and cited the DPRK as a possible model for development.
8. From 2003 the government relaxed its attitudes toward official cross-border trips and began to issue passports to North Koreans intending on traveling overseas as private citizens for the first time in its history (Lankov 2013, 92). Illegal border crossing into China, previously considered a serious crime was reclassified as a minor offence (Lankov 2013, 93).
9. Hazel Smith argues that "North Koreans moved from being without hardly any economic agency to being more proactively involved in the market than most people living in market democracies…" (Smith 2015, 234).
10. Hazel Smith argues greater female participation in unofficial market activities occurred because the authorities generally gave women wider berth when it came to absenteeism from work due to traditional child-rearing duties. In addition, the state believed women's self-help activities on behalf of their families were not politically threatening (2015, 206).
11. Attempts to suppress markets by devaluing the won for example, largely failed because they were subverted by local officials (see Lankov 2013, 123).
12. The 12th World Festival of Youth and Students had been organized in Moscow.
13. For other examples of low-level DPRK cultural diplomacy campaigns to reach out to the South Korean population see Kim (2015) and Szalontai (2009).
14. Inoki was a disciple of legendary founder of Japanese pro-wrestling Rikidōzan (Kim Sin-rak, 1924–1963) who was of Korean extraction.

15. My thanks to Roald Maliangkay for this information.
16. Szalontai also provides the example of a sudden celebration of Buddhist historical artefacts that had previously been condemned as the primitive tools of a repressive ruling class (2009, 156).
17. Ch'oe co-directed the film with Shin, but she received the direction award.
18. My thanks to Im Il for this information (December 2020).
19. My thanks to Vladimir Tikhonov (Pak No-ja) for this information (May 2016).
20. The exception is Robert Winstanley-Chesters' article on the North's fishing industry which is the only essay to deal directly with commerce but is noteworthy for its discussion of the continuity of approach that has defined the North's international dealings since its 1948 creation.
21. Young-Key Kim-Renaud on the language of the two Koreas, Min Hye Cho on identity formation among Japanese Koreans, and Robert Winstanley-Chesters on North Korean fishing.
22. However to include post-famine changes in the DPRK, Andrew Jackson's chapter covers social shifts resulting from unofficial overseas contacts by North Koreans as reflected in film.

References

Abrahimian, Andray. 2018. *North Korea and Myanmar: Divergent Paths*. Jefferson, NC: McFarland.

Ahn, SooJeong. 2011. *The Pusan International Film Festival, South Korean Cinema and Globalization*. Hong Kong: Hong Kong University Press.

Armstrong, Charles K. 2013. *Tyranny of the Weak: North Korea and the World, 1950–1992*. Ithaca: Cornell University Press.

Baker, Donald. 2009. "Introductory Notes." In *Korea Confronts Globalization*, edited by Chang Yun-shik, Seok Hyun-ho, and Donald Baker, 169–172. New York: Routledge.

Berry, Chris. 2002. "Full Service Cinema: The South Korean Cinema Success Story (So Far)." In *Texts and Context of Korean Cinema: Crossing Borders*, edited by Young-Key Kim-Renaud, R. Richard Grinker, and Kirk W. Larsen, 7–16. Washington, DC: George Washington University, Sigur Center Asia Paper, no. 17.

Brun, Ellen, and Jacques Hersh. 1976. *Socialist Korea: A Case Study in the Strategy of Economic Development*. New York: Monthly Review Press.

Chang Yun-shik. 2009. "Introduction: Korea in the Process of Globalization." In *Korea Confronts Globalization*, edited by Chang Yun-shik, Seok Hyun-ho, and Donald Baker, 1–39. New York: Routledge.

Chang Yun-shik, Seok Hyun-ho, and Donald Baker, eds. 2009. *Korea Confronts Globalization*. New York: Routledge.

Choe Sang-hun. 2018. "North Korea's Would-Be Olympics: A Tale of a Cold War Boondoggle." *The New York Times*, February 4. Last accessed January 16, 2021. https://www.nytimes.com/2018/02/04/world/asia/north-korea-olympics.html.

Choi Jin-hee. 2010. *The South Korean Film Renaissance: Local Hitmakers, Global Provocateurs*. Middletown: Wesleyan University Press.

Choi Yong Sub. 2017. "North Korea's Hegemonic Rule and its Collapse." *The Pacific Review* 30 (5): 783–800.

Chua Beng Huat. 2012. *Structure, Audience and Soft Power in East Asian Pop Culture*. Hong Kong: Hong Kong University Press.

Chung, Steven. 2014. *Split Screen Korea: Shin Sang-ok and Postwar Cinema*. Minneapolis: University of Minnesota Press.

Davis, Darrell William and Emilie Yueh-yu Yeh. 2008. *East Asian Screen Industries*. London: BFI Publishing.

Foster-Carter, Aidan. 1977. "North Korea: Development and Self-Reliance: A Critical Appraisal." *Bulletin of Concerned Asian Scholars* 9 (1): 45–55

Fuhr, Michael. 2016. *Globalization and Popular Music in South Korea: Sounding Out K-Pop* London: Routledge.

Gills, B. K. 1996. *Korea Versus Korea: A Case of Contested Legitimacy*. London: Routledge.

Gray, Kevin. 2007. *Korean Workers and Neoliberal Globalization*. London: Routledge.

Hall, Nick. 2020. "Collision in Korea: Pyongyang's Historic Socialism and Spandex Spectacular." *N.K. News*, April 29. Accessed April 6, 2021. https://www.nknews.org/2020/04/collision-in-korea-pyongyangs-historic-socialism-and-spandex-spectacular/.

Hassig, Ralph, and Kongdan Oh. 2015. *The Hidden People of North Korea: Everyday Life in the Hermit Kingdom*. Lanham: Rowman and Littlefield.

Häussler, Sonja. 2015. "Disco Music and Folklore: Cultural Aspects of the 13th World Festival of Youth and Students in Pyongyang." Paper presented at the 27th Conference of the AKSE (Association of Korean Studies in Europe) Conference. Bochum, July 10–13.

Häussler, Sonja. 2016. "North Korea and the World Festival of Youth and Students in 1989." Paper given at "Understanding the Other Korea: North Korea" Workshop, Copenhagen University, April 9.

Howard, Chris. 2008. "Contemporary South Korean Cinema: 'National Conjunction' and 'Diversity.'" In *East Asian Cinemas: Exploring Transnational Connections on Film*, edited by Leon Hunt and Leung Wing-Fai, 88–102. London: I.B. Taurus.

Kim, Immanuel. 2015. "*Snow Melts in Spring*: Another Look at the North Korean Film Industry." *Journal of Japanese and Korean Cinema* 7 (1): 41–56.

Kim, Kyung Hyun. 1996. "The Fractured Cinema of North Korea: The Discourse of the Nation in Sea of Blood." In *In Pursuit of Contemporary East Asian Culture*, edited by Tang, Xiaobing, 85–106. New York: Routledge.

Kim, Kyung Hyun. 2004. *The Remasculinization of Korean Cinema*. Durham, N.C.: Duke University Press.

Kim, Samuel S. 2000a. "Korea and Globalization (Segyehwa): A Framework for Analysis." In *Korea's Globalization*, edited by Samuel S. Kim, 1–28. Cambridge: Cambridge University Press.

Kim, Samuel S., ed. 2000b. *Korea's Globalization*. Cambridge: Cambridge University Press.

Kim, Sang Ki, and Eun-ju Choi. 2021. "The Fallacy of North Korean Collapse." *38 North*, February 1. Accessed March 16, 2021. https://www.38north.org/2021/02/the-fallacy-of-north-korean-collapse/.

Kim, Soyoung. 2005. "'Cine-Mania' or Cinephilia: Film Festivals and the Identity Question." In *New Korean Cinema*, edited by Chi-Yun Shin and Julian Stringer, 79–91. Edinburgh: Edinburgh University Press.

Kim, Young-Chan, Doo-Jin Kim, Yŏng-jun Kim, and Young Kim, eds. 2008. *South Korea: Challenging Globalisation and the Post-Crisis Reforms*. Oxford: Chandos.

Kim, Young-jin. 2019. "A Review of Korean Cinema in 2019: The Enormous Success of *Parasite*, and the Shadow of Polarization." In *Korean Film Report 2019*, edited by KOFIC, 8–15. Busan: KOFIC.

Lankov, Andrei. 2013. *The Real North Korea: Life and Politics in the Failed Stalinist Utopia*. Oxford: Oxford University Press.

Lankov, Andrei. 2017. "As New Sanctions Bite, They'll Hurt North Korea's Few Entrepreneurs, Resolution 2375 Represents a Major Blow to the DPRK's Private Sector." *NK News*, November 22.

Lewis, James. 2002. "Introduction." In *Korea and Globalization: Politics, Economics and Culture*, edited by James B. Lewis and Amadu Sesay, 1–9. London: Routledge

Lewis, James, and Amadu Sesay, eds. 2002. *Korea and Globalization: Politics, Economics and Culture*. London: Routledge

Macias, Monique. 2014. "In North Korea, China's Tiananmen Square Protests Stirred Hope for Change." *The Guardian* (UK), June 4. Accessed January 16, 2021. https://www.theguardian.com/world/2014/jun/04/north-korea-china-tiananmen-square-protests.

Merkel, Udo. 2013. "The Grand Mass Gymnastics and Artistic Performance Arirang' (2002–2012): North Korea's Socialist–Realist Response to Global Sports Spectacles." *The International Journal of the History of Sport* 30 (11): 1247–1258.

Myrseth, August. 2016. "Beyond Politics of Revenge: Recontextualizing the 13th World Festival of Youth and Students." MA diss., SOAS, the University of London.

Noland, Marcus. 2009. "The (Non-)Impact of UN Sanctions on North Korea." *Asia Policy* 7: 61–88.

Paquet, Darcy. 2009. *New Korean Cinema: Breaking the Waves*. London: Wallflower Press.

Parc, Jimmyn. 2017. "The Effects of Protection in Cultural Industries: The Case of the Korean Film Policies." *International Journal of Cultural Policy* 23 (5): 618–663.

Park, Joseph Sung-Yul. 2015. *The Local Construction of a Global Language: Ideologies of English in South Korea*. Berlin: De Gruyter, Inc.

Park, Mi Sook. 2015. "South Korea Cultural History Between 1960s and 2012." *International Journal of Korean Humanities and Social Sciences* 1: 71–118

Potter, Pitman B. 2009. "Foreword." In *Korea Confronts Globalization*, edited by Chang Yun-shik, Seok Hyun-ho, and Donald Baker, xv–xvii. New York: Routledge.

Schönherr, Johannes. 2012. *North Korean Cinema: A History*. Jefferson, NC: McFarland.

Smith, Hazel. 2015. *North Korea: Markets and Military Rule*. Cambridge: Cambridge University Press.

Szalontai, Balázs. 2009. "Expulsion for a Mistranslated Poem: The Diplomatic Aspects of North Korean Cultural Politics." In *Dynamics of the Cold War in Asia: Ideology, Identity, and Culture*, edited by Tuong Vu and Wasana Wongsurawat, 145–164. New York: Palgrave Macmillan.

Vaish, Viniti. 2010. "Introduction: Globalization of Language and Culture in Asia." In *Globalization of Language and Culture in Asia: The Impact of Globalization Processes on Language*, edited by Viniti Vaish, 1–13. London: Bloomsbury.

Yecies, Brian. 2007. "Parleying Culture against Trade: Hollywood's Affairs with Korea's Screen Quotas." Korea Observer, 38(1), Spring, 1–32.

Young, Benjamin R. 2021. *Guns, Guerillas, and the Great Leader: North Korea and the Third World*. Stanford: Stanford University Press.

PART I

Film

INTRODUCTION

Andrew David Jackson

This opening section turns its attention to film from the two Koreas in the new millennium. Cinema is perhaps the most prominent of Korea's cultural industries; its success is a significant source of patriotic pride and a vital way to influence the population's view of national self.[1] The motion pictures examined below appeared when the cinematic industries of the two Koreas were heading in very different trajectories: the South's cinema experienced enormous success after a period of decline, while the North's was stagnating. These contrasting paths occurred while filmmakers in the North and South were strongly pushing to maximize their audience sizes and achieve domestic and international success in a transformed global market.

South Korean film had been dealing with an existential crisis between the late 1980s opening of the market to direct distribution from Hollywood majors (see the general introduction to this volume) and the release of *Shiri* (Kang Je-gyu 1999, ROK). In *Shiri*, South Korean filmmakers developed a lucrative formula that continued with subsequent big-selling box office hits over the next two decades.[2] The producers used canny marketing and mass distribution strategies to maximize their audience sizes (Howard 2008, 90). The film proved appealing to both domestic and international audiences because it provided Hollywood-style spectacles, first-class production values, and exciting deadline-driven narratives. However, South Korean filmmakers also added specific touches that differentiated the domestic industry from Hollywood. For example, these major productions had storylines that, unlike Hollywood fare, often featured "nihilistic, tragic" endings in which protagonists only "partially achieve their goals" (Choi 2010, 48). Most importantly, these films increased their appeal by treating Korean historical subject matter (for example, *Shiri* examines the North–South conflict; Davis and Yeh 2008, 16). Producers drew local audiences back to domestic cinema by:

> evoking a sense of crisis – the encroachment of the domestic market by the "foreign" companies. Consumer nationalism – the idea that consumers' choice should be based on national interests – is achieved through the producing of nation-specific (not necessarily nationalistic) contents. (Choi 2010, 38)

Shiri's release signaled the start of a turnaround in the fortunes of South Korean cinema. It performed well abroad and began a trend for South Korean commercial genre films to be exported into regional cinema markets. Most importantly, it scored a symbolic victory over imported Hollywood movies, which the Korean film industry feared were about to swamp the domestic market and crush local movies, as had occurred in Taiwan and Hong Kong (Davis and Yeh 2008, 10, 19).[3] *Shiri* ended up outselling Hollywood big-budget spectaculars[4] and ushered in a new era of South Korean blockbusters that created a buzz among ordinary film viewers and drew increasingly large audiences back to the cinema. Within a couple of years of *Shiri's* release, 10 million admissions at the domestic box office became the holy grail for many South Korean commercial film producers. The past twenty years have seen many of these mass-selling films passing that threshold, including *Silmido* (Kang Woo-suk 2003, ROK), *Myŏngnyang (The Admiral: Roaring Currents*, Kim Han-min, 2014, ROK—17.6 million admissions) and *Amsal (Assassination,* Choi Dong-hoon, 2015, ROK—12.7 million entries). These enormous audiences were vital since domestic ticket sales account for most of the revenue generated by South Korean films (Howard 2008, 90).[5] While not the only part of the South Korean film renaissance, blockbusters represent a significant factor in the success of the domestic cinema industry.[6] The South Korean film industry had transformed itself in response to global forces of commerce and became a global model for success (Parc 2017).

Like *Shiri,* many of the most domestically successful films also took Korean history or the reality of peninsular political division as the subject of their narrative. *The Admiral: Roaring Currents* looks at the historical exploits of Korean hero Admiral Yi Sun-sin, who, despite being vastly outnumbered, managed to defeat a Japanese invasion force at the Battle of Myŏngnyang in 1597. *Assassination* tells the story of attempts by Korean independence fighters in China to assassinate key figures in the Japanese colonial administration that ruled Korea between 1910 and 1945 (Won 2015). The national focus of Korean films is also an important avenue that allows the country's artists and audiences to revisit an often traumatic past.[7] James Lewis (2002, 6) argues that when "modern Koreans look beyond the Peninsula, the first people they see are the Japanese. The Peninsula and archipelago have been joined from antiquity …", and this close and often fraught relationship has provided some of the most painful historical moments for the Koreans. It is no surprise that two mass-selling South Korean films, *The Admiral: Roaring Currents* and *Assassination*, cover different historical conflicts between the two countries. The Korean historical and geopolitical subject matter, combined with its appeal to consumer nationalism, proved to be a particularly potent marketing tool that greatly contributed to the rejuvenation of South Korean cinema. The nation-specific historical subject allows South Korean cinema to survive and prosper in the face of the opening of the Korean film market to globalization.

In the early part of the 2000s, when South Korean film was reversing its cinematic fortunes, the North Korean film industry was experiencing an existential crisis. Even before the international and domestic success of the Shin Sang-ok era, the country had a robust industry since it regarded cinema as a vital means to mobilize and socialize the population (Lee 2000, 33). North Korea had one of the highest motion picture attendance rates in the world in the mid-1980s, although many of these were not feature films, but public information pictures screened at factories with an explicit indoctrination function (Kim 1996, 89). The vital role of film to mobilize and inculcate duties and discipline to the population may explain why North Korea continued to produce large numbers of motion pictures throughout the devastating famine despite the virtual economic collapse. According to Johannes Schönherr, films made during this period specifically reflected elite concerns about the fragmentation of society caused by economic collapse (2012, 124–142). By the time the worst of famine was over, state funding for films appeared to have dried up, and only a meager output of films saw the light of day from the early 2000s onwards (Schönherr 2012, 158). A large number of those movies produced were also international co-productions because of the prohibitive costs involved—North Korean film was in crisis.

As the introduction to this volume makes clear, the Kim Jong Il-led North Korean film industry had attempted to make movies appealing to international audiences in the 1980s as part of a soft policy strategy. In the Sunshine Policy period of warmer ties between the two Koreas, the DPRK repeated on a smaller, less ambitious level its 1980s' cultural diplomacy attempt, and this time attempted to project a softer image to the international community through cinema.[8] However, international audiences of the early 2000s were very different from cinema-goers from economically ailing socialist countries of the 1980s. As Andrew David Jackson's chapter clarifies, DPRK filmmakers struggled to make films that satisfied three audiences—domestic and international viewers, as well as the watchful state authorities. Each of these groups often had conflicting expectations. The difficulty faced by filmmakers outside the DPRK was that international audiences struggled to accept hagiographic representations of the leadership with the cinematic depictions of post-famine society. Jackson's essay looks at the case of one film that depicts the social and economic changes in North Korea resulting from marketization from below and greater contact with world beyond the border and which squared the circle by appealing to both domestic and international audiences in addition to the state authorities.

The two other essays in this part focus on films taking Korea's historical situation as their subject and which have done so much to transform the fortunes of South Korean films domestically and internationally. Russell Edwards' chapter explores perhaps the most traumatic of Korea's historical experiences focusing on representations of Japan in South Korean film made during the presidency of Park Geun-hye. By examining a number of recently-made films covering Korea's historical relationship with Japan, he explores the many ongoing controversies associated with this relationship and its cinematic representation. Park Geun-hye, of course, is part of this controversy because of her attempt to negotiate a treaty with the Japanese Government that would resolve the Comfort Women issue once and for all. In this agreement, there are clear parallels to the actions of her father, the dictator Park Chung Hee, who in 1965 had also negotiated an unpopular reparation deal with the Japanese authorities and normalized diplomatic relations. The 1965 Treaty provided critical financial benefits that helped kickstart the South Korean economy and initiate three decades of significant growth, but in the minds of many, the agreement never sufficiently compensated the Koreans for the collective historical trauma they had suffered during the colonial period. Niall McMahon's chapter also treats a film that revisits a traumatic domestic past, this time the 1980 Kwangju Uprising—a massacre of civilians protesting the military dictatorship. This was a crucial event in South Korean history that redefined the country's relationship with the United States, which was blamed by many for tacitly approving the killings. The film *Isipyungnyŏn* (*26 Years*, Cho Kŭn-hyŏn 2012) was deemed too controversial for mainstream movie company production, and as a result had to be crowd-funded, although it ended up attracting large audiences. It is further evidence of the significant place that historical film occupies in the South Korean cinematic landscape.

Notes

1. Film can also offer a snapshot, as Hyangjin Lee argues, into the understandings of gender, nationhood and class of societies at any historical moment (2000, 1).
2. The film was made for less than US $3 million but went on to gross over $26.5 million in domestic box offices alone, selling almost 2.5 million tickets in Seoul and 5.8 million nationwide in a country of 50 million.
3. Taiwan averaged over 200 local films in the 1970s but only managed 17 local release by 2006; Hong Kong saw the release of 100 local films in 1996, in 1997 domestic films took 50% of the total box office but by 2006, this had dropped to 27% (Davis and Yeh 2008, 10, 19, 30–33).
4. For example, *The Mummy* (Stephen Sommers, 1999) and *The Matrix* (Lana and Lilly Wachowski, 1999, US).
5. Between 2001 and 2004 for example, 74–75% of revenues came from domestic box offices. Only between 3 and 10% of income came from overseas exports and ancillary sales, suggesting that in contrast to Jinhee Choi's claims, the nationalistic content of films did not always appeal to viewers abroad (Howard 2008, 88–89).
6. Films like *Yŏpkijŏgin kŭnyŏ* (*My Sassy Girl*, Kwak Chae-yong, 2001) were also domestic and international successes (Davis and Yeh 2008, 23).
7. This focus on historical subjects is also a important feature of (domestically) successful North Korean films as Steve Chung (2014, 172–174) observes. The majority of DPRK films until the end of the 1980s depicted the historical period between the late-1920s and 1953 end of the Korean War. He argues that domestic audiences found pleasure in "returning to the moment of [historical] humiliation" (Chung 2014, 172–174).

8. See Jackson's chapter in this volume and Schönherr (2012, 148–164) for further details about the films produced in this period. Kim Dae Jung introduced a Sunshine Policy (1998–2008) aimed at improving ties between Seoul and Pyongyang.

References

Choi, Jin-hee. 2010. *The South Korean Film Renaissance: Local Hitmakers, Global Provocateurs*. Middletown: Wesleyan University Press.

Chung, Steven. 2014. *Split Screen Korea: Shin Sang-ok and Postwar Cinema*. Minneapolis: University of Minnesota Press.

Davis, Darrell William and Emilie Yueh-yu Yeh. 2008. *East Asian Screen Industries*. London: BFI Publishing.

Howard, Chris. 2008. "Contemporary South Korean Cinema: 'National Conjunction' and 'Diversity.'" In *East Asian Cinemas: Exploring Transnational Connections on Film*, edited by Leon Hunt and Leung Wing-Fai, 88–102. London: I.B. Taurus.

Kim, Kyung Hyun. 1996. "The Fractured Cinema of North Korea: The Discourse of the Nation in *Sea of Blood*." In *In Pursuit of Contemporary East Asian Culture*, edited by Xiobing Tang and Stephen Snyder, 85–106. London: Routledge.

Lee, Hyangjin. 2000. *Contemporary Korean Cinema: Identity, Culture, Politics*. Manchester: Manchester University Press.

Lewis, James. 2002. "Introduction." In *Korea and Globalization: Politics, Economics and Culture*, edited by James B. Lewis and Amadu Sesay, 1–9. London: Routledge.

Parc, Jimmyn. 2017. "The Effects of Protection in Cultural Industries: The Case of the Korean Film Policies." *International Journal of Cultural Policy* 23 (5), 618–663.

Schönherr, Johannes. 2012. *North Korean Cinema: A History*. Jefferson, N.C.: McFarland.

Won, Ho-jung. 2015. "'Assassination' an Ode to Korea's 1930s Independence Fighters." *The Korea Herald*. June 22. http://www.koreaherald.com/view.php?ud=20150622001025. Accessed January 17, 2021.

CHAPTER 2

The Dictator's Daughter and the Rising Sun: Scars of Colonialism in South Korean Cinema During the Park Geun-hye Era

Russell Edwards

When compared to nations that were colonized by European powers, the legacy of the Japanese colonial period in South Korea is cloaked by the latter country's progress in factors such as independence of government, a strong economy and reclamation of the original language. The extent of the country's decolonization is also evident in South Korea's film industry. With its strong domestic support base South Korean cinema has created a comfortable (though vigilant) position in its home market alongside Hollywood films and shows no signs of being overwhelmed by contemporary Japanese cinema despite the 1998 relaxing of trade embargoes which had prohibited the distribution of Japanese films (and other cultural products) in South Korea (Paquet 2009, 2). Significantly, South Korean cinema's percentage of domestic box office share has not dropped below

R. Edwards (✉)
RMIT University, Melbourne, VIC, Australia

© The Author(s), under exclusive license to Springer Nature Switzerland AG 2022
A. D. Jackson (ed.), *The Two Koreas and their Global Engagements*, https://doi.org/10.1007/978-3-030-90761-7_2

35

30% since 1998 and typically, as *Variety* reported on March 19, 2019, local box office share hovers around 55% each year (Kil and Frater 2019).

However, regardless of these postcolonial facts, the impact of the Japanese colonial period is often highly visible, and it is clear that South Koreans are emotionally invested in the lingering impact of the Japanese colonial period. Between July 2014 and September 2017, a financially successful run of South Korean films managed to combine their pointed interest in South Korea's and Japan's relationship with frequent reference to the Japanese colonial period. Drawing on studies of film cycles, this chapter demonstrates how the truncated Presidency of Park Geun-hye which ran from February 2013 to her ousting in March 2017, was shadowed by what I call the Rising Sun cycle. Making allowances for the gestation period of filmmaking, this chapter argues that the Rising Sun cycle owes at least part of its existence to Park's influence (intentional or otherwise).

Hyangjin Lee observes, "the Korean film industry is inseparable from the political situation of the country" (2001, 16). While Lee examined film across the Korean Peninsula since cinema's beginnings, the revelations that surrounded the 2017 deposition of Park ensures that this statement still strongly resonates. The extent of the Park government's involvement with the South Korean film industry was rarely spoken of publicly until, as reported by *Screen International*, South Korean newspaper *Hankook Ilbo* (*Han'guk Ilbo*) published revelations of a blacklist (Noh 2016a). On January 10, 2017, Seoul-based *Variety* reporter Sonia Kil described the blacklist as further evidence of Park's corruption; and in a subsequent May 9, 2017 report on the election of the new President Moon Jae-in, the blacklist was regarded as a contributor to the unraveling of Park's administration and her resulting impeachment alongside other factors including Park's tardy response to the Sewol Ferry disaster (Kil 2017a, b). The existence of the blacklist and its political consequences suggests that popular films released and developed during Park's Presidential term should be scrutinized.

Politically conservative Park was elected to the Presidency in 2013 via direct presidential elections established in South Korea in 1987. However, as the daughter of the dictator, Park Chung Hee, who ruled South Korea as President from 1963 to 1979, Park Geun-hye was sensitive to, and about, her father's legacy—positive and negative. While from the late 1990s to 2007 South Korea had left-wing governments, it was the

Chaebol structure consisting of conglomerates controlled by elite families which thrived under Park's dictatorship that could take credit for the foundations of the economic prosperity (including the local film industry) that now makes South Korea the tenth largest economy in the world (*Statistic Times* 2020).

Park Geun-hye was a first-hand witness to the economic transformation of South Korea; and her political profile began in 1974 when the assassination of her mother, Yuk Young-soo [Yuk Yŏng-su], thrust her into the role of the country's substitute "First Lady" at the age of twenty-two. Despite the assassination of her father in 1979 and South Korea's subsequent shift from dictatorship to democracy a decade later, Park developed a legitimate political career arc, which assured many that it was inevitable that she would eventually aim to become the country's President. When campaigning for the Presidency in 2012, Park Geun-hye, in an opinion piece in *The Wall Street Journal*, drew parallels between the post-World War Two reconciliation in Europe and the path ahead for Northeast Asia:

> Northeast Asia also requires corresponding steps from the region's main historical and wartime transgressor. The lingering pain of Asia's victims, including Korea's and other countries so-called comfort women, as well as outstanding historical legacies must be fundamentally addressed. Only then will Japan be welcomed as a respectable and leading Asian country. And if Northeast Asia is to skilfully overcome its historical legacies while contributing to global norms, it has to champion open nationalism that enhances the spirit of community building while safeguarding universal values and democratic governance. (Park 2012)

While Park was forthcoming about her geopolitical concerns, she was less public about her issues with the South Korean film industry. Due to its associations with the 1980s democracy movement (Paquet 2009, 15), the South Korean film industry of the democratic era has not always been kind to the memory of Park Chung Hee. For example, Mark Morris (2009) outlines how the release of *Kŭttae Kŭsaramdŭl* (*The President's Last Bang*, Im Sang-soo [Im Sang-su], 2005)—a depiction of the dictator on the last night of his life—was legally contested as defamation of character by Park's surviving family for its linking of satirical fiction with political fact. The film depicts the dictator carousing with young women, cowardly in the face of danger and fond of Japanese culture, often speaking Japanese to his Korean colleagues. The film was still released, but for a time until the legal decision was overturned, some footage was blacked out including newsreel footage of Park Chung Hee's funeral. Notably, it was the production company MK Pictures that had to pay damages to the Park family and not the Chaebol that distributed and exhibited the film, CJ Entertainment (Morris 2009, 208–211).

Presently known as CJ ENM (CJ Entertainment aNd Merchandising, hereafter CJ), this corporation, which began as a sugar refinery company spun off from the Samsung empire, is South Korea's most influential film Chaebol. Paquet (2009), Russell (2008), and Yecies and Shim (2016) have all provided in-depth descriptions of how CJ has dominated South Korea's film business with its vertically integrated structure. The company owns multiplex theaters in which the films it distributes are provided to South Korean audiences, before the films are shown on CJ's cable TV channels. CJ also has a steady relationship with a number of production companies which—through seed investment—are essentially affiliate components of the Chaebol. CJ's largest competitor Lotte entered the film business after a 1996 deal between CJ and the Department Store/Hotel chain went sour. Lotte created its own cinema franchise single-handedly and followed CJ's lead of creating film productions to also distribute domestically and internationally (Russell 2008). Along with CJ and Lotte, similarly vertically integrated companies Showbox (which began investing in film production in 2002) and Next Entertainment World (aka N.E.W., established 2008) make-up the "big four" corporate (and dominant) players in the industry (Yecies and Shim 2016, 11). According to an April 27, 2019 *Yonhap News Agency* report, CJ and Lotte between them control nearly 80% of South Korean movie screens (Park 2019).

As CJ had distributed *The President's Last Bang* and had also raised the ire of the new President with their local version of *Saturday Night Live*, which (like its American namesake) satirized politicians including Park herself, it is unsurprising that the Chaebol became a focus for President Park's attention. *The Straits Times* reported on November 17, 2016 that phone recordings leaked to cable news network MBN indicate that, via her economic secretary Cho Won Dong (Cho Wŏn-dong), President Park pressured CJ Chairman Sohn Kyung-shik (Son Kyŏng-sik) to remove CJ's Vice-chairwoman, Miky Lee (Yi Mi-gyŏng), in July 2013 (*Straits Times* 2016; Noh 2016b). Furthermore, as reported by Jin-hae Park for *The Korea Times* on January 16, 2017, in November 2014, Park Geun-hye personally visited Sohn to further communicate her concerns about the

South Korean film industry's perceived "anti-government" stance. Sohn allegedly offered multiple apologies and said: "I've cleaned up everything. From this moment, our direction will change. We are currently making movies such as *The Admiral: Roaring Currents* that give priority to the national interest." CJ also made other moves to appease the government. In their cinemas, CJ screened prior to the main features, "three-minute-long promotional videos supportive of the administration's Creative Economy policy" (Park 2017). In addition, CJ also further invested in blockbuster films that would appeal to nationalism such as *Inchŏn Sangnyukcha'kjŏn* (*Operation Chromite*, John H. Lee [Yi Chaehan], 2016) about General MacArthur's pushback against communist invasion during the Korean War (Park 2017; Kil 2017b).

As Claire Lee reported in *The Korean Herald* on December 26, 2013, South Korea was already experiencing a general boom in period films when *The Admiral: Roaring Currents* (hereafter *Roaring Currents*) went into pre-production (Lee 2013). Fitting comfortably with Park's political aims for the local film industry, *Roaring Currents* domestically remains the most successful South Korean film ever, selling a total of 17.6 million tickets. It was no accident that *Roaring Currents* was already in preproduction when Park Geun-hye came to power. In many ways, Sohn's meeting with Park merely formalized the political reality. On December 6, 2016 multiple Chaebol CEOs admitted to feeling pressured by Park's administration (Reuters 2016) while later, on February 16, 2018 the *Asian Nikkei Review* reported that the Chairman of Lotte Group, Shin Dong-bin was jailed as a contributor to Park's slush fund (Suzuki 2018).

Sohn's nomination of *Roaring Currents* as proof of loyalty to the government was almost guaranteed to hit a chord with Park. The story of Yi Sun-shin and his repelling of a Japanese invasion in the sixteenth century had been filmed before. Just before Park Chung Hee came to power, Yu Hyŏn-mok made *Sŏng'ung Yi Sun-sin* (*Great Hero, Lee Sun-sin*, 1962) at a time when, as Moon Seungsook describes, Admiral Yi was elevated to the position of a "sacred hero" (Moon 1998, 43). Yu's script was remade as *Sŏngung Yi Sun-sin* (*Yi Sun-sin the Hero*, Yi Kyu-ung, 1971) when, as Kim Kyung Hyun states, Yi's "iconicity was cinematically reproduced to appease the government" (2004, 16). This version was successful enough to inspire yet another dramatization of Yi's military career later in the decade entitled *Nanjung Ilgi* (*The Diary of the Korean-Japanese War*, Jang Il-ho [Chang Il-ho], 1977). It was Park who suggested the placement of an iconic statue "of a person most admired and feared by the Japanese" at a major intersection of Sejongno close to the former Japanese General Government Building that had been the seat of Japanese power during colonization, and the links from Admiral Yi to Dictator Park were strengthened in the South Korean imagination when the President unveiled the statue in 1968 (Kim 2015).

Cycles, Currents, and the Rising Sun

According to genre theorist Steve Neale, a film cycle consists of "groups of films made within a specific and limited time-span, and founded, for the most part, on the characteristics of individual commercial successes" (2000, 9). With that definition, it should not be surprising that a film as popular as *Roaring Currents* can be easily positioned as part of a cycle of period films. However, the film also possesses elements that distinguish it from previous period films in that cycle. In particular, what distinguishes *Roaring Currents* from director Kim Han-min's previous period blockbuster, *Ch'oechongbyŏnggi Hwal* (*The War of the Arrows*, 2011) and that in fact more than doubled the box office of the earlier film, is the latter film's attitude toward its villains, the Japanese.

From the outset, *Roaring Currents* seems designed to stoke anti-Japanese sentiment. The film opens with a title card that reads: "1592, First Japanese invasion." Then, over a map graphic of Eastern Asia, a red mark resembling blood appears on Japan's main island Honshu. As Korean titles explain that, "when his free passage to China was rejected, Chancellor Toyotomi declares war on Chosŏn," the bloody smudge moves paintbrush-like across the screen. The red blemish then smears the Korean Peninsula, implying the bloodshed that Japanese forces brought to Korean shores. This image of a wound that envelops Chosŏn is emblematic of how colonization is represented, and as I will show, has its echo in a number of Rising Sun films. While the events depicted in *Roaring Currents* are almost five centuries old, its links to contemporary South Korean perceptions of Japan are clear in its stereotyping of Yi's adversaries as loathsome figures and the film's noticeable emphasis on early versions of the 日の丸 *Hinomaru* that serves as the contemporary national flag for Japan.

Advancing on Neale's work which also places financial drivers as a central characteristic of film cycles, Amanda Ann Klein stipulates that cycles come in two forms: the intrageneric cycle and intergeneric cycle (2011, 9). The most relevant to Rising Sun films is the intergeneric cycle, which typically consists of films that are released by several studios around the same time—therefore *not* subject to a house style. Klein writes of how intergeneric cycles can be initiated by a single film—such as *Roaring Currents*—before attaching itself to other genres such as horror and thrillers as the cycle continues.[1] Klein further points out that similarities in early films in a cycle can occur due to "some socio-cultural cue — new artistic trend, a social problem, a political movement, or a defining world event — that several film-makers decide to address independently of one another" (Klein 2011, 12). It is my contention that, along with other factors, Park's Presidency fulfills the stimulating criterion that Klein mentions. There are almost twenty films that I have identified in this Rising Sun cycle, most of which debuted in the number one position at the South Korean box office, authenticating the cycle's popular appeal.[2]

Naturally, there have been earlier instances of South Korean films concerned with Japan, and as my earlier citing of Lee (2001) indicates, the idea that the South Korean film industry has been in lockstep with government policy is not new. Popular films such as *Swiri* (*Shiri*, Kang Je-gyu [Kang Che-gyu], 1999) and *Kongdong Kyŏngbi Kuyŏk JSA* (*Joint Security Area*, Park Chan-wook [Pak Ch'an-uk], 2000) have been identified as helping to pivot South Korean attitudes toward North Koreans in line with the Sunshine Policy of Kim Dae Jung (Paquet 2009, 71–74). Interestingly, soon after these Sunshine films emerged, there was a small cycle of films dealing with the Japanese colonial period that Frances Gateward (2007) described as "anti-Japanese."[3] This was not a one-time event. Jinsoo An (2018) indicates that there had been previous cyclical cinematic manifestations of anti-Japanese sentiment in the Manchurian Westerns, *Kisaeng* films and Korean gangster films of the 1960s and 1970s. While he doesn't describe it as such, Kim Kyung Hyun (2011) notes a similarly small cycle of films about the Japanese colonial period appearing again during the presidential term of Lee Myung-bak (Kim 2011, 59).[4] At that time, the spectacular box office failure of *Maiwei* (*My Way*, Kang Je-gyu [Kang Che-gyu], 2011) and its story of a troubled relationship between a Japanese soldier and a Korean soldier underlined how far away the possibility of South Korean and Japanese reconciliation over postcolonial issues sat from the public mood. While Kate Taylor-Jones felt that *My Way*'s failure was "likely a rejection of war drama" (2017, 144), director Kang thought otherwise. In a *Korea JoongAng Daily* interview published October 10, 2012, Kang said: "Blockbusters are centered on themes that appeal to the public, and a friendship between a Korean and a Japanese man during the colonial rule probably appeals to a handful of people" (Sunwoo 2012). In Kang's comment lies the germ of difference between his flop and *Roaring Currents*' distinctive success: its approach to Japan. What further distinguishes the Rising Sun films from the "anti-Japanese" films that Gateward identified and most of the colonial films of the Lee Myung-bak era is that the Rising Sun films were profitable and prominent on South Korea's box office chart. I argue that this background, which combined a conservative political environment, a boom in non-Japan-related period films, and an example of what not to do in the form of the box office failure of *My Way*, paved the way for the creation of *Roaring Currents*. This, in turn, prompted the new cycle of Rising Sun films, which echoes earlier anti-Japanese sentiments noted by Gateward but with box office success similar to the 1960s and 1970s films highlighted by An.

Consistent with Klein's definition of an intergeneric cycle, the Rising Sun films of the Park Geun-hye era are spread across different genres: action movies, thrillers, biopics, melodrama, gothic horror, and in the case of *Ai K'aen Sup'ik'u* (*I Can Speak*, Kim Hyun-seok [Kim Hyŏn-sŏk], 2017), even a comedy/drama. Most of the films share an interest in the Japanese colonial period that is not intrinsic to their individual genre classification. Having attached themselves to multiple genres, Klein emphasizes how these cycles often peter out within five to ten years, as they tend to reuse plots or to repeat the same images within a short period of time. In the case of Rising Sun films there are multiple examples of such repetitions of imagery. Such repeated images include the 旭日旗 (*Kyokujitsu-ki*) aka Rising Sun flags, the stereotype of evil Japanese and upon occasion, even the token "good" Japanese characters. Building on my description of the blood painted across a map of Korea that appears in the opening of *Roaring Currents*, this chapter highlights the recurring imagery of wounds and scars in Rising Sun films.

In contrast to the idea that decolonization can become "a search for an essential cultural purity" (Ashcroft et al. 1991, 41), the Rising Sun films do not envisage a return to a paradise before Japanese Occupation, but illustrate the marks of colonization as still healing. To use the words of Trauma Studies theorist Linnie Blake, these films depict: "the diverse ways in which traumatic memories have been inscribed as *wounds* on the cultural, social psychic and political life of those that have experienced them, and [are] those cultural products that seek to represent such experiences to those who have not" (2008, 1. *My emphasis*). While Blake is concerned exclusively with horror films, the repeated images of wounds and scarring in these South Korean films suggests that such images are a valid starting point for analyzing the Rising Sun cycle.

It has been attributed to Russian filmmaker and theorist Sergei Eisenstein that films are "wounds" due to the "original act of tearing a piece of the world from its 'natural' place" (Redmond 2013, 38; Rothman 2004, 350). In turn, Nick Hodgin and Amit Thakkar emphasize that they "believe that the scar motif is helpful in avoiding terms which evoke a teleological process of 'healing' that risks underplaying the permanence of the damage done by trauma" (2017, 12–13). They emphasize two key aspects of a scar's structure as "lack of resolution and the need for explicatory narrative" (Hodgin and Thakkar 2017, 14).

Citing several medical sources to point out that scars are only 70–90% as strong as the original skin tissue, Hodgin and Thakkar build their case for using wounds and scars as metaphor for postcolonial trauma: "Films acting much like scars in their formation, as a present and ongoing process of organised engagement with the original wound in which it is implicitly accepted that what is reproduced is not the wound itself but a simulacrum of it" (16). Thus, while the widely quoted adage from *Le Petit Soldat* (*The Little Soldier*, Jean-Luc Godard, 1963) "cinema is truth twenty-four times a second" is appealing, writers from Hodgin and Thakkar to Rosenstone (2001) would confirm that South Korean representations of the colonial era are not true representations of the time or their participants, but a simulacrum of the era and by definition a distortion of the time period remembered and the wounds sustained. Quoting Gilles Deleuze's declaration that a scar is not the sign of a past wound but of "the present fact of having been wounded" (Hodgin and Thakkar 2017, 16), Hodgin and Thakkar imply that the existence of scars means that the original wounds of the past cannot be completely healed and that all postcolonial wounds are susceptible to a kind of scurvy of the soul that endangers them to re-opening, thus: "Scars can be passed from generation to generation, making them polytemporal" (Hodgin and Thakkar 2017, 19). This idea indeed fits with Gateward's observation of her "anti-Japanese" cycle that these films were made for and by people who had no direct experience of the Japanese colonial period (2007, 194). Before looking at specific examples of wounds in the Rising Sun cycle, one difference must be highlighted: in contrast to Hodgin and Thakkar's emphasis that their volume is not directly about scarring or the scar motif (Hodgin and Thakkar 2017, 23), this chapter is precisely about the repeated representations of such motifs as well as their place in a cycle of films made and released during Park Geun-hye's Presidency.

THE SILENCED, THE COMFORT WOMEN AND THE TURNING OF THE CYCLE

Within a year of *Roaring Currents* being released, Lotte distributed horror film, *Kyŏngsŏng Hakkyo: Sarajin Sonyŏdŭl* (*The Silenced*, Lee Hae-young [Yi Hae-yŏng], 2015). Lee's film is the story of a sickly Korean high schooler who arrives at a sanatorium/boarding school for teenage girls operated by a collaborationist headmistress who uses her charges for Japanese genetic experiments investigating physical prowess. Two images highlighted by Taylor–Jones are especially relevant (2017, 146–147). The first is a tapestry map of Korea embroidered with Japanese cherry blossoms unfurled near the film's beginning. This foreshadows a second, more shocking image that appears at the film's climax and which has echoes of Japan's notorious *maruta* experiments.[5] When the girls turn on their torturers/carers, the headmistress has her own skin embellished with the same embroidered cherry blossom motif that decorated the tapestry. Taylor-Jones describes this as a literal representation of the headmistress' desire to become Japanese. I would agree, but I also consider this image in the context of disfigurement of Korean citizens in other films that represent the "scar" of Japanese colonialism including *Amsal* (*Assassination*, Choi Dong-hoon [Ch'oe Tong-hun], 2015), *Sŏkcho Chŏt'aek Sarin Saŏn* (*The Tooth and the Nail*, Jung Sik, Kim Whee [Chŏng Sik, Kim Hwi], 2016), and *I Can Speak*. I acknowledge that as an act of retribution, the embroidery of skin differs from the scarring presented in other films: but whether it be an act of revenge or as the recipient of sadism, there is no removing the scar once it has been made.

Taylor-Jones also observes that the girls in *The Silenced* "are both the victims of colonial rule but also the means via which it can be defeated" (2017, 148). This accurately reflects the film's plot, which has the Korean schoolgirls develop superpowers as a result of Japanese medical experiments. But more than this, the virginal girls, who represent both sullied purity and Korean power, are a stand-in for the real-life Comfort Women who were often girls themselves. The Comfort Women were also created by the Japanese: and though the now-aging women do not possess superpowers, the continuing pressure applied by South Korea on Japan about the justness of a formal Comfort Women apology acts as another way to defeat the legacy of the colonial period. Furthermore, by using schoolgirls as Comfort Women stand-ins, *The Silenced* manifests Kim and Choi's (1998) observation that anti-colonial nationalism re-constructs the Comfort Women as "national virgins" (1998, 5). The revenge the schoolgirls take on their collaborationist headmistress may be extremely violent, but is metaphorically consistent with widespread South Korean anger about the Comfort Women issue and compatible with Park's own (previously quoted) call for Japan to address "historical legacies" (Park 2012). *Roaring Currents* and *The Silenced* were both shot and released *before* Park's meeting with the CJ Chairman. While Park clearly tried to influence the local industry, film cycles have their own energy and can serve purposes contrary to, or in conflict with, the political agendas of those who would seek to steer them.

On December 28, 2015, Park announced—with Japan—a final deal on the Comfort Women issue (Choe 2015). However, in the wake of her more private request that CJ make "national interest" films, there came a series of films from CJ and other Chaebol that heightened the Comfort Women issue. Instead of complementing Park's Comfort Women deal with Japan, these films further fuelled dissatisfaction and heightened the tragedy of the Comfort Women experience both in the past and in the present. Coming mere weeks after the bi-lateral announcement, the popularity of the low-budget, independent film *Kwihyang* (*Spirits' Homecoming*, Cho Chŏng-rae, 2016) in February 2016 can be read as a public rebuke to Park's agreement with Japanese Prime Minister Abe Shinzo, and a signal that the South Korean public were unwilling to embrace Park's diplomatic efforts. The irony about this eruption of anti-Japanese movies is that, despite Park's desire to overcome "historical legacies" by settling the Comfort Women issue, the film-makers' version of nationalism often ran counter to Park's own vision of films in the "national interest" and her ideas of how issues with Japan should be resolved.

Partially due to Taylor-Jones' writing, *The Silenced* is steadily acquiring an academic profile that is greater than its box office performance. However, given that cycles are driven by box office success rather than box office failure, the rest of this chapter will emphasize the wound and scar imagery in Rising Sun films which resonated with local audiences during the Park Geun-hye era as reflected by most of them reaching the number one position in the box office charts. About five weeks after *The Silenced* was released, Showbox espionage film *Assassination* opened. This film has an equally confronting image of colonization's wound.

Largely an extended flashback related by a witness against a former double agent, *Assassination* tells the intersecting stories of several Korean insurgents as they position to assassinate Japanese officials and a wealthy Korean collaborator. Prior to the opening titles of *Assassination* (2015), that same collaborator, Kang In-guk (played by: Lee Kyoung-young [Yi Kyŏng-yŏng]) realizes that his wife (played by: Jin Kyung [Chin Kyŏng]) is hiding a Korean insurgent, Yŏm Sŏk-jin (played by Lee Jung-jae [Yi Chŏng-jae]). As Kang's awareness dawns, she taunts him by saying, "Japan conquered us without a fight. Don't we deserve better? We were just handed over by people like you." To avoid being implicated by the presence of the insurgent in his house, Kang allows his wife and the insurgent to escape, but instructs his butler (Kim Eui-sung [Kim Ŭi-sŏng]) that they must be pursued and killed. The subsequent execution of the wife shows her from behind as she sits in a rickshaw with the butler taking aim with a pistol. When the butler shoots, the blood spurting from the woman's head wound creates an eerie red blotch on the rear flap of the rickshaw that is a bloody subversion of the *Hinomaru*. Although there are no Japanese characters present in this scene, there is no mistaking the imprimatur of the Japanese military as delivered by their Korean agents. Like the blood that smears the map of Korea during the *Roaring Currents* opening, this *Hinomaru* bloodstain envelops the viewer's eye, offering no escape from its offensiveness and positioned as an object that must be confronted. As a stain, this *Hinomaru* also echoes the embroidered cherry blossoms as evidence of Korea being tainted by the Japanese presence.

While Kang's wife of course does not survive the *Hinomaru* wound, Yŏm, the insurgent she was protecting, escapes and emerges as one of the film's key players. In the course of *Assassination*, Yŏm becomes a covert collaborator himself, and whether he will successfully keep his Japanese informant status secret becomes central to the narrative. In a flashback within a flashback, the audience is made privy to the circumstances of Yŏm's conversion to the Japanese empire, where his fellow insurgents are killed and his own body is covered in wounds and blood. As the film draws to a close, Yŏm's body is revealed once again at his 1949 trial at the "War Crimes Investigation." The mysterious death of a key witness indicates both the degree of Yŏm's unwillingness to admit the truth and the omnipresent extent of pro-Japanese factions even within an independent Korea. In response to heckling from the courtroom gallery who believe him to be guilty, the now aged Yŏm strips to the waist for a flamboyant reply. Much to the shock of the court, Yŏm lists and physically indicates the locations of each of his bullet wounds and knife scars and recounts the patriotic circumstances under which the injuries were acquired. Yŏm offers his body and the accrued scars as physical evidence of his loyalty to Korea. While the film's audience knows Yŏm was a collaborator, they are as unable as the courtroom audience to determine which injuries were acquired in the fight against the Japanese and which were perhaps acquired while protecting the colonial forces.

Although not as dramatic or as extensive as Yŏm's scars, the protagonist of the legal thriller *The Tooth and The Nail*, Yi Sŏk-jin (played by: Ko Soo [Ko Su]) also bares a scar for all in the courtroom to see. Overlooked by many Western writers on South Korean cinema, *The Tooth and The Nail* is based on a 1955 pulp crime novel of the same title, and it is somewhat of a mystery in itself how this little known book by Bill S. Ballinger, a writer better known for his 1960s American television scripts for shows such as *Alfred Hitchcock Presents*, came to be adapted by the South Korean film industry. Regardless of its pre-production development, the script by co-director Jung Sik (Chŏng Sik) and Lee Jung-Ho (Yi Chŏng-ho) does an excellent job of transferring events from New York City to the Liberation-era Korea of the late 1940s. Like *Assassination*, the story of *The Tooth and The Nail* has its roots in the Japanese colonial period even if much of the action takes place in the Liberation era. The film, like the book, is split into alternating chapters which detail significant events of a murder trial and the earlier circumstances that spurred the trial into existence.

In the last chapter of the pre-trial events, the film reveals how Yi acquired the scar. Seeking revenge for his wife's death, through the course of the film Yi, a magician creates a false identity of Ch'oe and then works as a chauffeur for the former Japanese collaborator Nam To-jin (played by: Kim Ju-hyeok [Kim Chu-hyŏk]) whom he believes to be the culprit. Hoping to frame Nam for murder by falsifying Ch'oe's death, Yi finds himself in a physical struggle with Nam before the plan reaches fruition. During the altercation, Yi (as Ch'oe) acquires a facial wound caused when Nam fires a revolver and the ejected bullet grazes Yi's cheek. With Nam imprisoned, the film's post-trial coda reveals Yi to have exchanged his magician's career for a new performing role as a clown.

In his dressing room after a show, Yi looks into a mirror. Yi's face has the traditional white greasepaint base of a clown. Unremarkable is the spherical red nose that Yi removes from his face, but its removal brings into visual prominence the wide red mouth of clown make-up that sits on the white foundation on Yi's face. This creates an effect of this Korean man wearing a *Hinomaru* mask. Cutting to a closer view of Yi's face, the film concentrates on the act of removing the red make-up—the sun of a *Hinomaru* flag—and the white greasepaint with a sponge (Fig. 2.1). The face paint imprint of Japan must be removed to reveal the Korean man underneath. After the removal of the *Hinomaru* face paint, the metaphor continues. The image dissolves to show Yi from behind. The red sphere of the clown's nose sits plainly visible on the right hand side of the dressing table, but it is diminished in comparison to the large *Hinomaru* mouth Yi's face sported seconds earlier. Shortly after, clean-faced Yi now dressed in civilian clothes, turns away from the mirror and the scar from the gun blast from Nam—Japanese colonialism's emissary—assumes a central place on the screen's image (Fig. 2.2).

Similar to Yŏm's flamboyant showing of scars in *Assassination*'s courtroom, scars are once again used as a form of legal proof in *I Can Speak*. Released a few months after the deposition of Park Geun-hye, *I Can Speak* was one of the last substantial box office hits of the Rising Sun cycle.[6] In its first half, this film uses a comedy premise about aging neighborhood busybody, Ok-bun (Na Moon-hee [Na Moon-hŭi]), who wants to learn English as a Trojan horse to deliver a powerful story about a Comfort Woman in its second half. During Ok-bun's testimony at the United States House of Representatives Inquiry on Human Rights Abuses by Japan during World War Two, the film cuts to a wide and high shot

Fig. 2.1 Yi removes his *Hinomaru* facepaint in *The Tooth and the Nail*

Fig. 2.2 The scar of colonialism is still present after "Japan" is removed

that implies the POV (point of view) of an official sitting in the building's upper balcony space. In this POV shot, when Ok-bun raises her jacket to reveal her midriff, there is a collective gasp, with some Senators rearing back in their seats. The film then cuts to an extreme close-up of Ok-bun's bare stomach to reveal why the US Senators' reactions were so strong. The switch from extreme wide shot to extreme close-up has a powerful, slingshot-like effect. The visual impact is reinforced by the marks visible on the surface of Ok-bun's skin, including several knife scars of varying depth. To the left of the screen there are tattooed Japanese hiragana characters *inu koro* いぬころ ("child of a dog"), while to the right of the screen is the greenish tinge of a partially faded tattoo of the *Kyokujitsu* (Fig. 2.3). The *Kyokujitsu* is not completely visible which suggests that there may be additional, unseen marks on Ok-bun's body. This startling representation of the Japanese military flag underlines precisely why the aging woman has come to the United States to protest against Japan. For around thirty seconds of screen time, there is no sound. This keeps the rawness of the image completely unfiltered, and adds power to Ok-bun's later words: "No evidence, you say? I'm the evidence!" The *Kyokujitsu*, a symbol of Japanese power becomes the symbol of Japanese culpability.

I Was Scarred, But…

However, while Rising Sun films frequently linger on the permanence of wounds and scars, particularly in relation to Japanese culpability for war crimes, at other times the film erases other, less convenient aspects of

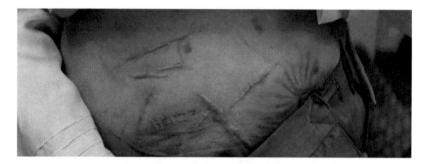

Fig. 2.3 Ok-bun reveals her scars and tattoos to the US House of Representatives in *I Can Speak*

South Korea's postcolonial story. The House of Representative sequences in *I Can Speak* leading to Ok-bun revealing her scars also provides a prime example of such erasure. In the film, the driving force of the US government's investigation into Japan's use of Comfort Women is Korean-American Michael Lee. Michael Lee only appears in the film a couple of times. His first appearance, seated at the House of Representatives, is the most prominent in that it is a shot where he is the only character in focus and alongside his image is a Hangul script indicating his name, his role as a Congressman, and his role in the drama as the person who introduced HR121 to the House. Unfortunately, Michael Lee did not exist. Examination of the Gov.Track.us website which records the activity of United States Congress reveals that the person who actually introduced the HR121 Bill is Japanese-American Congressman Michael "Mike" Honda.

In creative terms, the film's erasing of Michael Honda in favor of a Michael Lee is understandable. Michael Lee allows for a consistency of representation of evil Japanese throughout the film that extends from the violent Japanese soldiers depicted in Ok-bun's colonial flashbacks to the film's contemporary Japanese obstacle, the political Lobbyists who attempt to undermine her testimony. Including Honda would muddy this film's anti-Japanese schemata and arguably diminish or otherwise minimize perceptions of the South Korean contribution to the Comfort Women issue: particularly as, in an effort to appease bi-lateral relations, the South Korean government had not, prior to Park's and Abe's agreement, formed an official body of support for the Comfort Women (Yoo

2012, 54). Given, as I have already argued, that the popularity of the low budget *Spirits' Homecoming* in January 2017 can be read as a rebuke to Park Geun-hye's Comfort Women deal with Abe Shinzo in December 2016, a decision to modify *I Can Speak*'s content is feasible even in the pre-production stage, as the comedy/drama's actual shooting occurred between March 29 and June 26, 2017. It would seem that the choice to erase Honda was made during *I Can Speak*'s post-production, as otherwise the casting of Hawaiian-born, Japanese-American actor Cary Yoshio Mizobe as Michael Lee would seem to be particularly perverse. Accordingly, this representation of a champion for Comfort Women by the erasure of a sympathetic Japanese-American is problematic. Like the removal of the *Hinomaru* make-up in *The Tooth and The Nail*, Honda's erasure still leaves a trace—a scar if you will—of Japaneseness.

This erasure of Honda parallels the way that Koreans themselves have often dealt with the Comfort Women issue. Hyunah Yang writes of the South Korean media's coverage of revelations about Comfort Women recruitment in the early 1990s:

> what was startling to me about these revelations was that the student records in question had existed in Korea for half a century, without being brought to light…. Until a Japanese person, supposedly an accomplice of colonial rule, reported the story, the records were ignored. Still the media focused only on the fact that the Japanese recruited such young girls through the elementary schools. (1998, 125)

And while the Korean media coverage of Comfort Women that Yang writes about occurred in the early 1990s, it seems that over two and a half decades later, not much has changed. Furthermore, given that Honda was an American citizen, the perceived advantage of erasing his Japanese heritage (and supplanting it with Korean identity and heritage) suggests that positive representation of Japanese—including Japanese who have acted on Korea's behalf and even at a remove of two generations—is still considered too challenging. This erasure has additional significance in terms of Park Chung Hee's own Japanese connections and the Park family lawsuit that tried to suppress the release of *The President's Last Bang*. That President Park sought to control the South Korean film industry via blacklists and a myriad of other means is particularly ironic when it comes to *I Can Speak*, as in that film's final moments it is Park who is erased.

A coda sequence, indicating that Ok-bun now frequently travels, obviously takes place well after the main story set in 2007. The sequence begins with Ok-bun lecturing Min-Jae, beginning with her remark: "Abe is talking lies again."[7] Although the film is set in the era of Abe's initial Prime Ministership of September 2006–September 2007, the film takes advantage of Abe's second stint as Japanese Prime Minister from September 2012 to September 2020, which covers the time of *I Can Speak*'s release in September 2017.[8] While a positive representation of Japanese-American Michael Honda could have undermined the film's anti-Abe coda, and therefore theoretically risk the film's potential for domestic box office success, the denigration of Abe does more than channel the growing South Korean dissatisfaction with Japan that was evident at the time of the film's release. The emphasis on Abe also serves to pass over President Park Geun-hye, who had been impeached seven months before the film's release, and to gloss over her unpopular Comfort Women deal which was rejected by the South Korean public. Even when corporations such as the Lotte Chaebol that distributed *I Can Speak* were speaking out about the political pressures that emanated from the by-then deposed President, such conglomerates are still unlikely to directly provoke their potential customers. However, by pointedly mentioning Abe, the film's postscript not only concretes Hyangjin Lee's observed connection between the cinematic and the political, but also gracefully performs another act of erasure by refusing to mention the deposed President. Whether Korean audiences are being trusted to read between the lines in the omission of Park Geun-hye's name, or whether this is purely to shift the blame for the unpopular Comfort Women agreement as Japan's sole responsibility remains open to debate. Whichever view one takes, the cinematic moment would not exist without Park's stimulus.

Conclusion

Park Geun-hye asked for films in the national interest—and she got them. Prompted into existence by the combination of an already conservative environment and the popularity of *Roaring Currents*, the Rising Sun cycle fell away soon after Park's deposition. Clearly, some of the films proved not to be in Park's political interests, as their nationalism kept Japan and the Comfort Women on the agenda even as she made moves to remove this issue from dominating South Korean discourse. After the former President's erasure from the narrative of *I Can Speak*, the next box office hit set in the Japanese colonial period was the Kim Gu (Kim Ku) biopic *Man Of Will* distributed in October, 2017. Thereafter, the few similarly themed films that followed, such as Next Entertainment World's *Heoseutori* (*Hŏsut'ori*) (*Herstory*, Min Kyu-dong [Min Kyu-dong], 2018) and the Showbox distributed, independently produced *Chajŏnch'awng Ŏmbokdong* (*Race to Freedom: Uhm Bok-dong*, Kim Yoo-sung [Kim Yu-sŏng], 2019), fared less well, although the Lotte-distributed *Malmo-i* (*Malmoe: The Secret Mission*, Eom Yu-na [Ŏm Yu-na], 2019) did good business in January 2019. This is despite there being thirteen number one box office successes touching on the colonial period during Park's Presidency. The next colonial period film to reach number one at the South Korean box office was *Hangŏ: Yugwansun Iyagi* (*A Resistance*, Joe Min-ho [Cho Min-ho], 2019) a biopic about celebrated young patriot, Yu Gwan-sun which had been strategically targeted to have its release coincide with the centenary of the 1919 March Uprising. Given that the independence martyr was known to be tortured—and erroneously rumored to be drawn and quartered—it is unsurprising that wounds are also a feature of that film. The success of *A Resistance* came two years after Park's impeachment and eighteen months after the popular success of *I Can Speak*. Although these outlier films fall outside the sphere of Park's influence, this does not negate the existence of the Rising Sun cycle. In fact, Klein stresses that "highly visible film cycles rarely disappear completely" (Klein 2011, 97). This is particularly the case when the subject is one in which audiences are emotionally invested (Klein 2011, 11). The high-profile "anti-Japan" boycott of 2019 and the popularity of the SK court's decision to repossess the South Korea-situated assets of Japanese companies in 2020, indicate that the South Korean public are still emotionally invested in themes related to the colonial period. Is it just a matter of time until the Rising Sun cycle rejuvenates and becomes a prominent feature of South Korean film culture once again; or will it remain a time-capsule portrait of concerns during the Park Geun-hye era?

Notes

1. Though Klein's work is mostly concerned with exploitation films, cycles can occur anywhere. One of Klein's chapters describes the changes to the cycle initiated by social problem film *Dead End* (William Wyler, 1936). While the first films featuring "the Dead End Kids" are social problem films, in order to maintain audience

interest, subsequent films keep the *Dead End* semantics (recurring actors, urban setting, similar plots) and place them within new generic syntax ranging from war propaganda (*Pride of the Bowery*, Joseph H. Lewis, 1940) to comedies (*'Neath Brooklyn Bridge*, Wallace Fox, 1943) to horror films (*Ghosts on the Loose*, William Beaudine, 1943).

2. CJ distributed: *Roaring Currents*; *Tongju* (*Dongju: Portrait of a Poet*, Lee Joon-ik [Yi Jun-ik], 2016); *Agassi* (*The Handmaiden*, Park Chan-wook [Pak Ch'an-uk], 2016); and *Kunhamdo* (*The Battleship Island*, Ryoo Seing-wan [Ryu Sŭng-wan], 2017). Lotte distributed: *Kyŏngsŏng Hakkyo: Sarajin Sonyŏdŭl* (*The Silenced*, Lee Hae-young [Yi Haeyŏng], 2015); *Haewŏrhwa* (*Love, Lies*, Park Heung-sik [Pak Hŭng-sik], 2016); *Tŏk'ye Ongjo* (*The Last Princess*, Hur Jin-ho [Hŏ Chin-ho], 2016); and *Ai K'aen Sup'ik'u* (*I Can Speak*, Kim Hyun-seok [Kim Hyŏn-sŏk], 2017). Showbox distributed: *Amsal* (*Assassination*, Choi Dong-hoon [Ch'oe Tonghun], 2015) and *Pak Yŏl* (*Anarchist From Colony*, Lee Joon-ik [Yi Jun-ik], 2017). Next Entertainment World distributed *Taeho* (*The Tiger: An Old Hunter's Tale*, Park Hoon-jung [Pak Hun-jŏng], 2015). Kidari Ent distributed both *Sŏkcho Chŏt'aek Sarin Saŏn* (*The Tooth and The Nail*, Jung Sik [Chŏng Shik] and Kim Whee [Kim Hwi], 2017) and *Daejang Kim Changsu* (*Man of Will*, Lee Won-tae [Yi Wŏn-ta'e], 2017). Independent film *Kwihyang* (*Spirits' Homecoming*, Cho Jung-rae [Cho Chŏng-nae], 2016) was distributed by WAW Pictures. *Miljŏng* (*The Age of Shadows*, Kim Jee-woon [Kim Chi-un], 2016) and *Koksŏng* (*The Wailing*, Na Hong-jin [Na Hong-chin], 2016) were distributed by their American production companies, Warner Brothers and Twentieth Century Fox, respectively. Films that failed to ignite with the South Korean public were: *The Silenced* and *The Tiger* which both debuted at No. 3, while *Dongju: Portrait of a Poet* debuted at No 5 on the Korean Box Office. There is also the special case of *Nungil* (*Snowy Road*, Lee Na-jeong [Yi Na-chŏng], 2015), a theatrical cut of a KBS1 television event. Debuting at number six at the box office, *Snowy Road* performed poorly. This was possibly because *Snowy Road* came near the end of the cycle and because it had already been widely seen on television. It was the first film of the cycle since *The Silenced* to achieve less than a million ticket sales.

3. Gateward nominates the following films as her "anti-Japanese" cycle: *SSaulabi* (*Saulabi*, Mun Jong-geum [Mun Chong-gŭm], 2004); *Anak'isŭt'ŭ* (*Anarchists*, Yu Yeong-sik [Yu Yŏng-sik], 2000); *2009 Rosŭt'ŭ Memori* (*2009: Lost Memories*, Lee Si-myung [Yi Simyŏng], 2002); *YMCA Yagudan* (*YMCA Baseball Team*, Kim Hyun-seok [Kim Hyŏn-sŏk], 2002); *Paramŭi P'aiŭt'ŏ* (*Fighter in the Wind*, Yang Yun-ho [Yang Yun-ho], 2004); *Yŏkdosan* (*Rikidozan: A Hero Extraordinary*, Song Hye-sŏng, 2004).
4. *Modŏn Poi* (*Modern Boy*, Jung Ji-woo [Chŏng Chi-u], 2008); *Wŏnsŭpŏn Ŏtaim* (*Once Upon a Time*, Jeong Yong-ki [Chŏng Yong-gi], 2008); *Radio Teijŭ* (*Radio Dayz*, Ha Ki-ho [Ha Ki-ho], 2008); *Choŭn Nom, Nappŭn Nom, Isanghan Nom* (*The Good, The Bad, The Weird*, Kim Ji-woon [Kim Chi-un], 2008) and *Kidam* (*Epitaph*, Jung Sik [Chŏng Shik] and Jung Bum-Sik [Chŏng Pŏm-shik], 2007). While the Kim Ji-woon film is undoubtedly the most successful of these films, *Epitaph* has received repeated examination by academic circles.
5. *Maruta*, the Japanese word for "wooden logs," was the dehumanising euphemism used to refer to prisoners who were subject to horrific medical experiments conducted by doctors, veterinarians and others sanctioned by the Japanese Imperial Army (see Yudin 2010).
6. It was not until January 2019, almost fifteen months after the box office success of *I Can Speak*, that *Malmoe: The Secret Mission* a film with a colonial topic once again held the top position. In the fifteen months prior to *I Can Speak*'s *release*, ten colonial-themed films reached the number one spot.
7. This is the subtitle in one version of *I Can Speak* I have seen. My understanding is that Ok-bun's language is more robustly scatological.
8. Abe stepped down in 2007 for reasons of ill health. Re-elected in 2012, Abe used the same explanation for stepping down in 2020.

References

An, Jinsoo. 2018. *Parameters of Disavowal: Colonial Representation in South Korean Cinema*. Oakland: University of California Press.

Ashcroft, Bill, Gareth Griffiths, and Helen Tiffen. 1991. *The Empire Writes Back: Theory and Practice in Post-colonial Literatures*. London: Routledge.

Blake, Linnie. 2008. *The Wounds of Nation: Horror Cinema, Historical Trauma and National Identity*. Manchester: Manchester University Press.

Choe, Sang-hun. 2015. "Japan and South Korea Settle Dispute Over Wartime 'Comfort Women.'" *The New York Times*, December 28. Accessed May 15, 2019. https://www.nytimes.com/2015/12/29/world/asia/comfort-women-south-korea-japan.html.

Gateward, Frances. 2007. "*Waiting to Exhale: The Colonial Experience and the Trouble with* My Own Breathing." In *Seoul Searching: Culture and Identity in Contemporary Korean Cinema*, edited by Frances Gateward, 191–218. New York: State University of New York Press.

GovTrack.us. 2020. "H.Res. 121 (110th): A resolution expressing the sense of the House of representatives that the Government of Japan should formally acknowledge, apologize, and accept historical responsibility in a clear and unequivocal manner for its Imperial Armed Forces' coercion of young women into sexual slavery, known to the world as 'comfort women,' during its colonial and wartime occupation of Asia and the Pacific Islands from the 1930s through the duration of World War II." Accessed May 14, 2019. https://www.govtrack.us/congress/bills/110/hres121.

Hodgin, Nick, and Amit Thakkar. 2017. "Introduction: Trauma Studies Film and the Scar Motif." In *Scars and Wounds: Film and Legacies of Trauma*, edited by Amit Thakkar and Nick Hodgin, 1–29. Cham: Palgrave Macmillan.

Kil, Sonia. 2017a. "Korean Minister Apologizes for Blacklisting Artists, Denies Involvement." *Variety*, January 10. Accessed May 15, 2019. https://variety.com/2017/film/asia/korean-minister-apologizes-for-blacklist-1201956816/.

Kil, Sonia. 2017b. "Election of New South Korean Presidents Heralds Film Industry Reforms." *Variety*, May 9. Accessed May 15, 2019. https://variety.com/2017/film/asia/film-industry-reforms-for-korean-president-moon-jae-in-1202421834/.

Kil, Sonia, and Frater, Patrick. 2019. "Korean Distributors Fight for Box Office Market Share." *Variety*, March 19. Accessed May 15, 2019. https://variety.com/2019/film/asia/korean-distributors-fight-for-box-office-market-share-1203166637/. Viewed 15 May 2019.

Kim, Elaine H., and Choi Chungmoo. 1998. "Introduction." In *Dangerous Women: Gender and Korean Nationalism*, edited by Elaine H. Kim and Chungmoo Choi, 1–8. New York: Routledge.

Kim Jong-pil. 2015. "Korea's Statues Without Limitations." *Korea JoongAng Daily*, October 5. Compiled by Chun Young-gi and Kim Bong-moon. Accessed April 2, 2019. https://koreajoongangdaily.joins.com/news/article/article.aspx?aid=3009977.

Kim Kyung Hyun. 2004. *The Remasculinization of Korean Cinema*. Durham: Duke University Press.
Kim Kyung Hyun. 2011. *Virtual Hallyu: Korean Cinema of the Global Era*. Durham: Duke University Press.
Klein, Amanda Ann. 2011. *American Film Cycles: Reframing Genres, Screening Social Problems, and Defining Subcultures*. Austin: University of Texas Press.
Lee, Claire. 2013. "Period Blockbusters to Fill Silver Screens Next Year." *The Korea Herald*, December 26. Accessed May 15, 2019. http://www.koreah erald.com/view.php?ud=20131226000859.
Lee, Hyangjin. 2001. *Contemporary Korean Cinema: Identity, Culture, Politics*. Manchester: Manchester University Press.
Moon, Seungsook. 1998. *Begetting the Nation: The Androcentric Discourse of National History and Tradition in South Korea*. In *Dangerous Women: Gender and Korean Nationalism*, edited by Elaine H. Kim and Chungmoo Cho, 33–66. New York: Routledge.
Morris, Mark. 2009. "Melodrama, Exorcism, Mimicry: Japan and the Colonial Past in the New Korean Cinema." In *Cultural Studies and Cultural Industries in NorthEast Asia: What a Difference a Region Makes*, edited by Chris Berry, Nicola Liscutin, and Jonathan D. Mackintosh. 195–211. Hong Kong: Hong Kong University Press.
Neale, Steve. 2000. *Genre and Hollywood*. New York: Routledge.
Noh, Jean. 2016a. "Top Korean Directors, Actors on Government Blacklist." *Screen International*, October 15. Accessed May 15, 2019. https://www.screendaily.com/news/top-korean-directors-actors-on-government-blacklist-/5110391.article.
Noh, Jean. 2016b "Korean President Park Geun-hye Implicated in CJ Chief Miky Lee's Exit." *Screen International*, December 12. Accessed May 15, 2019. https://www.screendaily.com/korean-president-implicated-in-cj-chiefs-exit/5112104.article.
Paquet, Darcy. 2009. *New Korean Cinema: Breaking the Waves*. New York: Wallflower Press.
Park, Boram. 2019. "Massive Popularity of '*Avengers: Endgame*' Rekindles Debate Over Cinema Regulations." *Yonhap News Agency*, April 27. Accessed May 15, 2019. https://en.yna.co.kr/view/AEN20190426009000315.
Park, Geun-hye. 2012. "A Plan for Peace in North Asia; Cooperation Among Korea, China and Japan Needs a Correct Understanding of History." *The Wall Street Journal*, November 12. Accessed May 14, 2019. https://www.wsj.com/articles/SB10001424127887323894704578114310294100492.
Park, Jin-hai. 2017. "CJ Made Several Films Pressured by President." *The Korea Times*, January 16. Accessed May 15, 2019. https://www.koreatimes.co.kr/www/art/2018/11/689_222208.html.

Redmond, Sean. 2013. *The Cinema of Takeshi Kitano: Flowering of Blood.* London: Wallflower Press.

Reuters. 2016. "South Korea's Corporate Chiefs Deny Seeking Favours for Donations During Parliament Hearing." *Straits Times*, December 6, 2016. Accessed May 15, 2019. https://www.straitstimes.com/asia/east-asia/samsung-group-leader-vows-to-avoid-future-political-scandals.

Rothman, William. 2004. *The 'I' of the Camera: Essays in Film Criticism, History, and Aesthetics.* 2nd ed. Cambridge: Cambridge University Press.

Russell, Mark J. 2008. *Pop Goes Korea: Behind the Revolution in Movies, Music, and Internet Culture.* Berkeley: Stone Bridge Press.

Statistics Times. 2020. "List of Countries by Projected GDP." Last modified November 6, 2020. http://statisticstimes.com/economy/countries-by-projected-gdp.php.

The Straits Times. 2016. "Former Presidential Aide Grilled in New Twist to Political Scandal Crippling Park Geun Hye's Presidency." November 17. Accessed May 15, 2019. https://www.straitstimes.com/asia/east-asia/former-presidential-aide-grilled-in-new-twist-to-political-scandal-crippling-park.

Sunwoo, Carla. 2012. "Director Owns up to Box Office Flop." *Korea JoongAng Daily*, October 10. Accessed May 15, 2019. http://koreajoongangdaily.joins.com/news/article/article.aspx?aid=2960539.

Suzuki Sotaro. 2018. "Lotte Boss's Jail Term Keeps South Korean Executives Feeling Trapped: Conglomerates Tiptoe Between Political Pressure and Public Anger." *Nikkei Asian Review*, February 16, 2019. Accessed May 15, 2019. https://asia.nikkei.com/Business/Business-trends/Lotte-boss-s-jail-term-keeps-South-Korean-executives-feeling-trapped2.

Taylor-Jones, Kate. 2017. *Divine Work, Japanese Colonial Cinema and Its Legacy.* New York: Bloomsbury Academic.

Yang, Hyunah. 1998. "Remembering the Korean Military Comfort Women: Nationalism, Sexuality and Silencing." In *Dangerous Women: Gender and Korean Nationalism*, edited by Elaine H. Kim and Chungmoo Choi, 123–139. New York: Routledge.

Yecies, Brian, and Shim Ae-gyung. 2016. *The Changing Face of Korean Cinema: 1960 to 2015.* New York: Routledge.

Yoo Hyon Joo. 2012. *Cinema at the Crossroads: Nation and the Subject in East Asian Cinema.* Lantham: Lexington Books.

Yudin, Boris G. 2010. "Research on Humans at the Khabarovsk War Crimes Trial." In *Japan's Wartime Medical Atrocities: Comparative Inquiries in Science, History, and Ethics*, edited by Jing-Bao Nie, Nanyan Guo, Mark Selden, and Arthur Kleinman, 77–96. London: Routledge.

CHAPTER 3

Fighting "The Man": The Production of Historical Knowledge in Cho Kŭn-hyŏn's *26 Years*

Niall McMahon

In the climax of Cho Kŭn-hyŏn's film *Isipyuknyŏn* (*26 Years*, Cho Kŭn-hyŏn, 2012) Kim Kap-se, an ex-soldier and CEO of a private security firm, sits across from a fictionalized portrayal of one of South Korea's most controversial figures. Known throughout the film as "Ex-president," "Big Man," "V.I.P," "Highest ranking personage," or as stated in the film's credits, "the man," this character sits oblivious as Kap-se gives him a gift: a statue with not one, but two faces; one facing forwards, the other facing backwards. After giving him this gift, Kap-se demands an apology from "the man" for his role in the nation-defining tragedy that occurred in 1980. Yet "the man" meets this demand at first with indifference, and then hostility, prompting Kap-se to draw a gun from a hidden compartment in the statue in an act of vengeance 26 years in the making. While not overtly specified, "the man" is a facsimile of the former South Korean

N. McMahon (✉)
Monash University, Melbourne, VIC, Australia

president Chun Doo Hwan, who is alleged to be the key player in the instigation of the Kwangju Uprising, otherwise known as the Kwangju Massacre. The statue that Kap-se gifts to "the man," which holds the instrument of his potential death, is "Janus-faced." Based on the mythic figure of Janus, a Roman god with both a forward and backward fronting face, items with this construction are said to look "both to the past and the present" (Burgoyne 2008, 11). Therefore, Kap-se, a symbolic representation of the South Korean populace, uses a weapon housed in an emblem of South Korea's past and present in order to kill a duplicate of Chun Doo Hwan. The narrative therefore reducing decades of distress, suffering, finger-pointing, and injustice to a bullet aimed at a solitary person; asserting that only through an act of retribution that the past and present of South Korean citizens may find solace in their collective historical trauma.

The Kwangju Uprising was an event of great violence and conflict; for ten days, the streets of a South Korean city were turned into a warzone. The conflict originated with the assassination of South Korean president Park Chung Hee in 1979 (Kingston 2014). Killed by the head of the Korean Central Intelligence Agency (KCIA), Park's death was viewed as a sign that the country would shift away from an oppressive, military dictatorship into a more democratic-focused system. Yet, this power vacuum was seized by Chun Doo Hwan, a South Korean Army major general, through a military coup which resulted in Chun appointing himself the new leader of South Korea and locking the country into martial law. On May 18, 1980, the martial law spread nationwide, "closing all universities [...] and restricting all political activities, including the parliament" (Kim 2019). In addition, Special Forces paratroopers were sent across the country, suppressing anti-martial law protests in cities such as Seoul and Pusan. While the paratroopers were successful in stopping protests in the majority of these cities, the citizens of Kwangju instead marched harder despite facing intense beatings from the soldiers. The protests grew from 200 to 200,000 between May 18 and May 20, with the violence escalating to the throwing of stones and Molotov cocktails, as well as the burning of cars. On May 21, Chun's government had the city cut off from all communication and transportation, effectively trapping the civilians in the city. Gathered outside of the South Chŏlla (Chŏllanam-do) Provincial office, an order was given to the soldiers to open fire on the protestors, sustained for ten minutes, killing an unfathomable number of civilians in the process (Kim 2019; Na 2010). To this day, it remains unknown who ordered the soldiers to shoot.

The protestors subsequently formed a citizen army and swarmed police stations and armories around the city. Armed with rifles, hand grenades, dynamite, and machine guns, the civilians eventually forced the army to retreat (Seol 2020). Seven days later, however, the army returned, this time armed with tanks and helicopters, and swiftly, yet brutally ended the conflict (Na 2010; Seol 2020). During the ten-day period that the Kwangju Uprising lasted, the official toll stated by the government was that "165 citizens died, 76 went missing, 3,383 were injured, and 1,476 were arrested, affecting 5,100 in total" (Kim 2019). The unofficial death toll however sits closer to 2,000 (Kingston 2014). In the aftermath of the violence, Chun Doo Hwan ruled as South Korea's president until 1987. In 1996, Chun, alongside his subordinate Roh Tae Woo, was imprisoned and sentenced to death for treason, mutiny, and bribery charges, both over his role in Kwangju as well the embezzlement of large quantities of money in slush funds during his presidency (Borowiec 2015; Lee 2017). Both Chun and Roh were later pardoned for their crimes, escaping the death penalty, but Chun was ordered to pay back 220 billion Korean won, or $229 million. Chun never paid back this money, claiming he only ever had 290,000 Korean won, or roughly US$250, to his name. To this day, Chun has never shown remorse for his actions, openly refusing to admit his role in the massacre. Chun Doo Hwan was brought to justice, but justice was not served, leaving the Kwangju Uprising (henceforth referred to as Kwangju) tragically, and frustratingly, unresolved to this day.

In the hole left by the tragedy, art, literature, and film arose in an attempt to make sense of the chaos. Films that have centered on Kwangju have been dubbed as "5.18 cinema," named for the date the Uprising began (Rhee 2019, 91) and have included *Kkotnip* (*A Petal*, Chang Sŏn-u, 1996), *Pakha Satang* (*Peppermint Candy*, Yi Ch'ang-dong, 1999), *Hwaryŏhan hyuga* (*May 18*, Kim Chihun, 2007), and *T'aeksi Unjŏnsa* (*A Taxi Driver*, Chang Hun, 2017). Subsequently, much academic discussion has arisen around these various representations of Kwangju in order to decipher both the meaning of these filmic texts and the place the Uprising has within the South Korean zeitgeist and artistic expression. A notable element to the South Korean films that depict Kwangju, as well as the academic discussion surrounding them, is that the historical event is not often the central focus. Despite being set during the time of Kwangju and depicting key events from the Uprising, both the texts and the discussion surrounding them speak to grander themes such as military violence, the failings of culture, and mankind's inherent cruelty. As a result, the historical occurrence of Kwangju itself, namely why it occurred, what happened, and who was involved, is not explored in detail.

Three noteworthy examples of this have occurred in the discussions surrounding *A Taxi Driver*, *Peppermint Candy*, and *A Petal*. David Shim articulates the universality of human rights and democratic struggle of Kwangju within *A Taxi Driver*, stating that the film is not about "Koreans shooting at Koreans [...] but of soldiers firing at protesters" (2020, 463). In this sense, Kwangju is not restricted to a Korean affair but a stand-in for all global struggles of a citizenry against an oppressive government. Shim notes that icons of "symbolic national imagery" are only present during scenes depicting protestors and entirely absent during scenes depicting the military or governmental institutions such as the police (2020, 462). Notably, the soldiers committing acts of violence against the citizens are often hidden, either by masks or camera angles, resulting in a military force that is not explicitly Korean and, in turn, elevated to a depiction of universal military violence. Therefore, *A Taxi Driver* as articulated by Shim becomes a stand-in for any country, where "an oppressive apparatus versus patriotic, pro-democratic citizens" (David Shim 2020, 463); a global problem with uneasy answers that is not limited to Kwangju. Similar to how Shim connected *A Taxi Driver* to military violence, Kim So-young analyzes the film *Peppermint Candy* from a gendered perspective, connecting Kwangju to South Korea's persistent militarization and how this alters male subjectivity (2011, 179–180). Kim pinpoints the mandatory military service of Korean males as blurring "the distinction between perpetrators and victims" (2011, 179–180), where the tragedy of Kwangju is not one of soldiers committing violence against the protestors, but how the structure and ideals of a nation's culture are built to turn its citizens against each other (2011, 180). The military perspective given to the South Korean men makes the culture one centered on military service, and as a result, gives them an anti-communist viewpoint which may be easily corrupted by those in power (2011, 180). Therefore, *Peppermint Candy* is less about the events of Kwangju and more about the fragility of the South Korean male and the systems that created him. Kwangju is becoming a universal narrative of how society fails the people and how a tragedy of this scale is inevitable when these systems are left unchecked. Finally, Kim Chun-hyo analyzes *A Petal* through a psychological and allegorical lens, one that uses Kwangju as a grounds to explore the "inner violence" of an individual (2008, 252). Through this study, the unspeakable physical and sexual violence the main female character endures during, and because of, Kwangju is elevated from a single event in history to a societal issue that pervades South Korean culture. Through the abuse this character faces during the narrative, by not only the main male character but other men she encounters, Kim argues that the film "discloses the severity and endless cycle of violence" inherent to South Korean culture through positioning Kwangju from the perspective of "private sadistic and masochistic impulses: cruelty, brutality, and anxiety" (2008, 248). In this regard, Kwangju becomes but one event in a long history of internalized South Korean malice, where events like the Uprising are not random but an end result of the citizen's capacity for violence. In short, the brutality of Kwangju was not the result of a specific set of historical conditions, but instead was the inevitable outcome of the savagery that lay within the hearts of all South Koreans. As made evident by these examples, the discourse surrounding Kwangju as depicted by South Korean cinema elevates the Uprising from an isolated incident to a critique of both South Korean society and a global suffering, trauma, and societal failure. Kwangju, therefore, is depicted as an inevitability of humankind's inherent cruelty and not as a single event with a definable cause and motivation. As a result, Kwangju becomes a thematic launching pad for greater discussion but is often ignored as a historical event worth examining in its own right.

A film that is curiously absent from this discussion regarding the cinematic representation of Kwangju is *26 Years*. Set in 2006, 26 years after the events of Kwangju, the film follows five people: Kim Kap-se, Kwak Chin-bae, Sim Mi-jin, Kwŏn Chŏng-hyŏk, and Kim Chu-an. This group, all of whom lost family in the massacre or were forced to kill during the chaos are brought together by Kap-se with one goal, make "the man" apologize for Kwangju or kill him if he does not. Despite not being set during Kwangju, *26 Years* is a film that is explicitly and singularly about the Uprising. It is a film with a laser focus, to unambiguously pinpoint "the man" as the sole reason for the bloodshed. As a result, the film's narrative, characters, and themes all stem back to the massacre in some regard, keeping the focus on a single, explicitly Korean traumatic event without elevating it to a cipher for global catastrophe as the above-mentioned films often do. Its portrayal of "the man" is simplified and at times dangerous, yet in doing so captures the complex suffering and unresolved trauma of the Kwangju survivors and their families towards the real-life figure this facsimile is based upon. Due to *26 Years*' narrative and thematic approaches to Kwangju, the historical event is arguably more explicit and dramatically central in this film than in those previously discussed. Yet, this film has entirely been left out of the discussion of 5.18 cinema outside of the most cursory of mentions. This, I argue, is a matter of categorization. Films such as *A Taxi Driver*, *Peppermint Candy*, and *A Petal* are films that are set during the historical event while being about issues tangentially connected to it. Due to this historical backdrop, these films are analyzed together with each contributing to the historical knowledge of Kwangju and the South Korean articulation of their past. *26 Years* on the other hand, is set during a contemporary time period but is unambiguously about Kwangju and why it occurred. Yet, due to the modern setting, it is left out of the discussion of 5.18 cinema because it is not an overt depiction of said event. On a superficial level, the former films become historical films of Kwangju while the latter do not. However, when analyzed under the context of historical film theory, *26 Years* not only becomes a historical film of Kwangju but also creates important and noteworthy historical knowledge of Chun Doo Hwan and the deep scar Kwangju left on the South Korean people. Therefore, this chapter argues that *26 Years* offers relevant and significant historical knowledge regarding Chun Doo Hwan and the Kwangju Uprising, and as a result, can be deemed a historical film pertaining to this event.

THE KWANGJU UPRISING AND THE HISTORICAL FILM

The historical film genre is curious, as though the definition of what may constitute a film of this type sounds simple, it is in fact, complex. The popular consensus of a historical film is that it is a narrative that is "consciously set in a past, sometime before the production of the specific work itself" (Parvulescu and Rosenstone 2013, 1). Yet, this broad characterization does not assist in understanding the genre because almost any film, apart from films with stories set after the year of production, could be included. A more specific definition of the historical film genre therefore is offered by theorists Natalie Zemon Davis and Robert Burgoyne. Davis posits that the historical film's narrative either has to be based on documented historical fact or have historical events play a centralized role within its story (2000, 5). For example, the South Korean films *Pohwa soguro* (*71: Into the Fire*, John H. Lee [Yi Chae-han], 2010) and *Irŭmŏbnŭn byŏldŭl* (*Nameless Stars*, Kim Kang-yun, 1959) could be considered historical, as the first sets its narrative within a recreation of the battle of P'ohang-dong, an actual battle of the Korean War, and the second has a fictionalized plot that reinterprets the Kwangju Student Independence Movement of 1929, a key demonstration in the Korean resistance against the Japanese colonial rule. However, a film such as *Kŭrimja sarin* (*Private Eye*, Pak Tae-min, 2009) which has a fictional plot set in 1910, the first year of the colonial period, would not be, by this definition, a historical film as it does not directly utilize the era within its narrative outside of a historical, esthetic setting. Burgoyne likewise asserts that the historical film is built upon "documentable historical events" as the film's narrative directly refers to relevant historical incidents (2008, 4). As Burgoyne elaborates: "The events of the past constitute the mainspring of the historical film, rather than the past simply serving as a scenic backdrop or a nostalgic setting" (2008, 4). Therefore, as long as a historical film uses a documented historical event as its dramatic core, and its narrative and formal elements such as character arcs, plot progression, and thematic elements in some way tie back to the event, it may be deemed as historical and create historical knowledge of the era. Historical knowledge is here defined as the confluence between two distinct elements: the core historical information a text contains, such as the names, dates, and timelines of events (for example, the start and end dates of a war, and when and in what order battles were fought), all of which is supported by archived historical evidence, and, on the other hand, the way in which a historical text has come to produce an understanding of the past it depicts. For example, the South Korean World War II film *Maiwei* (*My Way*, Kang Che-gyu, 2011) contains historical information, such as the start and end dates of the war, alongside depictions of actual historical battlefields, such as the Normandy beach landings. Yet this information is filtered through the thematic ideal of unity between Korea and Japan, rewriting the historical record through a fictional narrative that symbolically calls for an end to the historical contention between the two countries. In short, while the information the film presents may be accurate to the historical record, the knowledge it produces about the past is subjective and unique to the text itself.

Davis' and Burgoyne's criteria for labeling a film as historical, as well as the definition of historical knowledge, is vital when discussing a film like *26 Years*. Despite not being set during Kwangju, the film can nonetheless be considered historical through its presentation of historical information and its understanding of history. As the film is primarily set in 2006, a general understanding of the historical film genre would posit that it cannot be deemed historical and is unable to create historical knowledge of Kwangju. However, when framed through the definitions of the genre granted by Davis and Burgoyne, *26 Years* is indeed a historical film. Kwangju is dramatically central to the film, with everything linking back to the event in some regard. The characters are driven by their trauma of the event, the assassination plot is fueled by their history with Kwangju, and the focus of the narrative is the facsimile of Chun Doo Hwan. Kwangju is not a mere backdrop to the narrative, but its core, with the knowledge and understanding of how and why these characters are still affected by this historical tragedy filling every frame.

Previous Kwangju set historical films, such as the aforementioned *A Taxi Driver* and *Peppermint Candy*, are similar in their narrative approach to the Uprising, namely to use the historical event as a cipher for universal issues. Furthermore, these films often share a more general black-and-white morality when depicting South Korean citizens. The populace are portrayed as either innocent or as "heroes, idealistic political activists who risked their lives in a noble attempt to build a democratic and just society on the Korean Peninsula" (Baker 2003, 91). Consequently, these films are primarily focused at the ground level; the citizens who lived through Kwangju. Neither is there any central antagonist, a villainous figure at the center of the massacre. Instead, the soldiers are shown to be a force of nature sweeping over the citizens without motive or reason, not acting as characters but as stand-ins for the themes, the film wishes to explore. *26 Years*, on the other hand, is different from this narrative focus. The film has an unambiguous antagonist in "the man," with every action or scheme the protagonists have been focused on him. "The man" is placed on a symbolic pedestal, with the narrative insisting that the trauma of Kwangju may be resolved once he is removed. As a result, *26 Years* is a film of uncomplicated morals and simple answers, not interested in exploring the human condition but is rather a narrative of pure, blind fury. While the figure who ordered the massacre of civilians at Kwangju has never been found, *26 Years* focuses on Chun's facsimile and uses its narrative and formal construction to create damning historical knowledge of "the man" in an attempt to rewrite the historical record to make him, and only him, the mastermind behind Kwangju.

The Production and Reception of *26 Years*

26 Years is based on a webcomic created by South Korean cartoonist Kang To-yŏng, under the pen name Kang Full. Released between April 3 and September 28, 2006, comprising of 30 chapters, the webcomic was created by Kang as a way to battle what he states as the "willed amnesia" of South Korean society towards Kwangju. While never completely falling out of the country's zeitgeist, Kang's indignation at the South Korean media's favorable stance towards Chun's presidency, specifically in regards to his economic management, was used as the motivation to create a piece that could help people remember the events of Kwangju within an entertaining framework (Petersen 2012, 40–41). The perceived political stance of the work by various South Korean production companies, and the South Korean government itself, led to a long, hard battle for the film adaption to be made. The film's producer, Ch'oe Yong-bae, has stated that his intentions behind the film adaptation aligned with that of Kang:

> I felt sorry and sad to see the main characters that lost their parents in [Kwangju] in the year 1980. I empathized with the victims and felt anger towards the inflictor. [...] Kang Full was astonished by these people's stories and wanted to show the young generation that couldn't tell the difference between 8.15 and 5.18. I felt the same way and wanted to make it into a movie and tell the world. (Song Ji-hwan 2012)

The first date that Ch'oe mentions is August 15, the National Liberation Day of Korea, the day Korea was liberated from Japanese colonialism. The second date is May 18, the first day of the Kwangju Uprising. Seemingly, according to Ch'oe, a national day of celebration and a national day of mourning were merging within the popular consciousness and the tragedy and significance of Kwangju were being lost. Both Kang Full and Ch'oe Yong-bae intended their creative works to be a way to remind audiences, both domestic and international, of what the South Korean government had committed against its citizens on those fateful days in 1980. However, the first attempt at a film adaptation of *26 Years* was halted only ten days into filming after investors started to withdraw their support (AsianWiki 2020; Song Ji-hwan 2012). As Ch'oe states:

> Everything was ready right before the shooting in 2008. But the main investor suddenly backed out. He came over and told us that he might

get fired so the investment can no longer be continued [...] the president of the investor company had been called in to the Blue House and was told to stop investing in *26 Years* and the rest of the investors eventually backed out as well. (Song Ji-hwan 2012)

The involvement from the Blue House is not surprising. The presidential elections the year prior resulted in president-elect Yi Myŏng-bak who was under investigation for "financial scam, money laundering and false reporting of personal assets" at the time of his victory (Kim 2007). Furthermore, a legislative election for control of South Korea's National Assembly, which heavily involved Yi's conservative Grand National Party (Chayuhan'guktang), was due to be held in April of 2008 (*Hankyoreh*, April 10, 2008). That *26 Years'* narrative revolves around the assassination plot of a controversial ex-president during the time of another contentious political figure allegedly courted a controversy that shut down the film for over four years.[1] Eventually, Ch'oe and the production turned to crowdfunding for finance. By the end of the campaign 15,000 donors had given the production 700 million Korean Won, or US$646,000. Through a combination of social media and the project's meld of history with a revenge-focused action narrative, the film was able to attract a curious and passionate audience that circumvented the politically charged production issues the film faced prior (Song Ho-jin 2012). The names of the donors consume 15 minutes of the film's total runtime with many of these people stating they were motivated to donate to the project, not because they were interested in seeing another action-thriller, but because of its historical connections. Some donors mentioned they helped finance the film due to their feelings of obligation to honor the victims of Kwangju and their sacrifice in the search for democracy; they viewed their small contribution as a way to pay back their debt to the people who died (Lee 2012). Upon release in 2012, the film sold over a million tickets in six days, gained 2,963,652 admissions, and made 21,242,367,145 Korean won or US$17,810,319 at the box office. At the time of writing this chapter, the film sits as the 135th highest-grossing film at the South Korean domestic box office (Kobis 2020).

The reactions among Western critics were mixed. The film was hailed as "not a work of easy solutions" (Orion 2014), a "fantastical narrative that pits spectators against their long-held traumas" (Conran 2013), and "among the most direct attempts Korean cinema has made to reckon with the traumatic recent past" (Scanlon 2018). The majority of the film's praise was reserved for its initial half-hour which contains both a graphically violent animated sequence set during Kwangju as well as a lengthy set of scenes set between 1980 and 2006 showcasing the after-effects the massacre had on the protagonists and their parents (Cho 2012; Scanlon 2018; *Tom's Reviews* 2018). Less successful was the film's ending, which sees the assassination team close to killing "the man," before cutting to black leaving the outcome ambiguous. Western audiences did not like the vague nature of the ending, with the fate of "the man" being met with accusations of laziness, disappointment, and being anti-climactic (LetterBoxd 2020; MyDramaList 2020). The film's characters sought blood; the audiences demanded blood; but the ending denied it to them both.

Yet, to a Korean audience, the citizens who both contributed to the film's funding and had direct links to the event through cultural and familial ties, their reception was not limited to a case of good or bad but reflected the narrative's ability to touch them on a deep, emotional level. As detailed by Song Ho-jin (2012), one audience member cried at the film, telling reporters that she wanted to hug the main characters, "ask them how much it hurt" and tell them she was "sorry for making you bear that pain alone." Another member said he felt angry and frightened by the film, infuriated that even in this imagined narrative Chun did not apologize for the tragedy he caused (Song Ho-jin 2012). Additionally, Ch'oe Yong-bae stated that many audience members approached him after the film and said "This really happened? I didn't know," "I cried really hard," "Thank you for making such a movie," and "It's enough just to have made this film" (Song Ji-hwan 2012).

The different receptions to the film, both Western and domestic, showcase two different ways the film can be interpreted. While both the webcomic and film were motivated by the desire to make South Koreans remember the event, for an international audience, its creation became a tool to get them to know the event had happened at all. Therefore, to audiences without a prior understanding of Kwangju, "the man" is an unambiguous villain that needs to be taken down. The ex-president is an obvious target for retribution and the failure of the characters to kill him by the film's end is viewed as a cheap cliff-hanger by lazy filmmakers. However, to an audience whose friends and families have lived with the trauma of Kwangju, and who have been infuriated by the lack of resolution and any accountability on the part of the real-life Chun and the government, this ending is entirely the point. Chun never truly faced punishment for his crimes and the specter of Kwangju and its victims still linger in the hearts of many Koreans. The film's lack of resolution is akin to South Korea's lack of resolution regarding the event itself. For an audience without this context, Chun's lack of comeuppance is confusing and frustrating. For an audience with this context, the film's lack of closure hits close to home and makes them cry. Yet for both, their urging for the characters to just kill "the man" and end the film in a satisfying way is one and the same.

The Narrative and Formal Construction of "The Man"

As the adage goes, "a society says a lot about itself in the way it treats its villains" (Scanlon 2018), and it is through this treatment where the agenda of *26 Years* comes to light. Within the narrative "the man" is so integral to the events of Kwangju that the film's proposed resolution of national trauma becomes worryingly simplified: closure and catharsis are all but guaranteed once he either repents or dies. In fact, so narrow-focused the narrative is on Chun Doo Hwan's facsimile that the other historical figure charged and imprisoned alongside him in 1996, Roh Tae Woo, is mentioned only once within the film's runtime and even then only referred to as a "former president"; the film all but ignoring a figure whose role in Kwangju awarded him a death sentence. "The man" is presented as an omnipresent, malevolent force, only appearing on screen to order violence, belittle traumatic citizens or act apathetic towards Kwangju. When he is not on screen, his presence looms large, with rarely a scene going by without one of the characters criticizing "the man," calling for his death or repentance, or wailing due to what they lost due to his actions. As Martin Petersen claims, "this unrelenting spotlight on a former president has the consequence of almost mystifying Chun as a hegemonic, near-transcendental enigmatic social agent, rather than making the former president understood as a product and manifestation of authoritarian history, or as a cynical manipulator of social codes" (2012, 44). *26 Years* is narrow-focused to a fault, blindly focusing on Chun's facsimile and his role in Kwangju rather than the system and the allies that supported the order at South Chŏlla. This is no more evident than within the film's prologue. The film opens with a text intertitle that provides audiences with a general background of Kwangju, followed by a ten-minute animated sequence that is set during the Uprising. What is significant about this is that "the man" is not shown or discussed during this time. The intertitle is the following:

> In May 1980, Kwangju, Korea, innocent civilians protesting for democracy were massacred by their own soldiers. With 4,112 killed or wounded, it was the most casualties since the Korean War. With that crime as a foothold, the head of the military became South Korea's 11th President. This is a work of fiction, using the above facts as its background.

The basic information that this text provides is correct. Civilians protested against the government. Many people were killed. Chun became the president of South Korea. However, two significant elements of this text turn the audience against "the man" before he is shown on screen. Firstly, through the use of emotive words such as "innocent," "massacred," and "crime" within this text, the historical information is focalized behind a viewpoint that positions the civilians as guiltless, untainted people with the South Korean government being contextualized as a merciless, evil entity. The second element is the presented death toll. As stated earlier, the official death toll of Kwangju stands at 165, with unofficial estimates believed to be as high as 2,000 (Kim 2019; Kingston 2014). The 4,112 number goes significantly beyond these numbers. While it is difficult to confirm the exact number of people dead or missing, no other source has the number this high. As a result, Kwangju is rewritten to more violent and deadly than official records, accentuating the crimes of "the man" before the film has even begun. In consequence of these elements, the audience is left with no choice but to hate Chun's facsimile and are swayed into sharing the film's emotive viewpoint without a chance to come to this conclusion by themselves.

The biased and emotive contextualization of Kwangju continues into the film's opening ten minutes. This animated sequence follows the perspective of all of the film's main protagonists during Kwangju and specifically hinges around a recreation of the massacre at the South Chŏlla Provincial office on May 21, 1980. During this sequence, the violence is extreme and graphic with countless depictions of explicit injuries, mutilated bodies, and acts of cruelty. A key example is when Chŏng-hyŏk's sister is shot in the back and a large, sustained blood geyser erupts from her body, pooling on the street. She staggers from a run, dropping to her knees as her intestines slowly fall out of her body with a prominent squelching noise as she weakly tells Chŏng-hyŏk to run. She whimpers in terror as a soldier runs up behind her, hitting her with a baton, blood spurting from her head. She falls dead in a pool of her blood. The small bullet wound on her back is visible on her dead body. The animation style throughout these ten minutes is rough and sketchy, with a lot of pencil marks, coloring outside the lines, and the implementation of a janky, dropped frame style of movement giving the events an uncanny, surreal effect. During moments of extreme acts of violence or emotional trauma the characters briefly flick to static, as if the suffering and pain of the event is bleeding through the frame, becoming a blinding white agony. Coupled with a body count of approximately 42, the animation is disturbing and confronting, briefly elevating *26 Years* into a pseudo-horror film.[2]

At the conclusion of this sequence, the animation ends and cuts to a wide shot of a live-action living room. The air is still and quiet, contrasting heavily against the noise and chaos of the preceding ten minutes. The shot slowly pushes into a television set, which blinks into life, turned on by no one, as documentary footage of Chun's presidential inauguration plays. Chun says, "Thank you to the National Council for Unification and the Korean people for choosing me as President," before the television turns off and the scene cuts away. The placement and stylization of this shot is curious, but when the Kuleshov effect is applied to the opening intertitle, the animated sequence and then this shot, their order becomes clear.[3] The animated sequence is bookended by the opening text describing the 11th president using Kwangju to gain power and concludes by showing this documentary footage of Chun's inauguration. As a result, all of the terror and violence that lay between these two scenes become attributed to him. The sudden silence of this final shot disrupts the flow and pace of the animation, creating a shocking moment of stillness, making the televised footage engrossing. When Chun is revealed on television shortly thereafter, this stillness is broken and produces an effect of astonishment and blame. As a result of this narrative and formal construction, the intertitle, animation, and documentary footage of the prologue narrows the scope of Kwangju to one discursive element, the action and graphic aftermath of violence, and is assigned to one source, Chun Doo Hwan.

Through juxtaposition and association, *26 Years* has already characterized "the man" in an unflattering and unsympathetic light before he has ever been presented on screen, and, as a result, has already begun to generate a highly emotive, yet simplified, historical knowledge of Kwangju. When he is eventually depicted on screen, this trend amplifies. Two notable scenes encapsulate his representation: one that details his cavalier attitude towards Kwangju; and one that highlights his penchant for violence. The first scene occurs just over 80 minutes into the film. At the beginning of the scene, documentary footage of a memorial ceremony at the real-life Kwangju Memorial Park is shown. An announcer states over the footage, "Today is the 26th anniversary of the May 18 Kwangju democracy movement. Over 4000 family members, politicians, and officials took part in the ceremony. Afterward, a line formed at the 5.18 graves to commemorate the departed." As the announcer speaks, the scene cuts to "the man" sitting in his office, his back turned to a TV playing the footage as he trims his toe nails with a razor blade. At the conclusion of the dialog, he nonchalantly turns off the TV and gets back to his task. The blade slips and he cuts his toe, grimacing, as a small amount of blood oozes from the wound. At this point, it is revealed he is using a newspaper article that shows the graves of Kwangju victims as a footrest. This is a casually damning representation of "the man." Before this scene, the character's consistent denial and ignorance regarding his role in Kwangju could have potentially been genuine, with him sincerely believing the Uprising was just a riot that the military had responded to. Yet after this action, any doubt is gone. In a matter of seconds, through one act of contempt and malice, *26 Years* visually reinforces the ideal of "the man" as someone who does not care about the trauma caused by Kwangju and, most importantly, as someone who actively disrespects the memory of the victims.

The next significant scene occurs during the film's climax. In this sequence, Kap-se and Chu-an attempt to assassinate "the man" from the inside of his compound as Chin-bae causes a riot outside and Mi-jin stands guard with a sniper rifle. During the scuffle, Chu-an is shot and killed by a character named Ma Sang-nyŏl, who is the head of security for "the man" and also served as a soldier alongside Kap-se during Kwangju. Kap-se is later shot and dies as he is being carried out into an ambulance. Finally, Sang-nyŏl is killed by another guard after he is driven crazy by the violence and threatens the ex-president with his gun. In all three cases, "the man" reacts with either little emotion or with a look that seemingly implies he is pleased with what is occurring in front of him. As Chu-an dies, "the man" stares stoically at the body and a grieving Kap-se, uncaring that a young man was killed in front of him. After Kap-se is shot, he stares at his lifeless frame with a smirk, unfazed, and seemingly happy at the outcome. Finally, when Sang-nyŏl is killed, he is initially shot by the guard and falls into "the man," clearly fading and not a threat. "The man" looks down at Sang-nyŏl with disgust and makes a head motion, prompting the guard to shoot him again. "The man" then kicks the body off of him without any respect or care, completely stoic to ordering the execution of a defeated man. All of this violence occurs in front of "the man," and significantly, because of him. Chu-an, Kap-se, and Sang-nyŏl are all killed in their pursuit of catharsis; to finally be free of their historical trauma. Yet, the demise of these three men means nothing to "the man," in effect highlighting his ease for ordering the deaths of defenseless people. Instead of attempting to diffuse the situation and deflate the tension, "the man" instead resorts to murder to resolve the conflict. When placed into the wider historical conflict of Kwangju and how the protests were fueled by citizens resisting his martial law, the leap to a massacre is depicted as not being out of character for "the man." Both the fictional assassination plot, whose primary goal was an apology, and the real-life protests, who wanted Chun Doo Hwan to step down as president, could have been resolved through conversation and peaceful solutions, no matter how hard or contentious they may have been. Therefore, when the first response of "the man" is violence and death in the former, the historical outcome of the latter snaps into focus. As a result, through this parallel between fact and fiction, historical knowledge regarding the real-life Chun is generated, namely that the likelihood of him ordering the massacre at South Chŏlla is both high and hard to refute.

Finally, the guilt of "the man" is supported by *26 Years*' use of fallacy, or in other words, how it constructs historical knowledge of Chun Doo Hwan through persuasive, yet consciously deceptive reasoning. There are two main issues regarding "the man" that are repeated throughout the film: his role in Kwangju and his economic management while president. The earlier discussed occurrence of Chun's criminal charge of embezzling money and his subsequent refusal to pay his fine (Borowiec 2015; Lee 2017) are repeatedly brought up during the film, notably through the use of documentary news footage in two key scenes. The first shows footage of "the man" greeting people at a local marketplace while a voice-over states, "Mr. President told the merchants his commitment to economic development," in turn, highlighting the economy as a major factor in his presidency. In a scene that follows shortly after, news footage shows "the man" leaving prison as the voice-over states, "After being jailed for the December 12 and May 18 Incidents and slush funds, the two former presidents were granted a special pardon today. Apologizing for having caused anxiety, Chun expressed his concern about the declining economy."[4] Through these scenes, the economic management of "the man" is both praised and demonized, cementing the idea that he was a good economic manager and used this knowledge to embezzle money. These scenes occur within five minutes of the aforementioned animated sequence set during Kwangju. Therefore, from a formal, stylistic perspective, the film presents Kwangju and Chun's economic management together, keeping them both as a central, integral focus. In a subsequent scene, Chin-bae sits in his mother's ramshackle, street-side noodle restaurant, carefully counting his cash. As Chin-bae literally counts his pennies, his TV announces the following:

Voice-over: Former President Chun stood before the court again after 6 years. The judge demanded he disclose his financial assets, and Chun claimed to have only 290,000 won.

"The Man": Why don't you check my bank account? There's only 290,000 won left!

This number of 290,000 Korean won is repeated throughout the film to the point where it is as embedded within the narrative as Kwangju itself. However, visually, everything about "the man" contradicts his claim of a lack of money: he lives in a large, enclosed compound that is protected by security 24 hours a day; he has an armed motorcade at his beck and call; he pays off the police force in order to gain preferential treatment, specifically to change traffic signals when he passes. Just one of these are the actions of a wealthy man, but all taken together showcase someone of unimaginable power and affluence. The contradiction between his claims of poverty and his splashes of personal wealth exhibit that "the man" is not to be trusted. The integral element to the film's claims is that the lies "the man" tells in regards to his lack of money is not a construction of the narrative, but a well-documented, factual occurrence. Like his filmic counterpart, Chun lives a lavish lifestyle: playing golf at exclusive clubs; hosting ceremonies at opulent hotels; and, similar to "the man," lives in a well-guarded compound, surrounded by "15-foot stone walls" (Harlan 2013). The use of documentary footage alongside the film's constructed images of wealth creates a clear connection between history and the film's characterization of "the man," one that can be verified on a meta-level. The earlier discussed documentary footage of "the man" being released from prison mentions both Kwangju and his embezzlement of money. Therefore, by heavily emphasizing the embezzlement throughout the film the narrative posits that the other issue it presents, "the man" as the mastermind of Kwangju, must also be true through association. Or put simply, as Chun's embezzlement is true, so must his role in Kwangju. This is important when the following exchange occurs between "the man" and Kap-se during the climax:

> *Kap-se*: 26 years ago today... exactly today, in May 1980. Do you remember?
> *"The Man"*: What?
> *Kap-se*: Your life depends on your attitude.
> *"The Man"* This man is talking ancient history! We discussed it all a long time ago. Listen. We invoked the military's power of self-defense. I knew nothing until they reported it to me.
> *Kap-se*: The military's power of self-defense? You knew nothing? I was a soldier of the martial law forces. The order came from you. Admit the truth and beg for forgiveness! Then we can finish this quietly.
> *"The Man"*: Everything has already finished quietly.
> *Kap-se*: It may be finished for you, but not me. To achieve power, you trampled on innocent citizens and cut them down bleeding, with guns and swords. And yet, throughout these 26 years, you never once said a word of apology.

By using the historical record to debunk any claims to poverty, the narrative has proven "the man" to be a liar and a fraud. Therefore, when Chun's facsimile starts to claim the same ideas as his real-life counterpart, specifically that of the military's power of self-defense and his ignorance about Kwangju, this is also put into question. The scene takes the factual claims of the real-life Chun and presents them as lies, furthered by using a character that has earned the audience's trust and sympathies to call them as such. The protagonist has the attention and benefit of the doubt, compared to the antagonist that has already been caught in a lie. As a result, what Kap-se says is positioned as the truth and the words of "the man" are presented as a fabrication. Therefore, through the use of fallacy, historical, documented truth is used as a weapon to push the film's agenda, and in the eyes of an uninformed audience, the guilt of "the man" becomes factual.

Conclusion

South Korean Grand National Party Member of Parliament, Wŏn Hŭiryong, said of the narrative of *26 Years*, both in webtoon and film forms, "It is not the victory of history to get retaliation by shooting a mass murderer [....] *26 Years* is not the right answer" (Petersen 2012, 55). While the veracity of Wŏn's statement is questionable due to the political color of his party and the ties of South Korea's conservative parties like his to the country's history of military dictatorship (*Redian* 2011), his point holds weight in regards to the film. By rewriting and recontextualizing Kwangju so Chun is its sole perpetrator, does the narrative allow for a catharsis from the historical trauma or does it intensify it? The answer the film presents to resolve this unresolved historical tragedy is black and white: kill Chun and free the people or let him live and continue existing under the weight of his tyranny. This binary choice is startlingly simple and a dangerous mindset. *26 Years* can be counted as a historical film of Kwangju due to its production of historical knowledge regarding the event. Yet the idea this historical knowledge generates is enough to twist and turn history until audiences, domestic and international, become likewise furious at a single source. For domestic audiences, the lack of names given to the fictionalized version of Chun is not an issue as his omnipresence and stature throughout the film is more than enough, "there is no need for more" (Orion 2014). For an international, globalized audience, the fixated historical knowledge, generated by juxtaposition, association, characterization, and fallacy is convincing enough to sway them onto the side of the narrative. As other Kwangju focused films such as *A Petal*, *A Taxi Driver*, and *May 18* retell this event through a lens of universal themes of violence and the failings of culture, no answer is offered to settle this historical tragedy, only to remember it and identify its trappings in both South Korea and other nations. Yet *26 Years* presents an option for resolution, a way to close the book on Kwangju forever. Yet like the film's controversial ending implies, meeting violence with more violence, no matter how justified, may lead to an endless cycle of cruelty that South Korea may never be able to escape from.

Notes

1. Yi was eventually found innocent of his charges and allowed to complete his full term in office. However, in 2018 Yi was given a 13 billion won fine and sentenced to 15 years in prison for bribery and embezzlement (Choe 2018).
2. The use of animation is not unique to *26 Years*, as over a decade earlier the Kwangju set *A Petal* utilized surreal and disturbing animated sequences, complete with a childlike art style, oddly proportioned characters and settings, and most notably, the portrayal of South Korean soldiers as grotesque insects, to likewise depict the trauma of the Kwangju survivors.
3. Named after Soviet filmmaker Lev Kuleshov, the Kuleshov effect is an editing principle that dictates meaning is created via the association, contrast or juxtaposition of two adjoining shots. As stated by Maria Pramaggiore and Tom Wallis, "the meaning of a shot was determined not only by the material content of the shot, but also by its association with the preceding and succeeding shot" or in other words, certain meanings are created for the viewer depending on what is cut to or cut from (2005, 162).
4. The December 12 Incident refers to Chun Doo Hwan's 1979 coup d'état against acting President Ch'oe Kyu-ha which resulted in him seizing control of both the KCIA and the South Korean government. Once appointed as president in May 1980, Chun and his government banned political activities, arrested political rivals, and deployed the army to maintain order, specifically against those protesting the government's martial law around the country (Breen 2010; Elizabeth Shim 2020). Therefore, the December 12 Coup directly correlates to the beginning of Kwangju.

References

AsianWiki. 2020. "26 Years." Accessed July 19. http://asianwiki.com/26_Years.

Baker, Don. 2003. "Victims and Heroes: Competing Visions of May 18." In *Contentious Kwangju*, edited by Shin Gi-Wook and Moon Hwang-kyung, 87–108. Lanham: Rowman & Littlefield.

Borowiec, Steven. 2015. "South Korea's Ex-Dictator Chun Doo-hwan Tries to Keep Low Profile in His Twilight Years." *Los Angeles Times*, November 29. Accessed September 20, 2020. https://www.latimes.com/world/asia/la-fg-south-korea-dictator-20151129-story.html.

Breen, Michael. 2010. "General Chun Doo-hwan Took Power in a Coup." *The Korea Times*, May 23. Accessed November 10, 2020. http://www.koreatimes.co.kr/www/news/nation/2016/11/117_66347.html.

Burgoyne, Robert. 2008. *The Hollywood Historical Film*. Oxford: Blackwell.

Cho, Seong-yong. 2012. "26 Years (2012) ☆☆(2/4): They Have Waited for So Long…" *Seongyong's Private Place*, November 30. Accessed September 20, 2020. https://kaist455.com/2012/11/30/26-years-2012/.

Choe, Sang-hun. 2018. "Former South Korean President Gets 15 Years in Prison for Corruption." *The New York Times*, October 5. Accessed November 9, 2020. https://www.nytimes.com/2018/10/05/world/asia/lee-myung-bak-south-korea-convicted.html.

Conran, Pierce. 2013. "The Ultimate Revenge Narrative: 26 Years (26년, 26-nyeon) 2012." *Modern Korean Cinema*, February 12. Accessed September 1, 2020. http://www.modernkoreancinema.com/2013/02/the-ultimate-revenge-narrative-26-years.html.

Davis, Natalie Zemon. 2000. *Slaves on Screen: Film and Historical Vision*. Toronto, ON: Vintage Canada.

Hankyoreh. 2008. "Political Apathy Leads to Record-Low Voter Turnout." April 10. Accessed November 11, 2020. http://english.hani.co.kr/arti/english_edition/e_national/281027.html.

Harlan, Chico. 2013. "South Korea Goes After the Fortune of Chun Doo-hwan, Its Last Military Strongman." *The Washington Post*, August 14. Accessed December 10, 2020. https://www.washingtonpost.com/world/south-korea-goes-after-the-fortune-of-chun-doo-hwan-its-last-military-strongman/2013/08/13/a3e2b35e-00be-11e3-9711-3708310f6f4d_story.html.

Kim, Chun-hyo. 2008. "Representation of the Kwangju Uprising—*A Petal* (1996) and *May 18* (2007)." *Asian Cinema* 19 (2): 240–255. Accessed November 30, 2020. https://doi.org/10.1386/ac.19.2.240_1.

Kim, Seo-yeon. 2019. "May 18 Gwangju Democratization Movement." *The Postech Times*, May 17. Accessed August 29, 2020. http://times.postech.ac.kr/news/articleView.html?idxno=20843.

Kim, So-young. 2011. "Gendered Trauma in Korean Cinema: Peppermint Candy and My Own Breathing." *New Cinemas: Journal of Contemporary Film* 8 (3): 179–187. Accessed December 3, 2020. https://doi.org/10.1386/ncin.8.3.179_1.

Kim, Tae-jong. 2007. "[Elect]President-Elect Faces Probe." *The Korea Times*, December 19. Accessed November 9, 2020. https://www.koreatimes.co.kr/www/news/nation/2007/12/117_15821.html.

Kingston, Jeff. 2014. "Dying for Democracy: 1980 Gwangju Uprising Transformed South Korea." *The Japan Times*, May 17. Accessed September 1, 2020. http://www.japantimes.co.jp/news/2014/05/17/asia-pacific/politics-diplomacy-asia-pacific/dying-democracy-1980-gwangju-uprising-transformed-south-korea/#.VNGOb52Udth.

Kobis. 2020. "Previous Box Offices (Based on Integrated Computing Network)." Accessed August 25. http://www.kobis.or.kr/kobis/business/stat/boxs/findFormerBoxOfficeList.do?loadEnd=0&searchType=search&sMultiMovieYn=N&sRepNationCd=K&sWideAreaCd.

Lee, Han-soo. 2017. "Korea's History of Arrested Ex-presidents." *The Korea Times*, March 30. Accessed September 20, 2020. https://www.koreatimes.co.kr/www/nation/2017/03/356_226661.html.

Lee, You-kyung. 2012. "Crowdfunding Rescues Provocative S.Korean Film." *The Seattle Times*, October 1. Accessed September 9, 2020. https://www.seattletimes.com/business/crowdfunding-rescues-provocative-skorean-film/.

LetterBoxd. 2020. "26 Years." Accessed September 20. https://letterboxd.com/film/26-years/.

MyDramaList. 2020. "26 Years (2012)." Accessed September 20. https://mydramalist.com/5146-26-years.

Na, Kahn-chae. 2010. "A New Perspective on the Gwangju People's Resistance Struggle: 1980–1997." *New Political Science* 23: 477–491. Accessed August 29, 2020. https://doi.org/10.1080/07393140120099598.

Orion, Vasia. 2014. "[HanCinema's Film Review] '26 Years.'" *HanCinema*, November 15. Accessed August 25, 2020. https://www.hancinema.net/hancinema-s-film-review-26-years-75454.html.

Parvulescu, Constantin, and Robert A. Rosenstone. 2013. "Introduction" to *A Companion to the Historical Film*, edited by Constantin Parvulescu and Robert A. Rosenstone, 1–8. Malden: Wiley.

Petersen, Martin. 2012. "26, 27, 28, 29, 30, 31, 32 … Years: The Politics of Kang Full's Webtoon 26 Years." *The Review of Korean Studies* 15: 33–65. Accessed July 30, 2020. https://doi.org/10.25024/review.2012.15.2.002.

Pramaggiore, Maria, and Tom Wallis. 2005. *Film: A Critical Introduction*. London: Laurence King Publishing.

Redian. 2011. "Asking Korean 'Conservatism.'" June 5. Accessed November 10, 2020. https://web.archive.org/web/20120402093123/, http://www.redian.org/news/articleView.html?idxno=22574.

Rhee, Joo-yeon. 2019. "Beyond Victims and Heroes: The 5.18 Cinema Across Gender Boundary: Introduction: The Problem of Representing Historical

Trauma in Cultural Productions." *Korean Studies* 43 (1), 68–95. Accessed November 30, 2020. https://doi.org/10.1353/ks.2019.0008.

Scanlon, Hayley. 2018. "26 Years (26년, Cho Geun-hyun, 2012)." *Windows on Worlds*, December 12. Accessed September 1, 2020. https://windowsonworlds.com/2018/12/12/26-years-26%EB%85%84-cho-geun-hyun-2012/.

Seol, Kap. 2020. "The US Didn't Bring Freedom to South Korea—Its People Did." *Jacobin*, June 25. Accessed September 1, 2020. https://jacobinmag.com/2020/06/gwangju-uprising-korean-war-seventieth-anniversary.

Shim, David. 2020. "Cinematic Representations of the Gwangju Uprising: Visualising the "New" South Korea in *A Taxi Driver*." *Asian Studies Review* 45: 454–470. Accessed November 30, 2020. https://doi.org/10.1080/10357823.2020.1837071.

Shim, Elizabeth. 2020. "U.S. Faced 'Tricky Choices' Following South Korea Coup, Documents Show." *UPI*, May 15. Accessed November 11, 2020. https://www.upi.com/Top_News/World-News/2020/05/15/US-faced-tricky-choices-following-South-Korea-coup-documents-show/1021589548521/.

Song, Ho-jin. 2012. "Small Budget Films Making Big Impressions." *Hankyoreh*, December 4. Accessed August 1, 2020. http://english.hani.co.kr/arti/english_edition/e_entertainment/563723.html.

Song, Ji-hwan. 2012. "26 Years Producer CHOI Yong-bae." *KoBiz*, December 28. Accessed July 30, 2020. http://www.koreanfilm.or.kr/eng/news/interview.jsp?blbdComCd=601019&seq=17&mode=INTERVIEW_VIEW.

Tom's Reviews. 2018. "26 Years (2012)." October 8. Accessed September 20, 2020. http://tomsfilmreviews.blogspot.com/2018/10/26-years-2012.html?m=1.

CHAPTER 4

Squaring the Circle: *The Schoolgirl's Diary* and North Korean Film in the Era of Marketization

Andrew David Jackson

Most researchers analyzing pre-millennium North Korean film agree that motion pictures made in the Democratic People's Republic of Korea (DPRK) are very different from the type of cinematic output produced and consumed in countries with more commercial film industries like South Korea or the USA. The state has traditionally dominated North Korean film production, distribution, exhibition, and regulation, and filmmakers operate according to a strict regulatory framework (Lee 2000, 41). Hyangjin Lee (2000) argues for a clear-cut distinction between state media in North Korea and the regulation of cinema and commercial filmmaking industries like that of South Korea:

A. D. Jackson (✉)
Monash University, Melbourne, VIC, Australia
e-mail: andy.jackson@monash.edu

© The Author(s), under exclusive license to Springer Nature Switzerland AG 2022
A. D. Jackson (ed.), *The Two Koreas and their Global Engagements*,
https://doi.org/10.1007/978-3-030-90761-7_4

> In most capitalist societies, including South Korea, film is viewed chiefly as a form of entertainment [...] in North Korea [...] it is conceived primarily as an instrument for socialization and effective political propaganda of the masses [...] the most important and powerful mass educational means. (Lee 2000, 30–31)

For Lee, North Korean films have always had an educational function—they ensure that audiences are aware of their duties and responsibilities to the country. In other words, films help to mobilize the population, encouraging them to make greater efforts on behalf of the industry and the military. For Kyung Hyun Kim (1996), the main difference between films produced in North Korea and in commercial industries also lies in the overt political messages of the texts:

> North Korean cinema simply does not conceal its political manifestation and chooses to externalize its hegemonic desires. In North Korean cinema, the political objectives are spelled out for the viewer without much ambiguity. (Kim 1996, 100)

Given the observations made by Lee and Kim, one key question is whether these historical differences in North Korean production still hold true in the light of the extreme social, political, and environmental challenges the DPRK has faced in the new millennium. The 1996–1999 famine ushered in a period (analyzed in more detail below) in which the authorities' political legitimacy was severely dented by social and structural breakdown as well as economic collapse. In the light of these socio-political changes, it is important to understand whether filmmakers were able to make audience-friendly feature films with less overt political content or whether films continued to serve as tools to indoctrinate the domestic population, as Lee argues. This chapter examines the relationship between text, producer, and audience within a state media context and focuses on cinematic representations of contemporary social issues. I have two assumptions in mind when I specify films about "contemporary" North Korean society rather than cinema about historical events or foreign settings, which has formed such an essential part of DPRK film production.[1] First, if the gap between fictional representation and the reality experienced by audiences is too large, then the text would require a suspension of disbelief too vast to be taken seriously. Second, any attempt to portray actual social structural problems accurately would result in state proscription. I answer this question in relation to *Han Nyŏhaksaengŭi Ilgi* (*The Schoolgirl's Diary* [*A Schoolgirl's Diary*] 2007, Chang In-hak) a film that garnered significant domestic and international attention while at the same time gaining the praise of the authorities, which raises the question of how this film managed to apparently square the circle and achieve this success. I analyze *The Schoolgirl's Diary* by taking into consideration the geopolitical context of the film's creation, the cultural and diplomatic history of the DPRK film industry, and scholarly understandings about how art is produced and meant to be consumed by the North Korean authorities.

A Transformed Post-Famine Social and Economic Context

The Schoolgirl's Diary was made during the first decade of the new millennium, a period when the North Korean economy had begun to stabilize after the catastrophic 1996–1999 famine. However, the post-famine economy was functioning along very different lines to the 1945–1994 Kim Il Sung (1912–1994) era, and some background explanation is required to account for the far-reaching social, economic, and political change that occurred in the DPRK after the mid-1990s.

The Collapse of the Public Distribution System (PDS)

The PDS was a system through which the DPRK authorities distributed state-produced food and goods to the general population (Hassig and Oh 2015, 45). Workers were provided with ration cards to obtain foodstuffs as long as they both worked in official industries and attended political indoctrination sessions (held at workplaces; Smith 2015, 174). The collapse of the Soviet Union meant that the DPRK was no longer able to source oil at "friendship" prices and was forced to pay the market rate, impacting the transport supplies to distribution centers. A series of disastrous harvests because of severe flooding in 1995 and 1996 and inefficient farming techniques exacerbated the pressures the PDS already faced because of excessively high transportation costs (Lankov 2013, 78). The system had been in decline for years, but these disasters combined to cause its total collapse in 1996. Remote areas remained cut off and received no supplies, and even the more privileged groups outside of Pyongyang often went without rations (Lankov 2013, 79). Estimates of the deaths caused by the famine range from 600,000 to over a million (Lankov 2013, 79).

Marketization from Below

With the state incapable of feeding the population, ordinary North Koreans began to rely on nominally proscribed private or informal economic activities to survive. Black markets or *changmadang* emerged in which labor, food, raw materials, and consumer goods were traded for profit (Ward 2016). Those who were unable to trade grew foodstuffs in farmer's markets or developed cottage industries preparing food or goods to be sold at markets (Hassig and Oh 2015, 68–69). North Koreans also crossed the northern borders into China to bring in goods to trade in such markets. Lower-ranking state officials, soldiers, and their dependents residing in rural locations, particularly remote border areas, were equally susceptible to privation and turned a blind eye to private enterprise or cross-border trade for a cut (Smith 2015, 212, 221, 328; Lankov 2016, 7; Hassig and Oh, 2015, 71). Between 1998 and 2008, these informal economic activities accounted for an estimated three-quarters of the total income for DPRK households (Lankov 2013, 82). Another vitally important change within DPRK society was the transformed economic and organizational role of women. The bulk of the market operators and pedlars, as well as many of the cross-border smugglers, were and are women (Lankov 2013, 83). This phenomenon was partly achieved because of women's accepted roles, duties, and activities according to the socialist division of labor within North Korea. Marketization gave women an economic agency that had been practically unknown before and led to a reversal of traditional gender hierarchies in the DPRK (Lankov 2013, 83). By 2005, largely thanks to unofficial marketization, the worst of the famine was over, although malnourishment still existed in the North (Lankov 2013, 122).[2] The marketization was accompanied by a shift in power in domestic politics from the Party towards the military. This was the advent of so-called "military-first politics" or *Songun* (Smith 2015, 235). This prioritization of the military was meant to ensure regime continuation in an era of increasing instability, and control was generally achieved through the threat of force (Smith 2015, 242).

Ideological Changes

Marketization in the DPRK did not just bring economic changes to the country; it also brought ideological changes. Smugglers engaging in cross-border trade brought in goods and they also carried information, media (DVDs and USBs of film and TV dramas), and images of life in the People's Republic of China (PRC) and the ROK (Choi 2017, 792). An estimated 350,000 DVD players were brought into the DPRK from the PRC in 2006 alone (Lankov 2013, 102). Close to 500,000 North Koreans visited the PRC between 1998 and 2013, and most returned (Lankov 2013, 102). Information entering the country as a result of market activities was supplemented with data about South Korea and the West transmitted by human rights organizations and religious NGOs via USBs, balloons, or other means (Baek 2016). This information brought a wider knowledge of the regime of scarcity and repression that North Koreans were living under in their home country (Baek 2016, 83). In addition to this influx of information, the DPRK authorities were less able to impose their own ideology on the population. Petty officials who themselves were reliant upon private economic activities to survive became less inclined to devote their time to ideological training (Smith 2015, 223). The collapse of the PDS also reduced the state's ability to indoctrinate the general population through meetings held at workplaces and distribution depots.

Overall, the combination of marketization from below and new information coming in from abroad resulted in significant shifts in the population's attitudes towards the DPRK leadership (Smith 2015; Hassig and Oh 2015; Choi 2017). The information filtering in meant that the DPRK population became more aware than ever of the poverty of their lives in comparison to their international neighbors (Smith 2015, 330). Hassig and Oh observe that the majority of people now pay little attention to official ideological pronouncements and regard officials with contempt (2015, 191). These changes have led to a general "disassociation" of the general population from the DPRK authorities, which is a worrying situation for the political elites (Smith 2015, 331). The seriousness with which the regime regarded the threat that marketization posed to their ideological control can be seen in the authorities' post-2005 attempts to reinstate the PDS, take back control of food supplies, and exert greater authority over the population. These measures culminated in the failed currency reform of 2009,[3] but all attempts to restrict black market activities and revive the PDS have failed due to the combination of unwilling local officials and popular pressure (Lankov 2013, 120–122).

It is against this immediate domestic economic and social background that *The Schoolgirl's Diary* was produced. Also important is an analysis of the different ways we can approach the interpretation of DPRK cultural output and the specific cinematic context of the period, all of which are discussed in the following section.

Understanding Film Consumption and Production in a Post-Famine North Korea

As stressed in the introduction to this chapter, many scholars have observed that there are specific peculiarities to be found within the type of artistic production of the DPRK, where art primarily functions, as Stephen Epstein contends, "as a tool of state ideology" (Epstein 2003; see also Kim 1996; Lee 2000). More than investigations into other forms of artistic cultural production, it is research within literary studies which has provided the most intensive interrogation of frameworks that help us understand the relationship between administrators, producers, and consumers of culture. Work by Epstein (2003), David-West (2009), and Petersen (2012) on North Korean fiction and graphic novels (comic books) provide insights into the connections between the producers of art, a state which enforces a clear political agenda, and the ordinary consumer of North Korean art, and this relationship is also relevant to our discussion of DPRK film.

Literary Studies: Frameworks for Understanding Cultural Production

Epstein (2003) and David-West (2009) observe that most analyses of North Korean artistic output almost invariably begin with an examination of a work's "relationship to official policy" (Epstein 2003). The implication is that if readers want to interpret the meaning of DPRK literature, then they need to look no further than official pronouncements on policy. David-West (2009, 23), for example, cites Pucek (1996) and Choi's (2008) examination of North Korean literature, which argues that writers serve as the mouthpiece of the regime, extolling the virtues of socialism while ignoring the grim realities of life within the DPRK. David-West argues this commonly held view characterizes the authorities writing via a proxy author, presenting the party-state as the "meta-author" (David-West 2009, 25).

The meta-authorial view of North Korean art is perhaps the most commonly held view of how to "read" DPRK cultural output for a good reason. Government policy directly impacts artistic production in the DPRK, since in order to publish their work, writers are obliged to join the Korean Writer's Union and are therefore subject to direct state influence (David-West 2009, 22).[4] The state obliges writers to consider official prescriptions and literary pronouncements from the voluminous work of Kim Il Sung and Kim Jong Il (David-West 2009, 3–9). One impact of this governmental involvement in literary production was the introduction of Soviet literary ideas, particularly Socialist Realism (David-West 2009, 8–11, 20). In terms of literary narratives, Socialist Realism is an intensely citational format inspired by Maxim Gorky's 1906 novel *The Mother*. Protagonists go from a position of acting according to their spontaneous desires to a state of consciousness in which they comprehend and embrace their responsibility to society (see Klark 1997). These protagonists are usually facilitated in their development from spontaneity to consciousness by a mentor-type figure.[5] The basic narrative trajectory of most Socialist Realist outputs played an important propaganda function for communist countries as a tool for the mass mobilization of society in the construction of communism. Socialist Realism proved an attractive framework for cultural production, partly because it was not a direct cultural imposition by the Soviets but was open to local adaptation, and the North Korean version included culturally nationalist elements (see Chung et al. 1996; David-West 2009, 8–9, 21).

Both David-West and Epstein observe problems within the meta-authorial perspective that inhibits its effectiveness as a means to explain all DPRK literary output. First, in assuming the state as meta-author, the approach invokes Wimsatt Jr. and Beardsley's intentional fallacy and is overly reliant upon political intentions revealed through official pronouncements rather than the "internal evidence" provided by closer textual analysis (Epstein 2003; David-West 2009, 26). Despite its "aesthetic, cognitive and sociological limitations" propagandist art still has some form of "art function" that must be revealed through critical examination (David-West 2009, 23). A more serious weakness of the meta-authorial approach is that it pays little attention to the interpretative possibilities offered to readers by ambiguities within the text. In his analysis of literature produced around the tail-end of the North

Korean famine, Epstein observes that instead of closed texts inviting a single reading with an implied reader, short stories reveal ambiguities in their narratives. These include conflict between families as well as overall evidence of "deep-rooted structural problems within" DPRK society that is often at odds with the official pronouncements (Epstein 2003). Epstein observes that the officially sanctioned message is often contained at the very end of a story, in a conclusion, which always "promises better if North Koreans are prepared to struggle through the present-day challenges" (Epstein 2003). The conclusions of such texts serve as a form of pay-off between the writer and the state in an implied contract in which authors must unambiguously reproduce official party lines but in return are accorded greater freedom in other narrative elements—such as the observation of general material poverty and familial conflict.

North Korean literary narrative, Epstein concludes, can offer "ample scope" for its audience to become "resisting readers" and to rebel against the standardized perspective imposed by the texts' conclusions (Epstein 2003). There is a contrast then between the meta-authorial approach and the possibility of "ironic readings" implied by Epstein in his focus on the moments of "indeterminacy" within narratives (Petersen 2012, 197; see also Lee 2000). The significant gap between fictional representation and daily experience results in an ironic or "uncontrolled response" on the part of the reader (Lee 2000, 253; Petersen 2012, 197). The state may be able to prescribe how writers *should* produce art and how readers *should* consume it, but the authorities are unable to control the readers' own responses.

Both approaches—the meta-authorial and ironic readings—provide us with insights into the functioning of North Korean literature and ways to visualize the tripartite relationship between state, author, and reader. Both approaches share one commonality—an assumption that the authorities lack much in the way of reflexivity about the artistic output of officially sanctioned authors. The meta-authorial approach assumes that the authorities can only conceive of artistic output in terms of a direct line of communication—one of output and uptake—between an omnipotent/omniscient state via a writer to a reader. On the other hand, Epstein contends that authors whose work encourages an ironic reading follow a "dangerous strategy" by offering readers sufficient scope to interpret narratives in potentially anti-authoritarian ways (Epstein 2003). However, Epstein does not include any analysis of whether administrators themselves *understand* the possibility of ironic readings. Neither does he explain whether the government's own artistic production machinery realizes that a by-product of the quarantine strategy (which limits explicit ideological content to the conclusion while allowing main narratives to reveal warts-and-all insights into DPRK life) can potentially elicit counter-state views amongst readers. According to both these ways of understanding the production and consumption of DPRK art, the state appears incapable of dealing with anything other than a complicit reader response.

To resolve this conundrum, Martin Petersen (2012, 200) proposes a third way of reading North Korean fiction, which he refers to as a "Reader-recognisant Meta-Authorial Reading." Petersen's study focuses on graphic novel representations of the 1996–1999 famine, and he argues that the authorities governing artistic production are fully aware of the possibility of "uncontrolled responses" on the part of readers and are therefore complicit in the creation of narratives that can elicit such responses. To minimize the impact of uncontrolled interpretations of DPRK literature, the authorities condone limited criticisms of North Korean society and life while sanctioning any direct attacks on their leadership. Petersen provides an example through his analysis of outside agitators who deliberately sabotaged the North Korean harvest to promote famine and discredit the authorities. In allowing the creation of such a scenario, the authorities admit that they failed to detect the presence of saboteurs and were not therefore in total control of the food distribution system. The author therefore indicates a tacit admission of failure on the part of what is supposed to be an all-powerful and all-knowing state (Petersen 2012, 199). By creating more nuanced depictions of contemporary society that allow for different interpretations, the authorities are attempting not to push the domestic readers' suspension of disbelief too far, and perhaps even claw back some support lost during the famine.

Petersen produces no evidence about how this strategy of allowing limited criticisms of North Korea's bureaucracy or structural problems is communicated to writers or whether this is part of an implied contract between the authorities and authors. However, the Reader-Recognisant Meta-Authorial approach is convincing in that it assumes that the authorities fully understand the limitations of overt political indoctrination through art and the possibility of multiple interpretations of texts. In addition, the approach also fits with strategies common in classical Soviet Socialist Realist narratives in which lower-ranking bureaucrats were often blamed for more general social failings (Petersen 2012, 200; Myers 1994).

Overall, these three approaches to literary texts offer a useful approach to considering DPRK film in the first decade of the new millennium, especially the relationship between the film regulating authorities, the artists, and the audiences. However, while these three approaches allow us to reflect on relationships within a state-dominated medium, there are some historical differences between literary and cinematic output which are essential to our understanding of DPRK film in the new millennium and its representations of a post-famine society.

Exhibition Contexts

One particularly important feature that distinguishes literary from cinematic production is the presence of a collective audience. This is important to any analysis of film made during a period of increasing disenfranchisement between state and society because the process of exhibition may have been factored into the authorities' analytical considerations of the content of films they would allow to be screened domestically. Unfortunately, as Dima Mironenko observes, few studies on North Korean cinema go beyond analyzing film texts to investigate the exhibition site, while his own study on the subject focuses mainly on a formative 1970s period in DPRK cinema (Mironenko 2016, 41). However, Mironenko's analysis is important because it reveals that far from being docile, brainwashed audiences, and despite constant state admonitions, the movie theater represented a space of significant "social nonconformism" in DPRK society, involving violent responses and open discontent against "poorly made propaganda films" (Mironenko 2016, 25, 41). The important point made by Mironenko's study is that North Korean cinemagoers have proved themselves to be discerning and demanding audiences, intolerant of inferior products, and desiring of well-made cinema. These factors also influenced the development of DPRK film beyond the 1970s into the 1980s. Thanks to the "popular demand" for "mass entertainment" from a public openly contemptuous of inferior product, cinema producers in the 1980s, began to create a film with a heavily reduced ideological content (Lee 2000, 39).

Shifting State Views of the Role of Culture as a Form of Soft Power

The demands of domestic audiences were not the only reason behind the creation of more entertaining films with a less didactic function. The 1980s DPRK film industry under Kim Jong Il's stewardship recognized the potential for cinema to appeal to an audience beyond the country's borders. Kim believed that cinema was a prestigious industry and that by raising the standards of filmmaking, movies could help raise the DPRK's international profile and exert influence overseas as part of a wider campaign of cultural diplomacy (Szalontai 2009). The primary targets of this campaign were fraternal socialist countries but also the South Korean public, whose opinion the North Koreans wanted to shape in support of policies that favored North Korean strategic interests (Szalontai 2009, 145).[6] The DPRK's efforts at soft power were challenging since there were few if any opportunities for direct interaction between the two Koreas until the late 1990s. The DPRK still targeted South Korean public opinion, but the most accessible targets for cultural diplomacy were the communist allies, which the North felt did not "wholeheartedly support Pyongyang's initiatives" (Szalontai 2009, 146). As part of this wider soft power campaign, Kim Jong Il initiated the production of films that could be exported, win prizes in prestigious international film festivals in former Eastern bloc countries, improve the name of North Korea abroad, and help achieve the DPRK's strategic interests more effectively than aggression.[7]

One important example of this campaign can be found in the production of the film *Pomnalŭi nunsŏgi* (*Snow Melts in Spring*, Rim Chang-bŏm and Ko Hang-nim, 1985, DPRK), a Romeo and Juliet-like narrative about division and reunification transplanted to Japanese Korean communities divided between pro-North and pro-South factions (Kim 2015, 53). Immanuel Kim argues that *Snow Melts in Spring* is important because it demonstrates that the level of overt political and didactic content within DPRK film could be altered according to target audiences and national policy priorities. *Snow Melts in Spring* was produced with a specific political function and international audience in mind. The picture was made when Pyongyang was intensively engaged in persuading Seoul to co-host the 1988 Olympic Games. In order to demonstrate its own earnest desire for the peaceful reunification of the Peninsula, the DPRK produced films like *Snow Melts in Spring* with a reduced level of pro-Pyongyang political content. The film features less hostility towards the US or the

South Koreans and none of the utopian presentation of socialist society[8] that commonly featured in other North Korean films and which carried the greatest likelihood of causing distaste to overseas audiences (Kim 2015, 42–43). Blatant pro-Pyongyang political propaganda is limited to the film's final 15-minute montage sequence, which features a visit of the protagonists to Pyongyang to celebrate Kim Il Sung's ideology.[9] However, this sequence was deleted from the film's international version, allowing audiences to infer that reunification could be achieved through mutual reconciliation rather than according to strict North Korean terms. Essentially, two versions of the movie were made, one for the domestic market and another, with a reduced didactic narrative, for overseas consumption (Kim 2015, 49).

The case of *Snow Melts in Spring* is important because it shows that DPRK authorities could subvert their own prescriptions about the domestic indoctrination function of cinema according to necessity. The desire for international cooperation to achieve diplomatic and national goals trumped the necessity for domestic indoctrination. *Snow Melts in Spring* also demonstrates a reflexive regime that is sensitive to a variety of potential audience responses and is prepared to reduce the specific political content of its national cinema. The restriction of the most prominent ideological messages in the film to the final 15 minutes of the film is significant for two reasons. First, by isolating potentially intrusive political messages to clearly signposted segments of the movie, their removal does not undermine the integrity of the narrative. Second, this quarantining of ideological content also reflects a feature of short-story narratives observed by Stephen Epstein, where the overt political messaging is often restricted to certain sections of the narrative (the conclusion). This appears to be an attempt at offering a payoff, a concession not only to the authorities but also to the audience, which acknowledges the idea that such propaganda is required while minimizing its impact on the actual narrative. The reduced political content and greater entertainment value of DPRK cinema is confirmed by defector accounts of this 1980s period of film (see Schönherr 2012, 191–192). Overall, the cinematic production of the 1980s indicates that filmmaking in the DPRK during this period was not monolithic and that the regime was also responsive to contingency and political function, as well as being sensitive to the needs of different audiences, all of which are important factors in our understanding of *The Schoolgirl's Diary*.

The Cinematic Context

During the build-up to the 1988 Seoul Olympic Games, the DPRK failed to engage with the South Korean public or achieve its diplomatic objectives. However, the late 1990s and early 2000s provided another opportunity for North Korea to use cultural diplomacy to further its international agenda. This was a period of détente between the two Koreas during which South Korean President Kim Dae Jung established a Sunshine Policy (1998–2008) aimed at fostering closer cooperation between Seoul and Pyongyang. However, it was also a time of increasingly frosty relations between the US and North Korea because of the breakdown of the Agreed Framework aimed at neutralizing the DPRK's indigenous nuclear program and preventing nuclear proliferation on the Korean Peninsula (Lankov 2013, 151). Making use of the worldwide coverage of the Seoul and Pyongyang rapprochement, North Korea began another cultural diplomacy drive in the early part of the 2000s by producing a greater number of films targeting the international market. In 2000, an updated version of the Shin Sang-ok film *Pulgasari* was the first DPRK film to be put on general release in Seoul, and it was also given a release on VHS video in the United States (Schönherr 2012, 148). The rights to *Sarainŭn yŏnghondŭl* (*Soul's Protest—The North Korean Titanic*, Kim Chun-song, 2000, DPRK) were purchased by a South Korean distribution company, and the film was shown at the Hong Kong International Film Festival (Schönherr 2012, 150–151). The picture covered the sinking of the *Ukishima Maru*, a ship carrying Koreans living in Japan back to the Peninsula following the end of World War Two. *P'urŭn Chudanesŏ* (*On the Green Carpet*, dir Rim Chang-bŏm, Chŏn Kwang-il, 2001, DPRK), a dramatization of a mass gymnastics event, was also shown at the 2004 Berlin International Film Festival. The release of *Soul's Protest—The North Korean Titanic* coincided with a renewal of South Korean-Japanese conflict over the publication of Japanese high school history textbooks, which revised the extent of Japan's culpability in its imperialist conquest of Asia in the 1930s and 1940s. The release also appears to have been an attempt to appeal to traditional animosity amongst South Koreans towards the Japanese.

The renewal of cinematic cultural diplomacy had several aims. On one level, the DPRK authorities were keen to appeal to a South Korean public opinion that was largely split over the benefits of greater cooperation between Seoul and Pyongyang in the early 2000s. The DPRK was also keen to show that the country was prepared for a limited and controlled opening up to the outside world and that the conciliatory aspects of the cooperation between Seoul and Pyongyang were its true face rather than the US assertions that North Korea was a rogue state. Despite the efforts to gain international attention, *Soul's Protest—The North Korean Titanic*, like *Pulgasari* and *On the Green Carpet*, failed to garner much interest from commercial buyers outside the DPRK. The films flopped, reportedly because audiences and journalists put off by "hagiographic" representations of people's devotion to the leadership and the unrealistically rosy representations of life in the DPRK. In addition, the technically inferior quality of production felt like a step back in time for film critics and spectators alike (Schönherr 2012, 150, 154).

International success and recognition did come for DPRK film, but not through 100% domestic productions. Two sports documentaries made by British filmmaker Daniel Gordon succeeded in garnering significant international attention for DPRK film where *Soul's Protest* and *On the Green Carpet* had failed (Schönherr 2012, 155). The first film, *Ch'ŏllima Ch'ukkudan* (*The Game of Their Lives*, Daniel Gordon, Nicholas Bonner, 2002, UK/DPRK), is a documentary about the performance of the North Korean football team at the 1966 World Cup finals in England when they reached the quarter-finals and defeated Italy. The film depicts the ordinary lives of the players who achieved remarkable results as well as their relationship with the industrial city of Middlesbrough, whose population took the North Koreans to their hearts. The second film, *A State of Mind* (Daniel Gordon, 2004, UK), closely follows the trials and tribulations of two North Korean child gymnasts and their families who are in training for the 2003 Pyongyang Mass Games. Both films were popular domestically, shown widely at international film festivals, distributed on the art house circuit, and critically well-received. Johannes Schönherr (2012, 156–157) argues that the films were particularly appealing internationally, partly because of their frank depictions of ordinary North Koreans in extraordinarily challenging environments. The films proved to be a major propaganda victory for the North Korean authorities, showing "North Korea as an interesting but unfortunately misunderstood country to the outside world." (Schönherr 2012, 156–157).

The Schoolgirl's Diary

Few of the small number of films produced in the DPRK between 2003 and 2007 were shown abroad or at the most important outlet for the international exhibition of North Korean film, the Pyongyang International Film Festival (PIFF, Schönherr 2012, 158–159). An exception was *The Schoolgirl's Diary*, which precipitated widespread domestic media attention (Schönherr 2012, 162). Press articles revealed that Kim Jong Il reportedly returned from his busy schedule inspecting frontline military units to help make improvements to the script. Eight million cinemagoers flocked to the film, which was widely praised by senior party members for its "truthful representation" of the lives of the protagonists (Schönherr 2012, 161–162; Elley 2007). The film was shown at the 2007 PIFF and given a limited release in France (Elley 2007). Despite boasting that the film had attracted a third of the population to watch it, in 2016 the DPRK authorities reportedly banned the domestic exhibition of the film (RFA 2016). All of this raises questions as to how a film like *The Schoolgirl's Diary* managed to garner international and domestic acclaim, as well as the approval (and subsequent disapproval) of the authorities?

The film tells the story of a teenage girl, Su-ryŏn, who lives in an unnamed rural area of North Korea with her extended family: her younger sister Su-ok, her mother Chŏng-nan, and her grandmother. Her father, a scientist, is constantly away from home and hard at work in a factory in a distant city on an undisclosed project of national importance. Su-ryŏn's dream is to live in an apartment in a city; she is unhappy with the quality of her family's existence and frequently voices her anger at the general material lack in their lives. The only relief from this cycle of deprivation is the intermittent visits of her uncle (*samch'on*), a businessman who brings brightly colored clothing as gifts to his two nieces. But Su-ryŏn's greatest complaint is the fact that her father is always absent, devoting himself to work, duty, and nation. He even ignores his family at the dinner table during the few moments when he does return for visits. The father's devotion to work and his neglect of his family comes to a head when he is informed that his wife is seriously ill with cancer and chooses to continue working on his project. In the film's conclusion, the mother's cancer is cured, and the father's project ends with his achievements recognized by the state. Su-ryŏn realizes how selfish she has been in her desire for a more close-knit family and material wealth, and finally understands the importance of her father's sacrifices for the country.

The overall tone and style give the film the flavor of the type of social reality film marketed for art house screens in Europe, North America, or even South Korea, and this is established in the opening title sequence. An analysis of the opening in particular provides insights into how the film's style is established, as the section also forms a reference point for critical narrative elements that appear later in the film. The film begins with a flashback and a tracking shot, with the camera following nine-year-old Su-ryŏn as she walks in her elementary school uniform through a rural setting on her way back home after class. This is followed by a close-up of her backpack, dominated by an image of Mickey Mouse that fills the entire frame (Fig. 4.1). As Su-ryŏn continues her quick pace, the camera slowly pans out to reveal other schoolchildren on their way home, wearing similar backpacks with images of animated Disney characters. The voiceover of 16-year-old Su-ryŏn reflects on how she had always envied people who lived in apartments and is spoken to the accompaniment of mournful harmonica music played extra-diegetically. The title sequence cuts to Su-ryŏn as a young teenager, with the same music and voiceover explaining how neighborhood children living in apartments actually envied Su-ryŏn's small house because a family of swallows had made a nest in their front porch. The film cuts to a close-up of the nest,

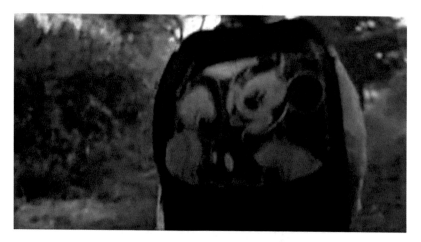

Fig. 4.1 Opening of *The Schoolgirl's Diary*, Su-ryŏn returning from school

which gives onto a medium-long shot of a crowd of local children clambering onto the porch to get a better view of the birds. The shot of the children cuts to a medium close-up of Su-ryŏn leafing through a family photo album, while the voiceover explains how her sister also grew up in the house. There is a close-up of family portraits in the book followed by a medium-long shot of her sister Su-ok attempting to keep the neighborhood children away from the swallows' nest. Some children fall into the house's vegetable patch, breaking a fence, at which point Su-ryŏn intervenes to scold the children and send them away. In the next scene, which shows a medium-long shot framed by the rectangular structure of the family home, Su-ok breaks down in tears because of the children's accident and is consoled by her grandmother. The accident and anger in the scene provide an indication that all is not well in the household. By way of explanation for the family's distress, the voiceover explains that Su-ryŏn's father practically lives at his office, leaving the four women alone in the house.

The swallow's nest scene cuts to a second flashback, this time a close-up of a 12-year-old Su-ryŏn standing looking out through a glass door at the school entrance, wearing her school uniform and her Young Pioneers red scarf (Figs. 4.2, 4.3). She is waiting in vain for her father to come to the parent's day meeting, watching with sadness and envy as the parents of other children file in one by one. She turns away in disappointment, and the camera pans into a close-up of Su-ryŏn's sad expression, as the

Fig. 4.2 Su-ryŏn waits in vain for her father to come to her school's open day

Fig. 4.3 Su-ryŏn waiting at school dissolves to an older Su-ryŏn returning from school

voiceover explains that her father's absence has resulted in a deterioration in her relationship with him. This school close-up dissolves to a medium-long shot of the 16-year-old Su-ryŏn walking back from high school and hearing her mother's voice speaking to the schoolteacher in front of the family home. The acousmatic voice of the mother apologizes to the teacher for Su-ryŏn's behavior, while Su-ryŏn herself hides in a bush to avoid the passing teacher and becomes upset because she realizes she has trodden in rabbit dung (Fig. 4.4). We are left in the dark as to what Su-ryŏn has done to warrant a home visit by her teacher, but the details come out in the next scene when Su-ryŏn is helping her mother with the ironing. Su-ryŏn's mother scolds her for lying to her homeroom teacher by telling him that her father had died (in order to account for his absence). During this ironing scene an electrical fire breaks out, electrocuting Su-ryŏn's mother. Su-ok returns from soccer practice to help extinguish the fire and prevent greater damage.

Especially notable in this opening sequence is the use of flashbacks and the subdued colors and hues of the *mise-en-scene*. The unity of costume and theme—the journeys to and from school establish a narrative bridge between the different timeframes. The rapid cutting between three time periods illustrates both the passage of time and the father's ongoing neglect of the family. Each period of Su-ryŏn's childhood depicted in the sequence is characterized by darker tones. The sky is permanently

Fig. 4.4 Su-ryŏn hides from her teacher who visits her home

overcast and subdued, the buildings—even the apartment block where Su-ryŏn yearns to live is shabby and gray—reflecting the intensity of her pain. The one exception to the drab colors is the vivid and bright pastels of the foreign-made goods symbolized by the Mickey Mouse image, a reference forward to the brightly colored clothes the uncle brings his nieces as gifts. This *mise-en-scène* covers the serious themes evoked at the start of the film about family relationships, growing-up, and social problems resulting from work and duty. Meanwhile, the film's style and lack of action establish the picture as one that might be distributed by independent firms interested in a limited release at art houses or international film festivals. The film achieved modest success by targeting this particular international market. After its screening at the PIFF, it was offered a distribution deal by a small independent French company, opened in five cinemas and also exhibited at the 2007 Cannes Film Festival as well as in Denmark and Romania (Elley 2007; Person 2008; Molen 2013).

Another feature of the film is that it is very much grounded in the changes that DPRK society was undergoing at the time, and in the real-life challenges that ordinary North Koreans were facing under Kim Jong Il's rule. The opening sequence features important elements that are developed throughout the narrative, notably the film's almost total focus on women. This was noted by Kim Suk-young in her commentary on the movie. Kim observed that the film depicted three generations of women each with varying expectations of their positions in society.

The grandmother is the provider, the mother is the carer for her children and husband, and the daughters are shown as young people with a less well-defined sense of their role in life (Person 2008). A primary driving force for the narrative is family conflict arising from this younger generation's indistinct social identity. Another focus of the film is on the actions of women as providers, organizers, carers, and workers, and this reflects the important transformation of the role of women in society in the wake of the famine. The film also reveals constant evidence of the broader change created by marketization. In the opening sequence, the contrast between the North Korean school uniform and Disney character indicates the juxtaposition of the foreign over the national and represents the influx of foreign goods, ideas, and influences brought about by increased marketization. In a later scene, the uncle tells Su-ok that she will be as good a soccer player as Pele in the new training kit he has given her. The implication here is that there is a generally more welcoming attitude from ordinary people towards the influx of foreign-made consumer goods due to marketization. These representations indicate a remarkable shift in a country with an aggressively nationalist cultural ideology (see Myers 2010).

The film reflects important changes that were ongoing within DPRK society through its constant references to social problems. The opening sequence makes reference to increasing levels of conflict between generations of women subject to different expectations about their roles and futures. The desires of the younger generation for greater material comfort often conflict with the notion of social responsibility held by their parent's generation. The material deprivation exemplified by the electrical fire in the opening sequence is reprised throughout the film, for example, when a door collapses during one of the father's rare visits. The shoddy living conditions experienced by ordinary North Koreans are displayed very clearly to the viewer. One feature of the film that is perhaps surprising is the constant references to food—or the lack thereof. Su-ok's first words as she returns home from sports practice in the opening sequence is "I'm really hungry" (subtitled as: "I'm starving."). The sisters later complain about the meager lunchbox rations that they were given for a school picnic outing. When the father returns home late one night, he eats cold food he finds in the kitchen so that it will not go to waste. All of this in a country where just a decade previously, there was no city in the DPRK that did not experience malnutrition, and in remote rural areas, people dropped dead in the streets from hunger.

Multiple Address Strategies

The question that remains is how a film that drew critical attention abroad as well as a large domestic audience managed to also receive official approval. The answer appears to lie in the film's ability to appeal to different audiences. It has what Chris Howard calls a "multiple address strategy" in relation to the mass appeal of South Korean commercial film in the era of the ten million ticket phenomenon (Howard 2008, 92). Of course, the difference is that such a strategy is not usually associated with didactic cinema produced by a state-controlled media, which should have a single, pliant audience in mind according to the "meta-authorial" interpretation of DPRK art.

Domestic Appeal

Defector testimony indicates that one reason why the late 1980s era of North Korean filmmaking was so popular is because of the reduced political messaging. As one defector explains: "Shin Sang-ok didn't go beyond the general outline of revolutionary propaganda, he did try to give hints and to show different things." (Quoted in Schönherr 2012, 191). Another important reason was that domestic audiences felt Shin Sang-ok created more accurate representations of their existence. A different defector explains:

> Shin Sang-ok brought a more realistic approach to cinema. His films were closer to real people's lives… [The films produced after Shin returned to South Korea were inferior because they] …didn't reflect our daily lives, they were not realistic movies. We didn't like them. (Quoted in Schönherr 2012, 193–194)

For cinemagoers in the DPRK, an important reason for watching film in addition to the increased entertainment value associated with the Shin Sang-ok era was the reduced propaganda content and narratives that reflected North Korean society. *The Schoolgirl's Diary* offered domestic viewers a more subtle and understated didactic content (see below), as well as a content that was more reflective of many people's lives. The film reveals the underlying dissatisfaction of a society in which the state had virtually abandoned the majority of the population to their own fate. The influx of material goods and ideas from abroad symbolizes some of the tensions that growing wealth disparities created, while the frequent accidents, shoddy building construction, and poor working conditions reflect the lives of many in this period.

International Appeal

The most notable response from international reviewers was how ordinary, commonplace, and universal many of the issues featured in the film were. For Derek Elley (2007) writing in *Variety*, Su-ryŏn is comparable to "an average teen dealing with peer pressure." For the French movie distributor James Velaise, who bought the film's international rights, the appeal of *The Schoolgirl's Diary* was that it showed "another side of North Korean culture… 'They're not all out to do nuclear crazy things. There are normal people in that country.'" (*National Review* 2008). This is certainly the impression we are given in the opening sequence by the sight of a child with a Mickey Mouse backpack. This could be any school-age child in the world. The producers of *The Schoolgirl's Diary* appear to have drawn lessons from Daniel Gordon's documentaries as well, with the focus on mundane, commonplace, and ordinary details. One clear international appeal of the film was, therefore, its focus on the quotidian. This was not a presentation of North Korea as exceptional or special or different, and indeed it was its sameness that attracted praise. This was not a depiction of North Koreans as being slavishly devoted to the leader, or as outstandingly disciplined and universally content with their lives; it was a representation of people that anyone in the international audience could relate to.

In addition to the universality of themes, a second aspect that interested Western critics was the technical superiority of the film style in comparison to previous DPRK offerings. The intricate opening sequence included a flashback to two previous periods in Su-ryŏn's childhood linked by a musical bridge and a voiceover from the present.[10] The complex coordination of the sonic and visual references to different characters (Su-ok, the teacher, and the father), drab *mise-en-scene* (dilapidated buildings and permanently gray weather), together with the graphic matches on action and the serious social issues in the subject matter, helped create a film that did not look out of place on the festival circuit or in art houses.

The producers of *The Schoolgirl's Diary* appear to have drawn lessons from the failure of films like *On the Green Carpet*, *Soul's Protest: The*

Korean Titanic, and *Pulgasari*, which were widely criticized for their technical inferiority, hagiographic celebration of the North Korean leadership, and rose-tinted representations of the DPRK (see Schönherr 2012). *The Schoolgirl's Diary* removes the more overt political references to the leadership, which instead is implied metaphorically through the invocation of the father-family relationship.

Overall, the film appeared to balance the necessary combination of originality and difference. It worked within the generic conventions of state media by featuring a didactic element and symbolic references to the leadership (albeit understated), but it also presented enough novelty to interest audiences internationally. Relatively open accounts about the gray lives of ordinary people, about material deprivation, and the lack of food were not what most viewers associated with the DPRK's official state media (See *National Review* 2008 for example) so the element of surprise appealed to many commentators (Demick 2008; Molen 2013). Audiences didn't expect Mickey Mouse to feature in a film made in the DPRK, and this juxtaposition of convention against novelty was a key difference in the movie and a reason for the attention it garnered.

Acceptance by the State

Perhaps the most surprising feature of the film is that it not only appealed to domestic and international audiences but at the same time it squared the circle by passing the authorities' ideological requirements. *The Schoolgirl's Diary* had enough of a politically correct message to satisfy the authorities, which can be seen in its narrative structure, symbolism, and overall payoff message at the film's conclusion. In terms of the narrative trajectory, the film is not that far from traditional Socialist Realist narratives in that it follows the heroine's progression from spontaneity to consciousness, from acting according to her personal desires to understanding her social role and collective responsibility. Explicit mentor figures who play a guiding role are exemplified by mother and grandmother, and the film also employs important stereotypical features of DPRK art, namely the symbolism of a father figure to represent the DPRK leadership. In her book on DPRK art, *Illusive Utopia*, Kim Suk-young (2010, 143–144) argues that in much North Korean art, there are two sets of fathers, one related by blood and the other the implied father of the state. In *The Schoolgirl's Diary* one father figure is represented by the uncle, a wealthy representative of the group of market traders or business entrepreneurs that emerged along with post-famine marketization. The film implies that the uncle, with his ostentatious wealth, is not the desirable patriarch whom Su-ryŏn and Su-ok should follow. Instead, their actual father is depicted as the true leadership figure. Kim Suk-young also notes that most DPRK conventions deprive the traditional patriarchs of their masculinity and turn them into secondary males, demonstrating that the people are in the final analysis children of the father Kim Il Sung (or Kim Jong Il) within the imagined family of the nation-state (2010, 143–144). *The Schoolgirl's Diary* shows that actual and implied fathers have both been deprived of their masculinity—at least temporarily. In the opening sequence, Su-ryŏn explains how the conflict with her mother arose because of the absence of her father. The father also apologizes for his absence from his family, as they have suffered because of it. Both actual and symbolic fathers regain their "strength" and masculinity at the end of the film. The metaphorical reading of the film is a tacit acknowledgment of the state's failure in its duty of providing for the people. As such, the symbolic and actual father relationship and the narrative's conclusion suggest that the film invites the Reader-Recognisant Meta-Authorial reading outlined by Martin Petersen. The Meta-author asks for a return of trust from a population that has been pushed to the brink. In showing awareness of their own failings, the authorities attempted to direct the domestic response of viewers away from "ironic" or unintentional readings of the film's narrative—for example, seeing the electrical fire and shoddy buildings as symbolic of state collapse.

For the authorities, then, the film was acceptable because it used typical narrative structures associated with Socialist Realism, it represents an essentially positive view of the political leadership through the allegorical use of the father figure, and it steers the viewers away from an ironic or uncontrolled response to the problems depicted in the narrative. This leaves the final question—why was the film subsequently banned in 2016? It is possible that the film's frank presentation of social problems and internal conflict in a society that is officially without such conflict was tolerated by the authorities as a strategy to gain international recognition for the country at the time the film was made. The film probably had a clear cultural and diplomatic aim. However, once the immediate needs of the DPRK's leadership had shifted and the country was no longer engaged in a mission of cinematic cultural diplomacy to present a more human face to the world, the film was banned.

Conclusion

Researchers investigating DPRK film from the Kim Il Sung era have noted that North Korean cinematic output was very different from filmmaking made in commercial cinematic contexts in terms of the didactic elements aimed to socialize and mobilize the population in the service of the country. Since Kim Il Sung's death and the catastrophic 1996–1999 famine, there have been some widespread social, political, and economic changes in North Korea. Marketization from below gave people more economic agency than they had ever had before, but it also helped bring in new material goods and ideas from abroad, which served to alienate the population from the ideological rule of the authorities. This chapter analyzed the domestic, international, and official reception of a state-produced film about contemporary life in the DPRK in the context of significant social changes within North Korea. It considered the geopolitical and historical cinematic context as well as theories about art produced by a state-controlled media to examine how *The Schoolgirl's Diary* succeeded in appealing to three different types of audience—international, domestic, and official. The film drew domestic audiences because it spoke to ordinary North Koreans about some of the problems impacting their lives, including poor housing, material deprivation, and social conflict arising from growing income disparities. International critics praised the film's style and its technical superiority to previous DPRK films marketed abroad. A European distributor targeted the film towards festivals and art houses because of its low-key style, technical superiority, and themes of social alienation. The depiction of North Koreans as ordinary but misunderstood aligned with state prerogatives, and the film could therefore be allied to a low-level cultural diplomatic campaign to shape more favorable international views of the DPRK. This is why the authorities were prepared to accept the film's reduced ideological content and greater honesty about the daily challenges faced by ordinary North Koreans. The film also encouraged a Reader-Recognisant Meta-Authorial reading in which the authorities attempted to control ironic responses to narratives through a limited acknowledgment of social problems in the hope that audiences would begin to trust their rule again.

Returning to the question of the character of DPRK film in the context of the widespread social and political change of the early 2000s, we see a pragmatic and purposeful approach to cinema exerted by the North

Korean state. The DPRK authorities are fully aware of the potential influence cinema has as a medium to further state foreign policy objectives. This cinema policy was enacted by Kim Jong Il in the mid-1980s and revived by Kim on a smaller scale with *The Schoolgirl's Diary*. In their use of cinema, the DPRK authorities also appear to understand the poor experience of autocratic governments with an inflexible approach to state media. Richard Hall (2000), in his investigation of the collapse of Eastern European socialism, argues:

> … control over public opinion attributed even to the most totalitarian regimes is frequently overstated. Authoritarian or totalitarian regimes may control the mass media and the flow of information to society, and they may be able to shape the understanding of the population, but they cannot completely control the interpretation of such information by the population or the connotation or meaning the population attaches to it, particularly not during times of crisis where the regime is already widely viewed as illegitimate. (Hall 2000, 1081)

In specific cases like *The Schoolgirl's Diary* the North Korean authorities reveal themselves to be reflexive, aware of audience needs and tastes, and able to meet them within certain limits.

Acknowledgements I wish to express my special thanks to Martin Petersen, James Velaise, Immanuel Kim, and Russell Edwards for their assistance and feedback, and to Bev Zalcock for her guidance on film.

Notes

1. See Steve Chung (2014) on the issue of historical representations in DPRK film.
2. It was not only ordinary people who were marketizing during this period but also state institutions, which meant that different branches of government were becoming increasingly responsible for sourcing their own funds (for more details, see Smith 2015, 12).
3. See Lankov (2013, 120–122) for more on the failed attempt to undermine unofficial marketization via the 2009 currency reforms.
4. Researchers differ over the extent of the influence of Soviet-style Socialist Realism on DPRK art. For example, Myers (1994) argues

that the DPRK failed to impose Soviet style Socialist Realism at all, while David-West (2009, 8) refutes this contention, arguing that Myers "overprivileges the national form and narratology of Soviet literature." Jackson (2016) argues that elements of Socialist Realist narratives continued to have an impact on DPRK film well into the 1980s.
5. For an analysis of a positive hero and mentor figure in a 1980s North Korean film see Jackson (2016).
6. For example, supporting the DPRK call for the withdrawal of US troops stationed in the South, or to support DPRK proposals for the reunification of the Peninsula.
7. Such as military threats, espionage and terrorist attacks, which were common in the run up to the 1988 Olympics (see Lankov 2013).
8. For an example of a conflict-free, utopian vision, see *Sagwa ttalttae* (*When we Pick Apples*, Kim Yong-ho, 1971).
9. Where propaganda is the "attempt to influence the public opinions of audiences … propaganda both confirms and 'converts' … through the transmission of ideas and values, it is thus distinguished from the more overt pressures, such as financial reward, or the threat or use of violence." (Taylor 1998, 15).
10. Elley calls the film "well-lensed" and a "slick snapshot" of contemporary life in the DPRK (2007); *DPRK Films* claims it has "technically proficient photography." (*DPRK* Films 2013).

References

Baek, Jieun. 2016. *North Korea's Hidden Revolution: How the Information Underground is Transforming a Closed Society*. New Haven, CT: Yale University Press.

Choi, Yearn-Hong. 2008. "North Korea's Literary Theory." *Korea Times*, April 23. Accessed December 10, 2021. http://www.koreatimes.co.kr/www/news/opinon/2008/12/246_22987.html.

Choi, Yong Sub. 2017. "North Korea's Hegemonic Rule and its Collapse." *The Pacific Review* 30 (5): 783–800.

Chung, Hilary, Michael Falchikov, Bonnie S. McDougall, and Karin McPherson, eds. 1996. *In the Party Spirit: Socialist Realism and Literary Practice in the Soviet Union, East Germany and China*. Amsterdam: Brill/Rodopi.

Chung, Steve. 2014. *Split Screen Korea: Shin Sang-ok and Postwar Cinema*. Minneapolis: Minnesota University Press.
David-West, Alzo. 2009. "The Literary Ideas of Kim Il Sung and Kim Jong Il: An Introduction to North Korean Meta-Authorial Perspectives." *Cultural Logic* 1–34.
Demick, Barbara. 2008. "No Stars, No Swag, But What a Crowd!" Los Angeles Times, October 11. Accessed January 22, 2021. https://www.latimes.com/archives/la-xpm-2008-oct-11-fg-film11-story.html.
DPRK Films. 2013. "Review: *The Schoolgirl's Diary*." DPRK Films. August 3. Accessed January 22, 2021.
Elley, Derek. 2007. "*The Schoolgirl's Diary*." *Variety*, May 17. Accessed January 22, 2021. https://variety.com/2007/film/markets-festivals/the-schoolgirl-s-diary-1200559318/.
Epstein, Stephen. 2003. "Encountering North Korean Fiction: The Origins of the Future." *Words Without Borders* (September). Accessed January 19, 2021. https://www.wordswithoutborders.org/article/encountering-north-korean-fiction-the-origins-of-the-future.
Finney, R. 2016. "North Korea Bans Formerly Approved Films Now Deemed Sensitive." rfa.org [online]. Accessed October 17, 2019. https://www.rfa.org/english/news/korea/films-07222016153114.html.
Hall, Richard Andrew. 2000. "Theories of Collective Action and Revolution: Evidence from the Romanian Transition of December 1989." *Europe-Asia Studies* 52 (6): 1069–1093.
Hassig, Ralph and Kongdan Oh. 2015. *The Hidden People of North Korea: Everyday Life in the Hermit Kingdom*. Lanham: Rowman and Littlefield.
Howard, Chris. 2008. "Contemporary South Korean Cinema: 'National Conjunction' and 'Diversity.'" In *East Asian Cinemas: Exploring Transnational Connections on Film*, edited by Leon Hunt and Leung Wing-Fai, 88–102. London: I.B. Taurus.
Jackson, Andrew David. 2016. "DPRK Film, *Order No. 27* and the Acousmatic Voice." In *Korean Screen Cultures: Interrogating Cinema, TV, Music and Online Games*, edited by Andrew David Jackson and Colette Balmain, 161–176. Oxford: Peter Lang.
Kim, Immanuel. 2015. "*Snow Melts in Spring*: Another Look at the North Korean Film Industry." *Journal of Japanese and Korean Cinema* 7 (1): 41–56.
Kim, Kyung Hyun. 1996. "The Fractured Cinema of North Korea: The Discourse of the Nation in *Sea of Blood*." In *In Pursuit of Contemporary East Asian Culture*, edited by Tang, Xiaobing, 85–106. New York: Routledge.
Kim, Suk-Young. 2010. *Illusive Utopia: Theater, Film, and Everyday Performance in North Korea*. Ann Arbor: The University of Michigan Press.

Klark, Katerina. 1997. "Socialist Realism with Shores: The Conventions for the Positive Hero." In *Socialist Realism without Shores*, edited by Thomas Lahusen and Evgeny Dobrenko, 27–50. Durham, N.C.: Duke University press.

Lankov, Andrei. 2013. *The Real North Korea: Life and Politics in the Failed Stalinist Utopia*. New York: Oxford University Press.

Lankov, Andrei. 2016. "The Resurgence of a Market Economy in North Korea." Carnegie Moscow Centre. Moscow: Carnegie Endowment.

Lee, Hyangjin. 2000. *Contemporary Korean Cinema: Identity, Culture and Politics*. Manchester, UK: Manchester University Press.

Mironenko, Dima. 2016. "North Koreans at the Movies: Cinema of Fits and Starts and the Rise of Chameleoon Spectatorship." *The Journal of Japanese and Korean Cinema* 8 (1): 25–44.

Molen, Sherri Ter. 2013. "Benoit Symposium: Capitalist Dreams in the Communist Utopia: North Korea's *The Schoolgirl's Diary*." *SinoNK*. September 30. Last Accessed January 22, 2021. https://sinonk.com/2013/09/30/capitalist-dreams-in-the-communist-utopia-north-koreas-the-schoolgirls-diary/.

Myers, Brian. 1994. *Han Sorya and North Korean Literature: The Failure of Socialist Realism XE "Socialist Realism" in DPRK*. Ithaca, NY: Cornell University Press.

Myers, Brian. 2010. *The Cleanest Race*. New York: Melville.

National Review. 2008. "Those Who Were Unable to Attend the 2006 Pyongyang Film Festival Missed a Treat: A Tender Dramedy Titled *The Schoolgirl's Diary*, One of the Two Films Produced in North Korea That Year." *National Review* 60 (2), February 11.

Person, James. 2008. "North Korean Film Screening: *The Schoolgirl's Diary*." *The North Korea Independent Documentation Project*. Last Accessed January 22, 2021. https://www.wilsoncenter.org/event/north-korean-film-screening-the-schoolgirls-diary-english-subtitles.

Petersen, Martin. 2012. "A New Deal: Graphic Novel Representations of Food Issues in Post-famine North Korea." *Korea Yearbook 2012*, 181–208. Leiden: Brill.

Pucek, Vladimir. 1996. "The Impact of Juche upon Literature and Art." In *North Korea: Ideology, Politics, Economy*, edited by Han S. Park, 51–70. Englewood Cliffs, New Jersey: Prentice Hall.

Schönherr, Johannes. 2012. *North Korean Cinema: A History*. Jefferson, N.C.: McFarland.

Smith, Hazel. 2015. *North Korea: Markets and Military Rule*. Cambridge: Cambridge University Press.

Szalontai, Balazs. 2009. "Expulsion for a Mistranslated Poem: The Diplomatic Aspects of North Korean Cultural Policies." In *Dynamics of the Cold War in Asia: Ideology, Identity, and Culture*, edited by Vu Tuong and Wasana Wongsurawat, 145–164. London: Palgrave Macmillan.

Taylor, Richard. 1998. *Film Propaganda: Soviet Russia and Nazi Germany.* London: Bloomsbury.

Ward, Peter. 2016. "What is Marketization and When Did It Begin in North Korea?" *NK News*, August 10.

PART II

Music

Introduction

Andrew David Jackson

The year prior to the 1994 promulgation of Kim Young Sam's *segyehwa* policy witnessed a formative moment in South Korean cultural history. The release of director Im Kwon-taek's movie *Sopyonje* (1993, ROK) produced a phenomenal and unparalleled public response in the history of South Korean cinema, encapsulating the complex relationship between modernity and traditional culture in the Korean context. The film's release provoked a moment of national self-reflection that revealed the ambivalence with which many South Koreans viewed modernity and its impact upon what is considered to be native cultural heritage. *Sopyonje* told the story of a family of *p'ansori* (Korean vocal art performed by a single vocalist and accompanying drummer) singers eking out a living in 1960s South Korea. It was the first South Korean-made film to sell over a million tickets at the domestic box office, where it had to compete with Hollywood blockbusters like *Jurassic Park* (Steven Spielberg 1993, US). Its release caused a media sensation for its representation of familial disintegration as a metaphor for declining cultural traditions like *p'ansori*. At the same time, the film helped revive widespread interest in Korean musical traditions (Cho 2002, 135). The movie is also important because it was supposed to be the event that would break Korean heritage on the world stage. Cultural commentators confidently predicted that the domestic success of the film would be repeated internationally, signaling the revival of South Korean cinema (Stringer 2002, 157). Others argued that overseas audiences (much like domestic ones) would embrace Korean traditional cultural forms like *p'ansori* due to the film (Cho 2002, 151). "What is the most Korean is the most universal" was an expression used to account for what many Koreans believed would be the global appeal of *Sopyonje* and the cultural forms it depicted (Cho 2002, 151).[1]

However, the spectacular domestic success was not repeated outside the country, and international audiences largely shunned the film's representation of traditional music.[2] 1993 was not the year in which the world embraced South Korea's cultural forms traditional or otherwise but this moment was not far off.[3] In the late 1990s, South Korean cultural producers began to export their work internationally in increasing quantities. South Korean film was followed by television dramas, popular music, online gaming, variety shows, and webtoons. More than any other cultural form, it is Korean music that has achieved the most significant global success. However, this success has not been achieved by the traditional music represented by the *p'ansori* of *Sopyonje*. Instead, global prominence has come with K-pop a form of popular music consisting of fast-paced, catchy, melodic dance tunes accompanied by flashy videos and performed by attractive multiple-member vocalists/dancers and marketed via highly capitalized, powerful management agencies. The K-pop phenomenon has been remarkable: K-pop exports from South Korea in 2016 totaled US$443 million. The South Korean industry employs approximately 78,000 people, and the domestic music market leaped from the 33rd largest in the world in 2005 to the 11th largest by 2012 (Woo 2018).

Researchers have attempted to explain the global appeal of K-pop in various ways, accounting for its success by arguing that diverse domestic and international audiences are drawn by the hybrid mixture of native and foreign cultural forms (Jin 2016, 113). Others like Choi and Maliangkay (2014, 4) account for the spread of K-pop by stressing the importance of obsessive fandom that social media can mobilize to support, fetishize and popularize its performers on a global scale. The international reach of K-pop from the late 1990s onwards followed significant legislative and economic shifts resulting from globalization processes within the East Asia region. These regional shifts, outlined by Chua Beng Huat (2012) and Shim Doobo (2005), saw the liberalization of cultural flows over previously sealed borders; they also resulted in K-pop management agencies deliberately targeting massive Chinese markets that had once been penetrated by J-Pop (Japanese pop). As well as resulting from important shifts in the international diffusion of popular culture (thanks to increased globalization), K-pop is also a part of South Korean state strategy aimed at increased global engagement. This strategy utilizes K-pop diplomacy to facilitate South Korea's foreign policy agenda;[4] it also uses performances to depict elements of Korean heritage such as *p'ansori* to portray South Korea as both modern and rich in tradition.[5]

This part of the book examines music in the era of South Korea's cultural internationalization, focusing on popular and official understandings of the importance of traditional musical culture in a modernizing society and on the global appeal of K-pop. Seung-hwan Shin's essay investigates the continued significance of *Sopyonje*, a film that started a debate about the place of tradition particularly music in a modernized South Korean reality. Roald Maliangkay follows with a chapter that looks at key difficulties in preserving traditions within South Korea. The process of rebuilding and modernizing created a cultural heritage system aimed at gaining international recognition while restoring pride in a transforming country. However, fewer people seeking a livelihood in the arts coupled with an increasingly aging population of artists keeping traditions alive have posed existential threats to Korea's musical heritage. Ute Fendler's essay examines the global spread of K-Pop, particularly how a musical form that has frequently been criticized as manufactured and manipulated continues to project a rebellious persona that appeals to international audiences.

Notes

1. This phrase is significant, as it would become central to Kim Young Sam's *segyehwa* policy (Cho 2002, 151).
2. For one account of why international audiences shunned *Sopyonje*, see Stringer (2002).
3. This moment came with the release of *Shiri* (see section two introduction of this volume).
4. See for example BTS's 2019 concert in Saudi Arabia that was organized despite the opposition of fans and human rights groups (*The Guardian* 2019).
5. See for example Hgordon (2019).

References

Cho, Hae Joang. 2002. "*Sopyonje*: Its Cultural and Historical Meaning." In *Im Kwon-Taek: The Making of a Korean National Cinema*, edited by David E. James and Kyung Hyun Kim, 134–156. Detroit: Wayne State University Press.

Choi, JungBong, and Roald Maliangkay. 2014. "Introduction: Why Fandom Matters to the International Rise of K-Pop." In *K-Pop—The International Rise of the Korean Music Industry*, edited by JungBong Choi and Roald Maliangkay. London: Routledge.

Chua, Beng Huat. 2012. *Structure, Audience and Soft Power in East Asian Pop Culture*. Hong Kong: Hong Kong University Press.

The Guardian. 2019. "K-Pop Group BTS Criticised for Saudi Arabia Concert." *The Guardian*. https://www.theguardian.com/music/2019/oct/12/k-pop-group-bts-criticised-for-saudi-arabia-concert. October 12. Accessed March 1, 2021.

Hgordon. 2019. "12 K-Pop Songs that Incorporate Elements of Traditional Korean Culture." *Soompi*. December 7. https://www.soompi.com/article/1367060wpp/12-k-pop-songs-that-incorporate-elements-of-traditional-korean-culture. Accessed March 1, 2021.

Jin, Dal Yong. 2016. *New Korean Wave: The Transnational Cultural Power in the Age of Social Media*. Urbana: University of Illinois Press.

Shim Doobo. 2005. "Globalization and Cinema Regionalization in East Asia." *Korea Journal* 45 (4): 233–260.

Stringer, Julian. 2002. "*Sopyonje* and the Inner Domain of National Culture." In *Im Kwon-Taek: The Making of a Korean National Cinema*, edited by David E. James and Kyung Hyun Kim, 157–181. Detroit: Wayne State University Press.

Woo, Jaeyeon. 2018. "Exports of Korean Cultural Content in 2016 Surpasses US$6 Billion for 1st Time." *Yonhap News*. June 1. https://en.yna.co.kr/view/AEN20180601004100315. Accessed March 16, 2021.

CHAPTER 5

Singing Through Impossible Modernization: *Sopyonje* and National Cinema in the Era of Globalization

Seung-hwan Shin

Sopyonje Reframed

Released in 1993, Im Kwon-taek's *Sopyonje* (*Sŏp'yŏnje*) quickly became a milestone in both Korea's film and cultural history. It was the first South Korean (hereafter, Korean) film that surpassed the million-admission mark, stirring up some hope for the local film industry's turnaround in the face of the ever-expanding dominance of the Hollywood machinery. More broadly, its far-reaching resonance over Korean society led to a thrust of animated discussions on national culture, which later came to be called the *Sopyonje* phenomenon. For many in Korea, *Sopyonje* was a ground-breaking event. Cultural anthropologist Cho Hae Joang (Cho Han Hae-joang), for instance, saw the film as a "triumph of a local movie within a locality" (Cho 2002, 151). For her, *Sopyonje* did not

S. Shin (✉)
University of Pittsburgh, Pittsburgh, PA, USA
e-mail: shs39@pitt.edu

© The Author(s), under exclusive license to Springer Nature Switzerland AG 2022
A. D. Jackson (ed.), *The Two Koreas and their Global Engagements*, https://doi.org/10.1007/978-3-030-90761-7_5

try to emulate the center or self-Orientalize for the attention of international viewers. Nor was it an attempt to overcompensate for colonial self-denigration by idealizing rediscovered traditions. Instead, it spoke to Korean people who had been ardently waiting for "words that resonate deep within their own lives" (Cho 2002, 151–152). In an attempt to put the film's legacy in context, Michael Robinson also noted that it marked both an end and a beginning in Korean film history. An eloquent figuration of Korean society's efforts to reckon with its national traumas, it was a culmination of the master narratives caught with the nation's deeply troubled modern history—from colonization at the dawn of the twentieth century to the Korean War and the ensuing reign of the Cold War paranoia, to decades of political repression under authoritarian rule up until the early 1990s. On the other hand, the film also opened a new horizon for Korean film as it laid the foundations for a liberation from the ponderous weight of national ordeals. Coming along with *Sopyonje*'s phenomenal success was the loosening grip of the weighty master narratives, which eventually led to an explosion of creative energies in the mid to late 1990s (Robinson 2005, 26–28).

Few would question *Sopyonje*'s standing as a major landmark in the history of Korean film and culture. Above all, it presented Korean viewers a moment of serious reflection on their deeply ruptured and highly compressed modern history—"deeply ruptured, highly compressed" in that Korea's modernization has not been indigenously or democratically developed but forcibly imposed and enforced from outside and above, first during colonial rule, then under the constellation of the Cold War paradigm, and after, through the authoritarian policies of military regimes. At the junctures of such drastic historical changes, Korean people had by and large little time to come to terms with those abrupt changes and their traumatic impact on individual lives. Then, how was the film able to successfully speak to the hearts of Korean people? How could it serve as a real catalyst for critical reflection?

Sopyonje's plotline itself is rather simple. At its core is the search for national culture and identity, which is dramatized through a family's struggle to preserve *p'ansori*, a dying traditional art form of story singing. A closer look, however, would prove that the film is riddled with a host of uncontainable tensions. Watching the film feels like confronting a conjuncture where a variety of distinct thematic and formal strains intersect or compete. Take the brother-sister reunion scene for example. It constitutes the climax, given that the film gravitates toward the search for the lost sister, an allegorical figuration of *p'ansori* or forgotten cultural roots. Tong-ho (Dong-ho), the brother who ran away from his family's impoverished itinerant life, travels around rural areas, looking for his lost sister Song-hwa, who has now mastered *p'ansori*, but at the cost of her youth and vision. He eventually finds her at a ragged tavern in a desolate rural town. Yet he does not reveal his identity to his blind sister immediately; he instead asks for her *p'ansori* and offers to accompany her with the drum. She, of course, recognizes him soon by his drumming style. Yet, without openly acknowledging it, she, too, continues her singing through the night. And as the day breaks, they part ways even without any promise to meet again. Rendered in this stoic way, the irresolute ending leaves us wondering why they have to be separated again after all the years of waiting for each other. Is Song-hwa found? Is *p'ansori* rediscovered? Or are they lost again? Is the film's premise of reconciling tradition and modernity fulfilled? The film defies any easy answer to such questions. Besides, halfway through the scene, modern music replaces the sound of *p'ansori*. At the climactic moment Tong-ho and Song-hwa reunite, their *p'ansori* as the very medium of their reunion is taken away. In other words, stripped of sound and now accompanied by a non-diegetic electronic score (Kim Su-chŏl's "Ch'ŏnnyŏnhak"), their *p'ansori* turns into an image. Is this *p'ansori* image a betrayal of the film's own promise to restore *p'ansori*? Or is it a reminder of the disparity between *p'ansori* as a traditional form of art rooted in oral culture and film as a modern medium of technically reproduced representation? Here again, the film does not lend itself to any rushed conclusion on the uneasy relation between *p'ansori* (sound) and cinema (image).

These uncontainable tensions at work within the text also leave us with some challenging questions at the contextual level. *Sopyonje* has largely been understood as a movie about national cultural roots. Yet would it really be fair to write its inward-/backward stance off as a rejection of modernization and globalization? Does Song-hwa's blindness simply symbolize willed blindness to the outside world? What does it really mean to turn inward toward local tradition when global and transnational interaction has increasingly become integral to our everyday social and cultural practices? If the film, as Cho observed, resonated deep within the lives of Korean people, exactly what was it in the film that made it possible? Was it *p'ansori* itself? In reality, *kugak* (traditional national music), as has often been noted, rarely creates a mass-market appeal and its audience has seldom expanded beyond the circular network of *kugak* schools—professors, students, graduates, and professional performers (Howard 2011, 200–201; Kendall 2011, 5; Um 2008, 42–43).[1] Then, it becomes precarious to think of *p'ansori* itself or rediscovery of its forgotten beauty as the main reason for the film's far-reaching resonance in Korean society. Perhaps, it may make more sense to say that *Sopyonje* spoke to the modern minds drawn toward things in danger of vanishing. Are we then also entitled to say that the film's inward/backward looking is, in fact, not antithetical to the urge to move on, or the effort to reach beyond the parameters of national culture and open up to a wider horizon?

Traditions, as Eric Hobsbawm and Terence Ranger (1983) pointed out, are not very old at all. They are a conscious product of modernization. Broadly, in the formation of modern nation-states, they serve as a key catalyst for the sense of commonness or distinct national identity. Yet their return to the present takes place for many different reasons and in various distinct manners. They often return through nostalgic sentiments or patriotic feelings. They are sometimes revered as national treasure. Other times, they are reproduced or reinvented as commodity. Some of them are hailed as precious heritage, while others are pushed aside. The thesis of tradition as a modern product thus requires us to stay alert to when and how a specific tradition is evoked and what use or relevance it gains at a certain historical juncture. *Sopyonje* borrows a traditional setting. With the old tradition, however, the film addresses new questions central to the contemporary lives of Korean people. In the film, tradition and modernity are not exclusive to each other; the film is as much about tradition as about modernity. Likewise, it is also as much about national culture as about cinema, and as much about national cinema as about the globalizing environments as a new condition to reckon with. The main concern of this essay thus rests with the complex ways in which the film works its way through the tensions emerging in between discrete thematic and visual strains—between tradition and modernity, between *p'ansori* (music) and film (image), and between local (inside, nativist) and global (outside, transnational). Through this rereading of the film, this essay also hopes to open up the national culture/cinema discourse to further discussion, particularly in conjunction with the question of globalizing or transnationalizing film culture.

Historical Rupture, Impossible Modernization

In the preface to *Im Kwon-Taek: The Making of a Korean National Cinema*, David James wrote, "In Korea, community and art alike have both been caught between an extraordinarily rich array of the preconditions of a national culture and the ruinous negation of them" and "a national cinema has been simultaneously an imperative and an impossibility" (2002, 11). Paul Willemen also argued in "Detouring Through Korean Cinema" that Korean cinema is "deeply preoccupied with its very own specific and 'impossible modernization'" (2002, 175–176). A similar view can also be found in Rob Wilson's writing on the 1990s Korean film: "It is as if South Korean film experiences [...] a kind of communication block toward explaining (or explaining itself to) the larger world of globalization forces" (2001, 309). What does "impossible modernization" mean? Why had modernization been impossible in Korea? In what sense had a national cinema been an impossibility in Korea? What communication block had Korean cinema suffered from?

Willemen found Korean cinema caught with a blockage between tradition and modernity: modernity repeatedly proves "undesirable" and tradition "no longer unproblematically available" (2002, 173).[2] Simply put, "both the way back to tradition and the way forward to modernity are blocked" (Willemen 2002, 175). Consequently, Korean cinema often appears impregnated with "impossible tensions," irresoluble conflicts between various differing perceptual and ideological directions immanent in both narrative and style. Herein also lies an explanation for why Korean cinema has had trouble in inserting itself into world cinema. Those uncontainable tensions have rendered Korean films feel too eccentric to the international audience; hence, their impossibility to reach the global markets (Willemen 2002, 173).

From today's perspective, Willemen's assessment may feel a little outdated, in that Korean cinema has grown to be one of the most robust national cinemas in the world for the past two decades or so. Written in the early 2000s when Korean cinema was still struggling for survival, Willemen's review indeed seems restricted to the works prior to the new millennium. Today, however, few would deny that Korean cinema is no longer a void in world cinema. Still it is mistaken to write off his remarks as obsolete. "Impossibility" is not simply a question of whether Korean culture/cinema can be made more palatable to the international audience. Making "impossible tensions" "possible" for global viewers to digest easily has often been the very attitude that has caused Korea's modernity to be deeply flawed. Pursuing a visa, or recognition, from the center such as Hollywood and European international film festivals would never be the ultimate way of modernizing Korean cinema even when we acknowledge border-crossing exchange as an indispensable aspect of national cinema. The validity of "impossible modernization" as a conceptual tool to reflect on Korean society and film would rather become evident when we have a good grasp on the deeply ruptured and highly compressed nature of Korea's modern history.

Modern Korean history has been anything but smooth and presents no linear narrative of progress. Modernity in Korea began with loss of independence and Koreans remained caught for decades with the "colonial double bind" that continued to drive the colonized to seek modernity, but indeed never fully let them be modern or other than colonial subjects (Hanscom 2013, 629). Then came the US-Soviet joint occupation, and a civil war that caused the death and dislocation of millions. Considering all the intense conflicts among Koreans after the Liberation, the Korean War was perhaps inescapable. Yet it was never a war purely among Koreans—which could have resolved internal conflicts resulting from colonialism and foreign interventions. The real tragedy was: first, the Cold War paradigm was prescribed, regardless of the shared desires of Koreans—that predated the rigid split along the ideological line—to remove colonial legacies and establish a modern independent nation (Choi 1993, 17); second, "the war solved nothing; only the status quo ante was restored" (Cumings 2005, 298); and third, the war resulted in a political pattern to be repeated in the following chapters of Korean history, that is, the profound divide between the autocratic state and repressed society (Choi 1993, 20). During the Cold War era, Korea achieved a rapid industrialization, but only at the cost of decades of political suppressions, social injustice, and economic inequality.

Then, in 1993, Korean society witnessed civilian administration finally in place after decades of authoritarian rule. Yet the 1990s was less an era of progress than a time of disorientation. For the decade, the word "collapse" carries a lot of weight—both in its physical sense (for example, the collapse of the Seongsu [Sŏngsu] Grand Bridge and the Sampung [Samp'ung] Department Store) and in the psychological aspect (for instance, the breakdown of the hope for change, as collusion between civilian leaders, including former democracy activists, and corporations laid bare civilian democracy's vulnerability to the legacy of previous authoritarian regimes). A more devastating blow, however, was yet to come. Korea was hit hard by the 1997 Asian financial crisis and the meltdown of the national economy. In the end, the government turned to the IMF for a bailout. The 1990s brought a realization of the costs of compressed modernity (Chang 1999, 31). Yet the opportunity was hijacked again as the national economy collapsed. The initiatives for democratic transition were superseded by the urgency of economic recovery and Korean society was driven again into the task of nation-rebuilding with old slogans like unity over difference and growth over justice.

In a nutshell, Korea's modern history is abundant in sudden breaks, particularly because the indigenous popular will has repeatedly been interrupted by forces from both outside (foreign intervention) and above (the authoritarian state). In other words, "historical rupture" has been an inescapable part of what has shaped Korean society and culture throughout the modern era. More importantly, this historical condition has continued to deny Korean society proper opportunities to come to terms with historical ruptures. Korean society, in Cho's words, has been "pushed and shoved in the rush toward colonial modernization to the extent that it has been difficult to create any space for critical reflection" (2000, 51). It is thus unsurprising to learn that overseas viewers have often found many Korean films caught in an impasse between the past and present. Indeed, this tendency can be traced back to *Ch'ŏngch'unŭi sipcharo* (*Crossroads of Youth*, An Chong-hwa, 1934), the oldest surviving film in Korea, in which young protagonists, stricken by poverty and frustrated with old traditions in their rural hometown, leave for Seoul, only to find the urban environments more malicious. Variations on this theme can also easily be found in a number of films in the second half of the century, such as Yu Hyun-mok's (Yu Hyŏn-mok) *Obalt'an* (*The Aimless Bullet* 1961), a much-touted postwar classic, which dramatizes the aimless life of a family of war refugees caught in between homelessness and hopelessness. In the early to mid-1990s when Korean society was gripped with the impetus to reconfigure its modern history with the newly found freedom of expression after democratization, historical rupture again became an urgent question for Korean society and cinema alike. *Sopyonje*, a figuration of the deep rift between tradition and modernity via the separation of Song-hwa and Tong-ho, stands as one of the most compelling cases. Here, before we go further, giving some thought to melodramatic sensibility as another notable aspect of Korean cinema may help to further our understanding of Korean cinema's struggle to account for the nation's deeply fragmented history.

There has already been much discussion about why the melodramatic mode of imagination matters in representations of Korean history and culture. Melodrama has specific relevance for Korea's history. Nancy Abelmann, for instance, found melodrama quite congenial to capturing Koreans' experiences; it "dramatize[s] issues central to rapidly changing societies" (2003, 23). Permeated with excesses like non-psychological character development, abrupt reversals in plot, implausible coincidences, and intense pathos, melodrama bears an affinity to Korea's history of abrupt and rapid changes, history riddled with breaks and traumas that rational language remains unable to explain. Herein lies a justification for the realism of melodramatic representations in Korea's context. According to Kathleen McHugh and Nancy Abelmann, the melodramatic nature of Korean history would be lost on few observers of Korea's postwar history and melodrama has been an "efficacious mode of realism" in Korea (2005, 4). It then becomes pointless to draw a distinction between realism and melodrama in Korea's case.

Korea's melodramatic narratives, however, pose serious challenges, especially to overseas audiences. What Koreans consider perceptually and ideologically plausible often comes across as implausible to them. The difficulties Korean cinema has had in reaching international audiences, as Willemen noted, have much to do with the blockage between tradition and modernity—which "feels to many like a 'no-way-out' situation"—and resulting "uncontainable tensions" at work in a variety of distinct and often conflicting narrative strains (2002, 173). It is worth noting here the bent in many celebrated Korean films to refuse to understand historical changes in other than melodramatic terms, even at the price of such principles as verisimilitude. This tendency, however, is not an indicator of Korean cinema's incompetence. Deposited in it is the struggle to articulate conundrums specific to Korean history or a recognition that melodramatic narratives are more suited than other modes of representation in accounting for the ruptures in Korea's compressed modernity. It is certainly not that anything can be allowed. Yet melodramatic imagination often serves as a suitable vehicle for a firm sense of local realism and logic. An intriguing case here is time travel melodrama.

Time travel film emerged as a prominent trend in Korean cinema around the turn of the century. Notable examples include *K'ara* (*Calla*, Song Hae-sŏng, 1999), *Tonggam* (*Ditto*, Kim Chŏng-kwŏn, 2000), and

2009: Rosŭt'ŭ memorijŭ (*2009: Lost Memories*, Yi Si-myŏng, 2002). These films largely conform to the conventions of melodrama, for example, by including heavy doses of coincidence, sudden twists of fate, emotional excess, and so on. Yet they also indicate a new development of melodramatic representation in Korean cinema. What sets them apart from their predecessors is, above all, the "decompressed narrative" or the use of the time travel theme in order to "decompress the process through which national identity was rapidly formed under 'compressed modernity'" (Martin-Jones 2007, 46, 48). These time travel films open the folds in the history of compressed modernity and thereby reestablish the continuity between past and present. In *Ditto*, for instance, So-ŭn, a college girl from 1979, coincidentally connects with In, a male college student living in 2000, through a ham radio. As their virtual meeting continues, the pleats of history between the two time zones unfold against the backdrop of military rule and democracy protests, and she, in the end, learns that In is the son of Tong-hŭi, her love, and Sŏn-mi, her best friend. Faced with the dilemma that if she continues to date Tong-hŭi, she will change the course of history and In will not exist, she eventually decides to give up Tong-hŭi for Sŏn-mi and secure In's life. Here, decompressed in this manner, history proves to be fraught with repressed desires and unrealized possibilities, which allows different continuities to be imagined.

Time travel, however, is ironic as it becomes the means to reconnect to the past and, at the same time, represents the impossibility of change. All the possibilities that time travel narratives evoke for reconciliation with the repressed past as they decompress history are repressed again when they give in to the pressure to conform to established historical events or the sentiment of "too late." To take *Ditto* for example, So-ŭn's sacrifice of personal happiness is inevitable for the continuation of historical events, no matter how questionable the ruling history is. In other words, the uncontainable tensions in compressed modernity become the very problem to be contained. It is here that *Sopyonje*'s legacy in Korean society and cinema becomes more tangible. It deserves our continued attention in that it leaves "impossible tensions" between tradition and modernity open to further reflection.

Singing Through Historical Impasse

Sopyonje accentuates the break between tradition and modernity, above all, through the conflicts within the itinerant *p'ansori* family. Yu-bong, the father figure, embodies the resolve to preserve tradition. Yet his commitment to *p'ansori*, although noble, turns into a pernicious obsession that traumatizes his children, or more broadly, the future generation. Yu-bong thus can be regarded as representing a tradition that proves repressive and destructive, despite its value. On the other hand, Tong-ho is at the other end of the spectrum. He runs away from his family and *p'ansori* in quest of a new life in Seoul. He later regrets this and begins looking for his family. However, even after the reunion with his lost sister Song-hwa, he ends up leaving for Seoul. In Song-hwa's case, she remains committed to *p'ansori*, as Yu-bong wishes. However, she still yearns for her brother, which leaves her caught in between the two opposing directions. She thus crystalizes the sense of impasse, as I will discuss in more detail later.

When schematically taken, however, this kind of linear topological analysis leaves some important questions untouched. The three main characters are far from fixed or one-dimensional. As they work through the break between tradition and modernity, their struggles register distinct aspects of the historical impasse. Yu-bong may come across as antimodern, as he is committed to the *p'ansori* tradition. On closer examination, however, one can learn that he is not antithetical to modernity. He is indeed a rebellious figure in his own right; he is expelled from his own *p'ansori* school after an affair with his master's mistress—due to his challenge to the patriarchal culture of the *p'ansori* world and his master's phallic authority. Due to his affair with a widow in a rural town, he is also ousted from the traditional community which is still under the spell of Confucian ethics. His itinerant life, in a way, is a consequence of his resistance against repressive traditions. On the other hand, his devotion to *p'ansori* is not so much a blind traditionalism as a criticism of fallacious forms of modernization—which is not simply a disapproval of modernity but rather an attempted critical intervention into modernization. His stubborn rejection of his friend's offer to join his *ch'anggŭk* theater in Seoul, for instance, invites us to consider the disparity between his *p'ansori* and *ch'anggŭk*, a new genre of the traditional singing opera created for the modern proscenium stage. The principal difference between them, according to Marshall R. Phil, is that *p'ansori* is solo performance and *ch'anggŭk* relies on multi-singer casting to fully realize all the characters in the story by different individual actors (1994, 10–11). The solo performer in *p'ansori* plays not only all the characters in the story but also the narrator. Therefore, *p'ansori*, by nature, creates a distance and tension between narrator and characters and also enables spontaneous interaction to arise between singer and audience. In contrast, *ch'anggŭk* deprives *p'ansori* performers of their mediating role, because their role is now restricted to a single character. Furthermore, as the full characterization requires costume, make-up, and stage setting, the spectacles created by all these theatrical effects replace unique virtues of *p'ansori* as folk art. Phil thus argues that *ch'anggŭk* is not so much a developmental stage of *p'ansori* as an imported theatrical format that draws upon *p'ansori* largely for its materials (1994, 12). We can then read Yu-bong's negation of *ch'anggŭk* as a valid critique of misguided uses (reproduction, consumption) of tradition in the modern era.

Yu-bong's position indeed reminds us of the *minjung* culture movement as a subset of the democracy movement (the *minjung* movement) particularly in the 1980s, which sought to revive indigenous folk culture as an antidote to colonial legacy and cultural imperialism and return it to the true owners—the *minjung* (people). Restoration of traditional culture was a major means for the authoritarian rulers to propagate national unity. The military juntas in the 1960s and 1970s were eager to preserve and promote indigenous artifacts, customs, and arts through mass media, public exhibitions, and the educational system. This institutionalization, however, often stripped traditional culture of its folkloric aspects and caused it to lose touch with the ordinary lives of the people. Faced with the objectification and museumization of popular cultural traditions, *minjung* practitioners responded by reversing the course and restoring the folkloric and communal nature of traditional cultures. A prominent example is *madanggŭk*—"*madang*" refers to an open shared place for communal activities and "*gŭk*" means drama. An effort to de-institutionalize *t'alchum* (mask-dance drama), *madanggŭk* sought to resuscitate key esthetic traits of mask-dance drama such as the polyphonic open structure and the active participation of the audience (Choi 1995, 115; see also Um 2008, 43). The birth of *madanggŭk* echoes Yu-bong's stance on *ch'anggŭk* where the proscenium stage and full characterization left little room for interactive performance and participatory spectatorship.

Recent debates over *kugak* fusion also attest to the lasting relevance the Yu-bong character has in the contemporary cultural milieu. *Kugak* has continued to struggle in the market and new generations of musicians have sought to innovate it to attract a wider audience, particularly young listeners, by adopting new elements from various different genres. While this new *kugak* has succeeded in expanding its audience, it also has provoked misgivings over whether it trades quality off with public appeal or if it just turns *kugak* into popular entertainment (Howard 2011, 210–211; Um 2008, 42–44). Is this a replay of the old fight between purist and innovator? Here, remembering Yu-bong, or the questions raised around the character, can lead our debate to a more advanced level. As noted above, he is not a blind traditionalist. His refusal of *ch'angguk* rather urges us to carefully historicize reconstructed tradition—when/how tradition is used or misused. Yu-bong defies both institutionalized and commodified *p'ansori*; he rejects his traditional *p'ansori* school and a modern simulacrum of *p'ansori* such as *ch'angguk*. What kind of *p'ansori* does he search for? "Authentic" is a dubious term. Traditions, as Kendall noted, "assume values as a consequence of contemporary concerns, needs and imaginings" (2011, 16). It is then wrong to think that only the past can prescribe the conditions for the use of tradition in the present. Then again, authenticity is not always an essentialist claim. In strategical use, it can help refine our positioning on various discrete ways in which the past is evoked and used in the present. It can work as a valid antidote to empty tradition simulacra stripped of any relevance to our present concerns or struggles. Yu-bong's quest of authentic *p'ansori* becomes meaningful to our contemporary life when we use it for critical reflection on the consumption of tradition.

This is not to deny that Yu-bong is not the ultimate answer to the break between tradition and modernity, although, as noted above, there is some truth to his own struggle. He fails to find a viable path between tradition and modernity and in the end, becomes dogmatic and destructive; after all, he is largely responsible for the plight of Tong-ho and Song-hwa. Yet we cannot readily brush his failure aside. It invites us to the complexity of the question of national culture. Indeed, Yu-bong's struggle is replayed in the lives of his children, if not in the same manner, with newly added tensions.

Tong-ho may come across as antithetical to Yu-bong. Then again, it is hard to disregard some unmistakable affinities between them. Above all, they are both rebellious figures. As Yu-bong protested against his master and Confucian tradition, Tong-ho, too, rises against Yu-bong. His break with his father, however, does not mean a total rejection of tradition. He is far from a one-sided figure. Struggling to work through the rifts between past and present in his own way, he is at once forward-moving and backward-looking. If Yu-bong allegorizes the break between past and present in the world of *p'ansori* performers, Tong-ho's struggle between tradition and modernity has more resonance in the minds of ordinary Koreans who have lived through deeply ruptured and highly compressed history of modernization. He represents the imperative to move on. At the same time, he is a mourner caught with a sense of loss. Yet his mourning does not sit well with conventional views. It does not conform to the established understanding of mourning in which the ego works through the loss, and eventually lets go of the loss.[3] Tong-ho may feel a little relieved after his reunion with his sister. But the reunion is transient, and his reconciliation with tradition is by no means complete. In other words, his mourning can never end.

The Song-hwa character, too, is a deeply polarized character, despite her devotion to the tradition of *p'ansori*. She sings through her own struggles between Yu-bong and Tong-ho, which embodies another strain of efforts to grapple with ruptured history. The subtlety of her position is signaled, first, in her relationships with both her father and brother. She chooses to remain on the road of *p'ansori*, as Yu-bong wishes. Yet is she simply a filial, passive daughter? As is often the case with characters in allegorical or melodramatic texts, she remains non-psychological. She is quite stoic and taciturn for the most part, which denies us access to her interiority, or because of that, prompts us to look at the details for the character. It is intriguing, in this respect, to note the intricate nature of her reaction to Yu-bong after his confession that he was the one that made her go blind. When asked if she knew, she replies with a slow nod. To the next question "Have you forgiven me, as well?" however, she just sits still, without giving any word or gesture. Yu-bong then says that he could not sense any grudge in her singing. Has she really forgiven him? Could she really transcend her resentment toward him? It is rather weak to argue that music or spiritual enlightenment solves suffering in the real world. A symbolic solution is an easy way to repress actual historical problems. Here my sense is rather that her motionless gesture attests to the difficulty of reconciling the past and the present and leaves the question open to further interpretation.

It is interesting, in this respect, to note the subtle reversal between father and daughter in the brother-sister reunion scene. It is perhaps not a coincidence that the father figure is absent at the moment when Tong-ho and Song-hwa eventually reconnect through *p'ansori*—or he is only present through the *p'ansori* piece that his children perform, *Tale of Shimch'ŏng*. In the song, the father is remembered but only through the mediation of the blind father figure in her singing. An irony here is that while in reality, the daughter is blind, it is the father that is blind in the song. In addition, Song-hwa's frontal shot at the end of the scene, where it seems as if she could actually see her brother, seems to insinuate that she has acquired her spiritual eye and now can see things through her mind. Juxtaposed with her wish in her song for her blind father to regain his vision, this scene brings back to our attention the tensions between Song-hwa and her father. Here, too, the film denies us any easy answer to her relationship with her father as if to suggest that there is not an easy solution to the problem of historical ruptures and that her *p'ansori* is indeed more about singing through it.

The final reunion scene is also where we can find the most nuanced representation of her struggles to sing through historical impasse. In this scene, the much-anticipated reunion between Song-hwa and Tong-ho unexpectedly ends after a single night, and following their brief reunion, they go their separate ways. Does this indecisive ending confirm the impossibility of reconciling tradition and modernity? For many overseas viewers, this narrative indeterminacy may feel like another instance of historical blockage and narrative impasse.[4] This irresolute closure, however, does not seem to have felt so irresolute to the Korean audiences. For example, Park Wan-sŏ, one of the most celebrated women writers in Korea, held it as a more mature way of accounting for Korean history. According to Cho Hae Joang,

> She [Park] didn't want the emotions built up during the movie to be suddenly lost by an ending in which the characters hugged, cried and recited lines such as "Sister! It's Tong-ho." The brother and sister's "meeting through music, hugging each other in their minds only, and stoutheartedly parting" is an "advance" and a "transcendence" that is superior to an "immature" meeting. (2002, 146)

What intrigues me about Park's take on the ending is that she saw it as "an advance" rather than a sign of Korean cinema caught in historical blockage. The indeterminate nature of the ending is not a failure to overcome the break between tradition and modernity but rather a consequence of a more rigorous reflection on ruptured history. *Sopyonje* is a film about *p'ansori* or tradition, but it is a modern film governed by the modern desire to reimagine cultural identity by reconnecting with the past. Scholars like Cho even suggested that *Sopyonje* marked Korea's long-overdue but real entrance into the modern age (2002, 148). Yet Park's advance (or Cho's modernization) has little to do with finding any clear solution to the tension in ruptured history, which would hardly be other than a false continuity between tradition and modernity. Rather, the real advance begins with careful reflection about historical ruptures. And a scene like the inconclusive ending offers the viewer opportunity for reflection.

Long Take to *P'ansori* Image

Im's mature stance on the break between tradition and modernity is also evident in his handling of the tensions between *p'ansori* and film. The search for the lost sister at the level of narrative runs parallel with the ambition to preserve *p'ansori*, a form of traditional music, through the film as a modern medium of technical reproduction. In other words, at the esthetic level, too, *Sopyonje* is suffused with tensions between tradition and modernity. To begin with Im's endeavor to bring *p'ansori* to the screen, perhaps the most compelling example is the *Chindo Arirang* sequence. In film, music has largely been treated as an accompaniment to image or narrative. In this sequence, however, their relations appear reversed. Inserted between scenes with no apparent connection, it rather feels like an independent segment solely devoted to the premise of preserving *p'ansori*. In the sequence, music is no longer derivative or complementary. It is not subordinated to image or narrative; they instead succumb to the authority of *p'ansori*.[5]

This sequence opens with Yu-bong's family slowly emerging from a distant corner of the backdrop of idyllic natural landscape. As they walk down the road that meanders through small patches of farming fields, singing *Chindo Arirang* together, the camera yields its movement to the song and the frame remains still for over five minutes. With this extremely long and static take, the viewing experience becomes theatrical.

We as the audience feel as if we were sitting in a concert auditorium. By doing so, this sequence invites us to scrutinize the ensemble that the song creates with *p'ansori* singers and the road. Particularly interesting is the way in which they blend with each other. As the *p'ansori* performing family gradually advance toward the foreground, their song also changes in both tone and tempo from sorrow to joy and *chinyang* (*adagio*) to *hwimori* (*vivace*). Herein lies a justification for the long take. It coincides with *Chindo Arirang*'s ability to embrace a wide range of themes and emotions. On the other hand, *Chindo Arirang*'s variable and improvisational nature also corresponds to both the long tortuous road and the itinerant life of the *p'ansori* artists. If the road serves as *p'an* (stage) for *sori* (song), the song responds by breathing rhythms into the road and the static long take offers time for them to blend.

A complication arises, however, as we consider the elusive nature of *p'ansori*. *P'ansori* as music is an art of time that has temporality as a fundamental quality in that its sounds unfold and move in and through time. Moreover, it grew out of traditional oral culture; until the modern era, it had only been passed down orally. From the start, thus, *p'ansori* is defiant of the ambition of the camera, a modern medium of reproducibility, to preserve or transcend time. Remarkably, the *Chindo Arirang* sequence ends with the empty road. After the *p'ansori* family walk out of the frame, the camera lingers for a while, as if to oblige the audience to meditate on the empty road. The scene is indeed saturated with a sense of transience. *P'ansori* remains elusive, just as Song-hwa does. Its elusiveness, however, is not just an ontological issue. It would be more accurate to understand it as a historical question. As a product of oral and artisanal culture, it is rooted in the experiences that have been dismissed in the system of modern knowledge production. It is worth noting here that one of the recurrent themes in *Sopyonje* is training, which does not simply mean gaining techniques but rather pickling *p'ansori* in the life of its singer long enough so that it can acquire the rich flavors from life.[6] Furthermore, the privileged places for *p'ansori* training are the roads. It is born and reborn on the roads. *Sopyonje* is a road movie and the search for *p'ansori* is virtually synonymous with wandering on the roads.[7] The road for *p'ansori*, however, is never an open highway or an urban street. As *p'ansori* has been marginalized by the modernization drive, remote areas have become the best places for *p'ansori* training. And in the face of this historical elusiveness of *p'ansori*, Im's camera becomes self-effacing. Instead of anxiously trying to arrest its object, his camera freezes itself and remains ascetic. Perhaps this cinematographic austerity is a way Im pays tribute to *p'ansori* that is fading into history. It is also an acknowledgment of the difficulty of bridging the ruptures between past and present. His camera stands still, or becomes counter-filmic, letting *p'ansori* slip out of its frame.

Im's handling of the tensions between *p'ansori* and film, however, takes a very different stance in the climatic reunion scene. In stark contrast to the *Chindo Arirang* sequence where the camera remains reserved for the sake of *p'ansori*, the reunion scene allows the camera to regain its mobility and actively engage with its objects: high-angle shots are employed to establish the setting; shot-reverse shots are also frequently applied for the interaction between the two main characters; and camera distance, too, alters from long-medium shot to close-up to capture their emotions. However, a more striking contrast comes at the moment when Tong-ho and Song-hwa reunite. At the climactic moment of their reunion, *p'ansori* as the very means of their reunion or reconciliation is taken away and an electronic mood music score takes its place (Stringer 2002, 164–165). In other words, *p'ansori* cannot be heard, but only seen in the scene. Does this mean that Im breaks his promise to preserve *p'ansori*? Yet isn't it also true that this kind of wariness often proves to be anchored in the desire to essentialize or romanticize it?

Technical reproduction, Walter Benjamin argued, detaches the reproduced object from the domain of tradition and replaces its unique existence with a plurality of copies. Yet this does not necessarily mean that the reproduced is a forgery. It can allow the reproduced object to meet its beholders in their own specific situations (1968, 220–221). Benjamin's remarks on technical reproduction divert us from claims of authenticity to the notion of transmissibility, that is, how the reproduced *p'ansori* meets its viewers or listeners in their own specific historical situations that have become so different from those responsible for the unique existence of *p'ansori*, or how it can be reconnected with the present that has become detached from it. In this respect, *Sopyonje* becomes a compelling text to discuss the ways in which technical reproduction is implicated in the making of a national culture. The new way of perception involved in the technical reproduction of *p'ansori* coincides with the urge to bridge the rupture between the past and present. Yet technical reproduction also attests to the challenges in grappling with historical ruptures. It comes with the endless interplay of contrary practices such as detaching-reattaching, decomposing-recomposing, deactivating-reactivating across temporal and spatial boundaries.

This double movement in technical reproduction brings us to a deeper understanding of the indeterminate nature of Im's stance on the tensions between *p'ansori* and cinema. It is not a symptom of the ultimate failure to reproduce *p'ansori* through film. This indeterminacy invites us to the complex interchanges between *p'ansori* and film rather than remaining caught in delusive queries such as whether *p'ansori* can really be filmed. A formal choice like the long take in the *Chindo Arirang* scene certainly confirms the film's aspiration to preserve *p'ansori*. However, it is the only scene where a long take is used. Indeed, Im does not seem to be a keen advocate of the long take. In an interview, he admitted that he had been very anxious about the long take in the *Chindo Arirang* scene even during the shooting due to the fear that a long take might discourage viewers from immersing themselves into *p'ansori* (Chŏng 2003, 279). Of his choice to make a film about *p'ansori*, he also stated:

> If I saw *p'ansori* on TV, I would change the channel to find something more pleasing. I had become so much removed from *p'ansori*. Yet, for some reason, I had the recurring urge to make a film about it, bring back things that are vanishing, and talk about them. (Chŏng 2003, 266; my translation)

This remark indicates that Im was not a *p'ansori* enthusiast, either. In embarking on a film about *p'ansori*, he was more concerned with capturing things that were disappearing, which is indeed a modern sentiment. In other words, what really mattered to him was not so much *p'ansori* itself as "the gaze" toward the dying tradition. It was also this modern way of looking that appealed to his contemporary viewers, who had become as much removed from *p'ansori* as he was, or far more so than him. In other words, it is fair to regard *p'ansori* as a vehicle that conveys the modern *sori* (voice) that arises from people's growing desire to work through the condition of impossible modernity. *Sopyonje*, as scholars like Young-Key Kim-Renaud observed, is "not so much about *p'ansori* as about the voice within all of us" (1993, 117). In this sense, we are also entitled to say that the switch from audible to visible *p'ansori*, or *p'ansori*-image, in the reunion scene does not necessarily indicate that *Sopyonje* turns against its own promise to bring *p'ansori* back to life. It rather serves as a warning against ill-advised assumptions about authentic *p'ansori*, or as a reminder that *p'ansori* can only prove authentic when it is in the service of people's struggles to find their *sori* (voice).

Globalization Through Strategic Localism[8]

In the minds of many Koreans, tradition was not so much lost as taken away by others—first, by colonial rule, and then, by industrialization and cultural imperialism of the West. The desire to reconnect with the past thus runs deep in Korean society. Understandably, the use of tradition or more broadly, the use of history has been an urgent question in Korean society—more so than in many other countries—and discussions of tradition in Korea often prove deeply permeated with nationalist sentiments (Kendall 2011, 6). However, the reproduction of tradition requires careful positioning because of the difficulty in distinguishing between simulacra deprived of any use or relevance to people's present struggles and traditions recalled for the real needs and concerns of our present life. Frantz Fanon cautioned: "You will never make colonialism blush for shame by spreading out little-known cultural treasures under its eyes" and uncritical fixation on tradition would mean "opposing one's own people" (1994, 41, 42). It is around people's struggles that national culture can take on substance, not around some specific idiosyncratic products (Fanon 1994, 45). In his writing on history, Benjamin also noted, "To articulate the past historically does not mean to recognize it 'the way it really was' […] In every era, the attempt must be made anew to wrest tradition away from a conformism that is about to overpower it" (1968, 255). *Sopyonje*'s success is remarkable not simply because it could successfully tap into Korean people's desire to reconcile with tradition. The film's enduring critical value lies in its ability to inspire us to reflect on ruptures in modern history by probing irrepressible tensions between tradition and modernity, rather than offering an imaginary solution to them.

Given these uncontainable tensions—and their effects such as narrative blockage, abrupt changes in plot, and affective excess—in its thematic and formal composition, for many distant viewers, *Sopyonje* may come across as a typical Korean melodrama riddled with unfamiliar and puzzling moves. As illustrated above, however, the film articulated an advanced way of handling ruptured history. In other words, it was through a shared sense of local realism and logic that the film could speak to the needs of the time. This brings us back to impossible modernization, and by extension, impossible globalization, that is, the impossibility of explaining Korean cinema to the global audience.

At the core of *Sopyonje* is the turn to local sensibility. Given the ever-globalizing world, including film production and culture, we cannot help wondering what it would mean to turn to trenchant localism. Can we consider Song-hwa's blindness as signifying the film's firm rejection of modernization and willed blindness to global and transnational dynamics of cultural formation today? My sense is that Im's introspective turn is not an antithesis, but rather a prolegomenon to global interactions and communications. Caught in between tradition and modernity, Song-hwa is illustrative of the impossible tensions at work in the film's narrative and visual representation. Thus, it would be challenging particularly for the international audience to have a good grasp of the tensions signaled through her reserved manner. As noted above, however, the indeterminacy in her stoic disposition is not a failure to find an answer to her struggles, but rather a recognition of the need to work through the ruptures between tradition and modernity without forging a false continuity between them. She proves that modernization is not impossible, but possible, yet only with continuously renewed struggles over fractured history. The localism conveyed in the Song-hwa character—more specifically, uncontainable tensions in the character—rejects the allure of making Korean films more palatable or marketable in global settings, for instance, through self-exoticization and particularism. On the other hand, hers is not a willed blindness to the global or transnational environments. It would be more accurate to think of Im's trenchant localism as an effort to find a path where the local is neither disqualified by the global nor overly compensated in opposition to the global, but properly revalued in global settings.

Notes

1. It is also worth noting that Im's other films devoted to *p'ansori*, *Ch'unhyangdyŏn* (*Chunhyang*, 2000) and *Ch'ŏnnyŏnhak* (*Beyond the Years*, 2007), failed to draw much public attention, despite all the warm receptions at international festivals. *Chunhyang*, for example, was the first Korean film to be commercially released in the US largely thanks to the acclaim it garnered at Cannes. However, the news from international film festivals had little impact on its lackluster reception in Korea (Lee 2005, 70; Kim 2011, 152). Its failure

to attract audiences in its own constituency is a somber reminder of the disparity between local sensibility and overseas film festival circuits. It is also an indicator that the *Sopyonje* syndrome, indeed, does not have much to do with *p'ansori* itself or its restoration, unless we simply assume that distant observers somehow understood the beauty of *p'ansori* films better than Korean viewers.
2. In a similar vein, Han Ju Kwak noted, "Tradition has been a long object of ambivalence for most Koreans. On the one hand, it was an obstacle to modernization that had to be removed as soon as possible. On the other hand, the immense impact of the modernization process forced Koreans to discard their heritage, on which national identity is anchored" (2003, 100).
3. In an effort to draw clear distinction between mourning and melancholia, Sigmund Freud wrote, "In mourning it is the world which has become poor and empty; in melancholia it is the ego itself" (1957, 246).
4. For a detailed discussion of the challenges *Sopyonje* poses to international viewers, see Stringer (2002).
5. This is not to say that the *Chindo Arirang* scene stands alone and disrupts the narrative flow. As Sato Tadao observed, in *Sopyonje*, *p'ansori* music often offsets discontinuity in the narrative and editing (2000; cited in Kim 2011, 157).
6. My thought here hinges on Walter Benjamin's notes on the storyteller: "The storytelling that thrives for a long time in the milieu of work [...] is itself an artisan form of communication, as it were. It does not aim to convey the pure essence of the thing, like information or a report. It sinks the thing into the life of the storyteller, in order to bring it out of him again" (1968, 91–2).
7. For more comments on the role of the road in *Sopyonje*, see Kim 2004, 53–54, 64; Chŏng 2003, 274, 277–278.
8. For this term, I draw on Gayatri Spivak and Rob Wilson. In "Subaltern Studies: Deconstructing Historiography," Spivak argues for "strategic essentialism" that allows the subaltern to represent themselves and develop into historical agency (1987, 205). Similarly, Wilson (2001) sees in Im's films a "strategic localism" for a critical engagement with the globalizing milieu, which diverges from such tendencies as hybridization, particularism, and self-Orientalization.

References

Abelmann, Nancy. 2003. *The Melodrama of Mobility: Women, Talk and Class in Contemporary South Korea*. Honolulu: University of Hawai'i Press.
Abelmann, Nancy and Kathleen McHugh. 2005. Introduction to *South Korean Golden Age Melodrama: Gender, Genre, and National Cinema*, edited by Kathleen McHugh and Nancy Abelmann, 1–15. Detroit: Wayne State University Press.
Benjamin, Walter. 1968. *Illuminations*. Edited by Hanna Arendt. Translated by Harry Zohn. New York: Schocken Books.
Chang, Kyung-Sup. 1999. "Compressed Modernity and Its Discontents: South Korean Society in Transition." *Economy and Society* 28 (1): 30–55.
Cho, Hae Joang. 2002. "*Sopyonje*: Its Cultural and Historical Meaning." In *Im Kown-taek: The Making of a Korean National Cinema*, edited by David James and Kyung Hyun Kim, 134–156. Detroit: Wayne State University Press:
Cho, Han Hae-joang. 2000. "'You Are Trapped in an Imaginary Well': The Formation of Subjectivity within Compressed Development—A Feminist Critique of Modernity and Korean Culture." *Inter Asia Cultural Studies* 1 (1): 49–69.
Choi, Chungmoo. 1995. "The Minjung Culture Movement and the Construction of Popular Culture in Korea." In *South Korea's Minjung Movement: The Culture and Politics of Dissidence*, edited by Kenneth M. Wells, 105–118. Honolulu: University of Hawai'i Press.
Choi, Jang Jip. 1993. "Political Cleavages in South Korea." In *State and Society in Contemporary Korea*, edited by Hagen Koo, 13–50. Ithaca: Cornell University Press.
Chŏng, Sŏng-il. 2003. *Imkwŏnt'aegi Imkwŏnt'aekŭl marhada 2 [Im Kwon-taek on Im Kwon-taek II]*. Seoul: Hyŏnsil munhwa yŏn'gu.
Cumings, Bruce. 2005. *Korea's Place in the Sun: A Modern History*. New York: W. W. Norton & Company.
Fanon, Frantz. 1994. "On National Culture." In *Colonial Discourse and Post-Colonial Theory: A Reader*, edited by Patrick Williams and Laura Chrisman, 36–52. New York: Columbia University Press.
Freud, Sigmund. 1957. "Mourning and Melancholia." In *The Standard Edition of the Complete Psychological Works of Sigmund Freud*, edited by James Strachey, vol. 14, 243–258. London: Hogarth.
Hanscom, Christopher P. 2013. "Modernism, Hysteria, and the Colonial Double Bind: Pak T'aewŏn's *One Day in the Life of the Author, Mr. Kubo*." *Positions* 21 (3): 607–636.
Hobsbawm, Eric, and Terence Ranger, eds. 1983. *The Invention of Tradition*. Cambridge: Cambridge University Press.

Howard, Keith. 2011. "Kugak Fusion and the Politics of Korean Musical Consumption." In *Consuming Korean Tradition in Early and Late Modernity: Commodification, Tourism, and Performance*, edited by Laurel Kendall, 195–215. Honolulu: University of Hawai'i Press.

James, David E. 2002. Preface to *Im Kown-taek: The Making of a Korean National Cinema*, edited by David E. James and Kyung Hyun Kim, 9–17. Detroit: Wayne State University Press.

Kendall, Laurel. 2011. "Introduction: Material Modernity, Consumable Tradition." In *Consuming Korean Tradition in Early and Late Modernity: Commodification, Tourism, and Performance*, edited by Laurel Kendall, 1–17. Honolulu: University of Hawai'i Press.

Kim, Kyung Hyun. 2004. *The Remasculization of Korean Cinema*. Durham: Duke University Press.

Kim, Shin-Dong. 2011. "The Creation of Pansori Cinema: *Sopyonje* and *Chunhyangdyun* in Creative Hybridity." In *East Asian Cinema and Cultural Heritage: From China, Hong Kong, Taiwan to Japan and South Korea*, edited by Kinnia Yau Shuk-ting, 151–171. New York: Palgrave Macmillan.

Kim-Renaud, Young-Key. 1993. "*Sŏp'yŏnje*: A Journey into the Korean Soul and Human Existence." *Korea Journal* 33 (4): 112–117.

Kwak, Han Ju. 2003. "Discourse on Modernization in 1990s Korean Cinema" In *Multiple Modernities: Cinemas and Popular Media in Transcultural East Asia*, edited by Jenny Kwok Wah Lau, 90–113. Philadelphia: Temple University Press.

Lee, Hyangjin. 2005. "Chunhyang: Marketing an Old Tradition in New Korean Cinema." In *New Korean Cinema*, edited by Chi-Yun Shin and Julian Stringer, 63–78. New York: New York University Press.

Martin-Jones, David. 2007. "Decompressing Modernity: South Korean Time Travel Narratives and the IMF Crisis." *Cinema Journal* 46 (4): 45–67.

Pihl, Marshall R. 1994. *The Korean Singer of Tales*. Cambridge: Harvard University Press.

Robinson, Michael. 2005. "Contemporary Cultural Production in South Korea: Vanishing Meta-Narratives of Nation." In *New Korean Cinema*, edited by Chi-Yun Shin and Julian Stringer, 15–31. New York: New York University Press.

Sato, Tadao. 2000. *Han'guk yŏnghwa wa Im Kown-taek* [*Korean cinema and Im Kown-taek*]. Translated by Ko Chae-un. Seoul: Hanguk haksul chongbo.

Spivak, Chakravorty Gayatri. 1987. "Subaltern Studies: Deconstructing Historiography." In *In Other Worlds: Essays in Cultural Politics*, 197–221. New York: Methuen.

Stringer, Julian. 2002. "*Sopyonje* and Inner Domain of National Culture." In *Im Kown-taek: The Making of a Korean National Cinema*, edited by David James and Kyung-Hyun Kim, 157–181. Detroit: Wayne State University Press.

Um, Hae-kyung. 2008. "New P'ansori in Twenty-First-Century Korea: Creative Dialectics of Tradition and Modernity." *Asian Theatre Journal* 25 (1): 24–57.

Willemen, Paul. 2002. "Detouring Through Korean Cinema." *Inter-Asia Cultural Studies* 3 (2): 167–186.

Wilson, Rob. 2001. "Korean Cinema on the Road to Globalization: Tracking Global/Local Dynamics, or Why Im Kwon-taek Is Not Ang Lee." *Inter-Asia Cultural Studies* 2 (2): 307–318.

CHAPTER 6

Valorizing the Old: Honoring Aging Practitioners of Korean Traditions

Roald Maliangkay

Since 1962, the South Korean (hereafter Korean) government has made considerable efforts to preserve and promote elements of its cultural heritage. It devised a system that recognized not only tangible but also intangible cultural properties, which entailed the selection of virtuosos—"holders" (*poyuja*)—capable of passing on and promoting traditional arts, crafts, and rituals. Considering many of the items that fall under its wings have since succeeded in gaining stature both domestically and overseas, the system has been broadly hailed. Indeed, to foreign visitors, Korea now promises considerable vibrancy and authenticity in both popular and traditional culture. UNESCO (United Nations Educational, Scientific and Cultural Organization) has played an important role in this. Its recognition of a range of Korean cultural properties as an essential part of world heritage since 2008 has led Koreans to valorize cultural items beyond what their own system could ever achieve on its own. Korean

R. Maliangkay (✉)
Australian National University, Acton, ACT, Australia
e-mail: Roald.Maliangkay@anu.edu.au

© The Author(s), under exclusive license to Springer Nature Switzerland AG 2022
A. D. Jackson (ed.), *The Two Koreas and their Global Engagements*, https://doi.org/10.1007/978-3-030-90761-7_6

heritage bolsters the Korean Wave and drives revenue from both local and foreign audiences. The importance of the foreign praise and engagement it fosters is encouraging the government to continue its pursuit of UNESCO listings.

Korea's heritage management constantly faces challenges, however, and in recent decades they include the aging of art, craft, or ritual practitioners. Korea's aging population is a nationwide problem that has placed the country's pension schemes under increasing scrutiny. The country's office of statistics has estimated that over the next 37 years, the number of those most likely to be fully employed, people between the age of 15 and 64, will decline by more than half to 17.84 million, while that of people aged 65 and over will more than double from 8.13 million to 18.27 million. The eventual tally would lead to a situation where one worker has to support one retiree. To prevent this, it is important that measures are taken early on. Seeing as pension funds are already expected to run in deficit from 2044 and be depleted by 2060 (Ch'oe 2020), it may be best not to focus on increasing premiums only; the pension age should be raised, too (Kim 2021). But although the average life expectancy in Korea has improved by more than 20 years since the late 1960s (United Nations Population Division 2019), in some professions, the demand for strong physical and mental health will make delayed retirement an unattractive solution. One might count the traditional performing arts to be among them, but recent developments suggest that even among artists fortunate enough to have one, a retirement plan itself is not embraced as readily as one would expect. One reason for this is that for many, the basic pension is insufficient. Another is the artists' sense of duty to their art and students.

In 2001 the government set up a pension scheme that allowed holders to retire as "honorary holders" and in 2019, in an effort to reward more senior practitioners and help promote traditional culture as a career option, the government decided to offer the scheme to aging assistant instructors, too. In the past few years, the new scheme has seen a large number of instructors designated and given the associated, higher stipend. Despite the increased financial support for aging practitioners in general, however, the efforts have not been unanimously embraced by the community. Concerns have been raised over the reduction in monthly income that retirement implies, over retirement restricting the involvement of senior practitioners in the transmission of their art, and over hierarchy issues that arise on account of assistant instructors being offered the same retirement package as holders. And yet, in part due to the fast-rising median age, job prospects in some areas of traditional culture have become slim, a situation not alleviated by the limited stipends the government pays to the practitioners recognized under its system. While some traditions have struggled to attract students, let alone of the gender to which they were originally (and physically) tied (see, for example, Maliangkay 2017, 94–95), there are others with only one aging practitioner who failed to become a holder and cannot afford to stop working either because of financial reasons, their commitment to passing on their knowledge, or both.

In this chapter, I deliberate the system of honorary holders and the causes of discontent. Since it is partly intended to encourage participation in traditions and promote them as viable career choices, the system may have to increase funding and incentivize earlier retirement. Their ultimate purpose as national icons could nevertheless motivate the government to redirect its investment toward newly listed traditions that are more likely to be favored by foreigners rather than in the preservation of cultural properties that have failed to organically grow in popularity since they were recognized. And yet, because cultural properties may lose in value when their number continues to grow, a policy that does not necessarily seek an expansion of its list of traditions could ultimately yield equal commercial and political returns. I argue that if UNESCO listings serve to make Koreans recognize the value of their own heritage and rekindle interest in traditions at risk of having no successors, then pursuing the organization's listing of existing traditions should be made a priority.

Growing Icons

In the early 1960s, Korea still reeled from the devastation of the 1950–1953 Korean War. The ongoing threat of North Korean aggression and the fast recovery of Japan underscored the urgency of political, cultural, and economic autonomy (Park 2010, 72; Maliangkay 2017, 5–6). Sustained economic growth would require a considerable sacrifice from the people, one that involved much hard work, long hours, and poor working conditions. To package that message persuasively at a time when the government's pockets were shallow posed a challenge. Faced with a decimated cultural sector and heavy reliance on US financial support for its recovery, the Park Chung Hee administration (1963–1979) had limited options to promise recompense. Nevertheless, by focusing on traditional Korean culture, it managed to establish an effective but relatively low-cost cultural policy. By building on existing esthetics and the notion that foreign aggression and interference had sought to do great damage to Korea's cultural heritage, it was able to boost both productivity and national pride and, in the process, create cultural icons that would largely hold their own in comparison with those of its neighbors, both esthetically and commercially.

The government devised its heritage management system around the Cultural Heritage Protection Act (*Munhwajae pohobŏp*), promulgated in 1962. Like the 1950 Japanese law after which it was named and modeled, it set out to designate both tangible (*yuhyŏng*) and intangible (*muhyŏng*) cultural properties (*munhwajae*), as well as sites of natural or historical significance, and indigenous animals, plants, and minerals (Maliangkay 2017, 38). On the basis of the law and its various amendments over the years, academics and officials have compiled reports on a wide range of traditions and customs from around the country. Following review and discussion of the reports, the Cultural Properties Committee (*Muhyŏng munhwajae wiwŏnhoe*; hereafter CPC), comprised largely of academics, could recommend an item to be designated as a National Intangible Cultural Property (*Kukka muhyŏng munhwajae*; hereafter NICP). To safeguard their transmission, however, holders of a cultural item were needed to teach and perform. As a reward for transmitting their art through teaching and, in the case of traditional performing arts, giving at least one public performance annually, since 1968 holders have received a monthly stipend that now at 1.5 million Won (equivalent to US$ 1371) sits approximately 15% below minimum wage (Munhwajaech'ŏng 2020d, 3, Shin 2021). Selecting these individuals involves choosing and thus foregrounding a limited number of styles and interpretations. Because the appointment comes with a stipend and considerable prestige, it has frequently caused friction between practitioners, especially where only one or a very small number of versions were selected from among many equally vibrant ones (see Sŏ 2003, 290; Lee 2011, 10, 17; Yates-Lu 2019, 52–54).

The number of NICPs has grown to 148, but the position of holders, who are frequently referred to as "human treasures" (*in'gan munhwajae*), has remained rather exclusive. While their current number of 173 shows that cultural items each have more than one representative on average, there are 38 traditions that have none (Munhwajaech'ŏng 2020a). And yet, finding appropriate representatives has rarely been easy. While the status associated with the appointment has led to a few instances of poor decision-making (see Hŏ Yun-hŭi 2014), much more often, the search for appropriate appointees has been complicated by a lack of candidates. A further complicating factor is the relatively small number of male practitioners of traditional performing arts. The gender imbalance may decrease in the near future as the number of single households grows, but for the past few decades, the competitive nature of Korea's job market led to few men taking the risk of seeking to provide for their (future) family through a career in the arts. Even in the case of traditions that have many practitioners, it is, however, not always easy to find people who have the talent, long-term commitment, and age required. The government has often appointed people quite late in their career, even though it has come to acknowledge that seniority does not necessarily guarantee authenticity while some traditions, such as tight rope walking and Korean wrestling, will always require a relatively younger holder capable of performing and teaching the art (Im 2006, 25). The average life expectancy in Korea has nevertheless risen considerably, from 52.9 in the late 1950s, to 59.3 in the late 1960s, when the first holders were appointed, to 82.8 in the late 2010s (United Nations Population Division 2019). Whereas it may not be necessary, therefore, to make drastic changes to the age at which holders are appointed, the current median age of holders is 72, which means some will be a little too old to take on all the chores and duties associated with the position (Paek 2020). Indeed, too often in the past, the position of holder was inherited rather than passed down. What is more, the very late retirement of holders limits career prospects to others interested in dedicating themselves to a cultural item.

Allowing holders to retire honorably would appear to be one solution. Following a public survey in which 78.1% of respondents gave their approval to an amendment of the system (Cho 2016, 166n24), the Cultural Heritage Protection Act was revised on March 28, 2001. Since then, holders have been able to retire and see their status converted to that of "honorary holder" (*myŏngye poyuja*). Before it was lowered to 75 in 2020 (Munhwajaech'ŏng 2020c, 19), holders were made to retire at the age of 80, presumably on the assumption that they would be too old by then to effectively carry out all duties (Inha taehakkyo sanhak hyŏmnyŏktan 2017, 72). But even younger holders can find it difficult to carry out all related duties. If a review finds that a holder is genuinely struggling to train students or to engage in activities to transmit the tradition, due to, for example, old age or poor health, the status can be converted earlier (see also Article 2, point 8 of the *Muhyŏng munhwajae pojŏn mit chinhŭng-e kwanhan pŏmnyul* (Act on the Safeguarding and Promotion of Intangible Cultural Heritage). This will usually be followed by a senior student being promoted to holder lest the NICP is dropped. The honorable retirement option was generally praised by practitioners. Assistant instructor of *Sŏdo sori* (Folksongs from the Western Provinces) Pak Chun-yŏng told me he was quite pleased with the measure as it allowed holders to retire while maintaining a degree of involvement and recognition (personal communication, December 10, 2020), though I suspect he also welcomed it on account of its increased support for non-holders like him, as I explain below.

The new measure has nevertheless been met with unease, too. *P'ansori* singer Choi Jin-sook, a graduate student (*isuja*) of NICP no. 5, expressed concern about the retirement age being mandatory when many would still be able to carry out their activities. She wondered whether their new status would end up having a curbing effect on their activities especially in light of the reduction in the monthly stipend it entailed (personal communication, December 10, 2020). Indeed, in a survey conducted among 126 senior practitioners within the system, 15.9% of respondents recommended raising the stipends while only 1.6% recommended bestowing the title of honorary holder on aging practitioners (Munhwajaech'ŏng 2018, 236). The new measure does not, however, make retirements automatic; they will still be based on an investigation by the CPC and take the intentions of the holders into account. Back in early 2005, for example, the CPC decided against the retirement of the then 84-year-old holder of NICP no. 11, Pak Ki-ha, on account of the holder himself having no desire to retire and being very motivated to continue teaching. Even so, upon further investigation conducted at the end of the year, Pak's deteriorating memory and physical condition were found to justify retirement (Munhwajaech'ŏng 2005, 19; 2006, 11–12). Equally, in early 2005 the CPC declined the application of the 68-year-old holder of NICP no. 26, Kim Chong-gon, on account of the holder's physical condition having been found sufficient to continue working. While an investigation conducted at the end of the year found that Kim was still healthy enough to work, a second review conducted in July 2007 found that it was finally time for him to become an honorary holder. Since it might negatively affect the quality of their work otherwise, I suspect that as long as they have a perfect track record and approach the required age, holders will be able to have their status conferred when they express a desire to retire (Munhwajaech'ŏng 2005, 22; 2006, 9–10; 2007, 122–123).

Despite the CPC's due diligence, many holders do retire late and usually only because poor health forces them to. Song Pang-ung (1940–2020), for example, holder of NICP no. 10 since 1990, became an honorary holder in March 2020, but died roughly four months later. Nam Hae-sŏng (1935–2020, NICP no. 5), Kim Tŏk-hwan (1935–2019, NICP no. 119), Chang Yong-hun (1937–2016, NICP no. 117), Kim Kwi-bong (1935–2013, NICP no. 81), and Min Nam-sun (1940–2013, NICP no. 61) all died roughly a year after they became honorary holders, while Kim Shil-cha (1928–2015, NICP no. 34), Yi Kŭnhwasŏn (1924–2015, NICP no. 15), Yi Mae-bang (1927–2015, NICP nos. 27 and 97), Kim Ch'ŏl-chu (1933–2015, NICP no. 35), T'ae Tŏk-su (1929–2014, NICP no. 43), and O Su-bok (1924–2011, NICP no. 98) all died roughly two years after their retirement. Although one might argue that loss of drive and status will be partly to blame for their short post-retirement life, it is more likely that the people had already struggled to carry out their duties as holder for quite some time. According to Im Sŏng-bong, the reduction in stipend by a third, to one million Won per month with funding for funeral arrangements up to 1.2 million Won, is the primary cause for the late retirement. She argues that because the amount has only increased by 100,000 Won since the first honorary holders were appointed makes retiring increasingly unattractive, which is why the number of new honorary holders dropped between 2013 and 2018 (Im 2018). Im Yŏng-ŭn agrees that many holders seek to postpone their retirement because the stipend is insufficient to carry out the vast range of activities required (Im 2019). Indeed, while senior students, holders, and honorary holders of relatively popular art forms will be able to add to their monthly income by demanding high private tuition fees, many others will not. And yet, teaching and public events require funding, especially when old age compounds the strain of travel, performance, and media engagements. In particular, very old holders who do not have a dedicated student will therefore struggle to involve themselves in such activities.

Retiring with Honors

On December 24, 2018 (Munhwajaech'ŏng 2020b, 239), a change in the law allowed assistant instructors who sit below holders and above graduate students in the official order of practitioners and are paid 700,000 Won per month, to also retire as honorary holders. A category of "future holders," who were paid half the monthly stipend given to holders, had been created in the past to support a larger number of senior practitioners and avoid antagonism between them (Munhwajae kwalliguk 1994, 768). But in 1994, the category was abolished, and all future holders added to the category of assistant instructors (Sŏ 2003, 294; Howard 2006, 10). Because the new scheme implies an additional 300,000 Won per month for retiring assistant instructors, in addition to funding for funeral arrangements, the scheme incentivizes being actively involved in a tradition until one is appointed as an assistant instructor, holder, or honorary holder, which can be crucial in the case of traditions that have none (see also Yi 2020). Considering only assistant instructors of 75 years of age or older with at least 20 years of teaching experience are eligible to apply for the change in status, the number of qualifying practitioners might appear to be small. However, on July 27, 2020, as many as 21 assistant instructors were appointed honorary holders. Seeing as the average age of the students was approximately 80, with Mr. Yi Ch'ang-ho of NICP no. 90 having even reached the age of 94, the law change was undoubtedly welcomed (see Kim 2020).

Some traditions have healthy student numbers. NICP no. 2, the mask drama *Yangju pyŏlsandae nori*, and no. 5, *p'ansori*, for example, have as many as 12 and nine assistant instructors, respectively (Munhwajaech'ŏng 2016, 2020a). And yet, the overall number of senior representatives appears to be decreasing. Although there is no cap on the number of possible appointees, holders tend to have only one or two assistant instructors on average. In 2016, when there were 290 assistant instructors across all NICPs overall, 21 traditions remained with only one senior representative. Since then, the list of NICPs has grown by 19 to a total of 148, but the total number of assistant instructors has decreased to 251, while 25 traditions remain that have only one senior representative (Munhwajaech'ŏng 2016, 2020a). By way of the improved retirement plan and the respectable title they share with retired holders, officially recognizing older representatives may help boost morale among senior practitioners and promise improved support to younger ones. Considering that by 2020, 54 of the 70 previously appointed honorary holders had died, decreasing the minimum age seems imperative.

Increasing the number of honorary holders will not, however, solve all problems. Ms. Bang So-Yeon (Pang So-yŏn) of the Cultural Heritage Administration's (Munhwajaech'ŏng, hereafter: Administration) Intangible Cultural Properties Division told me that the system appeared to be working well without any issues immediately arising (Bang So-Yeon, personal communication, December 24, 2020). Even so, albeit without specifying on what specific grounds, in 2019, Sŏng Ki-suk argued that most of the practitioners of traditional dance objected to the new scheme. I suspect their objection related to the controversy over the Cultural Heritage Administration's selection of a new holder for NICPs nos. 27, 92, and 97, which began in 2016 and carried on into 2019 until it was finally settled in September, some six months after Sŏng wrote her piece (Kim 2016; Sŏng 2019; Munhwajaech'ŏng 2019a). According to Im Sŏng-bong, one of the sources of concern is that the broadening of eligible practitioners represents no more than the introduction of a financial scheme, rather than a system that provides for an honorable retirement (Im 2018). Another source of discontent is the term "holder" itself. Since the Korean word for holder uses the generic character *cha/ja* (people), rather than the more respectful "sa," which is used in the words for doctor and nurse, it has been suggested to replace it with the unofficial term "human treasure" (Im 2006, 48; 2018). Holders are said to have also asked the Administration to replace the term *myŏngye* (honorary) with *wŏllo* (elder) (Im 2018), presumably in the hope of distinguishing themselves from retired assistant instructors.

Some have argued that it may not be appropriate to place honorary holders, who have not had to meet the same criteria as holders and have never served as one for any length of time, in the same category as holders upon retirement, and pay them the same stipend until death (see Sŏng 2019; Son and Yi 2015, 182). Indeed, until they end up in the same category as their assistant instructors, holders carry more responsibility and wield considerably more power. Senior students and assistant instructors generally regard them as their mentor, culturally, esthetically, and socio-politically. They rely on them for work opportunities and recommendations and will not openly pursue their retirement. Once they have retired, they usually continue to hold their mentor in high regard (see Maliangkay 2017, 47–48) and will not regard retired instructors as their equals. The responsibility to select holders is, however, still carried by the CPC, who have sometimes selected someone against the wishes of the retiring holder. For example, Yi Ŭn-ju, late holder of NICP no. 57, *Kyŏnggi minyo* (Folksongs from Kyŏnggi Province), had once tried unsuccessfully to get the CPC to drop one of her graduate students from the official order of practitioners (Maliangkay 2017, 113–114). A more recent case related to the same NICP involved late holder Muk Kye-wŏl (1921–2014), who became honorary holder in April 2005. Her physical condition had been poor for years, so when in early 2005, her ability to carry on her official duties came under review, she submitted a letter to the CPC asking to retire and her assistant instructor Yu Ch'ang to be appointed holder in her stead. In response to her eloquent, well-structured letter, which I suspect Muk had help composing, the committee granted Muk's wish to retire and assume the position of honorary holder but noted that it was unable to bypass the official selection process and allow Yu Ch'ang to take her place (Munhwajaech'ŏng 2005, 25–26). Bang So-Yeon assured me that while cases like these have come up a few times in the beginning, they have not continued (Bang, personal communication, December 24, 2020).

A Game of Numbers

In spite of the challenges it has faced over the years, Korea's comprehensive heritage management system has paid off, at least from a policy viewpoint (see Howard 2006, 38–39). Not only have Koreans embraced a large number of NICPs as symbols of the Korean identity, but many NICPs have also become recognized overseas, in part due to the international rise of Korean popular culture, which they helped foster. Korean heritage has become a source of hard cash and soft power. Foreign policymakers may look at Korea's heritage management and the Korean Wave (*hallyu*) as ideals worth following, but both phenomena have required considerable government funding (see Howard 2006, 13; Jin 2016, 29–30), and they could have both failed. The Wave was ultimately the culmination of a wide range of factors, including a major economic crisis, Korea's political past, the presence of a vibrant and easily identifiable traditional culture, and Korea's proximity to China and Japan, culturally and geographically. The commercial successes of Korean culture are owed partly to positive and negative associations with the culture of Japan overseas.

Some of those associations are made by Koreans themselves (see Maliangkay 2008, 55). Despite the Wave having firmly placed Korean culture in the limelight, many Koreans continue to feel a sense of competition with Japan, presumably spurred on by the ongoing dispute with Japan over its stance on Korea's Comfort Women. It is easy to see why one would make comparisons. The two nations' geographical proximity and Japan's colonization of Korea, among other things, account for a wide range of cultural and administrative similarities. And it was during the colonial period that the foundations for Korea's system of heritage management were laid. When it comes to funding holders, however, the current systems differ significantly. Sŏ Han-bŏm argues that the stipend given to holders in Korea is much too small compared to that given in Japan (Sŏ 2003, 281). But while Japanese holders have been given an annual stipend of two million yen since 1964 (approximately US$ 19,200), in 2020, Korea's Administration announced that it would raise the stipend to 16 million Won per annum (approximately US$ 16,000), which reduces the difference considerably (see Aikawa-Faure 2014, 41; Munhwajaech'ŏng 2020d, 3). What is more, Japan does not provide financial support to students, and it doesn't have a retirement scheme. According to Article 72 of the Japanese Law for the Protection of Cultural Properties (*Bunkazai hogohō*), when holders become physically or mentally incapable of continuing in their role, the Minister of Education, Culture, Sports, Science, and Technology may terminate the designation. Although one would think that this would be done on the basis of a report, the regulations do not stipulate this (see Ministry of Internal Affairs and Communications 2020), and Aikawa-Faure writes that because appointments are for life, the annual stipend sometimes ends up serving as a modest pension when a senior holder is no longer active, even when younger and more active practitioners are available (Aikawa-Faure 2014, 44).

Besides boosting business and preserving heritage, Korea's cultural policy is also aimed at nurturing national pride and increasing the nation's soft power. In addition to opportunities for diplomatic engagement, it is these objectives that drive Korea's considerable efforts to have its cultural properties recognized by UNESCO (Cho 2016, 164). Over the past decade, UNESCO's "Representative List of the Intangible Cultural Heritage of Humanity" has come to resemble an all-time Olympic Games medal tally. While in its current definition UNESCO regards intangible cultural heritage as that which "provides them [communities and groups] with a sense of identity and continuity, thus promoting respect for cultural diversity and human creativity" (UNESCO 2018, 5), the Olympic charter states that it seeks to promote "a peaceful society concerned with the preservation of human dignity ... in the Olympic spirit, which requires mutual understanding with a spirit of friendship, solidarity and fair play ... without discrimination of any kind" (International Olympic Committee 2020, 11–12). The mission statements of both organizations thus include respect for difference, even though they are sites of considerable competition and globalization processes (see Askew 2010; Cwiertka 2019; see also Cho 2016, 170).

In East Asia, examples of this competition, for what ultimately amounts to intellectual property rights, abound. Following China's recognition of the folksong *Arirang* as part of its national intangible cultural heritage in 2009, the Administration doubled its efforts to have the folksong added to UNESCO's list. It succeeded in 2012. But in 2014, the song was listed again, now as a repertoire of songs with that title sung in different provinces in North Korea (Maliangkay 2017, 41–42). Surprisingly, Korea's quintessential kimchi-making tradition was not added to the list until 2013, soon after a failed application for "Royal cuisine of the Joseon [Chosŏn] dynasty." The experience once again prompted North Korea to put forward a similar application, which led to another UNESCO listing of the Korean food practice in 2015. In the same year, having learned from Korea's failed bid, Japan's packaging of a food-related practice called Washoku proved successful, too (Cwiertka 2018, 2019, 75). The inclusion of traditional sports like Taekkyeon (T'aekkyŏn) in 2011, and Ssireum (Ssirŭm)—a shared listing with North Korea—in 2018, a year after Korea added it to its list of NICPs, forebodes the listing of sports in neighboring countries. Okinawa's local intangible cultural property *karate*, for example, may be the subject of a future application in spite of its foreign origins (Johnson 2012, 62, 66). This might encourage Korea to follow suit with its partly *karate*-inspired *taekwondo*. It's hard to imagine this competition boosting any party's soft power, but it may nevertheless strengthen Korea's image as a country that is rich in traditions. It is with this picture in mind that Lee Bae-yong [Yi Pae-yong], former head of the Presidential Council on Nation Branding, and her team dressed up in traditional Korean costume (*hanbok*) and bowed to the international committee when UNESCO approved their application for the addition of neo-Confucian sŏwŏn academies to its list in 2019 (Yoon 2019, 15).

To most Koreans, recognition by UNESCO is a crucial international accolade, one that outweighs the importance of national cultural property. Since 2008, both Korea and UNESCO have added 21 Korean cultural items to their respective lists. That international acknowledgment is considered of primary importance to Korea is demonstrated by the country having recognized kimchi preparation, the culture of female divers in Cheju province, and *Arirang*, a folksong in its myriad forms, only after they were added to UNESCO's list (Munhwajaech'ŏng 2020c, 19–20). Yeondeunghoe (Yŏndŭnghoe), on the other hand, a lantern festival celebrating Buddha's birthday, had been recognized by Korea in 2012. Whereas its addition to UNESCO's list in 2020 has not raised many eyebrows, the festival was revived in 1996 (Chŏn 2008, 367) and has only been a prominent feature of Seoul's daily life since the mid-2000s, when large lanterns suddenly appeared in the middle of Chŏnggyech'ŏn stream from November onward in partial celebration of the re-opening of the stream and adjacent promenade. Prior to that, the lantern festival was noticeable only outside Buddhist temples, like the Chogye Temple along Ujŏnggungno (a road in Seoul's central Chongno District). It was not a major feature of Korean daily life, and even today, it is a false claim that "the entire country lights up with colorful lanterns" as the application claims (UNESCO 2020, 3). Studies of the origins of the festival show that it evolved during the Koryŏ dynasty but lost its religious purpose from the middle of the Chosŏn dynasty; when it re-emerged in the colonial period, it came under significant influence from Japanese Buddhism, imperial politics, and Korean Christianity (Chŏn 2008, 332, 363; Kim 2011, 60, 72–73). Placing the festival in the same category as other modern constructs like Christmas, Hwan-soo Kim argues that today's version was partly inspired by the Korean Wave (2011, 76–77). Many Koreans will feel pride over the listing, but few will dispute that the festival has really only come to prominence when it was successfully turned into a tourist attraction. Korean traditions, it would seem, constitute little value without foreign valorization. Even the general public applies foreign yardsticks to indigenous traditions. Indeed, in explaining the importance of UNESCO to Korean traditions, Lee Bae-yong suggests that Koreans don't value their own heritage until it is recognized by UNESCO: "There are traditions that are priceless, yet are on the verge of disappearing because people don't know about it. By finding these traditions and preserving them, sending them to the [sic] UNESCO, we can find values that are worth sharing with the rest of the world" (Quoted in Yoon 2019, 15).

By not being overtly religious in nature, the festival attracts tourists in general, regardless of their religious beliefs. Considering the lack of a prominent Buddhist culture and the unlikelihood of Korean churches becoming a major tourist destination in the near future, it does not serve only as a tourist destination but crucially helps to portray Korea as diverse. The English-language website of the Korea Tourism Organization supports this image. Featuring photos of natural sites, modern constructs, and temples in different seasons as well as snapshots of food, shopping, K-pop, and traditional costumes under the tagline "Imagine your Korea," the picture of Korea it presents seeks to appeal to a wide range of travelers. Building a comprehensive package under a particular slogan is a form of country branding (see Kotler and Gertner 2002, 256, 259), which the Korean government has actively engaged in since the early 2000s (Lee 2018, 75). The drive to add to the plurality of traditions may in future years foster the development and appropriation of cultural items that while authentically Korean in concept (see Cohen 1988) may have opaque historical timelines as far as their development within national borderlines is concerned. The "K-" brand has nevertheless served to promote cultural products, both old and modern, as part of this vibrant cultural nexus Korea, irrespective of their foreign origins. A good example of this is music categorized as "K-classic": Western classical music performed by a renowned Korean virtuoso. Jocelyn Clark has found that while fewer Koreans are familiar with traditional Korean music (*kugak*) than ever before, university students are now associating it with the Wave. The problem with that, she finds, is that this inevitably leads to the adoption of Western esthetics and disconnects the musicians from their audience: "*Gugak* [*kugak*], and classical music, and new music, as well, are losing an audience that may be from Korea, but is no longer *of* Korea" (Clark 2018, 140, 154). In its efforts to find instant appeal, country branding may end up replacing indigenous cultural roots with foreign ones.

The honorary holder scheme is intended partly to remedy the inability of some traditions to become self-sustainable in terms of succession. If Koreans are, however, becoming less interested in preserving traditions whose value is not recognized abroad, the government may come under pressure to plant more seedlings of future traditions rather than tending to the roots of existing ones. Their ultimate purpose being national icons, recognizing a broader range of traditions may garner more support than securing numbers of practitioners of traditions that appear to have lost their relevance. Considering, for example, that the majority of Koreans have long considered Western classical music a more distinguished traditional form of art than their own *kugak* (see Clark 2018, 136, 148–149; Choi 2018, 147), one might consider investing in the latter as much of an interference as efforts to revive a Buddhist festival. Authenticity and uniqueness in tourism are nevertheless becoming ever harder to find, a situation not remedied by the proliferation of UNESCO listings, NICPs, and regional cultural properties. Across the country, provincial and municipal governments now recognize a total of 572 traditions in addition to the national and international ones (see Munhwajaech'ŏng 2019b). In the future, locals and tourists may become impervious if not averse to the heritage branding of products and practices and all-too-convenient tourist destinations. While some may embrace the diversity and the convenience, or even the inevitability of simulations (Ritzer and Liska 1997, 72, 78–79), others may still look elsewhere. The more Korean heritage is recognized, the more it risks losing in appeal as a whole. Rather than promoting the wide range of alternatives, therefore, there may be value in highlighting their increasing absence and pushing, instead, for the valorization of (careers in) once vibrant cultural properties at risk of being lost.

Conclusion

My brief deliberations here may be regarded as a critique of the ways in which the Korean government manages its intangible heritage. Conscious of the hierarchies that exist and are usually earned over a lifetime of dedication and hard work, I am indeed concerned about the implications of a system that does not distinguish between retiring practitioners: most holders take the responsibilities they carry very seriously and continue to teach and perform after retirement in spite of poor health. But their decision to postpone retirement will be driven by a lack of successors or the limited pension made available, rather than a desire to avoid being placed in the same category as retiring instructors. What is more, most practitioners retire in the twilight of their lives when the lack of a graded pension scheme ought not to be an issue. In light of this, the scheme should be commended for allowing succession to be more dependable. By allowing senior practitioners to retire at a particular age, it goes some way toward guaranteeing opportunities for younger hopefuls. In line with the national pension scheme, therefore, the Administration may wish to consider further lowering the retirement age for senior practitioners as it would improve opportunities, despite the undeniable added cost.

In the immediate future, the Administration plans to pursue more UNESCO listings and expand its efforts to promote regional cultural heritage (Munhwajaech'ŏng 2020d, 2, 4). The listings will be intended to nurture nationalism, to strengthen the nation's diplomatic position, and to preserve Korean heritage partly for the purpose of boosting tourism. But the number of cultural properties could eventually grow at the expense of the cultural value associated with them. Locals and foreigners may become impervious to their alleged significance, especially if their timelines are relatively short, their esthetics contentious, or both. It would be amiss, however, to deny that some traditions may never attract a large audience or a steady stream of students, and that only a minority of the people cares about foreign valorization of their achievements. If having them added to UNESCO's list is the best way to make Koreans valorize their own traditions, then I hope the Administration will prioritize pursuing the addition of all existing NICPs, rather than future ones.

References

Aikawa-Faure, Noriko. 2014. "Excellence and Authenticity: 'Living National (Human) Treasures' in Japan and Korea." *International Journal of Intangible Heritage* 9: 37–51.

Askew, Marc. 2010. The Magic List of Global Status: UNESCO, World Heritage and the Agendas of States." In *Heritage and Globalisation*, edited by Sophia Labadi and Colin Long, 19–44. New York: Routledge.

Cho, Sun-ja. 2016. "Han'guk muhyŏng munhwajae chedo pyŏnch'ŏnsa yŏn'gu — Kukka muhyŏng munhwajae-rŭl chungshim-ŭro" [A Study of the Transformation of Korea's System of Intangible Cultural Properties Over Time—With a Focus on National Intangible Cultural Properties]. *Ŭmak-kwa minjok* [Music and People] 52: 147–176.

Ch'oe, Kyu-min. 2020. "Kungmin yŏn'gŭm kaehyŏk sonnohŭn chŏngbu, kaehyŏg-an 1-lyŏn-nŏmge kukhoe pangch'i" [Government Revisiting National Pension Reform More Than a Year After a Reform was Last Deliberated]. *Chosŏn Ilbo* [Korea Daily], June 23, A10.

Choi, Hye Eun. 2018. "The Making of the Recording Industry in Colonial Korea, 1910–1945." Ph.D. diss., University of Wisconsin-Madison.

Chŏn, Kyŏng-uk. 2008. "Yŏndŭnghoe-ŭi chŏnt'ong-gwa hyŏndae ch'ukchehwa-ŭi pangan" [The Tradition of Yŏndŭnghoe and How to Turn It into a Modern Festival]. *Namdo Minsok Yŏn'gu* 17 (17): 329–379.
Clark, Jocelyn. 2018. "Relevant in the Digital Age: 100 Years of (Re)defining Gugak," *Asian Musicology* 28, 128–160.
Cohen, Erik. 1988. "Authenticity and Commoditization in Tourism." *Annals of Tourism Research* 15 (3): 371–386.
Cwiertka, Katarzyna J. 2018. "Serving the Nation: The Myth of *Washoku*." In *Consuming Life in Post-Bubble Japan: A Transdisciplinary Perspective*, edited by Katarzyna J. Cwiertka and Ewa Machotka, 89–106. Amsterdam: Amsterdam University Press.
Cwiertka, Katarzyna J. 2019. "From Military Rations to UNESCO Heritage: A Short History of Korean *Kimchi*." In *Culinary Nationalism in Asia*, edited by Michelle T. King, 73–90. London: Bloomsbury Academic.
Hŏ, Yun-hŭi. 2014. "T'ukha-myŏn chajil nollan… nugu-rŭl wihan in'gan munhwajae-in'ga" [Always Something to Critique… Who Are Human Cultural Properties for?]. *Chosŏn Ilbo*, February 12, A21.
Howard, Keith. 2006. *Preserving Korean Music: Intangible Cultural Properties as Icons of Identity (Perspectives on Korean Music Volume 1)*. London and New York: Routledge.
Im, Chang-hyŏk. 2006. *Chungyo muhyŏng munhwajae wŏnhyŏng pojon-gwa chaech'angjo kaidŭrain* [Guidelines for the Preservation and Reinvention of Important Intangible Cultural Properties]. Daejeon: Munhwajaech'ŏng [Cultural Heritage Administration].
Im, Sŏng-bong. 2018. "Mal-ppunin myŏngye poyuja… 'tanmul-man ppaemŏkko pŏrina'" [An Honorary Holder in Name Only… 'Do They Give Up on the Reward?']. *Newspim*, October 2.
Im, Yŏng-ŭn. 2019. "Muhyŏng munhwajae pojon-e p'yŏngsaeng pach'in myŏngye poyuja-ga pannŭn ton" [The Stipend Received by Honorary Holders Dedicated to the Preservation of Intangible Cultural Properties]. *OhmyNews*, September 18.
Inha taehakkyo sanhak hyŏmnyŏktan [Inha University Industrial-educational Cooperative]. 2017. *Muhyŏng munhwajaebŏp mit kwan'gye pŏmnyŏng kaejŏng-ŭl wihan yŏn'gu: Ch'oejong pogosŏ* [A Study of Revisions of the Cultural Properties Protection Act and Related Laws: Final Report]. Daejeon: Cultural Heritage Administration.
International Olympic Committee. 2020. *Olympic Charter*. Lausanne: International Olympic Committee.
Johnson, Noah C. G. 2012. "The Japanization of Karate?: Placing an Intangible Cultural Practice." *Journal of Contemporary Anthropology* 3 (1): 60–78.
Jin, Dal Yong. 2016. *New Korean Wave: Transnational Cultural Power in the Age of Social Media*. Urbana: University of Illinois Press.

Kim, Chi-hyŏn. 2020. "Myŏngye poyuja chedo ch'ŏt shihaeng 'Koryŏng chŏnsu kyoyuk chogyo chŏnsŭng hwalsŏnghwa'" [First Implementation of the Honorary Holder System "Activating the Transmission of Senior Training Assistants"]. *Seoul Culture Today*, February 10. Accessed December 6, 2021. http://www.sctoday.co.kr/news/articleView.html?idxno=31839.

Kim, Hwan-soo. 2011. "A Buddhist Christmas: The Buddha's Birthday Festival in Colonial Korea (1928–1945)." *Journal of Korean Religions* 2 (2): 47–82.

Kim Su-yŏn. 2021. "'Ch'ŏngnyŏn 1-myŏng-i noin 1-myŏng puyang' shidae tagawa… yŏn'gŭm pohŏmnyo 3-bae ttwil su-do" [An Era in Which "One Young Person Supports One Elderly Person" Is Approaching… Pension Premiums May Be Tripled]. *Tonga Ilbo* [East Asia Daily], January 12, A8.

Kim, Tong-uk. 2016. "Munhwajaech'ŏng, T'aep'yŏngmu in'gan munhwajae Yang Sŏngok-ssi yego nollan kayŏl" [Controversy Over the Cultural Heritage Administration and T'aep'yŏngmu's Human Cultural Property Yang Sŏngok Heats Up]. *Tonga Ilbo*, March 1, 20.

Kotler, Philip and David Gertner. 2002. "Country as Brand, Product, and Beyond: A Place Marketing and Brand Management Perspective." *Journal of Brand Management* 9 (4/5): 249–261.

Lee, Hoon Sang. 2011. "Reflections on the Intangible Cultural Heritage Policy and Folk Culture Politics in the Postmodern Era: An Autoethnographic Account of the Reconstruction of Kasan Ogwangdae." *Korean Social Sciences Review* 1 (1): 1–35.

Lee, Katherine In-Young. 2018. *Dynamic Korea and Rhythmic Form*. Connecticut: Wesleyan University Press.

Maliangkay, Roald. 2008. "Staging Korean Traditional Performing Arts Abroad: Important Intangible Intercultural Performance Issues." *Sungkyun Journal of East Asian Studies* 7 (2): 49–68.

Maliangkay, Roald. 2017. *Broken Voices: Postcolonial Entanglements and the Preservation of Korea's Central Folksong Traditions*. Honolulu: Hawai'i University Press.

Ministry of Internal Affairs and Communications. 2020. e-Gov Japan. Last modified November 24. https://elaws.e-gov.go.jp/document?lawid=325AC1000000214.

Munhwajaech'ŏng [Cultural Heritage Administration]. 2005. *Munhwajae wiwŏnhoe hoeŭirok 2005* [2005 Proceedings of the Cultural Properties Committee] 2005, vol. 2-1. Daejeon: Cultural Heritage Administration.

Munhwajaech'ŏng. 2006. *Munhwajae wiwŏnhoe hoeŭirok 2006*, vol. 2-1. Daejeon: Cultural Heritage Administration.

Munhwajaech'ŏng. 2007. *Munhwajae wiwŏnhoe hoeŭirok 2007*, vol. 2-1. Daejeon: Cultural Heritage Administration.

Munhwajaech'ŏng. 2016. "Kukka muhyŏng munhwajae chŏnsŭngja hyŏnhwang" [Status Quo of NCIP Transmitters]. June 30. Accessed

January 30, 2021. http://www.cha.go.kr/cop/bbs/selectBoardArticle.do?nttId=30629&bbsId=BBSMSTR_1045&mn=NS_03_09_01.

Munhwajaech'ŏng. 2018. *2018-lyŏn munhwajaech'ŏng chŏngch'aek manjokto kyŏlgwa pogosŏ - Part I* [Cultural Heritage Administration Policy Satisfaction Report—Part 1]. December. Daejeon: Cultural Heritage Administration.

Munhwajaech'ŏng. 2019a. "Podo charyo" [Press Release]. September 6. Accessed January 30, 2021. https://www.cha.go.kr/newsBbz/FileDown.do?id=TVRjNE1UYz0=.

Munhwajaech'ŏng. 2019b. "Chijŏng munhwjae ch'onggwal" [Summary of Designated Cultural Properties]. December 31. Accessed January 30, 2021. https://www.cha.go.kr/html/HtmlPage.do?pg=/cultural_info/cultureTotal_ccrebasi_kor.jsp&mn=NS_03_07_02.

Munhwajaech'ŏng. 2020a. "Kukka muhyŏng munhwajae hyŏnhwang" [Status Quo of NICPs]. October 31. Accessed January 30, 2021. http://www.cha.go.kr/cop/bbs/selectBoardArticle.do?nttId=78568&bbsId=BBSMSTR_1045&mn=NS_03_09_01.

Munhwajaech'ŏng. 2020b. *Munhwajae kwan'gye pŏmnyŏngjip* [Collection of Laws on Cultural Properties]. Daejeon: Cultural Heritage Administration.

Munhwajaech'ŏng. 2020c. *2020-nyŏndo chuyo ŏmmu kyehoek* [Major Business Plan for the 2020s]. Daejeon: Cultural Heritage Administration.

Munhwajaech'ŏng. 2020d. *Kungmin-gwa hamkke nuri-nŭn munhwayusan, munhwajaech'ŏng-i mandŭrŏ kagessŭmnida* [The Cultural Heritage Administration is Working to Create Cultural Heritage That Can Be Enjoyed by the People Together]. Flyer. Daejeon: Cultural Heritage Administration.

Munhwajae kwalliguk [Cultural Heritage Management Office]. 1994. *Munhwajae wiwŏnhoe hoeŭirok 1993* [1993 Proceedings of the Cultural Properties Committee]. Seoul: Munhwajae kwalliguk.

Paek, Sŏg-wŏn. 2020. "Muhyŏng munhwajae poyuja p'yŏnggyun yŏllyŏng 72-se, hwaldong-e chŏkhaphan nai-in'ga?" [The Average Age of Holders of Intangible Cultural Properties Being 72, Is It an Appropriate Age for Activities?]. *Culture Times*, May 19. Accessed January 30, 2021. http://www.ctimes.co.kr/news/articleView.html?idxno=7561.

Park, Sang Mi. 2010. "The Paradox of Postcolonial Korean Nationalism: State-Sponsored Cultural Policy in South Korea, 1965–Present." *The Journal of Korean Studies* 15 (1): 67–93.

Ritzer, George and Allan Liska. 1997. "'McDisneyization' and 'Post-Tourism': Complementary Perspectives on Contemporary Tourism." In *Tourism: Critical Concepts in the Social Sciences*, edited by Stephen Williams, 96–109. London: Routledge.

Shin, Ji-hye. 2021. "Why Do Old People Pick Up Cardboard in Seoul?" *Korea Herald*, February 26, 3.

Sŏ, Han-bŏm. 2003. "Muhyŏng munhwajae chŏngch'aek: ki, yenŭng chŏnsŭng-ŭi haengjŏng kwalli-rŭl chungshim-ŭro" [The Policy for Intangible Cultural Properties: Focusing on the Administrative Management of Technical and Artistic Transmission]. *Han'guk minsok hakhoe* [Korean Folklore Studies] 38 (12): 279–320.

Sŏng Ki-suk. 2019. "Muhyŏng munhwajae poyuja injŏng shimsa pulgongjŏng nollan" [Controversy Over the Unfair Recognition of Intangible Cultural Properties], *Seoul Culture Today*, March 27. Accessed January 30, 2021. http://www.sctoday.co.kr/news/articleView.html?idxno=27651.

Son, T'ae-do and Yi Chong-suk. 2015. "Munhwajae pohobŏp unyŏng kwajŏng-esŏ-ŭi chaengjŏmdŭl-gwa kŭ nonŭi" [Issues and Their Discussion Related to the Carrying Out of the Cultural Property Protection Act]. *Han'guk chŏnt'ong kongyŏn yesulhak* [Journal of Korean Traditional Performing Arts] 4: 161–191.

UNESCO. 2018. *Basic Texts of the 2003 Convention for the Safeguarding of the Intangible Cultural Heritage—2018 Edition*. Paris: UNESCO.

UNESCO. 2020. "Nomination File No. 00882 for Inscription in 2020 on the Representative List of the Intangible Cultural Heritage of Humanity." Accessed January 30, 2021. https://ich.unesco.org/en/8b-representative-list-01146#8.b.1.

United Nations Population Division. 2019. *World Population Prospects 2019—Special Aggregates, Online Edition, Rev. 1*. New York, NY: United Nations.

Yates-Lu, Anna. 2019. "When K-Pop and Kugak Meet: Popularising P'ansori in Modern Korea." *Yearbook for Traditional Music* 51: 49–71.

Yi, Pyŏng-jae. 2020. "75-se isang koryŏng chŏnsu kyoyuk chogyo orhae myŏngye poyuja injŏng chedo shihaeng" [The System of Recognizing Senior Assistant Instructors Older than 75 Who as Honorary Holders Will Be Put into Effect This Year]. *Chŏlla Ilbo* [Jeolla Daily], February 12, 12.

Yoon, Min-sik. 2019. "'What Is Korean Is What Is Most Global.'" *Korea Herald*, October 3, 15.

CHAPTER 7

The Transmedial Aesthetics of K-Pop Music Videos: References to Western Film Cultures

Ute Fendler

Many of the increasing numbers of publications on the Korean Wave are dedicated to the analysis of K-pop (Choi and Maliangkay, 2015; Lee and Nornes, 2015; Dal, 2016). This reflects the importance of the global spread of the phenomenon over the last ten to fifteen years and the flourishing cultural economy it has engendered. Marketing strategies fueling K-Pop focus mainly on the iconic value of artists (Maliangkay, 2013) and performance, including choreographies and fashions that highlight the visual aesthetic of the groups. (Willoughby, 2006) Music videos have therefore become a crucial component of sales strategies, while constructing a particular aesthetic for domestic and overseas audiences. This chapter will focus on music videos as an important interface between the product and the international public through their use of aesthetic and visual references to Western and other film cultures in the process of developing their own recognizable style.

U. Fendler (✉)
University of Bayreuth, Bayreuth, Germany
e-mail: ute.fendler@uni-bayreuth.de

© The Author(s), under exclusive license to Springer Nature Switzerland AG 2022
A. D. Jackson (ed.), *The Two Koreas and their Global Engagements*, https://doi.org/10.1007/978-3-030-90761-7_7

Youna Kim gives a short overview of the evolution of the Korean Wave since the 1990s. The term "Korean wave" or "*hallyu*" was first used by Chinese media in 1998 (2013, 1), and served as a catch-all concept for Korean transnational popular culture products like music, TV dramas, and films which were first exported to Asian countries and America (Howard, 2014), then later Europe and Australia (Kim 2013, 3). In the 1990s, the Korean government set out to "[...] sell a dynamic image of the nation through soft power" (Kim and Rioo 2007, 122–123), which coincided with a broader plan, as Kim stresses:

> [...] the current focus on "culture" by governments in Northeast Asia is the product of a neoliberal ideology espousing a global free market and the linking of globalized consumerism to individual freedom and social well-being. (Kim, 2013, 5)

It is important to keep in mind the dual evolution of popular music in South Korea (Howard, 2006), which was the planning and design of trends to represent and sell the image of a modern and dynamic state highly canalized by political settings and the economic interests of liberalized markets. (Kim and Kim, 2011)

The ongoing and increasing success of K-pop is, therefore, the result of an underlying process of hybridization, or rather "transculturalization," of popular music (Fuhr, 2016), which allows the integration of a range of cultural practices as long as they can find sympathetic resonances (Kim, 2012, 12). The major influences in music are recognized as being Japanese and American, but K-pop is increasingly acknowledging its indebtedness to hip-hop and rap (Shin and Lee, 2017), as the success of the TV show "Show me the money" since 2012 suggests, and as Myoung-Sun Song argues in her book *Hanguk Hip Hop. Global Rap in South Korea* (2019).

K-pop exemplifies many of the core characteristics of pop music, including ready accessibility and pattern repetition that integrate different elements (Anderson, 2014, 2020). This process provides a platform on which the interaction between various cultural positions and values takes place, although the foreign influences have stirred questions about the "K" in K-pop, as John Lie formulates it. Lie offers an overview of how and when Western music slowly took over in South Korea, from the first half of the twentieth century until 2010. The period saw the predominance of popular music over classical music in economic terms. Based on his description, Lie questions what the "K" might stand for in an economy of mass production, drawing attention to the conflictual relationship between notions of classical and popular in different contexts and highlighting the lasting influence of the idea of the Romantic artist as an idealized individual genius. This concept runs contrary to ideas linked with market orientations and contemporary studio systems, and Lie reflects on the (non)appreciation of K-pop:

> If we can move beyond the fact of K-pop as an unabashed culture industry, and if we can liberate our senses from Romantic ideology and its associated shackles, then it may become possible for us to appreciate K-pop's interesting and innovative features. (2014, 145)

Combining music with the artist's good looks—highlighted by fashionable designs and well-staged performances—music videos have become an ever more important part of a production system that highlights the hybridity of K-pop and reflects the strong commercial and economic interests behind it (Epstein and Joo, 2012). As Kim Chang Nam has emphasized, the most recent evolution of K-pop from the beginning of the 2000s was the idol group "meticulously managed through a production system that maximizes commercial profits." (Kim 2012). Only five years later, Hyunjoon Shin stressed the specificities of idol groups in relation to the production companies, highlighting that the companies strive to build their own recognizable brand in this extremely competitive field.

> The K-pop industry does not necessarily produce cookie-cutter idols who are indistinguishable from one another. Some local critics observe different idol types based on company cultures (Cha and Choi 2012, 146–150). For example, while the "hard-trained model student type" idols come from SM, YG produces the "hip-hop influenced, wild, and self-boasting type," and DSP does the "boys/girls next door type." The critics also highlight the "artistic achievement and generational difference" of "the second generation idol groups" since the late 2000s [...]. (Shin 2017, 117)

The K-pop phenomenon is thus strongly hybridized in the way it draws on various musical styles and economic and marketing strategies reaching out to international markets. As well as economic aspects (Kang, 2015), the media space allows a diversity of roles to co-exist, and that diversity in role models has an impact on society. Meanwhile, the importance of music videos has grown, and they have increased in quantity and improved in quality. It is against this very complex mediascape that K-pop culture must be set. The music videos contribute to the creation of an imaginary identity that draws on a multitude of cultural representations and values, and they strongly influence the transcultural processes that began some two decades ago.

Music Videos Between Economy and Art

Popular music linked to fashion and consumerism is closely related to ideas of individual freedom, which can clash with predesigned and market-orientated concepts. In contrast to the idea of the individual artist, big entertainment production companies (Fendler, 2017) introduced a "trainee system" from the 2000s onwards to recruit and train young talents for K-pop idol groups. (Ho, 2012) Heavy investment over the years has led to lengthy contracts to ensure a return on investment once the groups become successful. In this context, the importance of music videos is constantly growing as the group can be displayed and showcased in these videos as a label that sells. Youna Kim states that South Korea is the first nation to become "a dream society of icons and aesthetic experience" (2013, 84) that intentionally constructs the saleable concept of a dream using icons that appeal to a global public. In this process, the visual plays an important role:

> [...] Korean popular music is driven by the visual, not only via live performance on television but in music videos [...] too. As Hoon-Soon Kim notes, "The music video has captivated the younger generation… and has changed the notion of music from that of something primarily auditory to something to watch as well." (2013, 316)

The preponderance of images in the popular music industry is taken into consideration by the trainee system, which aims toward perfection in the idols' performances (Kim 2013, 8). Epstein and Turnbull go even further in their appreciation of the performance of K-pop idols:

> In this environment, music videos become not an autonomous expression of performer sensibility but a marketing tactic concocted by managers to sell a cultural product. In order to be effective, a music video (M/V) must resonate with the zeitgeist in the way it conforms to, or in some cases

challenges, normative expectations; [...]. (Epstein and Turnbull 2014, 317)

The points Epstein and Turnbull make here are very important, as they indicate the large range of themes that music videos deal with in spite of the economic interests and the rigid organization of the companies. The concept of Zeitgeist becomes a process of exchange between producers and the public.

Vannini and Myers underline the importance of music videos as "cultural agents":

> As such, its producers and consumers are interpreters belonging to the same social context in which music content and cultural values interplay to constitute socially constructed realities. It is this dual capacity of music to be at one time both reflective of common popular beliefs and influential in moving and shaping the same beliefs that make it such an important cultural agent. (Vannini and Myers 2002)

The dual character of music videos captures the dynamic and dialogic character of the format so that despite the strong control—economically and conceptually—the construction of meaning is always part of an ongoing exchange between the producers and artists and the potential public.

The format of music videos has evolved to match the rise in the number of television stations, greater access to the Internet, and the sharing of images and videos on YouTube and other sites. In the process, two main categories can be distinguished. The first covers most productions. The clips accompanying the release of a new album present the concept of the album or of the songs on it, which might range between "cute," "sexy," and "dangerous." (Sun, 2010) Whatever style is deemed fashionable is given added value by presenting a music genre and/or visual performance that is different from previous productions. Such music videos are part of a larger marketing concept that aims to sell the group to diverse target groups. These videos seldom include a storyline and pay little attention to filmic features. They usually offer a set of stages on which the groups perform each time in different outfits, showcasing each group's label and that of the production company.[1] Meanwhile, a smaller number of videos focus on a more developed storyline. In general, music videos entail a massive investment trying to reach a high level of aesthetic quality.

The sheer quantity of video production has also risen steadily over the last decade as a round of promotion accompanies the release of each new song, preceded by one or more teasers. Mini albums with a maximum of three songs and at least one music video have also made a comeback, as well as full albums. The high demand for videos has also led to the proliferation of production enterprises. While there were two major enterprises fifteen years ago, companies such as Zany Bros (which specializes in perfect photos of the idols in close-ups) and Digipedi (known for its avant-garde style) have set the conventions we associate with K-pop. Zany Bros—which at one time produced up to 70% of South Korea's music videos—has contributed significantly to the image of K-pop groups in the local and international market. At their peak, the label released up to three videos per week, and as cooperation with Japan, China, and other Asian countries continued to grow, the company's successful model was exported via distribution and collaboration.

The specific style that Zany Bros established persists in the majority of videos. This includes the combination of accelerated rhythms and a constantly moving camera that rushes through settings with cozy or luxurious interiors, futuristic decor, or impressive landscapes depending on the song and its visual concept. The general concept of the production is combined with the visual elements of seductive commercials and simplistic cinematographic stories set at a video game-like pace. Over the last decade, new techniques and styles have emerged based on the influence of work by new companies. Meanwhile, the performing idols represent ideal characters that populate a dream world designed according to the dictates of fashion and stardom. All such videos are produced using high-end technology and slick post-production, assuring a high-quality product in terms of light, focus, angle, and color. Despite the high aesthetics and excellent cinematographic work, music videos are still often accused of being simple commercials for the product, although some, such as Jullier and Péquignot (2013, 92), claim that music videos can also be considered as works of art in their own right.

Music Videos and Intermediality

Intermediality is defined by Irina Rajewsky (2005, 46) as a "generic term for all those phenomena that (as indicated by the prefix *inter*) in some way take place *between* media." Drawing on pre-existing visual formats is, therefore, an integral part of each production, and entertainment companies will create a concept (or commission production companies to create one) for each music video. For the first step in this process, visual references are the most important integral component. Stills from films, fashion photos, or advertisements often provide the base material for a new idea for a song, which means that each production results from a mediation process between the enterprise and the realization of ideas suggested by the music video production. This in turn, must consider the song and the image of the idols and the company while finding a balance between cutting-edge popular trends.

The references to the film are particularly complex, as they can inspire visual aesthetics that include the use of light and shadow as a way of creating atmosphere. Intermedial processes can also relate to montage and framing, which may echo cinematographic processes. The use of black stripes, for example, reflects the images of older films due to the comparative size and aspect ratio of the screens, and these limitations can be turned into aesthetic factors. Examples of such techniques can be seen in Seventeen's *HIT* (2019) and VAV's *She's Mine* (2017). Carol Vernallis (2013, 447–458) offers an overview of the most widely used techniques, which have come to set music videos at the same level as films in terms of technical and aesthetic production. Music videos copy rhythms through shots, editing, narrative and large-scale forms as well as performance and sculptural spaces. Vernallis also highlights the importance of intertextuality in making music videos, drawing on Bakhtin's idea of "dialogicity," which in turn builds on the concept of marginalized voices in a monolithic community with specific reference to the groups and their differences from the dominant culture. Bakhtin would consider dialog as the presence of a silenced voice that is heard and that can subvert a more dominant discourse. As the variety of media and formats grew, intermediality became central to the interrelationships between different media, including text, film, radio, music, television, and animation (Rajewsky 2002). As well as its close affinity with cinematography, intermediality can also occur at the level of content and narrative structure. The possibilities are endless and can range between a simple reference to a film genre (for example, the Western), the borrowing of a character (such as Alice in Wonderland in IU's *Twenty-three*) or references that function as quotes as they place concrete visual, audial or verbal references (a painting or sculpture, as in T.O.P.'s 2014 *Doom Dada*), or a quotation by Nietzsche in BTS' 2018 song *Blood, Sweat and Tears*) into the video.

As previously mentioned, many productions undergo different degrees of remediation. This chapter focuses on two examples and two major intermedial practices. First, I discuss videos that explicitly reference cinematographic genres in their aesthetics and narrative structure. Second, I use a number of examples to illustrate the intermedial procedures that construct spaces for critical dialog through their references. The concluding section provides examples that offer a glimpse into the trends which have emerged in 2019–2020 regarding music video as a short art form.

References to Cinematographic Genres: Music Videos as Short Films

Super Junior produced a series of music videos that used references to various film genres. The process began as early as 2012 with *Spy*, which uses elements of the main theme of James Bond films, easily recognizable because of the white spotlight on the silhouette of the figure appearing in front of the camera who turns and points at the spectator with a gun. In 2014, Super Junior released the song *Mamacita* along with a video produced by Zany Bros. In a 32-second introduction accompanied by a melody echoing soundtracks from old Western films, each band member is presented as a bartender, a barber, a bullfighter, and a sheriff, which freeze into a still image that turns into a "wanted" poster. The video sets expectations for its narrative structure right from the start by borrowing techniques from the Western genre and using a defined number of central characters and the basic plot of a manhunt. The sheriff is reading a newspaper, the headline of which reports a runaway thief. The detail of the headline offers narrative information, signals the end of the introduction, and initiates the plot, which intertwines performance settings and the storyline against a typical Western movie backdrop (a saloon and a sheriff's office). Meanwhile, the setting for the performance is reminiscent of a ballroom in an old mansion where elegantly dressed men perform. Their red suits connect with the bullfighter's bright garb and cape to create a continuity with the Western setting presented in a long shot of the street. Characters are then presented in medium and medium-long shots: a chivalrous *toreador*, the town blacksmith, gamblers, and a jeweler. The plot unravels in a series of short scenes: the traveler shows off a crown in his luggage and is attacked by a thief, who escapes with the loot. The next shot features the sheriff sitting in the saloon being alerted by the noise of the robbery. He rushes out to the street, where the thief reappears and shoots him. The camera angles stylistically reflect classic Hollywood Westerns: the medium shot for the interaction between the two men, the close-up of the dying sheriff on the ground, accelerating the rhythm until he dies. In the middle of the video, the dance performance is shifted from the mansion to the dusty street of the Western town, bringing the two narrative lines closer together and intensifying the growing suspense leading to the confrontation between the two men. The lyrics of the song—which is about lost love and deception—are linked to the Western movie plot by the title *Mamacita* and the merging of the two sets at the halfway point of the video. This demonstrates the links between the Spanish title and the Western narrative elements, suggesting a story that takes place in southern US states near the Mexican border. The video's action-packed story of betrayal and remorse becomes fused to the lyrics of a love song.

Further examples of productions that use film genres as the basis for music videos include *Chase me* (January 2017) and *Good night* (March 2017) by the girl-band Dreamcatcher, produced by Digipedi. In line with the group's overall aesthetic, the videos deal with dreams and imagined worlds that are reflected in the lyrics, which can sometimes carry a duality of meaning as a song about a dramatic relationship. This is also the case with *Chase me*. The lyrics tell a story about the seduction of a man who has fallen in love with the narrator (one of the members of the group), who keeps toying with him. The plot of the video strengthens the image of the group members as dreamcatchers, and the video itself develops an atmosphere of suspense by creating frightening scenarios that the protagonist—played by famous actor Cho Tong-hyŏk—has to endure.

The opening scene sets the tone of a horror film. The camera follows a man down a long corridor, with a slight creaking sound effect intensifying the growing feeling of suspense as the camera moves closer as if someone is approaching the man from behind. He stops in front of a door and lifts up the camera he is holding so that the following close-up shows the plate with the room number on it fixed above the door. Medium shots and reverse shots are used when he tries to open the door, which is locked. At the end of the corridor, a girl appears, holding a doll. The next shot shows one of the band members singing, building up the story at the hotel and a performance in the lobby and one of the rooms as a flow of scenes alternate with the storyline of a haunted hotel. The man directs his camera at the girl, but nothing appears on his screen. While the band sings and dances in the lobby, the man enters his hotel room. The parallel montage between the lobby and his room is strengthened by a blend of colors that insinuate continuity in space and time. He takes out old sepia photographs of different girls, shown in extreme close-up to reveal the details of their faces. The rhythm speeds up, showing a medium shot of the corridor turning dark, followed by a medium shot of the vanished girl with the doll before cutting to the girl sitting on the window ledge swinging a watch on a long chain above the man. The shot and reverse shot come at extremely high and low angles, respectively.

   This detailed description of the first one and a half minutes of the video (which is 4:08 min long in total) clearly illustrates the use of cinematographic tools such as camera angles to convey cinematic meaning, with the high angle perspective representing domination and control. Basic horror film genre elements are also used like the rapidly flickering images that blur the boundary between reality and dreams, linking the man's dream to what he had seen before. We see the empty corridor, then the corridor with a girl sitting on a rocking chair, then the empty chair. The strange happenings accelerate, accompanied by faster-paced cuts from medium shots to close-ups in rapid progression: the man spying on the events occurring in the corridor, the girl ripping an eye from a teddy bear, and the man's eyes magically disappearing. The parallel montage is punctuated by a mirror connecting the two worlds until it turns into a window for the ghostly girls while remaining a mirror for the man. He eventually gains access to the neighboring room, where the photo of the group of girls he was carrying with him is now hanging on the wall. The video ends with a black screen and an intertitle that states: "to be continued." The next music video, *Good Night*, begins with the same actor in a study room. Sequences from the past show the girls running through a forest, and the mirror/window link between the parallel worlds is continued. Meanwhile, sequences in sepia tones and black and white evoke the past as well as parts of other dreams, and stories are once more arranged into an accelerating rhythm, alternating between worlds and colors and shot lengths to highlight the entanglement of both worlds to create an atmosphere of anxiety and fear. The styles of both videos are very close to horror films in terms of montage and *mise-en-scene,* as well as the use of light and motifs that create a narrative of a haunted house through cinematic elements. The fact that there is a continuation between the two videos with no overall finale stirs the viewers' expectations of more to come.

Music Videos with "Critical Messages"

While the examples mentioned before strengthen the brand image of the group (as in the case of Dreamcatcher) or serve as an additional attraction for fandom (in the case of Super Junior), some music videos use intermedial references to open a dialogic space that brings into question the themes dealt with in the video.

The music video *Fantastic Baby* by Big Bang was released in 2012 and won several awards, including the 2013 Japan MTV Music Video Award. *Fantastic Baby* is about the pleasure of dancing, spontaneity and atmosphere, and the moment at which people come together and claim the dance floor. The video starts with G-Dragon sitting on a throne, looking straight into the camera and inviting the audience to join him in dancing. There is a strong visual message of rebellious intent. Special police forces protect a territory behind a high fence where signs indicate the prohibition of music. On the other side of the fence, people are wearing what looks like gas masks, which might also allude to the appearance of aliens or outsiders. The masked rebels intend to bring the fence down and attack the police forces to reclaim "free music" and dance. During these sequences, the chorus "I wanna dance" repeats, while the four stanzas emphasizing the concept of dancing as a way of freeing oneself from conventions and restrictions is linked with the concept of youth. This idea of freedom is strengthened by the *mise-en-scene* of the opening sequence, which is reminiscent of the setting of the South African film *District 9* (2009) by Neill Blomkamp, in which aliens live in an isolated suburb that looks like an end-of-the-world scenario. Assuming the reference in the video of Fantastic Baby is deliberate, then the film represents a significant metaphor for a free space created by music and dance in the face of an oppressive system, an aspect reinforced by sequences in which one group member tries to free himself from heavy chains. At the same time, another is brought back to life as the white frost on his frozen body slowly melts. The message of the video is that the power of music can create a free space for expression, dance, and individual styles by referring to the five members of the group, who are all very distinct in style and appearance. This is reinforced during the closing sequence, in which the rebels remove their masks and become recognizable individuals within a group of dancers. In this closing part, the melody and rhythm change, growing closer to the type of Korean folk song commonly played when dancing. At the same time, two bearers of traditional lion masks join in the dancing.

This feature links the video to the *Pukch'ŏng sajanorŭm* ceremony, a ritual to chase away bad spirits by dancing and singing during the night of the first full moon of the New Year. The folk song is *Ta katchi nolja*, a popular children's song that carries the message "let's all play and dance together."[2] *Fantastic Baby* closes by linking back to traditional music and dance, evoking the spirit of Korean resistance to centuries of colonization and oppressive politics.

Another music video that might have some critical undertone is *Nillili Mambo* (2012) by Block B. The title refers to an old Korean folk song that invites people to dance and suggests that the music will impart energy, life, and enjoyment. This message is also expressed in the lyrics as the band invites the audience to join in the dancing as they "take it to the next level" and as the "gritty boys are back." However, the visual narrative of the music video picks up on the rebellious elements of the "gritty boys," challenging the music scene as the group members appear as modern pirates in a harbor city dealing with treasure, gambling, and violent encounters with thugs. The opening sequence shows the group leader, Zico, sitting in a beauty salon next to a wanted poster with his portrait on it by the mirror. A parallel montage of Zico and men dressed in black suits with diamonds in dark cases sets a gangland tone before the insert announces "Blockbuster," (the title of the first album) followed by "Nillili Mambo" (the title of the song)—accompanied by the sound of crossing knife blades. The next establishing shot shows a high-angle panorama of a ship leaving a harbor, followed by a medium-long shot showing the group members from behind. Then a medium shot from a low angle of the group/gang on the boat's bridge shouting. This series of images pick up the ideas of "being loud," "let's shout" of the lyrics, and "lift the anchor" as a metaphor for starting something new and to raise attention. At the same time, the sequence evokes the *Pirates of the Caribbean* film series, even going as far as allowing it to provide the main motif for the song. The songwriter and group leader Zico, with blond dreadlocks, looks a lot like Jack Sparrow, the iconic captain played by Johnny Depp. The character of Jack Sparrow is a positive figure situated as a rebel and outcast who—in his sometimes clumsy way—parodies the outlaw, who could also reflect characters such as Robin Hood, a rebel who subverts the system from outside.

Another film reference comes in later when Block B member Kyung sharpens a knife. Ironically in this context, it is not for a fight but to kill a chicken that escapes. This sequence brings to mind the opening scene of the Brazilian film *Cidade de Deus* (*City of God*, 2002, Brazil) by Fernando Mereilles, in which the members of the gang from the favelas chase after a chicken. This motif announces the pursuit of men at various levels during the film: citizens by the gangs, gang members by rivals, or by the police. It also sets the fast pace for the rhythm of the film, evoking a life lived on the run. The video uses similar extreme camera perspectives (high and low angles) in narrow spaces like corridors or staircases, which evokes a sense of being blocked or imprisoned, as in *Cidade de Deus*. This reference places the video within the tradition of films that deal with the injustice of neoliberal and postcolonial societies, creating parallel communities forced into illegality and violence by an uncaring state.[3]

The lyrics of *Nillili Mambo* promote the idea that dancing can help you forget state control for a while and dance away some of your feelings of repression ("get frantic instead of being calm"). Here again, music and dance create a space where the individual can be free and show emotions. At the same time, the parody of pirate films might suggest a link to the ironic tone of the music video as well as to piracy in the Asian region, which could be seen as a metaphor of American Wild West practices that seem to reach out to the shared dream of wealth and freedom. This invites parallels between emerging states which all share the same growth objectives and appear willing to sacrifice social measures in return for fast economic development. The chorus "Ooh yeah, everyone's surprised and intimidated/ Everyone wake up! Get frantic instead of being calm" is underpinned by close-up shots from a low angle of the singers performing in a narrow staircase that gives the impression that they are being imprisoned and controlled. The song then also acts as an incitement to break free from the control of this prison-like space.

The main message linking the lyrics and the videos of both *Nillili Mambo* and *Fantastic Baby* is an invitation to join the dance in order to free oneself and to rebel against the forces, and to join or support marginalized groups. Music and dance turn into a channel that conveys messages of pursuing individual freedom. In this respect, the references to iconic films from the Global South have some impact on the contextualization of the song texts; both deal with music as an art form that aims to construct and support social consciousness and as an invitation to dance, to move as part of a project that transcends social boundaries. It is also remarkable that both songs refer to folk songs that embody traditional values that have not been influenced by the politics of the postwar period.

B.A.P. (Best Absolute Perfect) is a boy group comprising six members who were with TS Entertainment from 2012 to 2019. At the start of their career, they released two music videos with a commitment to social justice: *Warrior* (January 2012) and *Power* (April 2012), both dealing with the issue of current social injustice status. The texts are explicit, and although the videos do not refer to specific Western films, they do use a set of canonical cinematic tropes—mainly from Hollywood productions—about soldiers and suburban gang warfare. The setting of *Warrior* is dominated by dark colors and cityscapes of graffiti, fires behind cracked windows, and abandoned cars, recalling socially disadvantaged neighborhoods.[4] Rows of television screens are installed in the background of the scene as well as posters on the walls on both sides of the scene that all show skulls. This set evokes a state of total control that entails the disappearance of individuality. The lyrics call for a "revolution"[5] against a system that will betray and kill, echoed in the violent choreography that integrates martial arts moves, as well as shooting, marching, and dancing in the streets as part of demonstrations.

The video for the song *Power* functions similarly, although the setting is no longer urban. Instead, a crashed spaceship in the desert constitutes the backdrop for the choreography, providing a similar potential for protest and revolution in the future. The setting links the video to dystopian scenarios in Hollywood films like *The Book of Eli* (Albert Hughes, Allen Hughes, 2010) or *In Time* (Andrew Niccol, 2011). The video opens with images of cables and pipes that resemble the inside of an engine before the group's leader is seen standing in a cell, shackled in metallic bonds and receiving an injection into his head by a computer-controlled robot arm. Rapid montage reveals the other group members dressed in futuristic clothing, apparently standing asleep in cells, where they receive similar automatized injections. The singing starts with the group leader opening his eyes abruptly. From the next shot onwards, the members are all in front of the cells, with the lyrics denouncing a system of social injustice ruled by financial avarice.[6] The song calls for rebellion against the dehumanizing control that is stressed by the desert setting, which reminds the viewer of post-apocalyptic and dystopian movies such as *Armageddon* (Michael Bay, 1998), and this helps underline the urgency of the action as the members of B.A.P. turn into freedom fighters. The full slow motion shot of the six band members dressed as warriors in black moving in a horizontal line toward the camera is a typical motif—in Westerns as well as war and action films—of the cowboys/warriors/saviors coming home from the battle that saved the community or the world.

As well as the sporadic socio-critical messages that can be found in a number of music videos (for example, BTS' *Not Today* [2017]), intermedial dialogs are also used to provide a kind of meta-perspective on the position of idols—for example in the work of one of the members of Big Bang, T.O.P, who wrote the text and co-directed the music video for *Doom Dada* (2013). Pre-release stills announced that the video would not appeal to majority tastes. It was feted as a very "special music video" with a personal touch, but surprisingly the song and the music video were very successful in various charts, possibly due to T.O.P.'s popularity as an actor. The story behind the video is complex and includes references to various films and epochs as well as the arts in general. In the opening sequence, a group of apes finds a microphone among a collection of bones in the sand, and in learning how to use it, they take an important step in the evolution of music. This is a reference to Stanley Kubrick's *2001: A Space Odyssey* (1968), which also uses apes to represent evolution. The way the idea of evolution and apes is shown in this music video brings to mind the silent film era, in which early photographic apparatus attempted to capture single pictures and present them in a series to represent our evolution from monkeys to human beings.

T.O.P. himself reveals his homage to Kim Chi-un's *Choŭn nom, nappŭn nom, isanghan nom* (*The Good, the Bad, the Weird*, 2008, ROK), a 1930s Manchurian Western that mixes elements of generic and film aesthetics. The zebra and bike scenes refer to this film, while the appearance of T.O.P. with a mustache riding a bicycle is drawn from the film *Un Chien Andalou* (1928, France/Spain) by Luis Buñuel and Salvador Dali. While the reference to Kim Chi-un's atmospheric desert filming underlines the mixing of genres in recent adaptation and transfer processes, the homage to the 1920s and 1930s stresses the link to surrealism and the Dadaist movement in art and film history. Both references contextualize the dream-like arrangement of sequences linked by iconic and/or symbolic connotations. There are also pieces of art such as the painting *The Deer* by Korean artist Kim Hwan-gi as well as a reference in the song lyrics to the African-American painter Jean-Michel Basquiat (1960–1988),[7] as the expression of individual stories turns into an avant-garde montage that contributes to overcoming the diktat of production policies.

A very similar message was offered by G-Dragon in *Coup d'Etat* (2013), two months before *Doom Dada*. *Coup d'Etat* was announced by pictures showing G-Dragon with his head wrapped in red cloth that covers everything but his eyes, which emit an intensive stare. One of the advertising posters showed G-Dragon with a tagline line saying "Coup d'Etat, coming soon" beneath his profile, as if the poster was announcing an impending revolutionary act. This impression was reinforced by the next poster, which added the date "Coup d'Etat. 2013-09-02." The album was released in two versions, one with posters in red, the other one in black, taking on the colors of the political posters of socialist or revolutionary movements from the early twentieth century to the Cuban revolution. The design clearly picks up on a global aesthetic, displaying iconic conventions for the call for rebellion or political upheaval.[8] The music video that accompanies *Coup d'Etat* is particularly interesting. Following discussions on blogs and on Facebook, most fans were impressed despite the video's somewhat fractured narrative line. Almost parallel to the release of the album, G-Dragon reinvented himself as a model for beauty products and fashion, in which he appears as a classically handsome man, for example, in the magazine *ELLE* (02/2014). In the music video, however, he appears in the opening sequences as a deformed creeping creature whose skin is wrinkled and appears too big for the body it covers. In *Coup d'Etat* and *Doom Dada* the singers appear not only as the handsome models usually associated with the Korean pop industry, but as ugly or even ape-like, mocking the importance of physical appearance and referring at the same time to the subversive power of music and arts in general by using a wide range of concrete "quotations" in the case of *Doom Dada* and index-like references in *Coup d'Etat*. A fierce critique of the mass media can be found in both songs, and the videos mark a break from the official discourse and representation of K-pop by underlining the ambiguity of the productions. This might again be part of a marketing strategy, but even if it is, the fact that questioning product concepts becomes part of the product itself foreshadows a turning point in the popular music scene that has developed over the last few years, for example, Rap Monster's *Awakening* (2015), Bobby's *Run Away* (2017), Seventeen's *Trauma* (2017), or even *Ugly* by 2NE1 (2011).

Bringing the Story up to Date: An Ultramodern Snapshot

The two poles between which the diversification and remediation processes take place in K-pop videos can still be observed in videos released in 2020, which will serve as an ending for this chapter as it may mark the beginning of a new style in this rapid production of concepts and aesthetics for a glocal market that is becoming increasingly transnational.

The first example is *Lit* (2020), a song performed by Lay, a Chinese member of the South Korean group EXO (SM Entertainment) who has also developed a career as a solo artist, particularly in South Korea and China. The production illustrates the evolution of music videos toward short cinematographic art forms. This video draws on historical epics, using panoramic shots of a huge cast in the immense courtyard of a palace. The video underlines the message of the lyrics, which examine the lotus flower growing from the mud as a parallel with the development of Lay's own career and his growth to superstardom. The video interweaves sequences, mainly in black and red, in a setting that looks like a royal court, with actors wearing costumes inspired by traditional uniforms, with sequences that show Lay and his dancers dressed in black and in a hip-hop style. The video appears to link an epic past with a bright future, represented by the animated sequences of the golden dragon into which the small flower symbolically turns.

The second example features the Korean-American singer and dancer AleXa, released under the ZB subsidiary of Zany Bros. The first video *BomB* was released in October 2019, followed by *Do or Die* in March 2020 and *Revolution* in October 2020. The storyline of the videos focuses on the re-activation of a cyborg version of AleXa, who is struggling to recompose fragments of her memories. She fights adversaries and monsters in extended martial arts sequences, and the lyrics of each song refer to the evolution of the reactivated cyborg: *BomB* describes the destruction of the world that turned it into a post-apocalyptic space, while *Do or Die* shows how AleXa must face dangerous situations. In *Revolution*, she finally defeats her adversaries. The narrative structure links the three videos and builds suspense from one to the next. The third video ends with AleXa facing herself dressed in armor that is reminiscent of medieval knights. In the logic of the episodic structure, this ending may hint at the continuation of the story in a different setting. As a protagonist, AleXa remains a strong female character. She starts out as a cyborg who turns into a warrior and has a strong resemblance to martyr figures like Joan of Arc. On a visual level, the aesthetics link the three videos to dystopic films. *Do or Die* resembles Fritz Lang's *Metropolis* (1927, Germany) with its large female statue, while *Revolution* has similarities to *Mad Max* (George Miller, 1979, Australia) with its desert-like environment and heavily customized vehicles. As well as the cinematographic aesthetics, the dance performances are surprising as the choreography is as complex and difficult as it once was for boybands. The video includes dances involving anything from six to twenty-one backup dancers, the kind of numbers that had previously only been seen in boy band videos. AleXa plays a strong character in all three videos, as a woman leading her special unit (the dancers) to fight the forces of evil. The role of cyborg has previously been almost exclusively reserved for male characters, with the exception of some rare female superheroes and game characters.

These productions show that music videos are always the result of a large team effort, often with international collaborations that use intermedial references and are always on the lookout for something new and thrilling. In this case, the producer Kim Chun-hong, one of the directors of Zany Bros worked together with creative director Angelina Foss and her assistant Maira Naba, who developed the storyline, the characters, and the performances. This type of collaboration sets new production standards for girl bands and for intermedial dialog, taking into consideration the respective local positions[9] which turn the videos into cosmopolitan productions rather than transcultural hybrids. The use of the term "cosmopolitan" for K-pop productions was suggested by Hyunjoon Shin in 2017. By striving for a globally collaborative process of content and imagery, and by using an international team to develop the strategy as a dialog, both *Lit* and *Revolution* show that production companies are in the middle of a remediation process that continues to accelerate and intensify in a very complex glocal media space.

Conclusion

The examples discussed in this chapter demonstrate the breadth and intensity of intermedial referentiality in K-Pop music videos. The music video as an art form appropriates older forms by using light-hearted parodies of a wide range of iconic cinematic and musical styles to construct new or different connections as variations or new perspectives on intermedial dialog. However, they can also be seen as the basis of a Korean hybridity in music video production, as they open up opportunities for other music and dance styles as well as diverse modes of narration. Meanwhile, references to the aesthetics and motifs of Western film culture can be seen as a strategy that is designed to help embed Korean output into a global setting through audiovisual production. This brings K-Pop international recognition while simultaneously building additional layers of meaning. While it was possible to observe a new wave of music videos that contained aspirations to filmic narratives and cinematographic aesthetics in the first half of the 2010s, we can also see new influences in music videos since 2020 taken from cinematic traditions. This is especially true of productions featuring boybands, such as *Home Run* (2020) by Seventeen, *On* (2020) by BTS, *Basquiat* (2020) by Pentagon, and *Burn It* (2021) by Golden Child. These traditions are also used by solo artists, notable examples being *Love me Harder* (2020) by Woodz and *Thank You* (2021) by U-know (a member of TVXQ). This is illustrative of trends that have come to dominate production flows, which through their intense intermedial practices engage companies with these trends, forcing them to contribute to them. *Basquiat* can be seen in relation to music videos that include rebellious messages, as the young African-American artist Jean-Michel Basquiat was considered an icon of the anti-establishment art scene. The title of the song *Basquiat* was a reference not only to the artist himself but also to the independence he came to symbolize, while the storyline covers the fight against violent oppression. The combination of the title, its historical background, and its narrative elements create a representation of the struggle for artistic freedom. The negotiation of musical, visual, performative, and cinematic elements that respond to trends and expectations while simultaneously creating new narratives and aesthetic trends remains the only constant in the rapid flux of K-pop music video productions. Nicholas Cook, speaking about the Eclectic Method, reflects on techniques used in multimedia mashups that seem to catch the essence of the process of music video creation. These reflect the flow of audiovisual products, fashion, music, and dance and their continuous contribution to changes in film aesthetics. According to Cook (2013, 56): "Meaning is negotiated in the act of reception, in the attempt to make some kind of sense of the constant barrage of digital information." This means that we can see the mixture of styles as a direct embodiment of these negotiation processes.

Notes

1. See for example the boy band VIXX with songs and videos like *Super Hero* (2012), *On and On* (2013), *Hyde* (2013) and *Error* (2014). Also Super Junior with *Sorry Sorry* (2009), *Mr. Simple* (2011) and *Sexy, free and single* (2012).
2. I am grateful to Park Sang Mi for the references to the song and the ritual.
3. In an interview with the first producer of Block B, Cho PD, in March 2014, he confirmed that these references played a role in developing the concept. In an interview with Zico, they wanted to be "pirates" in this story.
4. Like the classic *Boyz n the Hood* (USA, 1991) by John Singleton.
5. The second stanza says "It's time to move and the anthem of the strong and weak will break that fight/This is a revolution, a Guernica flow/So everybody keep your head up." http://www.kpoplyrics.net/b-a-p-power-lyrics-english-romanized.html#ixzz3Nld2y69G (last accessed December 30, 2020).
6. The reference to dystopian films to approach the harsh living conditions for the younger generation in a neoliberal system and a very strict education system is frequent in music videos, for example, BTS' *N.O* (2013), Nu'East with *Face* (2014).
7. See for example Marc Mayer's 2005 *Basquiat*: "[…] he painted a calculated incoherence, calibrating the mystery of what such apparently meaning-laden pictures might ultimately mean." (2005, 50). A more recent reference to this artist is the music video entitled *Basquiat* (2019) by Pentagon, which uses him as an icon for creative independence.
8. See for example: King (2012) and Cushing (2003).
9. The cover was designed by South African artist Malcolm Wope. Hairstyle and dance were developed by Foss (Sweden/Chile), Naba (Germany/Burkina Faso) and the African-American choreographer Batina Mosley. I had the chance to stay in contact with the team after my first interviews in Seoul in April 2014 so that I could have some insight in the production process.

REFERENCES

Anderson, Crystal S. 2014. "That's My Man! Overlapping Masculinities in Korean Popular Music." In *The Korean Wave. Korean Popular Culture in Global Context*, edited by Yasue Kuwahara, 117–132. New York: Palgrave Macmillan. https://doi.org/10.1057/9781137350282_7.

Anderson, Crystal S. 2020. *African American Popular Music and K-pop*. Jackson: University Press of Mississippi.

Choi, JungBong, and Roald Maliangkay. 2015. *K-Pop*. New York: Routledge.

Cook, Nicolas. 2013. "Beyond Music: Mashup, Multimedia Mentality, and Intellectual Property." In *The Oxford Handbook of New Audiovisual Aesthetics*, edited by John Richardson, Claudia Gorbman, and Carol Vernallis, 53–76. Oxford: University Press.

Cushing, Lincoln. 2003. *Revolución! Cuban Poster Art*. San Francisco: Chronicle Books.

Dal, Yong Jin. 2016. *"New" Korean Wave. Transnational Cultural Power in the Age of Social Media*. Chicago: University of Illinois Press.

Epstein, Stephen, and Rachel M. Joo. 2012. "Multiple Exposures: Korean Bodies and the Transnational Imagination." *The Asia-Pacific Journal* 10 (33/1): 1–17.

Epstein, Stephen, and James Turnbull. 2014. "Girl's Generation? Gender, (Dis)Empowerment, and K-Pop." In *Korean Popular Culture Reader*, edited by Kyung Hyun Kim, 314–336. Durham/London: Duke University Press.

Fendler, Ute. 2017. "SM Entertainment: From Stage Art to Neo Culture Technology (NCT)." *Culture and Empathy* 2 (3): 206–219. https://doi.org/10.32860/26356619/2019/2.3.0005.

Fuhr, Michael. 2016. *Globalization and Popular Music in South Korea. Sounding out K-Pop*. New York: Routledge.

Ho, Swee-lin. 2012. "Fuel for South Korea's 'Global Dreams Factory:' The Desires of Parents Whose Children Dream of Becoming K-Pop Stars." *Korea Observer* 43 (3): 471–502.

Howard, Keith. 2006. *Korean Pop Music. Riding the Wave*. Kent: Global Oriental.

Howard, Keith. 2014. "Mapping K-Pop Past and Present: Shifting the Modes of Exchange." *Korea Observer* 45 (3): 389–414.

Jullier, Laurent, and Péquignot, Julien. 2013. *Le Clip—Histoire et esthétique*. Malakoff : Armand Colin.

Kang, Inkyu. 2015. "The Political Economy of Idols. South Korea's Neoliberal Restructuring and Its Impact on the Entertainment Labour Force." In *K-Pop. The International Rise of the Korean Music industry*, edited by JungBong Choi and Roald Maliangkay, 51–65. New York: Routledge.

Kim, Chang Nam. 2012. *K-Pop. Roots and Blossoming of Korean Popular Music*. Seoul: hollym.

Kim, Do Kyun, and Min-Sun Kim. 2011. *Hallyu. Influence of Korean Popular Culture in Asia and Beyond*. Seoul: Sunpress.

Kim, Eu Min, and Jiwon Rioo. 2007. "South Korean Culture Goes Global: K-Pop and the Korean Wave." *Korean Social Science Journal*, 34 (1): 117–152.

Kim, Kyung Hyun. 2014. *The Korean Popular Culture Reader*. Durham: Duke University Press.

Kim, Youna. 2013. *The Korean Wave: Korean Media Go Global*. London/New York: Routledge.

King, David. 2012. *Russian Revolutionary Posters: From Civil War to Socialist Realism, from Bolshevism to the End of Stalin*. London: Tate Modern.

Lee, Sangjoon, and Abé Mark Nornes, eds. 2015. *Hallyu 2.0. The Korean Wave in the Age of Social Media*. Ann Arbor: University of Michigan Press.

Maliangkay, Roald. 2013. "Catering to the Female Gaze: The Semiotics of Masculinity in Korean Advertising." *Situations* 7 (1): 43–61.

Mayer, Marc. 2005. *Basquiat*. New York: Brooklyn Museum.

Nam, Kim Chang. 2012. *K-Pop: Roots and Blossoming of Korean Popular Music*. Seoul: Hollym.

Rajewsky, Irina O. 2002. *Intermedialität*. Basel/Tübingen: A. Francke.

Rajewsky, Irina O. 2005. "Intermediality, Intertextuality, and Remediation." *Intermediality: History and Theory of the Arts, Literature and Technologies* (6): 43–64.

Shin, Hyunjoon. 2017. "K-Pop, the Sound of Subaltern Cosmopolitanism?" In *The Routledge Handbook of South East Asian Popular Culture*, edited by Koichi Iwabuchi, Eva Tsai, and Chris Berry, 116–123. London: Routledge.

Shin, Hyunjoon, and Seung-Ah Lee. 2017. *Made in Korea. Studies in Popular Music*. New York: Routledge.

Song, Myoung-Sun. 2019. *Hanguk Hip Hop. Global Rap in South Korea*. Palgrave Macmillan.

Sun, Jung. 2010. *Korean Masculinities and Transcultural Consumption. Yonsama, Rain, Oldboy, K-Pop Idols*. Hong Kong: Hong Kong University Press.

Vannini, Phillip, and Scott M. Myers. 2002. "Crazy About You: Reflections on the Meanings of Contemporary Teen Pop Music." *Electronic Journal of Sociology* 6. Last Accessed February 2, 2021. https://www.sociology.org/ejs-archives/vol006.002/vannini_myers.html.

Vernallis, Carol. 2013. "Music Video's Second Aesthetic?" In *The Oxford Handbook of New Audiovisual Aesthetics*, edited by John Richardson, Claudia Gorbman, and Carol Vernallis, 437–465. Oxford: University Press.

Willoughby, Heather A. 2006. "Image Is Everything: The Marketing of Femininity in South Korean Popular Music." In *Korean Pop Music. Riding the Wave*, edited by Keith Howard, 99–108. Kent: Global Oriental.

Yoon, Kyong. 2018. "Global Imagination of K-Pop: Pop Music Fans' Lived Experiences of Cultural Hybridity." *Popular Music and Society* 41 (4): 373–389.

PART III

Transformed Language

INTRODUCTION

Lucien Brown

The two chapters in the linguistics part of this volume provide contrasting—but at the same time—complementary analyses of the position of the Korean language vis-à-vis questions of Korean identity on the contemporary world stage. The first is authored by Professor Young-Key Kim-Renaud, Professor Emeritus of Korean Language and Culture and International Affairs at The George Washington University and one of the most eminent international figures in Korean linguistics. Her essay is titled *Korean Language, Power and National Identity*. The second, authored by Ms. Soyeon Kim and myself at Monash University is titled *Swearing Granny Restaurants: An International Perspective on Rudeness in Korean*.

Kim-Renaud's chapter provides a comprehensive and poignant overview of how the Korean language has emerged over the past 100 years or so as an important marker of Korean national identity. The author locates the emergence of nationalistic sentiment in the Korean language in the Japanese colonial period, during which the Korean language was oppressed by the colonial powers, who were very much aware of the power of linguistic symbolism. During this period, the Korean linguist and patriot Chu Si-gyŏng (1876–1914) coined the term Hangul (The Korean/Great/Unique Script) as a new name for the Korean script and maneuvered the Korean alphabet as what Kim-Renaud refers to as the "ultimate symbol of Korean identity." In the postcolonial and postwar era, Korean scholars turned their attention to restoring the purity of the Korean language, for instance, by removing Japanese loan words.

What is remarkable about Kim-Renaud's approach is how she manages to link these historical accounts to the linguistic lives of younger generations in South Korea today, who are increasingly cosmopolitan and outward-looking in their perspectives. These new generations of South Koreans reject Sino-Korean words and the study of Chinese characters, which are seen as outmoded, unfashionable, and impractical. At the same time, they embrace linguistic innovation, including the inventive use of English and other loanwords in neologisms, and creative expressions used in online environments and marketing. This proliferation of neologisms and English-based expressions is viewed by some as a new threat to the "purity" of the Korean language. Kim-Renaud, however, has a different perspective. She sees this creative language usage as indicative of a new linguistic security and self-esteem of a younger generation fortunate enough to have an independent and flourishing language of their own. Seen from this perspective, the younger generations' ability to innovate with the modern language is the ultimate privilege afforded to them by the struggles of their predecessors dating back to the colonial period.

In contrast to the expansive overview of Korean linguistic identity offered by Kim-Renaud, Kim and Brown's chapter focuses on just one phenomenon, and one which is a rather more unlikely symbol of Korean linguistic identity. The phenomenon in question is the emergence of "swearing granny restaurants" (*yokchaengi halmŏni ŭmshikchŏm*): eating establishments in which elderly female owners replace the more customary use of honorifics and polite niceties with swearwords and personal insults. Through analyzing YouTube videos that portray Korean content creators visiting a "swearing granny restaurant" in Korea and a supposed US equivalent, we gain a perspective on how rudeness is perceived in cross-linguistic contact. The authors demonstrate how Korean "swearing granny restaurants" make use of tropes of kinship that result in the use of the swearing by the "grannies" being perceived as an elder being endearing and intimate toward her younger customers, rather than impoliteness per se. As Korean culture becomes more globalized, the authors argue that rude language and slang more generally can emerge as alternative symbols of Korean culture, as shown by the appearance of the term "K-Slang" in recent years.

Although these two chapters are quite different in their content matter and, most notably, in their scope, there are important similarities in their approach. Both of the chapters see language not merely as a grammatical and phonological system used for conveying information, but also as a resource for communicating social messages and a form of cultural capital. As such, the approaches taken in these chapters are consistent with indexical approaches to sociolinguistics (e.g., Agha 1993; Ochs 1990; Silverstein 2003) in which language is seen as indexing social meanings. The symbolic cultural value of the Korean language was previously summarized in Harkness (2015) who recognized four of what he dubs "linguistic emblems" of South Korea: (1) Deference and demeanor indexicals (i.e., honorifics and politeness), (2) Hangul, (3) English, and (4) slang. The fact that these four areas of Korean language have particular power as linguistic emblems is confirmed by the chapters appearing in this volume, the content of which corresponds very closely to what Harkness proposed. These chapters thus follow Harkness in seeing certain fractions of linguistic repertoire as standing for or representing society through a formal resemblance or shared quality as linguistic *emblems*. These emblems may be dominant ones (as is the case with Hangul), or emergent ones (as in the case with English-based neologisms and impoliteness). I hope that these two chapters will play a role in heralding in a new wave of studies into the indexical properties of the Korean language.

References

Agha, Asif. 1993. "Grammatical and Indexical Convention in Honorific Discourse." *Journal of Linguistic Anthropology* 3 (2): 131–163.
Harkness, Nicholas. 2015. "Linguistic Emblems of South Korean Society." In *The Handbook of Korean Linguistics*, edited by Lucien Brown and Jaehoon Yeon, 492–508. Malden, NJ: Wiley-Blackwell.
Ochs, Elinor. 1990. "Indexicality and Socialization." In *Cultural Psychology: Essays on Comparative Human Development*, edited by James Stigler, Richard Shweder and Gilbert Herdt, 287–308. Cambridge: Cambridge University Press.
Silverstein, Michael. 2003. "Indexical Order and the Dialectics of Sociolinguistic Life." *Language & Communication* 23 (3–4): 193–229.

CHAPTER 8

Korean Language, Power, and National Identity

Young-Key Kim-Renaud

Language is a fundamental human faculty shared by all people, but at the same time, it is what distinguishes one person from the other. Language is often referred to as if it were a person. Thus, one talks of "language family," "ancestral language," "sister language," "daughter language," "related languages," "language divergence," "language mixing," and even "language death." Language is, for most people, the first and the most common representation of personal identity. In modern Korean discourse, it is a matter of empowerment to a degree not commonly observable in other languages. These two aspects of language, identity, and empowerment, make an important but unexplored focus in Korean Studies today, especially with a considerable number of Koreans residing all around the world, in addition to the divided nation of North and South Korea.

Y.-K. Kim-Renaud (✉)
George Washington University, Washington, DC, USA
e-mail: kimrenau@gwu.edu

© The Author(s), under exclusive license to Springer Nature Switzerland AG 2022
A. D. Jackson (ed.), *The Two Koreas and their Global Engagements*,
https://doi.org/10.1007/978-3-030-90761-7_8

Korean Language Purification Movement

History has taught us that some languages do undergo "natural" death (Crystal 2002), and that all languages transform themselves through time and space in different ways, although the change usually follows a set of principled possibilities available to human beings. A language also borrows constantly from other languages regardless of the way the contact may have been made. This is essentially what most modern, especially Western, linguists accept as the nature of language and make it an essential subject of their scientific inquiry (Fromkin et al. 1974/2014; Jackson and Stockwell 2011).

However, both in North and South Korea, linguistic independence, which has been guarded jealously by many as the ultimate sign of political independence, has been closely connected to nationalism. As King (1997, 109) notes, "National pride needs language as a resource at both the practical and sentimental levels." As South Koreans have become determined to find a significant place on the world stage, backed by their recent economic, political, and societal development, Korean people have evolved in their attitude toward their own language and also toward foreign languages. There is a direct relationship between the degree of the national sense of self-esteem and that of people's linguistic open-mindedness. The level of Korean language maintenance among different groups across the Korean diaspora is varied as different equations, including the social status they enjoy in the societies they live in, are at work in calculating their linguistic and cultural power.

In the postcolonial and postwar era, on both sides of the 38th parallel, there has been a specific movement to "purify" the Korean language, to make it shed all traces of what most, if not all, Koreans considered a shameful colonial past, and most urgently, the foreign—especially Japanese—elements that have seeped into the language. S. Robert Ramsey wonders about this fixation and provides an answer to his own question as follows:

> ...We Americans, with our laissez-faire attitude about language, have great difficulty understanding why Koreans would care so much about word origins. Why on earth would they want to purge perfectly good words from their language just because the words happen to come from Japanese? (I suspect all Westerners with any knowledge of the two languages have thought about this matter.) In a discussion Professor Lee [Yi Ik-sŏp] and I had about the subject one day, I remember vividly a poignant story he

told me about how, as a first grader in a country school, he was given strict order to stop using his Korean name. Cultural and linguistic identity becomes more important to a people who have had theirs threatened. (Lee and Ramsey 2000, x–xi)

One of the world classics which every contemporary Korean has grown up reading is "La dernière classe [The Last Class]" by Alphonse Daudet (1840–1897) published in 1888, not long after the Franco-Prussian War, 1870–1871. This war was provoked by the Prussian chancellor Otto von Bismarck as part of his ambition for a unified German Empire. As a result of the war, Alsace, except the Territory of Belfort, and a large part of Lorraine were ceded to Germany, which on Jan. 18, 1871, in the Hall of Mirrors at Versailles had been proclaimed an empire under Wilhelm I (Encyclopedia.com).

"The Last Class" by Alphonse Daudet (1888/1930) is a simple but dramatic story told, through the mouth of a young French schoolboy named "Franz," of the day his people were notified that their language would be taken away from them. This is one of the stories in a collection called *Contes du lundi* [Monday Tales], which demonstrates the author's power of controlled bleakness at its height. What moves Koreans deeply is much more than Daudet's touching narrative style with vivid and realistic sensitivity. Korean readers embrace this story, literally replacing the word "French" with "Korean." They take this story as their own. They collectively are reminded of the days when Koreans were told that they could no longer use the Korean language in any official and even some social situations. Koreans had to change not only their given names, but even their family names into Japanese or Japanese-sounding ones. The little Franz is the little Ik-sŏp. When Franz mentions how his teacher, Monsieur Hamel, in his most solemn tone wearing his formal garb, said, "il fallait la garder entre nous et ne jamais l'oublier, parce que, quand un peuple tombe esclave, tant qu'il tient bien sa langue, c'est comme s'il tenait la clé de la prison [You must keep (our language) among ourselves and never forget it, because when people become enslaved, as long as they hold on to their language, it's like holding a key to their prison.]" (Daudet 1888/1930, 6), Koreans listen to Monsieur Hamel, as if he were speaking to them.

Korea had its own voice. Speaking to its people simply but with great power and eloquence, Han Yong-un (1879–1944), a patriot, reformer, and prophetic Buddhist-monk, who helped draft the 1919 Declaration of

Independence and was one of its signers, gave courage and hope through his poetry to his people who had lost their country. Han writes his feelings about the Korean-alphabet Day, which was designated and celebrated as "Kagya Nal [ABC Day]" by the Korean Language Society (*Chosŏnŏ Hakhoe*, now called *Han'gŭl Hakhoe*) since 1926, in a letter to the *Tonga Ilbo* published on December 7, 1926. The following are two excerpts from the letter whose full text is given in Kwon (2013):

> <가갸날에 대하여>
>
> -한용운
>
> ... 가갸날에 대한 인상을 구태여 말하자면, 오래간만에 문득 만난 님처럼 익숙하면서도 새롭고 기쁘면서도 슬프고자 하여, 그 충동은 아름답고 그 감격은 곱습니다. ˆ 한편으로는 쟁여 놓은 포대처럼 무서운 힘이 있어 보입니다. ...
>
> On Kagya (ABC) Day
> ... If you insist that I tell my impressions of the Kagya Day,
> I'd say it is at once so familiar and yet so novel,
> just like a nim (loved one) that suddenly appeared after a long separation.
> At once joyful and sad,
> the passion of the moment is beautiful,
> and the overwhelming emotions pure and lovely.
> At the same time, it seems to possess formidable power
> like a battle-ready turret ...
>
> - by Han Yong-un

The letter contains a poignant poem, also titled "Kagya Nal," and its words are memorable:

> <가갸날>
>
> -한용운
>
> ... 그 속엔 우리의 향기로운 목숨이 살아 움직입니다.
> 그 속엔 낯익은 사랑의 실마리가 풀리면서 감겨 있어요....
>
> Kagya Day
> ... In it our fragrant life breathes and moves.
> In it I see the end of the thread that coils around the familiar love....
>
> - by Han Yong-un

Hangul (The Korean/Great Script) was the new name for the Korean alphabet connoting a highly nationalistic tone made up by a patriotic linguist, Chu Si-gyŏng, in 1910 when Korea lost its independence to Japan, replacing its original name, *Hunmin Chŏng'ŭm*, is commonly viewed as the ultimate symbol of Korean identity (Kim-Renaud 1997, 1).[1] In this poem, Hangul—referring to both the spoken and the written Korean language—is identified with the *nim* "loved one," a metaphor for the motherland. Here the word, *nim*, the object of respect, affection, and pride, is compared to a departed or lost lover. For Han Yong-un and many other independence fighters, holding on to the national language was more than holding the key to the prison, but it was like guarding an invincible stronghold that made them secure, powerful, and victorious.

The Japanese were very much aware of this linguistic symbolism and considered Korean linguists and language teachers as dangerous agitators and rebels that had to be suppressed, especially from 1937 to 1945. The Japanese persecuted not only those Hangul scholars and teachers, who carried out a massive campaign against the colonial policy to abolish the Korean language, symbolically and actually annihilate Korean national identity itself, but also those who did no more than compile the Korean language dictionary. Some Japanese linguists became the active agents of the Japanese imperial policy, keen on absorbing the Korean nation into the Japanese. As early as 1910, a highly respected Japanese linguist Kanazawa Shōzaburō concluded that the Korean language was a dialect of Japanese—something like Rukyuan (Lee and Ramsey 2000, 131), which thus meant, for Koreans to learn Japanese was nothing more than regional dialectal speakers learning the standard language.

It is no wonder that Korean scholars' attention turned to "restoring the Korean language to its former sovereign status" when the country was finally liberated. In both North and South Korea, the first agenda in linguistic restoration was to "eradicate the Japanese infiltration" in the Korean language. Often, rather than going back to old words, new expressions were formed. For example, in South Korea the Japanese loanword *chabuttong* from Japanese *zabuton* "cushion to sit on" has been replaced by a new word, 方席 *pangsŏk* "(lit.) square seat," constructed out of two Sino-Korean roots, 方 *pang* "square" and 席 *sŏk* "seat," but in North Korea, the neologized word is *kkalgae* "(lit.) spreader [something to spread on the floor to sit on]." While South Koreans have continued to enjoy eating "sushi" and "takuan," which are definitely of Japanese origin, newly coined words such as *kimpap* "(lit.) laver-rice" / *ch'obap* "(lit.) vinegar-rice" and *tanmuji* "sweet-pickled radish" replaced the Japanese loanwords *sŭsi* and *takkuang* respectively. Even some words with negative meanings, which Koreans could have kept for the purpose of propaganda saying such words had not even existed in Korean before the Japanese came, were replaced by neologisms. Thus, the Japanese words such as *suri* "a pickpocket," and *yokkodori* "cutting in" have been replaced by neologisms such as *somaech'igi* "(lit.) a sleeve-hitter," and *saech'igi* "(lit.) crevice-hitting" respectively in South Korea, but in North Korea by *konggyŏksu* "(lit.) attacker" and *saich'igi* "(lit.) crevice-hitting [with an earlier orthography 사이 *sai* for "crevice"]" respectively. The Japanese word *bento* for "lunchbox" has been replaced in South Korea by *tosirak*, retrieving the native word *tosŭlk*, and by a neologized *kwakpap* (lit. "boxed rice") in North Korea. For Koreans, whatever sounded Japanese in their language was seen as a legacy of the Japanese occupation and a painful memory of their recent past. So, even some loanwords from other foreign languages that came through Japanese have been replaced, often by what Koreans thought was closer to the pronunciation of the original language or the Korean-style pronunciation of it. Thus, *k'at'eng* "curtain" has been replaced by *k'ŏt'ŭn*, although in North Korea it was replaced by another neologism, *ch'anggarimmak* "(lit.) a screen hiding the window."[2]

As the above examples show, various strategies at getting rid of Japanese loanwords and Japanese-sounding expressions resulted in major differences, including the foreign words that were introduced to Korean via Japanese, such as *patteri*, which now seems to coexist with the form *paet'ŏri*, which is a more direct borrowing from English word *battery*.

In spite of similar goals, there is a fairly large gap between the standardized languages of South and North Korea, *P'yojunŏ* "Standard Language" and *Muhwaŏ* "Cultured Language" respectively. The reason is not just their years of no contact with each other, but because standardization was not achieved before the country was divided, and divergent language policies since the separation have led them farther apart. Many linguists, including King (1997, 143), see linguistic unification in Korea as a difficult goal to achieve.

New Consciousness and Pride in the Korean Writing System

Attempts to purify the Korean language have gone beyond weeding out the Japanese element in Korean. With a new consciousness and pride in the simple and efficient Korean writing system, many realized that doing away with the Chinese writing not only freed them from the long cultural domination of Chinese over Korean, but provided a way of eliminating illiteracy. As King Sejong said in his Preface to *Hunmin chŏng'ŭm*, writing in Chinese has been a major stumbling block for literacy in Korea not only because it is a writing system for a foreign language but also because of its inherently complex makeup as a script with an overwhelming number of characters, each containing an indication of pronunciation as well as that of meaning. (Kim-Renaud 2000, 20).

There is, both in North and South Korea, a general aesthetic appreciation of the native words, compared to Sino-Korean based expressions, perceived as overly formal, aloof, and unfriendly, even for those who are far from being nationalistic. From eliminating Chinese characters, North-Korean language planners went further to eradicating Sino-Korean-based expressions from the language, often by "translating" them into artificially "pure" Korean. J. Song (2005, 172) reports that by one count, as many as 50,000 new words have been created in the process.

The neologisms concocted in this manner are sometimes unintelligible or hilarious to South Koreans. Such extreme measures taken by North Koreans are often watched with apprehension by North Korean observers in the South. However, in my view the few new lexical creations will be only a small part of the problem in the case of reunification. Words like *ton chari* "(lit.) money seat" in place of *kyejwa* "bank account" to refer to the bank account and *pokkŭm mŏri* "(lit.) fried hair" in place of *p'ama* "perm" introduced to Korean via Japanese, however, could be easily accepted with repeated hearing, even if they may sound quite strange and unnatural to an unaccustomed ear at first.

In North Korea, purification in this narrow sense is complicated by the existence of nativized Sino-Korean lexis and Sino-Japanese vocabulary. There is an inevitable decision to be made as to which of the Chinese borrowings is perceived as having Sino-Korean roots. The choice is rather arbitrary—and it has got to be. As is well known, the long and deep cultural relationship with China, in which China was a dominant force, resulted in the Korean language being filled with expressions either directly borrowed from literary Chinese or created using Sino-Korean roots. Once embraced as Korea's own, Chinese words and roots have become part of the Korean lexicon, subject to the Korean linguistic rules and change over time. Some words came not only through written Chinese but spoken forms so long ago that their Chinese origin is completely beyond the speakers' consciousness. Some by now famous examples include *put* 붓 "brush," *mŏk* 먹 "calligraphy ink (stone)," and *chimsŭng* 짐승 "beast." Some words traditionally thought of as very Korean such as *munŭi* 무늬 "pattern" and *kŭl* 글 "writing" are now hypothesized as originating as Chinese borrowings by historical linguists, as noted by K. Lee (1991, 227). These and other words are so nativized that it would be almost impossible and incorrect, or awkward to write them in Chinese characters when writing in mixed script.

Koreans, including the purification zealots, did not realize that many Sino-Korean words were direct importations of newly coined words by the Japanese using Sino-Japanese roots. Many of them were new concepts from the West, for which no East-Asian equivalents existed, e.g., 民主主義 "democracy," 教育 "education," 先生 "teacher," 科學 "science," 企業 "enterprise," 哲學 "philosophy," and 政治 "politics," came to be used in Chinese, as well. Since Japan opened its doors to the West first, it was natural that such new words were created there, and Koreans have just left them unchanged, as they should be.

As in all language use, the question of naturalness and appropriateness does play a role. Naturalness is closely connected to familiarity and aptness in the society in question. Formal terms, especially academic and scientific, sound more natural when they are based on Sino-Korean roots rather than pure Korean roots, in the same way that Greco-Roman roots rather than local language roots are in Indo-European languages. Thus, early anti-Hangul-*only* (*han'gŭl chŏnyong*) advocates ridiculed those engaged in the language purification movement with comical-sounding examples such as *pŏn'gae-ttalttari* 번개딸딸이 "(lit.) lightening ring-ringer" for "telephone," *omsari* 옴살이 "(lit.) moving life" for "animal" and *paekkot kyejip k'ŭn paeum cip* 배꽃계집큰배움집 "(lit.) a big pear blossom learning house for women" for *Ewha Womans University* (Kim 1988, 559). Nevertheless, many newly coined words such as *mŏrimal* 머리말 "(lit.) head word" or *tŭrŏgamyŏ* 들어가며 "(lit.) entering" for "preface" and *maejŭmmal* 맺음말 "(lit.) concluding word" or *nagamyŏ* 나가며 "(lit.) exiting" for "conclusion" have become regular dictionary entries and now lead a peaceful coexistence with their original equivalents *sŏron* 서론 "preface" and *kyŏllon* 결론 "conclusion," the difference being perhaps the gentler and more intimate feeling conveyed by the native-sounding neologism.

In South Korea, some of the internet-related words such as *padanaerim* 받아내림 "(lit.) receiving from a higher place" for "download," have become a part of the basic vocabulary, but even there, direct Koreanization of foreign words like 다운로드 *taullodŭ* /taun'lodŭ/ "download" is more common now. This may be viewed as part of the globalization phenomenon involving information technology and other smoother communication between different nations. In fact, it is now considered well-educated and "modern" to mix English and other foreign expressions regardless of the context in South Korea. This clearly suggests that South Koreans, especially younger generations, who have enjoyed a long period of peace and prosperity, feel no longer linguistically threatened and are poised to use whatever seems more appropriate, more appealing, and more exotic. Most importantly, they feel it is natural to mix loanwords as they increasingly participate in global life, as will be discussed below.

Use of the Chinese Script and Misunderstandings of Korea-China Relations

The immediate question on this purification movement is: why only recently has the Korean alphabet been valued in North and South Korea? The Korean alphabet has been available since 1446, and the Chinese script has remained essentially the same in its basic nature. Why did Koreans embrace Chinese so readily and proudly (!) in premodern Korea? Was the prevalent use of Chinese characters a sign of *Sadae chuŭi* (the ideology of "Serving the Great") in reality, as many have claimed both in North and South Korea (e.g., Kim 1978, 455; *DailyNK* 2008; Ku 2011; Chŏng 2016)?

Koreans were never forced by the Chinese to write in Chinese or use Chinese expressions, just as European nations never were ordered to utilize Latin or Greek. Koreans adopted Chinese writing and Chinese expressions, as words carrying new concepts, and as the results of participating in the Great Sinitic culture and civilization. New ideas and belief systems were usually first studied and then imported by curious and "open-minded" Koreans. In the area of philosophy and religion, too,

Koreans were not proselytized but they themselves embraced foreign thought and belief systems out of their own curiosity and zeal for learning. Early Koreans did not seem to worry about their own identity becoming confused or threatened, because they saw Chinese linguistic and philosophical influence as enriching their own culture. Something that was practiced by the Chinese was deemed "proven" worthy of learning because of the Koreans' recognition of the richness of Sinitic culture. Earlier Koreans didn't want to miss what they saw as the best in the world, just as today's Koreans have been fascinated by the US and the Western languages and cultures. A good command of Hantcha has always been a sign of good education and erudition—a status symbol until recently (Lee and Ramsey 2000, 56; Cho 2002; Song 2005, 47 and 60).[3] The same can be said of English for contemporary Koreans.

Koreans also loved being recognized by the Chinese as their worthy, civilized brother, even if only a younger one. Ch'oe Ch'i-wŏn (857–915) was sent to China to study at the age of twelve, which was common practice at the time. Ch'oe was given a post in the Tang provincial government after passing the extremely difficult civil service exam in 874. He served in China for more than a decade and returned to Korea in 885 as an official envoy of Emperor Xizong (Ancient History Encyclopedia). It is said that by the twelfth century, "the Chinese considered Korean celadon the best under heaven and more valuable than gold" (Smith 2000). The fame of Hŏ Nan-sŏrhŏn (1563–1589) spread over Japan and China through her works published by her brother long after her death (K. Kim 2004, 94).

Here, it is necessary and important to reconsider the concept of the so-called *Sadae chuŭi* 事大主義 "Sadaeism," commonly and mistakenly referring to "Korea's subservience to 'the Great [China].'" The expression, "tributary relationship" used by Fairbank • Reischauer and other Westerners, including Hamel, Isabella Bishop, Maurice Courant, also needs to be revisited and corrected, as D. Kim (2010) and others have said.[4] This particular terminology is due to an error resulting from the failure to understand the East Asian, Confucian concept of *li* (禮/礼, Kor. 예) of the diplomatic tribute system, 朝貢 (Kr. *chogong*), which was clearly distinguished from *chogong* (租貢), which is a kind of tax demanded by an overlord state (大君主國, Kr. *taegunjuguk*) of a vassal state (藩國, Kr. *pŏn'guk*). Not only Western scholars but many Koreans themselves took this conceptual error as fact. Koreans for a long time were extremely ashamed of their ancestors for having a subservient position vis-à-vis China, and many tried to justify it as a diplomatic survival tactic (Lee 1984, 189).

Younger scholars, including Holcombe (2001, 165–182) are trying to correct the prevalent distortion as they study the Confucian order which is based on propriety, decorum, ceremony, and rites. The diplomatic tribute system was also an opportunity for Confucian nations to engage in trade, although they regarded it basically a non-productive and base practice. It is interesting to note some definitions of 朝貢 (chōkō ちょうこう in Japanese), which carry the same idea, as quoted below[5]:

- [朝貢/朝貢貿易] 中国の王朝に対する周辺諸国の貢物の献上という形態を採る一種の貿易。["tribute/tributary trade": A kind of trade that takes the form of neighboring countries' presenting tribute to the Chinese dynasty and the Chinese offering gifts in return] (History.net)
- 朝貢 (ちょうこう) は、皇帝に対して周辺諸国 (君主) が貢物を献上し、皇帝側は恩恵として返礼品をもたせて帰国させることで外交秩序を築くもので、使節 (朝貢使) による単なる儀礼的外交にとどまらず、随行する商人による経済実体 (朝貢貿易) を伴うこともあり経済秩序としての性格を帯びることもある [In tributary practice, neighboring countries (monarchs) present tribute to the [Chinese] emperor, and the emperor in return offers a gift for them to bring home, establishing a diplomatic order in effect. The tributary mission is not only a ceremonial one, but entails economic activities by the accompanying merchants and takes on the character of an economic order as well.] (Japanese-Language Wikipedia, n.d.)

It is clear that Sadae (事大 사대 "Serving/Doing the Great") is not a humiliating and gutless behavior but on the contrary, reflects pride in being part of the Great civilization, of which China played a central role. Just as today's Koreans want to be on top of the newest and most advanced forms of discovery and life on the world stage.

The anti-alphabet memorial by Ch'oe Mal-li, vice-director (Pujehak) of the *Chiphyŏnjŏn* (Hall of Worthies), submitted in 1444, soon after King Sejong (1397–1450, r. 1418–1450) revealed his invention of the new alphabet in 1443–1444, offers us a clue as to why people used Chinese characters and respected those who did:

... Only types like the Mongolians, Tanguts, Jurchen, Japanese, and Tibetans have their own graphs. But these are matters of the barbarians and not worth talking about... To now separately make the Vernacular Script is to discard China and identify ourselves with the barbarians. This is what is called "throwing away the fragrance of storax and choosing the bullet of the preying mantis." This is most certainly a matter of great implication for our civilization!

—Tr. by Gari Ledyard

King Sejong treated those who had objected to the alphabet in 1444 with light and brief chastisement, because Ch'oe Mal-li's disapproval exemplified an abhorrence and contempt of the new writing system that was clearly shared by officials and scholars. Most important, Sejong never actually suppressed this dissent, and his royal answer to Ch'oe and his colleagues ended the next day (Ledyard 1997, 73):

> Unlike Khubilai Khan who may have tried to make the newly created 'Phags-pa script replace the Uighur alphabet that was in use among the Mongols since the early thirteenth century without success (Ledyard 1998, 406), King Sejong never issued an edict requiring the use of the Korean alphabet instead of Chinese. While he was empowering the weak and the uneducated with his new invention, he never intended to change the power structure through the written language.

The prescient king knew consciously or subconsciously that trying to completely replace Chinese characters with Hangul would lead the latter's fate to that of the 'Phags-pa script.

Chinese was an important key to social and political power in a meritocratic system, in which literacy meant knowing Chinese classics and being able to analyze them and compose treatises in Chinese, as shown by three facts:

1. Kwagŏ, the national civil service examination system, first administered during the Silla dynasty in 788, and established in 958 during the Koryŏ dynasty and lasted to the end of the Chosŏn dynasty, tested candidates' humanistic knowledge and their analytic power, based on literary Chinese and Chinese classics.
2. All "serious/official" documents were written in Chinese characters. Those who did not know them had no agency in legal, political, and social affairs.[6]

3. Because only the well-born could afford to devote long hours to learning Chinese characters and Chinese classics, it was one way of maintaining the class system and the prevailing power structure.

If knowledge in literary Chinese was a prerequisite to becoming a gentleman-scholar, speaking the Korean language never really was considered a shameful or "vulgar" act by the Koreans, as has often been stated or implied (Kim 2005). The power and respect Chinese competency enjoyed was for classical, literary Chinese. Having oral proficiency in Chinese impressed no one. On the contrary, a handful of those who did, such as interpreters, were held in a rather low social status and were even barred from the civil service examinations that served as the gateway to a life of political and social prestige (Wang 2014, 58). King Sejong, who studied spoken Chinese, was a clear exception. Socially, there is every indication that the proper use of grammatical honorific markings, clearly Korean and not Chinese, was a sign of proper upbringing (Kim-Renaud 2000).

While knowing literary Chinese and Chinese classics served Korean leaders' self-esteem, empowerment, and identity as part of the general "greatness," their true dignity and identity as Koreans came from and was enhanced by such Korea-specific behavior as the proper use of honorifics.

Impact of the Korean Diaspora on Language and Identity

Korea's strategic geographic location in the epicenter of Northeast Asia has been a crucial factor in its political and cultural history–at times a blessing and other times a curse. Korea has figured importantly in East Asia, contributing to and benefiting from a great tradition shared across the region, but also falling prey to her neighbors' ambitions at times. Korea's recent unhappy history has led to the emergence of the Korean diaspora with a vital impact on Korean culture and civilization. For the first time in their long history, during the twentieth century, Koreans started migrating to foreign lands en masse, whether for personal reasons such as professional advancement and marriage or in search of a more favorable political and economic environment, or forcefully driven by foreign powers. There are 7.4 million Korean nationals, expatriates, and descendants living outside Korea as permanent migrants or sojourners as of December 2020 (Wikipedia, n.d.), which is about 10% of the total Korean population in the world.

Although North Korea has remained the most closed nation in the world since 1945, many of its people have crossed the border to the South or escaped to China. South Koreans, freer to travel and emigrate to another country, have also done so. Although children's education is often given as the top reason for emigrating more recently, the continued threat of war and personal desire for freedom from poverty and injustice have also caused many Koreans to voluntarily move to another country, the US in particular.

Since the Korean War, South Korea has been in frequent and substantial contact with foreigners, especially with Americans, who have facilitated much of the 70-year globalization of Koreans. By the end of the twentieth century, South Korea had established diplomatic relations with 175 countries, each with Korean residents (Sohn 1997, 56). Many Koreans have gone to study in the US and returned with advanced degrees in practically all fields. Increasingly, Koreans have come to think that their education is not really complete without study abroad. The United States continues to lead in popularity, but Koreans' study-abroad destinations have now become very diversified. Some chose Europe when they began looking elsewhere than the United States, partly for novelty but also as a form of personal independence movement from American hegemony. Soon, Koreans' consciousness as members of the Asian region led them to Taiwan and Japan, and then to Australia. Russia and China, forbidden territories to anti-communist Koreans during the entire Cold-War era, have also attracted students as places to experience newly accessible, different cultures in order to gain experience and wisdom.

Korea's relationship with Japan has seen rapid and positive progress. However, historical issues including the textbook controversy resulting from a Japanese (ultra-) conservative movement to change their "dark history" of colonial legacies such as Korean Comfort Women and forced labor for Japanese firms as well as the Japanese claim for Tokto Island (called "Takeshima" by the Japanese) occupied by South Korea, keep coming back to rub the wounds that do not heal.[7] However, there have been active exchanges both at public and private levels between Korean and Japanese peoples, who share so many cultural and social values. Korean universities began offering Japanese language and literature courses only in the 1990s, but by April 2010, there were 107 departments offering Japanese language, literature, and Japanese Studies

(Cho 2010). In Japan, where Korean language education has a much longer history, there were 375 colleges offering Korean language courses as of 2003. At the Tokyo University of Foreign Studies, Korean enrollment was the fifth of all foreign languages taught and still increasing (Hideki 2003, 85–86).

Korea's image abroad, especially in Japan, has been uneven and mostly negative for a long time until the late 1980's around the time South Korea hosted the Olympics. Some early Korean emigrants may have excelled as individuals, but they were often dismissed or called "unusual." As a group, Koreans have essentially been treated as unwanted guests even when they were guest workers or forced to live there, as in the case of South Korean nurses and miners in Germany. In addition to the terrible political and economic situation at home, linguistic and cultural differences made them appear "defective" to their hosts.[8] Nevertheless, there seem to be significant differences in attitude among the Japanese, depending on which generation a person belongs to and how conservative a person is.

Until the 1990s, there was little impetus for the education and the use of the Korean language by Korean expatriates and their descendants: They were eager to integrate in their current society, and many thought that alienating themselves from their country of origin in which they had little pride would expedite their assimilation process. As someone who has devoted her entire life to research and education of Korean language and culture as well as to enhancing Korea-US relations, I have observed a sharp turn in this attitude since the 1988 Seoul Olympics, when South Korea began receiving worldwide attention. Koreans became increasingly recognized for their present and past achievements, of which Hangul is a major one. Of course, this change was a direct reflection of how they are viewed by the society in which they live in and quite relatedly, how they view themselves.

Beginning in the early 1980s, the Korean language has been taught in colleges in the US, and the ROK government's financial support has played an important role. By the end of the twentieth century, as many as one hundred colleges and universities offered the Korean language as part of their regular curriculum; and there were 832 informal/community schools at lower levels (Sohn 1997, 68–70). This explosive expansion was due to a combination of related factors: Korea's increased economic, social, academic, sports, and cultural power, combined with growing interest, first by Korean immigrant communities and then by students who had had direct experience with Korea and Koreans or become interested in Korean culture and civilization as part of their knowledge base and future opportunities. The growing recognition of the importance of incorporating Korea in the Asian Studies field and in world history as well as the continued peninsular issues and related job opportunities also contributed to the interest in and the vitality of Korean Studies. More recently, various aspects of Korean pop culture have attracted global attention, especially among young people, many of whom wanted to learn Korean as the first step to learning more about Korea. According to the official ROK government statistics report, foreign students studying in South Korean institutions of higher education have also been steadily increasing. In 2019, there were more than 160,165 foreign students studying in South Korean colleges (Statista.com, n.d.).

Recent Trends in the Use of Hangul

More recent Korean emigrants to the US come from all strata of society. They are generally better educated, and are also better informed about the society they emigrate to, thanks to modern communication channels. Marcus Noland notes that the third wave of Korean immigrants in the US after 1965, "appears to be distinct both from most other national immigrant groups and previous Korean immigrants in that they have high levels of educational attainment, with rates of college education nearly twice the US national average" (Noland 2002, 61). Their number has also increased rapidly. Whatever their original social classes or year of emigration, these emigrants all share their zeal for education, which has been their core value and the most important goal, wherever they have gone. As a result, either they or their descendants have established themselves as respectable members of their new homes through their educational attainment and diligence.

Koreans have been studying Western culture and Western scholarship with ardor since the end of the nineteenth century, just as they studied Chinese classics and adopted many aspects of Chinese culture and civilization previously. Today South Koreans consider themselves world citizens, and many have excelled in various scientific and humanities endeavors. South Korea, where Western Classical music is greatly appreciated, has produced world-famous performers such as the Chung siblings, violinist Kyung-hwa Chung (Chŏng Kyŏng-hwa), pianist/conductor Myung Hoon Chung (Chŏng Myŏng-hun), and cellist Myung-hwa

Chung (Chŏng Myŏng-hwa), and pianists Paek Kŏn-u, Seong-Jin Cho (Cho Sŏng-jin), and Sunwoo Yekwon (Sŏnu Ye-gwŏn); Sopranos Hei-Kyung Hong (Hong Hye-gyŏng and Sumi Cho (Cho Su-mi), composers Yun I-sang and Unsuk Chin (Chin Ŭn-suk), and violinists Sarah Chang (Chang Yŏng-ju).

Thanks to the worldwide activities by musicians such as Hwang Byungki (Hwang Pyŏng-gi), composer and performer of kayagum music, traditional and innovative Korean music performances are no longer a rarity on the global stage. Artists like Kim Hwan-gi, Yi Ung-no, Nam Kwan, Chun Kyung-ja (Ch'ŏn Kyŏng-ja), Nam June Paik (Paek Nam-jun), and Bang Hai Ja (Pang Hye-ja) have shown some of the most creative contemporary artworks in major exhibition halls of the world.

Now we can add very popular K-Pop artists, movie directors Im Kwon-taek (Im Kwŏn-t'aek) and Bong Joon-ho (Pong Chun-ho). The same goes with other fields, including dance, sports, science, and humanities. South Korean politician and diplomat Ban Ki-moon (Pan Ki-mun) served as the eighth Secretary-General of the United Nations from January 2007 to December 2016. As of January 2021, there are four Korean-American members of the US House of Representatives: Andy Kim, Young Kim, Michelle Park Steel, and Marilyn Strickland.

Some South Koreans have continued to be fiercely nationalistic. A handful of people, such as active members of the *Hangul hakhoe* (The Korean Language Society) even look as if they are still fighting for independence. As recently as February 2001, a writer proposed replacing the common loanwords such as *ap'at'ŭ* (apartment) with *sadari chip* "(lit.) ladder house"; *t'erebijŏn* (television) with *sorikŭrim* "(lit.) sound picture"; *pijŏn* (vision) with *kkum kŭrim* "(lit.) dream picture" (Hyŏn 2001, 15).

In plain contrast, younger people are much more open and even enthusiastic toward different cultures. Neologisms based on "pure" Korean roots are made constantly, not because they are nationalistically motivated, but because new words made of pure Korean roots are understood and accepted more readily, even if people are not familiar with what they refer to initially. The motivation and intended effect are of a completely different nature from those held earlier by the "Purification Movement" activists.

Seemingly "natural" reasons for using native Korean words and writing come from:

1. Simplicity and ease in speaking and writing, as there is a one-to-one correspondence between the spoken and written languages when using Hangul;
2. Aesthetic: native words evoke the sentiment of pure, simple, unpretentious, and innocent beauty, compared to Sino-Korean-based expressions;
3. Emotion: Closer to heart and mind;
4. Branding: "Made in Korea".

Increasing International Life, Globalization, and Neologisms

Studies in Murata and Jenkins (2009) show that modern globalization has been both facilitated and reinforced by the spread of English. Chang (2018) demonstrates how the English textbooks reflect the goals of the South Korean government's global education. Their language policies purport to enhance the younger generation's competence in the globalized world by "introducing various cultures of the world into Korea and constructing the historical Korean identity by promoting Korean culture and tradition in the world" (Chang 2018, 83).

For both intellectual and practical reasons, English enjoys prestige and respect. Knowing some more foreign languages in addition to English would inspire awe. Today's relaxed and secure South Koreans, especially young people, not only see nothing wrong with mixing borrowed terms from English, the international language of globalization, but feel they stand out by doing so. Foreign language mixing now also extends to some other European languages, including French.

An interesting phenomenon is that South Koreans are playing with their own language to make it sound foreign. Some very creative names for business outfits in Korea are neologisms made completely out of the native language but they sound like foreign words. Rather than usual nouns or compound nouns for the names of business outfits, phrases and sometimes complete sentences are used. Linguistically, these forms usually consist of open CV (Consonant–Vowel) syllables—often at the expense of orthography and speech protocol of politeness—which are known to be an "unmarked" or a kind of "default" syllable structure naturally preferred universally.

A survey by a daily newspaper (*Hanguk Ilbo*, January 30, 2001) reports the existence of such signs as *panjirang p'inirang* "(lit.) rings and pins, etc.," which is a hanging form with more things to be said as a list, rather than a usual noun form that is used for titles, for example, *changsin'gu* (accessories); *mŏgŭllae sagallae* "(lit.) Wanna eat here or take out?", an interrogative sentence instead of a simple noun like *punsikchŏm* "fast-food store," to be even more shocking, with a highly informal, terse form of address, *panmal*, which would have normally been inappropriate and impertinent to a customer as overly intimate-sounding, instead of more polite, *yŏgiesŏ chapsusigessŭmnikka, ssagasigessŭmnikka* "Would you like to consume it here, or take it out?" In both cases, they sound French.

The same effect is sometimes achieved by manipulating the orthography with an intentional misspelling. For example, I noticed once that a casual-dress store was called 누네띠네 *nu-ne-tti-ne* "(lit.) It catches the eye!", also in a sentence form in *panmal*, which sounds and looks like French or Italian with a wrong spelling and spacing instead of the expected 눈에 띄네 *nun-e ttŭi-ne* with the correct spelling and a space between two words. Another sign 막파라 *mak-p'a-ra* "(lit.) Sells like crazy!", again in a *panmal* sentence form and misspelled, instead of what would have been correctly spelled with the word and syllable boundaries as in 막 팔아 *mak-p'ar-a*, resulting in a form that looks more like Spanish than Korean.

Structural dissection or merger also occurs. The title of a popular song is 올래 *Ol-lae* "(lit.) Will ya come?", which is a complex (verb + ending) form and a part of an interrogative sentence, sounds like the simple Spanish interjection, ¡Olé! A dialectal form in a question sentence, 무까마까 *mukkamakka* "(lit.) Shall I bite/eat it or not?", is without doubt a name for an eatery with a casual/fast-speech form of what would have been written/spoken in Standard Korean as 먹을까 말까 *mŏgŭlkka malkka* with a space between two words, resulting in a single Japanese-sounding word. The English word *utopia* is cut after the first vowel/syllable, and another foreign or Korean word is attached to make a compound noun, for example, *pukt'op'ia* (book-topia), *matt'op'ia* (taste-topia), and so forth, interestingly similar to the rather unusual English neologism shown in words like *dystopia*.

Young South Koreans seem to enjoy appropriating foreign expressions as their own. Examples abound showing how South Koreans Koreanize loanwords with liberty, sometimes in a way incomprehensive to the speakers of the donor language. For example, *A/S* is for "after-sale service," meaning "service under guarantee," and *memo* means "(phone) message." They readily abbreviate words and expressions that seem too long, for example, *rimok'on* for "R/C, remote (control)," *temo* for "(street) demonstration/protest," *terebi* for "TV, television," and *eŏk'on* for "A/C, air conditioner" (Tyson 1993, 30). Meanings change by narrowing or widening the scope or by extension as in the cases of *mit'ing* for "meeting" but meaning "blind date," *sŏbisŭ* for "service" but meaning "a bonus/gift free of charge," and *maensyŏn* for "mansion" but meaning "a big apartment" (Tyson 1993, 32).

Such word plays are particularly popular among the younger generation when communicating electronically. Even a quick look at some electronic chats these days will leave the uninitiated completely lost at the new cyber dialect of Korean that has been created. Dialectal speakers also eagerly participate in e-neologism, creating an e-dialect (Lee 1997). Young people find it novel, chic, humorous, cute, and close to the heart, if a little silly. They usually apply abbreviations and contractions, using the linguistic process commonly used in casual and fast speech, but in a far more radical way both in form and meaning, and also with some semantic representations, not unlike the methods used in shorthand writing. More than anything, it is for young people to exercise their agency and empowerment by having their own language.

Similar things happen in punk music. These youths, in various ways, are constructing new identities for themselves, whether directly connecting to a global youth subculture or becoming completely original, as noted by Stephen Epstein. Epstein offers an interesting analysis on the emergence of punk rock in South Korea, reflecting on various strategies by which "a new generation is appropriating external cultural forms in order to redefine its own position within society" (Epstein 2000, 2–3). These subcultures are not those of stone-throwing demonstrators on the street but they are just as loud and forceful as those who protest against the establishment. These developments reflect breathtaking changes that South Korean society has been undergoing recently.

N-generation[9] products and moods are (re)exported to the United States and neighboring countries. Various Korea towns in big cities of the United States have many entertainment outlets and shops which try to emulate the ambiance of Seoul's Kangnam/Gangnam district. Korean Americans wear Korean-made clothes and carry hairstyles and personal accessories following the fashion in Korea. In Taiwan, Japan, and China, there has been a so-called "Korea Wave (*hallyu*)" or "Craze for all things

Korean" among the young people who appreciate Korean food, movies, dramas, and popular songs, now labeled "K-X" as part of "K-Culture." Many actually study the Korean language. Some of these youths go as far as redefining the very notion of aesthetics. For example, for a long time, Western features were sought after in plastic surgery, but it is reported that Japanese people often choose the "Korean look" (Takayama and Itoi 2001; Yi 2001). Pop music and fashion models also find fans in Taiwan in an unprecedented way (Song 2001).

Chinese and former Soviet Russian Koreans have also shown renewed respect and pride in South Korea's development, since the normalization of their relationships with South Korea and particularly since the Seoul Olympics. However, their relationship with Korea is not as deep, due to their previously strong and now ambivalent relationship with North Korea and also due to the long period without contact. Many Yanbian Koreans in Northeast China have come to South Korea as workers, and some of them have experienced cultural and societal problems. Former Soviet Russian Koreans have also been coming to Korea, but most of them have little familiarity with Korean language and culture. Over time, they have developed a dialect, which they prefer calling *Koryŏmal* (Koryŏ language), which is harder to understand for mainland Koreans, causing them to feel more alienated even when they migrate to Korea (Jo 2018).

Impacts of the Internet on Communication and Attitudes Among Younger Koreans

The internet is transforming how people work, study, shop, and play, as well as stay in touch with each other. In Korea, it is changing how people talk. People are appropriating this technology with a new attitude toward their own language and others' languages, and behave freely in an unprecedented way. Even internationally, there seems to be no longer any reason why things should flow in one direction. Young users are ready to create a new dialect almost instantly, which previously would have taken generations, even centuries. Fouser quotes an example, which would have been unintelligible to most people without his translation. The sentence "Chon sol 2t'ong3ban taeding 010" apparently means "Chŏnŭn Seoule salgo 23sal imyŏ taehaksaeng igo namja" (I am a 23-year-old male university student living in Seoul) (Fouser 2000, 15).[10]

Scholars and policy makers often worry about dialectal differences if and when the Peninsula is reunited. It is hard to imagine what North

Korean youths would think of their South Korean brothers and sisters when they read what appears to them as a wild corruption of language written by their compatriots. After an initial shock, they might even join the creative process, just as some older South Koreans have done. Once they adapt to a new ideology of freedom and individuality, they might do so with a vengeance, just as they would accept and exploit the market economy. Many *kyop'o* (overseas Korean) students and some foreign nationals who have learned the Korean language exchange e-mail messages with young Koreans frequently.

When trademarks with pleasant-sounding CV (Consonant–Vowel) syllables such as *Nayana* "(lit.) It's me, me!" [name of a talent show] reach the international market, it is possible that these neologisms are received by non-Koreans as less strange but just exotic enough to attract their attention. After all, CV syllable types are the most common in all languages of the world. This is the very reason why young Koreans began making up such new forms. If these neologisms are any indication, then globalism and nationalism need not be incompatible.

The young Koreans are in general not fond of using Chinese characters, nor are they well versed in them. They are in some ways victims of capricious educational policies, which seesawed between teaching Chinese characters and not teaching them (Jang 2001). But it is also by choice. It is interesting to note that while those "purification movement" fighters regard Chinese characters as a colonial power, the computer generation, which now includes most South Koreans, simply does not want to use them; it is not only because of their inherent complexity and difficulty, but because they are so cumbersome to use electronically. Publishers avoid using Chinese characters even for academic book titles, which are clearer when written in Chinese, claiming that Chinese-titled books turn people away and do not sell as well. Some critics contend that this is part of a generation that avoids the three D's: "difficult," "dirty," and "dangerous." But most agree with those who say, if things are said and understood without the need to look up the characters as in a live conversation, so can they be read and understood even if written only in Hangul.

Will the Rise of Asia Affect Communication and Identity?

As Asian nations become more influential, Chinese-character education is becoming a renewed issue for the Korean government. Asian visitors and Westerners who know Chinese are surprised at the paucity of Chinese writing in Korea. It is noteworthy that in North Korea, which has been fiercely promoting a Hangul-only policy, learning 3000 Chinese characters is compulsory for seven years from the age of ten. This number contrasts sharply with 1800 studied by secondary school students in the South, which furthermore is subject to an off-and-on implementation (Kim 1999, 93–94). A colleague of mine who served on a panel for the prestigious Asian-Artbook award expressed her frustration at Hangul's "parochial" character. Of course, the books' title and general synopses had to be translated into English, the international language. However, if at least the title page of a strong Korean candidate had Chinese characters, it would have had a universal appeal and a better chance at attracting immediate attention. Nearly all East-Asian art historians, including those from Western countries, read Chinese characters.

Obligatory Chinese-character education: Pros (a) and cons (b):

1. a. Homonyms often result in ambiguity or confusion when written only in Hangul.
   b. Contexts disambiguate most cases, and people have no problem understanding each other, even though Korean vocabulary is heavily based on Sino-Korean roots.
2. a. Premodern literature and historical records might be severed from contemporary Korea. The case of Turkey is a warning in this regard.
   b. These texts can be translated by those who can read Chinese characters and ordinary Koreans can read translated texts as in the case of Annals of Chosŏn dynastic records (朝鮮王朝實錄). The Chinese have successfully converted classic texts into simplified characters.
3. a. Important common knowledge shared with other Sinitic cultures may be lost by Koreans.
   b. Koreans can study Chinese characters separately in order to achieve the same. In fact, there has been a dramatic increase in the number of students studying Chinese.

Some linguists have taken sides on the issue. For example, Young-mee Yu Cho (Yu Yŏng-mi) believes "it is not only all right but better not to use Chinese characters." She notes how Yun Heung-gil (Yun Hŭng-gil) in his short story "Home" written in the 1970s depicts the "weak and incompetent father" clinging to the "pathetic" and "incomprehensible" use of Chinese characters in writing a letter of petition to the authorities to save his family's shack (Cho 2002, 13).

Knowledge and usage of Chinese characters, once a direct mark of competence and power, are now viewed by some younger-generation Koreans as outmoded and useless like uninteresting antiques. King (2015, 8) is very critical of Cho and similar "nationalistic" thinking, which he finds "in stark contrast to the more positive understanding of Cho Dong-il ([Cho Tong-il] 1999, 645), who warns that such simplistic rejection of Korea's cultural heritage is doomed to invite intellectual poverty."

There has been a movement by scholars such as Hyun-bok Lee ([Yi Hyŏn-bok] 1992) to make Hangul a kind of International Phonetic Alphabet with a modification of letters in its inventory. It certainly is feasible to create what may very well be a more logical and practical writing system than the one by the IPA (International Phonetic Alphabet). It is noteworthy that a few Koreans have been on a mission to save unwritten languages from extinction and to ensure linguistic and cultural diversity (Choe 2009). A patriotic sponsor, a lady by the name of Lee Ki-nam (Yi Ki-nam), and a Seoul National University Professor of Linguistics, Kim Ju-won (Kim Chu-wŏn), along with a few other colleagues have tried to showcase the power, science, beauty of the Korean writing system by applying it to write down other unwritten languages. In 2009, finally, an Indonesian minority people of Cia-Cia, has officially adopted the Korean alphabet for writing their own language.[11]

Within Korea, the use of English is becoming widespread. It seems that a modern Korean sense of power derives from being proficient in English (Lee 2006, 2014; Park 2009; Baratta 2014, 54). Contemporary South Koreans are great travelers, and Chung (2011, 9) claims that the use of English on Korean TV is increasing because more and more episodes occur in an English-speaking country or environment. As J. S. Lee (2014, 33) observes, English is a source of stress as well as a medium of humor and may become another determinant of social stratification in Korea. This recent development in South Korea is reminiscent of those days when literary Chinese enjoyed prestige. However, traditional Koreans had a much better grasp of the Chinese classics, even though the transmission was mostly through written language. Although English is freely mixed among educated Koreans, who know both the written and spoken language, Koreans rarely create new words based on English or even Latin or Greek roots, but they still do based on Sino-Korean roots.

Linguistic Empowerment as a Political Issue

Language as a key element of identity is a widely accepted criterion. Linguistic empowerment, whether it is speech or writing, is an influential force and often becomes a political issue. Even in France where "La dernière classe" was produced, suppression of regional native languages continued. For example, as recently as the 1960s, it was prohibited for the people of Brittany (Bretagne) to speak Breton or for Corsicans to speak their own language. It is only today that they are given the option, when native speakers have become rare. Linguistic chauvinism, like any other kind of bigotry, is a sign of insecurity. And as we saw in Daudet's and Han Yong-un's works, this insecurity is at its strongest when that identity is threatened by such things as war or other forms of foreign aggression.

However, "self-interest" is not always what one chooses to push. When one is not just insecure but completely lacking in self-confidence, one does not dare to be nationalistic. Thus, many early immigrants took the road to hide or change their identity, to the extent possible rather than to assert themselves and protest against their wrongful treatment by others. It is well known that many Jewish immigrants changed their names upon their arrival in the States. How Korean immigrants Romanized their names exemplifies some of these variations, which may reveal the psychology behind the choice.

Compared to most immigrants from China who have adopted an American name until recently, few postwar immigrants from Korea did. Only some Catholics felt it made perfect sense for them to use their *ponmyŏng* (original/main name) or Christian names without feeling self-conscious about it. Many Koreans have tried to Romanize their names in ways that their identity might not be obvious. Thus, for the most popular Korean name "Kim," we see various alternate spellings such as "Khim," "Khimm," "Kimme," "Kiem," "Keam," "Kihm," "Gim," "Ghiem," and "Gihm." The famous Korean enlightenment leader and patriot Sŏ Chaep'il chose an apparently unrelated name "Philip Jaisohn" to go by in the US. It is not clear whether he did it to hide his identity or to fit in better in his new society, or even, if he simply wanted to make it easy for Americans to pronounce/remember. What he did was to reverse the order of the three syllables of his Korean name and slightly change the spelling to arrive at a name that sounded like an ordinary American name. Regardless of the reason for his new name, it is significant that he somehow kept his original Korean name there, even though it may not have been easily discernable.

Koreans living abroad thus have been reluctant to change their names completely. It was in part because of the colonial legacy, when Koreans lost their name and through it their identity. More importantly, however, it was a function of how it made sense or felt natural for an adult Korean to be called by another name than originally given. The first-generation Korean immigrants typically aren't comfortable to be called with Western names, which don't fit their "nature," of which face is an important part. Many Catholic Koreans, however, feel it is totally natural and "justified" to use their *ponmyŏng* "Christian / (lit.) original name" in adopting them as their new names. Of course, if one were born in another country, it would be completely natural to give the person a name popular in that country, although a Korean name would typically be given as a middle name.

Korean given names usually consist of two Sino-Korean syllables. Over the recent decades, however, many Koreans began to choose completely native names with no Chinese characters attached to them, such as 빛나 *Pinna* "It is shiny!" All of a sudden, beginning just a couple of decades ago, I have been coming across Western names on name cards and e-mail messages for Korean people who do not meet any of the above criteria. This might be their idea of globalization, or is simply an effort to make it easy for non-Koreans they associate with. This certainly shows how eager Koreans are to be international.

There has even been a controversial proposal to make English the official language in Korea. Proposed as a device for Koreans to participate in global life fully, the idea was first presented in a book by an activist writer, Pok Kŏ-il, in his 1998 book entitled *The National Language in the Age of the Global Language* as a measure of "taming the beast of nationalism," as described by Y. Cho (2002, 15). This certainly is not a pure symptom of Koreans becoming "open-minded." As J. Song (2011, 35) rightly points out, "English in South Korea cannot be understood fully unless it is recognized that its importance has not been as much engendered by globalization as it has been resorted to as a subterfuge to conceal where the responsibility for inequality in education lies within the society."

An increasing number of Korean-American writers are native speakers of English. Richard E. Kim, a near-perfect bilingual, and Chang-Rae Lee, who is only comfortable in English, have won international critical acclaim. They often write about Korean identity and the sense of alienation in one way or the other, but Chang-Rae Lee's *Native Speaker* (Lee 1995), is of particular interest to us in that language is an important metaphor in the matter of a person's identity. This novel received more than eight honors and prizes, including the PEN/Hemingway Award, the American Book Award, and the Barnes & Noble Discover Award. *Time* magazine named the novel one of the Year's Best Books of 1995. The narrator in the book, Henry Park, lists words identifying him that his departing wife left behind in the beginning of the novel. Of the 18 items, the last and the most important, which he calls "her signature" is "False speaker of language." As he struggles between the American identity and the Korean, he spends all his energy to become a native speaker—a true American. Although he speaks perfect English, he is obsessed with the possibility that his non-nativeness might somehow show through.

In the entire novel language and ethnicity or "face," in the case of Korean, are intricately intertwined. It is poignant when Henry says he senses that "some of them [English as a Second Language learners] gaze up at me for a moment longer, some wonder in their looks as they check again that my voice moves in time with my mouth, truly belongs to my face." He finally becomes a native speaker in the end of the novel when he hears his wife "speaking a dozen lovely and native languages, calling all the difficult names of who we are" (Lee 1995, 324).

The language metaphor applies particularly well to members of the 1.5 generation[12] as well as the first-generation immigrants who have gone through the major part of their school education abroad. Facing the urgent necessity to learn the language of the adopted land, the use of their native language is even suppressed by their own parents and teachers. In many cases, they are proficient and functional in neither language, falling right through the cracks. Language handicap is exactly what hampers social advances for nonnative speakers, as soon as managerial positions become a possibility. Some Korean companies, hiring immigrant returnees, also discover that they cannot write a decent memo in Korean, either. Even in the Yanbian area in Northeast China, where

Korean language maintenance has been remarkable, Koreans are discovering that speaking good Chinese advances them far better in their career and social status, and an increasing number of them are leaving the Korean-concentrated area.[13]

Some Koreans still get emotional when their younger relatives from a foreign country visit Korea and cannot communicate with them at all in Korean. They feel sad and resentful, as if their very being were despised or worse, ignored. Not only Koreans in their native land but also some neighbors in their non-Korean-speaking environment may expect them to speak Korean because of how they look. With time, language maintenance will be more and more difficult. In the end, what one has to do is what comes most naturally: descendants of immigrants must become native speakers of the country they are born in. Learning the language of one's ancestors, the language that matches one's face, is a natural act. More important, knowing another language empowers one, and does not diminish one. Also, being a little different by having a second language at hand should be counted as a blessing.

One is always a native speaker when one is comfortable with oneself. A native speaker does not have to learn and speak just his or her native language. Language is power. If more Koreans know other languages than others know Korean, it empowers them so much more. At the same time, unless more non-Koreans learn Korean, Korean native speakers will always have to work in a nonnative language, which puts them at a disadvantage. The need for foreign language studies cannot be overemphasized in a global era. In contemporary South Korea, multilingualism is increasingly admired. In 2018, it was reported that with globalization, an increasing number of K-Pop multilingual idols are entering the industry and it's not just English and Korean that they speak. At least eighteen of them speak more than three languages (Koreaboo.com).

Finally, talking about linguistic empowerment in general, one cannot leave out the North–South relations. If and when Korea is reunified, language power games will immediately start. What will the new country be called—*han'guk, chosŏn, koryŏ*, hannara [country of Han], *urinara* [our country]? In some ways, none of them sounds ideal. What would one even call the Korean language? *han'gugŏ, chosŏnŏ, koryŏŏ, hannara mal* [language of the country of Han], *urinara mal* [language of our country]? These are minor problems that could fire up emotions, and we would be adding more dialects and regions to the existing list. Wishfully, having more language varieties might be one way of getting rid of intolerance toward difference. We should feel lucky at least we do not have to decide which language we should choose as the official language. Standard dialects of the two Koreas are not so different, at least structurally, from each other. Koreans do have one language. They must, therefore, have one identity, even with many variations, which make human beings interesting. The danger is that once Koreans become reunified, they might begin to focus on their differences rather than the commonality they have emphasized so much for so long as *Paedalminjok*, unique people belonging to the same nation.

Conclusion

Language defines the image Koreans have of themselves and want to manifest to others. Their attitudes toward other languages and writing systems have constantly evolved and will continue to change. A modern-day Sadae persists, that is basically a positive and healthy ideal. Yet, there is a general switch in the notion of linguistic empowerment in that the greatness they would like to emulate or be part of is not monolithic. They recognize once again that knowing one more language does not make you lose your own identity. Linguistic power strengthens and frees you as a human being.

Knowledge of English in the current global world may bring immediate material gains, but one cannot underestimate the desire of today's cognoscenti not to miss the boat of US intellectual and cultural power. But the Korean language does not face any danger of extinction because of the use of English, just as the use of Chinese characters for more than a millennium has not annihilated Korean. On the world stage, Koreans are now at ease with themselves, and actively participating in world civilization.

The challenge is to do the same with linguistic diversity domestically. Koreans have always boasted their homogeneity, but it was more an ideal than reality. A healthy language planning with equality, fairness, and compassion as a guiding principle should be carried out as scientifically as possible, based on solid socio-linguistic analysis of languages of the people. Continued open-mindedness toward loanwords and neologisms would seem to enrich the language and culture of the people, but it is granted that continued language standardization, not prescriptive teaching, would guarantee the precious linguistic fit between the spoken and written forms of language the Korean speakers have been able to enjoy since the invention of the great writing system almost six centuries ago.

Notes

1. This chapter is a revised version of the paper presented at the Korean Studies Conference "Reimagining Korean Identity through Wars, Money, Ideas and Exchanges: 70 years' Identity Transformation," Monash University, Melbourne, Australia, August 17–19, 2018. An earlier version of this research, titled "Linguistic and Cultural Identity and Global Partnership," was delivered at the Annual Conference on "Korea: Korea and the Four Major Powers in Northeast Asia," University of South Carolina Center for Asian Studies of the Richard L. Walker Institute of International Studies, Columbia, South Carolina, May 18–20, 2001, and later published as Kim-Renaud (2010). I thank Micky Droy, Andy Jackson, and other conference participants for their very helpful comments and suggestions. Translations are mine unless otherwise indicated. In North Korea, however, they now refer to the Korean alphabet by a different name, *Chosŏn'gŭl* [script of Chosŏn] (Kim-Renaud 1997, 2).
2. North Korean examples are from various sources including *Naver Dictionary*.
3. Recent studies (e.g., Kim 2005, Kim 2015) show that in practice Hangul has been used much more prevalently than thought, including in formal documents, by commoners as well as upper class members, when the general understanding has been that the use of Hangul was limited to informal writing.
4. This was a response of influential nationalist intellectuals during the Japanese colonial period to the loss of sovereignty, as well (Schmid 2002, 61–64). I thank Micky Droy for drawing my attention to this point.
5. I thank Shoko Hamano for checking my translation.
6. J. Kim (2015) shows ample evidence that people, including commoners and slave women, exercised agency using Hangul, as observable in legal documents.
7. See Masalski (2001) for a critical review of the Japanese history textbook controversies.

8. A senior Japanese scholar-official recently made a casual remark in a social occasion, "Korean residents in Japan after all are just their 'former slaves'" directly to the author to her astonishment.
9. Generation N is a "cohort of children, teenagers, and young adults who have been immersed in digital technology and the digital way of thinking since their conception." (Garfinkel 2003).
10. Apparently "010" is supposed to be a pictorial representation of the male organ, according to Lee Jong-bok (personal communication).
11. This special case is not a "natural" development in the history of Korean language or usual Korean speakers' relationship with another language, and is beyond the scope of this paper. Note, however, after ten years since it started, the program has not faded away but in fact is prospering and even expanding (Sŏng 2019).
12. The 1.5 generation refers to the cohort of immigrants, who are foreign born but came to the US as young children.
13. It is interesting to note that when language is not involved, first-generation Koreans can go to the very top of the field without any problem, as shown by various prominent artists most of whom are first-generation Koreans.

References

Ancient History Encyclopedia. n.d. Accessed April 4, 2021. www.ancient.eu/Choe_Chiwon.

Baratta, Alex. 2014. "The Use of English in Korean TV Drama to Signal a Modern Identity: Switches from Korean to English Within Korean TV Dramas Signal an Identity of Modernity and Power." *English Today* 30 (3): 54–60. Accessed April 4, 2021. www.cambridge.org/core/services/aop-cambridge-core/content/view/S0266078414000297.

Chang, Bok-Myung. 2018. "Korea's Language Policy Responses to Globalization." *Journal of Pan-Pacific Association of Applied Linguistics* 22 (2): 71–85.

Cho Nam-Sung. 2010. "Hangug-esŏ ŭi ilbonŏ kyoyuk ŭi pyŏnhwa – irŏilmunhakkwa kyokwa kwajŏng-ŭl chungsim-ŭro" [Changes in Japanese Language Education in Korea—With a Focus on the Curriculum of the Japanese Language and Literature Department]. *Ilbonŏ Kyoyuk Yŏn'gu* 19: 23–34.

Cho Tongil (Cho Dong-il). 1999. *Kongdongmunŏ Munhak kwa minjogŏ munhak* [Literature in the Common Literary Language and Ethno-National Literature]. Seoul: Chisik Sanŏpsa.

Cho, Young-mee Yu. 2002. "Diglossia in Korean Language and Literature: A Historical Perspective." *East Asia: An International Quarterly* 20 (1): 3–23.

Choe, Sang-Hun. 2009. "South Korea's Latest Export: Its Alphabet." *New York Times*, September 11. Accessed April 4, 2021. archive.nytimes.com/www.nyt imes.com/2009/09/12/world/asia/12script.html.

Chong Daham [Chŏng Ta-ham]. 2009. "Yŏmal sŏnch'o ŭi tong asia chilsŏ wa chosŏn esŏ ŭi hanŏ, hanimun, Hunmin chŏng'ŭm" [The East Asian Order During the Late Koryŏ and the Early Chosŏn Period; and the Chinese Language, Hanimun/Hanliwen (the Language of Diplomatic Protocol in Use Since Yuan), and Hunmin chŏng'ŭm in Chosŏn Korea]. *Han'guksa hakpo* 35: 269–305.

Chŏng In-t'aek. 2016. *Ch'oe Mal-li sangsomun haesŏl* [Interpretation of Ch'oe Mal-li's (Anti-Alphabet) Memorial]. Seoul: Alda.

Chung, Kayoun. 2011. "Korean English Fever in the U.S.: Temporary Migrant Parents' Evolving Beliefs About Normal Parenting Practices and Children's Natural Language Learning." PhD dissertation. University of Illinois, Urbana-Champaign, IL.

Crystal, David. 2002. *Language Death*. Cambridge: Cambridge University Press.

DailyNK. 2008. "Pukŏhakji 'Hantcha.woeraeŏ sayong'ŭn sadaejuŭi'" [North Korean Linguistics Scholars (Say) "The Use of Sino-Korean or Foreign Words Is Lackeyism"]. April 23. Accessed April 4, 2021. https://www.dai lynk.com/%E5%8C%97%EC%96%B4%ED%95%99%EC%A7%80-%ED%95% 9C%EC%9E%90%EC%99%B8%EB%9E%98%EC%96%B4-%EC%82%AC%EC% 9A%A9%EC%9D%80-%EC%82%AC%EB%8C%80%EC%A3%BC/.

Daudet, Alphonse. 1888/1930. "La Dernière Classe." *Contes du lundi*. Paris: G. Charpentier. Reprinted in Alphonse Daudet. *Œuvres Complètes Illustrées IV, Contes du Lundi*, Librairie de France, 1930, 1–10.

Encyclopedia.com. Accessed April 4, 2021. https://www.encyclopedia.com/his tory/modern-europe/wars-and-battles/franco-prussian-war.

Epstein, Stephen. 2000. "Anarchy in the UK, Solidarity in the ROK: Punk Rock Come to Korea." *Acta Koreana* 3: 1–34.

Fouser, Robert J. 2000. "Online Korean Dialect." *Korea Now*, February 26, 15.

Fromkin, Victoria, Robert Rodman, and Nina Hyams, 1974/2014. *An Introduction to Language*. 10th ed. Boston, MA: Wadsworth, Cengage Learning.

Garfinkel, Simson. 2003. "The Myth of Generation N." *MIT Technology Review*, August 8. Accessed April 4, 2021. https://www.technologyreview.com/ 2003/08/08/234134/the-myth-of-generation-n/.

Hideki, Noma. 2003. "Ilbon taehakkyo taehagwŏnesŏ ŭi hangugŏ kyoyuk - tonggyŏngoegugŏdaehak daehagwŏn ŭi kyoyuk hyŏnhwang-ŭl chungsimŭro" [Korean Language Education in Japanese Colleges and Graduate Schools - Focusing on the Status of Education at the Graduate School of Tokyo University of Foreign Studies]. *Hangugŏ Kyoyuk* 14 (2): 83–106.
History.net. n.d. Accessed April 4, 2021. http://www.y-history.net/appendix/wh0301-080.html [A Japanese-language World History site].
Holcombe, Charles. 2001. *The Genesis of East Asia: 221 B.C.–A.D. 907*, 165–182. Honolulu: Association for Asian Studies & University of Hawai'i Press.
Hyŏn Nam-sŏp. 2001. "*Urimal sinjoŏ-rŭl p'ungbuhi haja*" [Let Us Enrich Neologism in Our Language]. *Hangul saesosik* 342: 15–16. Seoul: Hangul hakhoe.
Jackson, Howard, and Peter Stockwell. 2011. *An Introduction to the Nature and Functions of Language*. 2nd ed. London: Bloomsbury Academic.
Jang Yeong-hui. 2001. "Hantcha kyoyug ŭi silt'ae wa panghyang" [Actual State and Direction of Chinese Characters Education]. *kwugŏ kyoyuk yŏn'gu* [The Education of Korean Language] 8: 165–189.
Japanese-Language Wikipedia. n.d. Accessed April 4, 2021. https://ja.wikipedia.org/wiki/%E6%9C%9D%E8%B2%A2.
Jo, Mi-Jeong. 2018. "Koryo Saram in South Korea: 'Korean' but Struggling to Fit in." *KOREA EXPOSE*, May 29, 2018. https://www.koreaexpose.com/koryo-saram-from-central-asia-and-russia-struggle-in-south-korea/.
Kim, Chin-W. 1988. "The Making of the Korean Language." *Sojourns in Language II: Collected Papers by Chin-W. Kim*. Seoul: Tower Press.
Kim, Djun-kil. 2010. "Han'gukhak ŭi kukjejŏk sot'ong-e kwanhan han yŏn'gu: han'gug-ŭi yŏksa wa munhwa kwallyŏn yong'ŏ mit kaenyŏm ŭi yŏng'ŏ p'yohyŏn-ŭl chungsim-ŭro" [A Study on the Cross-Cultural Communication of the Korean Studies—Korean Studies Scholars and Their English Terminologies]. *The Journal of International Korean Studies* 4 (12): 51–91.
Kim, Jisoo M. 2015. *The Emotions of Justice: Gender, Status, and Legal Performance in Chosŏn Korea*. Seattle and London: University of Washington Press.
Kim, Kichung. 2004. "Nansorhon and 'Shakespeare's Sister.'" In *Creative Women of Korea: The Fifteenth Through the Twentieth Centuries*, edited by Young-Key Kim-Renaud, 78–95. Armonk, NY: M.E. Sharpe.
Kim Min-su. 1999. "Pukhan ŭi hantcha kyoyuk" [North Korea's Chinese-Character Education]. *Saegugŏ saenghwal* [New Korean Language Life] 9 (2): 93–124.
Kim Sŭr-ong. 2005. *Chosŏnsidae ŏnmun ŭi chedojŏk sayong yŏn'gu* [On the Systematic Use of Hangul in the Chosŏn Era]. Seoul: Han'gukmunhwasa.

Kim Yong-hwang. 1978. *Chosŏnminjogŏ palchŏnryŏksayŏn'gu* [On the History of the Development of the Korean National Language]. Pyongyang: Kwahak paekkwasajon ch'ulpansa [Science and Encyclopedia Publishing House].

Kim-Renaud, Young-Key, ed. 1997. *The Korean Alphabet: Its History and Structure*. Honolulu: University of Hawai'i Press.

Kim-Renaud, Young-Key. 2000. "Korea's Place in the Age of Globalization." Commentary in response to "The Korean Language and Literature in the 20th Century: A Historical Perspective" by Young-mee Yu Cho and to "Representing Korean Visual Culture to Western Audiences" by Jonathan W. Best. Presented at the Annual Conference on Korea: "Projecting Korea and Its Culture to the Outside World," the Center for Asian Studies, University of South Carolina, May 19–21.

Kim-Renaud, Young-Key. 2010. "Linguistic and Cultural Identity and Global Partnership." In *Contemporary Korean Linguistics: International Perspectives in Honor of Professor Sang-Oak Lee*, edited by Robert J. Fouser, 171–198. Seoul: T'aehaksa.

King, Ross. 1997. "Language, Politics, and Ideology in the Postwar Koreas." In *Korea Briefing: Toward Reunification*, edited by David R. McCann, 109–144. Armonk, NY and London, UK: M.E. Sharpe.

King, Ross. 2015. "Ditching 'Diglossia': Ecologies of the Spoken and Inscribed in Pre-modern Korea." *Sungkyun Journal of East Asian Studies* 15 (1): 1–19.

Koreaboo.com. n.d. Accessed April 4, 2021. www.koreaboo.com/lists/18-multilingual-kpop-idols-who-may-speak-your-native-language.

Ku, Pŏp-hoe. 2011. "*Tasi kogae tŭnŭn hantcha sadae chuŭi*" [Resurging Chinese-Character Worship/Sadaeism]. *The Kyunghyang Shinmun*, June 15.

Kwŏn Yŏngmin. 2013. "Kagyanal (ABC Day)." Kwŏn Yŏngmin's Literary Commentary on Poems, October 24. Accessed April 4, 2021. http://www.muncon.net/entry/%EA%B0%80%EA%B0%B8%EB%82%A0.

Ledyard, Gari. 1997. "The International Linguistic Background of the Correct Sounds for the Instruction of the People." In *The Korean Alphabet: Its History and Structure*, edited by Young-Key Kim-Renaud, 31–87. Honolulu: University of Hawai'i Press.

Ledyard, Gari. 1998. *The Korean Language Reform of 1446*. Seoul: Sin'gu Munhwasa.

Lee, Chang-Rae. 1995. *Native Speaker*. NY: Riverhead Books.

Lee, Hyun-bok. 1992. "Korean Phonetic Alphabet: Theory and Application." *Malsori* [Phonetics], *Journal of the Phonetic Society of Korea* 21–24: 123–143.

Lee, Jamie Shinhee. 2006. "Linguistic Constructions of Modernity: English Mixing in Korean Television Commercials." *Language in Society* 35 (1): 59–91.

Lee, Jamie Shinhee. 2014. "English on Korean Television." *World Englishes* 33 (1).

Lee, Ki-baik. 1984. *A New History of Korea*. Translated by Edward W. Wagner with Edward J. Shultz. Seoul: Ilchokak.
Lee, Ki-Moon. 1991. *Kugŏ ŏhwisa yŏn'gu* [The History of the Korean Lexicon]. Seoul: Tong-a Publishing Co.
Lee Iksop, and S. Robert Ramsey. 2000. *The Korean Language*. Albany, NY: State University of New York Press.
Lee Jong-bok. 1997. "Pangsong ŏnŏ ŭi karik'immare nat'anan him kwa kŏri" [Power and Distance Represented by the Terms of Reference in Broadcast Language]. *Korean Sociolinguistics Association* 5 (2): 87–124.
Masalski, Kathleen Woods. 2001. "Examining the Japanese History Textbook Controversies. Stanford Program on International and Cross-Cultural Education (SPICE)." *Japan Digest*, November. National Clearinghouse for United States-Japan Studies, Indiana University, Bloomington. Accessed April 4, 2021. https://spice.fsi.stanford.edu/docs/examining_the_japanese_history_textbook_controversies.
Murata, Kumiko and Jennifer Jenkins, eds. 2009. *Global Englishes in Asian Contexts: Current and Future Debates*. London: Palgrave Macmillan.
Noland, Marcus. 2002. "The Impact of Korean Immigration on the U. S. Economy." In *The Korean Diaspora in the World Economy*, edited by Inbom Choi and C. Fred Bergsten, 61–72. Washington, DC: Peterson Institute for International Economics.
Park, Joseph Sung-Yul. 2009. *The Local Construction of a Global Language: Ideologies of English in South Korea*. Series: *Language, Power and Social Process* [LPSP] 24. Berlin: DeGruyter Mouton.
Schmid, André. 2002. *Korea Between Empires, 1895–1919*. New York, NY: Columbia University Press.
Smith, Roberta. 2000. "ART REVIEW; Serenity Made Visible: Korea's Ceramic Art." *New York Times*, January 28. Accessed April 4, 2021. www.nytimes.com/2000/01/28/arts/art-review-serenity-made-visible-korea-s-ceramic-art.html.
Sohn Ho-min. 1997. "Migugesŏ ŭi han'gugŏ yŏn'gu wa han'gugŏ kyoyuk – hyŏnhwang, hyŏnan mit kwaje" [Korean Language Research and Education: the Current Status, Pending Issues, and Tasks]. *Kyoyuk Hangul* 10: 55–90.
Sŏng Hye-mi. 2019. "Tsia Tsia jok han'gŭl ch'aet'aek 10nyŏn… hŭjibuji andoego ohiryŏ hwaksan" [Ten Years Since the Cia Cia Tribe Chose Hangul—It Didn't Fade Away; on the Contrary It Is Expanding]. *Yonhap News*, October 2. Accessed April 4, 2021. https://www.yna.co.kr/view/AKR20191001202700104.
Song, Ho-jin. 2001. "Hot Wind from Korea Blowing in Taiwan." *Sports Today*, May 9.
Song, Jae Jung. 2005. *The Korean Language: Structure, Use and Context*. London and New York: Routledge.

Song, Jae Jung. 2011. "English as an Official Language in South Korea: Global English or Social Malady?" *Language Problems & Language Planning* 35 (1): 35–55.

Statista.com. n.d. Accessed April 4, 2021. https://www.statista.com/statistics/876030/number-of-foreign-students-in-south-korea/.

Takayama, Hideko, and Kay Itoi. 2001. "Japan Finds its Seoul," *Newsweek*, April 11.

Tyson, Rod. 1993. "English Loanwords in Korea: Pattern of Borrowing and Semantic Change." *El Two Talk* 1 (1): 29–36.

Vacheck, Josef. 1973. *Written Language: General Problems and Problems of English*. The Hague: Mouton.

Wang, Sixiang. 2014. "The Sounds of Our Country: Interpreters, Linguistic Knowledge, and the Politics of Language in Early Choson Korea." In *Rethinking East Asian Languages, Vernaculars, and Literacies, 1000–1919*, edited by Benjamin A. Elman, 58–95. Leiden, Netherlands: Koninklijke Brill.

Wikipedia. n.d. Accessed April 4, 2021. https://en.wikipedia.org/wiki/Korean_diaspora.

Yi Cha-yŏn. 2001. "Korea Mania: 'I Like Seoul Better Than New York.'" *Chosun Ilbo*, April 4.

CHAPTER 9

Swearing Granny Restaurants: An International Perspective on Rudeness in Korean

Soyeon Kim and Lucien Brown

Across service industry interactions in many cultures ritualized polite language has emerged as the norm. To be sure, the way that service staff perform politeness may be culture-specific; for instance, whereas American service staff are trained to be friendly and smiley, those in Japan receive extensive training in deferential and demure modes of politeness (see Dunn 2013). There may also be some cultures where expectations of politeness are lowered; for instance, Pan and Kádár (2011, 141) show that Chinese service interactions have traditionally been characterized by a relative "lack of politeness." But despite these different orientations, the overall picture is one of service staff being polite to customers as a general

S. Kim (✉) · L. Brown
Monash University, Clayton Campus, Melbourne, VIC, Australia
e-mail: soyeon.kim@monash.edu

L. Brown
e-mail: lucien.brown@monash.edu

© The Author(s), under exclusive license to Springer Nature Switzerland AG 2022
A. D. Jackson (ed.), *The Two Koreas and their Global Engagements*,
https://doi.org/10.1007/978-3-030-90761-7_9

rule. The need to be polite to customers is captured in idiomatic sayings such as *the customer is always right* in English and *sonnim-ŭn wang-ida* (the customer is king) in Korean.

But norms of politeness rarely go completely uncontested, and such is the case for ritualized politeness in service encounters. For the service staff involved, adopting a polite persona at work is a stylized display, which often requires the suppression of emotion. This kind of "surface acting," defined as "a type of emotion regulation that involves faking emotions, such as smiling or expressing cheerfulness," is linked to emotional exhaustion, lower job satisfaction, and low self-esteem (Wessel and Steiner 2015). This "surface acting" may be interpreted as insincere, and part of a display aimed at coercing customers into paying higher prices or making unnecessary purchases. In addition, the excessive use of politeness in the service industry is seen as symptomatic of a social situation where customers are becoming increasingly demanding of special treatment, placing ever greater demands on the psychological well-being of service staff. This final observation applies particularly to South Korea, where the issue of customers abusing their power over service industry workers has become part of a recognized social problem referred to as *kapchil*, defined by Shin and Moon (2017) as "the powerful picking on the weak."

Against this background, we conducted an integrative pragmatics study of language usage in food industry establishments where staff purposefully depart from polite protocol, and instead use flagrantly impolite language, including swearing. We look at two establishments: Yangp'yŏng sondubu siktang (Yangp'yŏng Handmade Tofu Restaurant; Yangp'yŏng Tofu, herein) in Kyŏnggi Province, South Korea and a hotdog restaurant called The Wiener's Circle in Chicago, USA. These two restaurants have attracted notoriety in their respective countries for the overt use of swearing by their serving staff, and have featured on various television programs and content produced by social media influencers. At Yangp'yŏng Tofu, customers are spoken to in *panmal* (non-honorific language) and frequently referred to as *nom* (jerk) or *saekki* (bastard), whereas at Weiner's Circle, customers are addressed as *asshole* or *mother fucker*. The use of obscene language has emerged as a subversive yet powerful linguistic emblem for these establishments to promote their businesses in the internet era. In South Korea, these restaurants, which are typically run by older women, are referred to as *Yokchaengi halmŏni ŭmshikchŏm* (swearing granny restaurants).

This paper sets out to explore how impolite language is used in these swearing granny restaurants in Korea and the US, and how it is perceived in cross-cultural contact. The materials used to explore these issues are drawn from two social media videos produced by South Korean content creators, one depicting Yangp'yŏng Tofu and one showing The Wiener's Circle. Both videos have a cross-cultural angle: the Yangp'yŏng Tofu involves the content creator taking two non-Koreans to the restaurant, whereas the video for The Wiener's Circle shows the South Korean content creator visiting the restaurant in Chicago, and also features comments from Korean viewers. We aim to show how, in neoliberal computer-mediated society, not only politeness but also impoliteness has become something that is consumed and commodified across online and offline spaces.

Background

We pause briefly to introduce impoliteness as a linguistic phenomenon, previous research on impoliteness in cross-cultural settings, and the concept of impoliteness in the Korean context.

Impoliteness

Politeness first emerged as a target of research in the linguistic field of pragmatics (the study of language use in context) during the 1970s in the work of language philosophers (e.g. Lakoff 1977; Leech 1977; Brown and Levinson 1978/1987). These early studies were chiefly concerned with establishing linguistic and cultural universals that could explain assumed preferences for speakers to use indirect and linguistically more complex utterances in situations that required politeness (e.g., "Can you pass the salt?" rather than "Pass the salt!"). Impoliteness was rarely discussed and was assumed simply to be inverse or opposite of politeness (Eelen 2001, 98). Whereas politeness was cast in a positive light as an important social lubricant, impoliteness was seen as causing social disruption (see Culpeper 1996).

More recent accounts of impoliteness view it not just as an absence of politeness, but as a type of "social practice" (Kádár and Haugh 2013, 65) in its own right, which is jointly constructed by participants during interactional exchanges. Speakers may perform impoliteness through certain types of language, which may typically include "intentionally gratuitous and conflictive … verbal acts" which are performed unmitigated and with some degree of deliberate aggression, and/or in an exacerbated or boosted way (Bousfield 2007, 2186). But impoliteness ultimately relies on the interlocutor validating the speaker's impolite intentions according to socially-constructed frames of expectation (Locher and Watts 2008, 81).

Speakers frequently use language that is heavily marked for impoliteness (e.g. swearing) not to attack face but for "mock impoliteness." This often takes place during ritualized bantering and teasing (e.g. Haugh and Weinglass 2020). Mock impoliteness can often be distinguished from genuine politeness by the reactions of the interlocutor. In the case of mock impoliteness, responses are more likely to involve a simple rejection of the mockery as untrue or exaggerated (Haugh 2010, 2109), or the interlocutor may choose to go along with the mockery either by elaborating on it or by countering it with increasingly preposterous forms of mockery (Haugh 2010, 2109). In the case of genuine impoliteness, the interlocutor may counter the impolite behavior (Culpeper et al. 2003, 1562).

As noted by Blitvich et al. (2013, 115), impoliteness is something that speakers employ rationally to perform part of their identity. Impoliteness is inherently connected to identity since it tends to involve instances where the identities and positioning speakers are trying to claim are attacked or questioned (Blitvich 2009). But beyond this, the use of impolite language also allows a speaker to frame a certain type of persona. Someone who uses impolite language can construct an identity not just as an impolite person who is uneducated, but also as someone who is down-to-earth, plain-speaking and honest, as well as irreverent, cynical, and humorous.

A wave of studies has shown that so-called reality TV shows frequently depict and indeed manipulate impoliteness and conflict for reasons of entertainment. Examples of Anglosphere TV programs explored in previous literature include *Dragon's Den* (Lorenzo-Dus 2009), *Idol* (Lorenzo-Dus et al. 2013), and *The Weakest Link* (Culpeper 2005). The phenomenon of impoliteness for entertainment has now spread to Korea in programs such as *Radio Star* (Lee 2020). The stars of these shows, such as Simon Cowell and, in the Korean context, Gura Kim (Kim Ku-ra), use language to create impolite personas that are popular to the audience for their brutal honesty and cruel wit.

One linguistic manifestation of impoliteness that is particularly closely linked to identity is swearing. Here, swearing is understood broadly as the taboo language which is used primarily for its expressive rather than referential meanings (Jay and Janschewitz 2008, 268), and which communicates emotional meanings which may range from disdain, disagreement, and shock, through to passion, sincerity, solidarity, and jocularity (Fägersten and Stapleton 2017). Swear words may appear propositionally in reference to the speaker (*I'm fucked*), the hearer (*you fucking idiot!*) or third parties (*he/she/it is fucking good!*), and also non-propositionally in what Jay and Janschewitz (2008, 270) "automatic emotional responses" (*fuck!*). Propositional swear words referring to the interlocutor are the most likely to cause offense (Jay and Janschewitz 2008, 270).

Swear words become strong markers of social meanings related to context and identity. Language users associate swearing not just with relaxed and informal environments but also with particular kinds of people. Within a university setting, for instance, Jay and Janschewitz (2008) show that speakers associate swearing with the speech of a student rather than with that of a dean, and also with male rather than female speech. Those in positions of respected authority are expected to exercise caution and restraint, and their avoidance of swearing in favor of "refined speech" becomes an indexical marker of their high social position. On the other hand, swearing can be a marker for lower social standing or lack of occupational prestige. Somewhat contradictory to this, those in positions of power (particularly men) may enjoy more freedom to use swearing or controlling who is allowed to swear (see White 2002).

Impoliteness in Cross-Cultural Settings

By using videos that feature both Korean and English impoliteness and cross-cultural perceptions, the current paper fits within a growing body of literature looking at impoliteness in cross-cultural contexts.

Correctly gaging the level of rudeness is challenging in an additional language since it "involves the difficult task of determining participants' identity, relationship, social norms, intentions and motivations" (Jay and Janschewitz 2008, 268). The general tendency is for language users to feel higher emotional intensity for insults in their first language (Dewaele 2010; Harris et al. 2003). In a study of Korean high schoolers who had moved to New Zealand aged 12–13, Kim and Starks (2008) found that some participants avoided swearing in Korean because it sounded "too real," "rude" and "intense," even though they frequently swore in English. Indeed, second language learners may underestimate the offensive nature of swearwords and use them inappropriately (see Ringbom's 2001, 66 for an account of a Finish student who returned from a year in the UK and frequently used *fucking* in class).

The tendency for the emotional intensity of impolite language to decrease in cross-cultural contexts also applies to the phenomenon of "other-language swearing": the use of swear words imported from other languages. A number of papers have looked at what Jaffe (2017, 87) refers to as "the global spread of fuck." In her paper "*Fuck* in French," Jaffe (2017, 88) contends that *fuck* is used in other languages "in a lighthearted way ... to take stances that convey some oppositionality, but limited association with the taboo nature of the word in English." The comparative lack of taboo of using *fuck* in other languages is illustrated by examples from Swedish in Fägersten (2017) including the slogan "FUCK CANCER" being used by the organization Youth Cancer and the movie title *Fucking Åmål*[1] (renamed *Show Me Love* for Anglophone audiences). In the case of Korean, Kim (2002, 232) notes that English curse words are frequently used by younger generations.

Impoliteness in Korean

Impolite language in Korean is referred to with a variety of terms including *sangmal/sangsori*, commonly defined as "vulgar language that is debased and undignified" and which was historically associated with the language of the *sangmin* (commoners) in the Chosŏn period (Kim 2002). Swearwords are referred to as *yok*, which is defined as "offensive language that disregards the character (*in'gyŏk*) of others" (Yon 2015, 2).

Consistent with these definitions, impolite language and swearing are traditionally assumed in Korea to be low-status forms of language that are used to attack others. However, as pointed out by Yon (2015, 2–6), swearing is also widely acknowledged as a device for relieving anger and stress, particularly for those who feel wronged by others. The control of abusive language in public spheres and the media in South Korea has started to relax in recent years. Lee (2020) notes that "'*being impolite*' on TV is one of the most distinctive recent changes from the old Korean TV programs."

Resources for abusive language in Korean show some important differences with English. Whereas high-frequency English swearwords tend to derive from bodily effluvia (for example, *shit*), sex (*fuck*), and religion (*hell*), common Korean swearwords often literally denote animals such as *kae saekki* (dog baby) and mental incapacity like *chiral* (go crazy), in addition to sex, such as *chot* (dick). Korean swearwords often occur in compounds or combinations; for instance, *nom* (jerk) and *nyŏn* (bitch) appear with modifying expressions such as in *michin nom/nyŏn* (crazy jerk/bitch) (Kim 2002).

In addition to swearwords, the intentional misuse of honorifics is a fertile area for expressing impolite meanings. As pointed out by Lee and Ramsey (2000), Korean speakers are highly sensitive to the deletion of honorific forms in contexts in which they are expected according to socially normative convention. The omission of honorifics for intentional impoliteness tends to be restricted to contexts where the speaker is the superior party (but using honorifics due to social distance), since using *panmal* to notable superiors is highly taboo (Brown 2015, 252). In interactions between intimates, on the other hand, speakers may strategically include honorifics in order to be sarcastic and impolite (see Brown 2013).

The use of address terms and pronouns can also be manipulated for displays of impoliteness. Korean operates what Kim (2003) refers to as a "taboo of name-calling avoidance" (Kim 2003), whereby status superiors and strangers are not typically addressed or referred to by their names. This means that speakers can intentionally include a name or pronoun as a deliberate signal of disrespect (Lee and Ramsey 2000, 226). For instance, the term *tangsin* "you" is quite frequently used for disrespect during verbal conflicts.

Methodology

Research Context

The current project involves the analysis of two YouTube videos depicting their content creators (and other participants) interacting with "swearing grannies" at restaurants in South Korea and the US, respectively. Before describing the videos themselves, a few words are in order regarding the phenomenon of "swearing grannies" and the restaurants involved.

Yokchaengi halmŏni ŭmshikchŏm (swearing granny restaurants) is a term that has become popularized in South Korea in recent years for referring to restaurants run by elderly female proprietors who engage in ritualized swearing and impoliteness with their customers. The term *yokchaengi* is a combination of the noun *yok* "swearing" and the bound suffix *–chaengi*, which denotes a human referent who takes on the attributes of the noun (often in a way that is excessive or notorious)— "someone who is renowned for their swearing." *Halmŏni* appears here as a generic term for an elderly woman, indexing an affectionate grandmother who might enjoy cooking for her grandchildren. In recent years, *Yokchaengi halmŏni ŭmshikchŏm* have grown in popularity thanks in some part to sympathetic portrayals in the media in programs such as *Pabŭn mŏkko taninya?* (*Are you eating?*). *Yokchaengi halmŏni* have become connected with an image not only of an elderly woman who swears, but also who are warm, caring, and honest working-class folk, and their restaurants are renowned for their delicious food.

The restaurant depicted in the video analyzed for this paper, Yangp'yŏng Tofu, is in the remote village of Sintan-ri, Kyŏnggi-do, about 80 km north of downtown Seoul and less than 10 km from the DMZ. Originally a restaurant frequented by hikers, it has become a popular destination for city folk these days due to the restaurant appearing on over 80 TV shows. The restaurant has been run for 40 years by a *Yokchaengi halmŏni*, whose actual name is never mentioned (note the "taboo of name calling avoidance" mentioned above). In the analysis, we simply call her Halmŏni. In the materials analyzed for this paper, she connects her reliance on swearing to her low education level (she did not complete primary school) and describes it as a defense mechanism she has used to protect herself from various twists and turns.

The American restaurant in the second video is The Wiener's Circle, a hotdog restaurant in the Lincoln Park area of Chicago, which opened in 1983. It has a female owner and appears to have predominantly female African American staff. The restaurant has featured on various US TV and radio shows (including *This American Life*). It also featured in the book *101 Places Not to See Before You Die* (Price 2010), where the author describes it as the top place that "makes me sad about humanity." The Wiener's Circle is one of several restaurants in the US that have developed cult followings for their rudeness, including the national chain Dick's Last Resort.

The Korean media has made frequent discursive connections between *yokchaengi halmŏni siktang* and rude American restaurants, with The Wiener's Circle being dubbed *miguk-p'an yokchaengi halmŏni siktang* (the American swearing granny restaurant).

Data

The data is comprised of two YouTube videos, one depicting Yangp'yŏng Tofu and one featuring The Wiener's Circle. Both videos are made by South Korean content creators (both young males) primarily for a South Korean audience, but with cross-cultural content.

The video depicting Yangp'yŏng Tofu is produced by "channel CKOONY," a YouTube channel with 119,000 subscribers and 24 million views as of December 7 2020. The videos mainly feature the channel's male content creator "CKOONY" (and occasionally other Koreans), partaking in light-hearted interactions with various non-Koreans, typically in South Korea. The video depicting the Yangp'yŏng Tofu restaurant was uploaded in May 2019 with a running time of 18:23.[2] It shows CKOONY and another male YouTuber, Trickid-z, going to the restaurant with two Korean-speaking women: Carson Allen (an American actress who has featured in minor roles in several South Korean dramas and movies, and who has lived in Korea since her early teens) and Maria Cernozukova (a YouTuber and social media influencer from Ukraine).

The video featuring The Wiener's Circle is on the channel Heechulism, produced by South Korean content creator Heechul Yoon [Yun Hŭich'ŏl]. The channel features Heechul traveling to interesting and sometimes controversial locations overseas, such as the red-light districts in Amsterdam and Bangkok and a "nude sauna" in Germany. The channel has 471,000 subscribers and more than 100 million views. The video depicting Weiner's Circle was uploaded in June 2019 with a running time of 11:37.[3] The video is filmed by Heechul himself, apparently using a selfie stick, and depicts him entering the restaurant and interacting with manager Evelyn Morris, after which he posts a monologic reflection on his experience.

The titles of both refer to the "swearing granny" trope with the first video using the Korean term *yokchaengi halmŏni*, and the second the English term *cursing grandmother*. The second video also uses the term *yokchaengi halmŏni* within the video itself to refer to Evelyn Morris, manager of The Wiener's Circle.

Data Analysis

In analyzing the data, we adopt an approach based on integrative pragmatics (Culpeper and Haugh 2014). Consistent with such an approach, our analysis consists of three distinct levels of analysis, which targeted three different perspectives.

We first analyzed the impoliteness strategies used by the swearing grannies themselves. This involved transcribing the videos and coding the different impoliteness strategies that occurred in a bottom-up fashion.[4] We then matched our labels to impoliteness strategies given in Culpeper's (1996) taxonomy of impoliteness strategies. As shown in Table 9.1, these strategies are divided into "positive impoliteness strategies" (strategies that show disapproval of the interlocutor) and "negative politeness strategies" (strategies that impinge on the interlocutor's territory and freedom of action).

Second, we analyzed qualitatively how the video creators and other participants in the videos assign interactional meanings to the use of these forms. This analysis involved identifying the spontaneous reactions of the participants, as well as commentaries provided by them following the

Table 9.1 Taxonomy of impoliteness strategies (Culpeper 1996)

Positive impoliteness strategies	Negative impoliteness strategies
– Ignore, snub the other	– Frighten
– Exclude the other from an activity	– Condescend, scorn or ridicule
– Disassociate from the other	– Invade the other's space
– Be disinterested, unconcerned, unsympathetic	– Explicitly associate the other with a negative aspect
– Use inappropriate identity markers	– Put the other's indebtedness on record
– Use obscure or secretive language	
– Seek disagreement	
– Make the other feel uncomfortable	
– Use taboo words	

encounter. We also looked at visual techniques that the content creators used to draw attention to impolite behavior and pass comment on it.

Third, we analyzed the viewer comments to look at how non-participating viewers of the video evaluated the impolite acts depicted in the videos. This final step involved sorting the comments into different opinion-based categories, following Kádár et al. (2013) and Okano and Brown (2018).

Data Presentation

Yangp'yŏng Tofu

The Korean video clip features CKOONY visiting Yangp'yŏng Tofu with Trickid-Z, Carson, and Maria. The main scene is filmed by CKOONY, and depicts Trickid-Z, Carson, and Maria interacting with Halmŏni as she cooks pork and tofu at their table. It is Trickid-z who takes the lead in the interaction, and who is the focus for all of Halmŏni's impoliteness.

Impoliteness Strategies
We identified four types of impoliteness strategies performed by Halmŏni.

The first was the use of swearing and obscene words, which occurred 44 times in total. These included *saekki* (bastard) (17 occurrences), (*tol*)*taegari* (bone head) (6 occurrences), *ssibal* (fuck) (4), *chŏmŏkta* (eat like a pig) (4), (*kae*)*chiral* (fucking around), *nom* (jerk) (2) and other combinations including *saekki* or *nom* (such as *ssŏgŏppajil-nom* [rotten jerk] and *sippal-saekki* [fucking bastard]) (11). Of the 44 total occurrences, 43 are used propositionally (Jay and Janschewitz 2008) with 39 referring to the hearer, Trickid-z. The frequent use of these kinds of expressions corresponds to impoliteness strategy of "using taboo words" under Culpeper's (1996) taxonomy.

Halmŏni also used casual language throughout the exchange. All of her utterances were in non-honorific *panmal*, frequently interspersed with interjections that only occur in casual language, including *ya!* (hey!) (6 tokens) and *ayu/ao/aissi*, which marks speaker frustration (10). Her speech was accompanied by vocal and nonverbal cues for casual speech, including varied pitch range and intensity and withholding of gaze (see Brown et al. 2014; Brown and Winter 2019). The use of inappropriate register corresponds to Culpeper's (1996) strategy of using inappropriate identity markers.

Halmŏni's use of *panmal* in interactions with customers also relates a wider strategy of flouting service industry routines. During the interaction, Trickid-z asks Halmŏni, for kimchi and then for lettuce. Since these are standard items that are provided (typically without charge) in a restaurant of this kind, it would be customary for the server either to provide the items, or otherwise apologize for the inability to do so. But instead, Halmŏni rebuts Trickid-z's requests and verbally insults him. She also refuses to meet his gaze during this sequence (Fig. 9.1).

(1)
1   Trickid-Z: *sangch'u hokshi innayo?*
               "Do you have lettuce, by any chance?"
2   Halmŏni: *ai chintcha i saekki-ya, sangch'u-nŭn wae tŭrŏga-nya? kimch'i-ga in-*
               nŭnde, i ssagaji ŏm-nŭn nom-a!
               "Oh, really, why would you need lettuce, you bastard? You already have kimchi, you ignorant jerk!"

This absence of ritual polite language constitutes another way in which Halmŏni applies the strategy of using inappropriate identity markers.

Fig. 9.1 Halmŏni does not meet Trickid-z gaze (Screen capture used with permission from CKOONY)

The fourth strategy was for Halmŏni to ridicule the utterances made by Trickid-z. In (2), Trickid-z asks Halmŏni if tofu is made from beans (line 1), which is met by Halmŏni's rhetorical reply (line 2) ending with the *-nya* interrogative, which tends to sound condescending or argumentative (Yeon and Brown 2019, 267). This is followed by Halmŏni uttering a series of swearwords as she questions Trickid-z's intelligence (line 4), his professional credentials (line 6) and implies that his own mother would be ashamed of him (line 8). Finally, in line 10 she repeats the rhetorical question and uses the vocative form *in'gan-a*, which literally means "you human" but is closer to "you fool" in illocutionary force.

(2)
1	Trickid-Z	*ŏ~ tubu-nŭn k'ong-ŭro mandŭ-nayo?*
		"Is tofu made from beans?"
2	Halmŏni	*kŭrŏm k'ong-ŭro haji, pab-ŭro ha-nya?*
		"Of course it's made from beans, do you think it would be made from rice?"
3	Trickid-Z	*a~ kŭraeyo? a~*
		"Ah, really? Ah."
4	Halmŏni	*ya, ssibal nŏ ae-saekki-rago ŏttŏk'e taegari-ga an toraga-nya?*
		"Hey, for fuck's sake, how can a little bastard like you be so stupid?"
5	Everyone	*hahahahaha*
		(laughter)
		[...]
8	Halmŏni	*aigo, nŏ, ni ŏmma-ga nŏ-rŭl na-k'o*
		"Oh, and think of the hardship your own mother went through giving birth to you."
9	Trickid-Z	*hahahahaha*
		(laughter)
10	Halmŏni	*a, kŭrŏm k'ongŭro haji, in'gana, pabŭro hanya?*
		"It's made from beans, you fool, would it be made from rice?"

Halmŏni's constant ridiculing of Trickid-Z is reminiscent of Culpeper's (1996) strategy of "condescend, scorn or ridicule." Notably, she does not treat the two non-Korean women in this way, and answers their (infrequent) questions patiently and with smiles.

Participant Reactions

Although Halmŏni's use of impolite language initially leads to some level of bewilderment for the YouTubers, it quickly becomes clear that the politeness is experienced by Trickid-Z and other participants as an act, which promotes intimacy and comity rather than causing offense. During an interspliced interview segment, Trickid-z notes that the Halmŏni's impoliteness was proof that "she adores me to that extent" (*kŭmank'ŭm chŏrŭl ippŏhae chushinŭn'guna*) and that "she swore at me like she was swearing warmly at her own grandson." This stance is also indexed in the telops, which note that he was just "too happy" (*manyang chŭlgŏun*) (Fig. 9.2). At the end of the visit, Trickid-z attempts to embrace Halmŏni, who playfully tries to hit him with a fly swatter, followed by which both are depicted smiling (Fig. 9.3).

Throughout the interaction, Trickid-Z and other participants maintain the use of honorifics and never reciprocate Halmŏni's swearing and impolite behavior. Trickid-z maintains gaze on Halmŏni throughout the interaction, which is also known as a marker of deference (see Brown and Winter 2019). This is not to say, however, that they do not play along with the mockery, but rather that they do it in a way that maintains respect for Halmŏni's advanced social standing. When Halmŏni refers to Trickid-z as *toldaegari* (bonehead) he responds in jest by saying, in the highest level of speech, that he is a university graduate (*Taehak chorŏp'aetsŭmnida*), which draws laughs from all of the participants. Going along

Fig. 9.2 The telop at the bottom reads "even though he is being sworn at, he is too happy" (Screen capture used with permission from CKOONY)

Fig. 9.3 Halmŏni and Trickid-z are all smiles at the end of the visit (Screen capture used with permission from CKOONY)

with the impoliteness is known to be a participant reaction associated with mock impoliteness (Haugh 2010).

The reactions of the two non-Korean participants toward Halmŏni's impoliteness are also largely positive. In an interview clip spliced in right at the end of the interaction, Maria comments that the grandma's swearing did not come from bad intentions and that it was cute. Both Maria and Carson comment on the fact that Halmŏni did not swear at them. Whereas Maria evaluated this positively and thanked Halmŏni for looking on them favorably (*yeppŭge pwajusyŏsŏ kamsahamnida*), Carson described this as "a bit of a shame" (*chogŭm ashwiwŏssŏyo*) and reported that Halmŏni refused to teach her any swear words.

The positive reactions of the participants should not belie the fact that the literal content of Halmŏni's utterances was extremely offensive. This is confirmed by the fact that Halmŏni's swear words are bleeped out, and also edited in the subtitles and telops, as in Fig. 9.1 where the second syllable of *kaejiral* is replaced with the letter X and followed by laughter marks "ㅎㅎㅎ" (ha ha ha). Since the utterance itself did not contain any laughter (and the other participants smiled but did not laugh), these laughter marks seem to function to soften the force of the utterance (Fig. 9.4).

Fig. 9.4 *Kaejiral* is censored in the telops and followed by laughter marks (Screen capture used with permission from CKOONY)

Viewer Comments

The video had been viewed 610,678 times as of December 7, 2020, and had attracted 888 viewer comments. We analyzed 196 of these comments which included reference to Halmŏni's behavior and/or the reaction of the participants.

The comments featured more frequent negative stances toward Halmŏni and her behavior. In total, 87 (45%) of the comments were negative, compared with 67 positive (34%) and 42 (21%) mixed/unclear. We then identified recurring ideas in the comments, and tabulated all of the opinions that occurred more than five times (Table 9.2). As shown in Table 9.2, six of the eight most frequently occurring opinion types were negative. Although some viewers found the swearing fun (19 comments) and warm (6), more reported that it was uncomfortable and crossed the line into genuine rudeness (19). Poster "Wŏnsŏngyŏn," for example commented that Halmŏni saying to Trickid-z that his mother would be ashamed of him was "not warm at all" (*chŏnhyŏ chŏnggamitchi an-ne*).

Table 9.2 Viewer opinions on Yangp'yŏng Tofu video

1	Halmŏni forces herself to swear, and only does it at particular customers	26
2	Trickid-z played the fool to get Halmŏni to swear at him	23
3	Halmŏni's swearing sounded (too) real and rude	22
4	Halmŏni's swearing and/or the video was fun and/or I would like to visit the restaurant myself	19
5	Halmŏni's swearing is uncomfortable and/or I would not like to visit the restaurant	15
6	I don't understand how people can eat/spend money at such a restaurant	13
7	Normal grandmothers do not swear at their grandchildren like this	7
8	Halmŏni's swearing sounds warm, and/or like she is talking to her grandchildren	6

Some commenters more specifically noted that swearing was in fact not a type of behavior that was becoming of a grandmother (7 comments). Commenter "kim dr," for instance, noted that they had never heard their own grandmother swear (*uri halmŏni-nŭn yok-ŭl hanbŏn-do han jŏg-i ŏp-kŏdŭnyo*). Instead, many commenters perceived Halmŏni's behavior as being forced (26 comments), and/or as being induced deliberately by the foolish behavior of Trickid-z (23). "Mŏlt'ip'ŏp'ŏsŭ" commented that Halmŏni had no choice but to continue swearing having chosen "swearing granny" as the concept of her restaurant.

In sum, the viewer comments rather diverged from the way that Halmŏni's impoliteness was portrayed in the video. Whereas the video portrayed her swearing as an act of endearment, this stance was only verified by a minority of the viewers. For the majority, Halmŏni's impoliteness was inappropriate and unbecoming for a grandmother.

THE WIENER'S CIRCLE

The second video features content creator Heechul entering The Wiener's Circle and ordering a hot dog from Evelyn Morris, the restaurant manager.

Impoliteness Strategies

We identified six types of impoliteness strategies performed by Morris.

The first was the use of swearing (26 instances in total), consisting entirely of words depicting sex and effluvia. *Fuck* (including *fucking*, *fucker*) appeared 17 times, followed by *shit* (6 times), *asshole* (2), and *pussy* (1). The middle finger gesture, which we consider a nonverbal form of swearing, is used 4 times. All of the 26 swearwords are propositional (Jay and Janschewitz 2008, 270), with 18 of them referring to Heechul, including vocative forms (*mother fucker*, *asshole*) and sentences featuring *fucking* for added emphasis (*turn your fucking camera off*, *eat your fucking food*). The use of swearwords corresponds to the impoliteness strategy of "use taboo words" (Culpeper 1996).

The second strategy is the use of *baby* as an address term toward Heechul (5 occurrences). This term is conventionally assumed to be a term of endearment (Leech 1999, 111). Morris' use of this term corresponds to "use inappropriate identity markers" under Culpeper's (1996) taxonomy.

The third pattern is Morris departing from the script of traditional routines in service industry interaction, including failing to respond to a complaint, and asking Heechul to pay a tip and then to increase it. On being served his food, Heechul observes that the food doesn't look good. In service industry interaction in America, we might expect responses such as reassuring the customer that the food will taste good, or even offering to do something to "make things right." Instead, Morris rejects Heechul's ostensive complaint, simply stating, "*fuck you, it's very good*" and then telling him to "*go and eat McDonalds.*"

Morris asking Heechul for a tip also departs from typical service industry routines. Since this restaurant does not have counter service, tips would not be expected in the US context. Besides, the custom is for tips to be left on the volition of the customer, rather than being dictated by the service provider. As seen in the following extract, Morris uses bald imperatives (lines 2, 4, 5, 9) and refers to Heechul as *mother fucker* (lines 10, 13) when telling him that he has to turn off his camera unless he increases his tip. Interestingly, in line 12, she frames the tip as being required for her swearing (*How much money you give me mother fucker for calling you mother fucker?*), thus identifying the swearing (rather than the food and service, or her time) as being the commodity that Heechul needs to compensate her for.

(3)
1   Morris   *No more camera.*
2   *Cut it off.*
3   Heechul   *Huhhuh.*

(continued)

(continued)

4	Morris	*Cut it off.*
5		*Cut it off!!*
6		*Yah, you got to give me more money.*
7		*Turn the camera off.*
8		*Let's talk.*
9		*Turn camera off.*
10		*How much, mother fucker?*
11		*How much!*
12		*How much?*
13		*How much money you give me mother fucker for calling you mother fucker?*

This part of the interaction features aggressive nonverbal behaviors. These include large open-palm gestures (Fig. 5a, c), the middle finger gesture (Fig. 5d), and also throat-slitting gestures synchronized with "cut off"

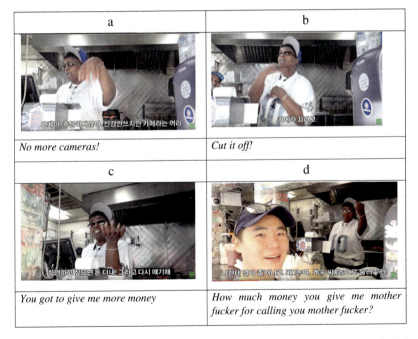

Fig. 9.5 Nonverbal behaviors produced by Morris (Screen captures used with permission from Heechulism)

(Fig. 5b). We analyze this departure from the norms of service industry interactions as being an extension of the strategy of "use inappropriate identity markers."

Fourthly, we see a total absence of mitigation across all speech acts. Morris performs two main speech acts: offers (of food and services) and requests (for Heechul to pay a tip and turn off the camera). In offers of services, formulas such as *Would you like ...?* never occur; instead, Morris uses *You need/want ...?* (5 occurrences) or simply a bare noun (e.g., *French fries?*) (3 occurrences). When making requests related to Heechul paying a tip or otherwise turning off his camera, Morris predominantly uses conventional imperative forms (6 occurrences) in addition to one unconventional imperative (*you* + verb), one occurrence of *no more* + *noun*, and one occurrence of the obligation statement *you got to* + *verb*. This lack of mitigation corresponds to traditional descriptions of impoliteness as the absence of politeness (Brown and Levinson 1987, 5), and to Culpeper's (1996) strategy of "put the other's indebtedness on record."

Fifth, when Morris asks Heechul where he is from, Morris pretends not to understand Heechul's response that he is from South Korea. She asks instead if he is from "West" Korea, before finally concluding that *I don't give a fuck*. This play at not understanding what Heechul is saying and the deliberate display of disinterest in Heechul's response corresponds to Culpeper's (1996) strategies of "be disinterested" and "snub the other."

Sixth and finally, Morris asks questions to Heechul about his personal life:

(4)
1	Morris	*Asshole*
2		*Where is your wife?*
3	Heechul	*Where, where is ma, my wife?*
4	Morris	*You don't get pussy?*
5	Heechul	[Heechul responds, but his response is muted out]
6	Morris	*You are a virgin?*
7	Heechul	[Heechul responds, but his response is muted out]

The use of personal questions falls under what Culpeper (1996, 358) refers to as the metaphorical invasion of other's space "speak[ing] about information which is too intimate given the relationship." Associating Heechul with the image of a virgin (line 6) and a man who does not "*get pussy*" (line 8) also corresponds to the strategy of "condescend, scorn, ridicule."

Participant Reactions

Heechul's interaction with Morris is largely depicted as entertaining rather than impolite. During the encounter, Heechul generally responds to Morris' impoliteness with laughs and smiles. He also attempts to play along with the impoliteness by criticizing the appearance of the food, teasing her for making a lot of money from the business and, on one occasion near the end of the encounter, reciprocating the use of *asshole*. At the end of exchange, Heechul comments that it was "fun," while the English description of the video on YouTube describes the encounter as "entertaining."

There are some signs, however, of mild discomfort or annoyance on the part of Heechul, particularly to Morris' demands for a larger tip. He does not respond to these demands besides for a short and tensed laugh, and then makes reference to the expensive price of the food and the large tip during an aside to the camera. He also displays discomfort to the questions about his personal life, and mutes out his own responses to these questions (see extract 4).

The video concludes with a monologic reflection by Heechul on the general phenomenon of "swearing grannies." He notes that no one in fact likes to be sworn at, hinting that he does not actually enjoy the experience himself. He observes that swearing grannies are able to escape censure due to their identity as grandmothers, who are physically weaker than the customers. In sum, Heechul displays a rather ambivalent attitude toward his visit to the restaurant, and toward the phenomenon in general.

The editing of the video displays contrasting perceptions of the impolite values of the English swearwords and their Korean counterparts. Whereas the English swearwords and associated hand gestures go uncensored, the translated equivalents in the subtitles are censored. For example, in Morris' question *How much money you give me mother fucker for calling you mother fucker?* (Extract 1, line 12), the obscenity *mother fucker* is not bleep censored, whereas the Korean equivalent *ssibalnom* is represented as *ssiXnom* in the subtitles.

Viewer Comments

The video depicting The Wiener's Circle had fewer views than the Korean video (318,427, compared with 610,678 as of December 7, 2020), but had attracted more comments (1091 compared with 888). We analyzed a total of 443 comments that included reference to Morris' behavior and/or the reaction of Heechul.

In contrast to the Korean video that attracted a majority of negative comments, the American video had more positive comments. In total, 261 (59%) of the comments were positive, compared with 81 (18%) negative and 101 (23%) mixed/unclear. The most frequently occurring comment type was that Morris (and/or the video) was funny, great, or cool (85 comments). A further 27 comments included emoticons depicting laughter (ㅋㅋㅋ) in the absence of any specific verbal mention of amusement. Viewers also playfully left their own comments using English swearwords, typically transliterated into Korean orthography (e.g. 퍽 *p'ŭk* [fuck] occurred 8 times) (Table 9.3).

Opinions were rather mixed, however, over whether Morris's use of swearing was "warm" (11 comments), or simply too real and rude (27 comments), scary (20 comments), or part of a money-making strategy (21 comments). Whereas for the Korean video commenters generally viewed the actions of the YouTubers negatively via observations that they were implicit in inciting the swearing from Halmŏni, viewers of the American video expressed emotional concern for Heechul who they noted was scared, embarrassed, and looked like he was going to cry. These comments confirm our earlier observations that Heechul displayed discomfort during the video.

Table 9.3 Viewer opinions on The Wiener's Circle video

1	Morris and/or the video is funny, great, cool, etc	85
2	It was a surprise to see that swearing granny restaurants exist in other countries	30
3	Morris's swearing sounded (too) real and rude	27
4	Morris's swearing is just a strategy to make money	21
5	Morris/the video is scary	20
6	Morris' swearing is simpler/weaker than that found in Korean	18
7	This behavior is risky in a country where guns are legal	14
8	I felt emotional concern for Heechul	14
9	Morris is warm and kind	11
10	Morris's swearing does not sound warm like that of a Korean swearing granny	10
11	I don't understand how people can eat/spend money at such a restaurant	5
12	Heechul (or other customers) might use racial slurs to Morris	5

A number of comments made reference to the American setting of the video, including explicit comparisons with Korean "swearing grannies." 11 commenters noted that Morris was not as warm as Korean swearing grannies, with a further 18 commenters noting that the swearing appeared to be weaker or simpler to that found in Korean. One poster named "Mr. Physio Hojumullich'iryosa" noted that Morris's swearing lacks the "delicate taste" (*kusuhan mat*) of Korean swear words, whereas "Hwangŭn'gi" observed that the swearing was repetitive and tiresome, lacking the "varied tastes" (*tayanghan mat*) of Korean insults.

Discussion and Conclusion

The analysis has shown that both of the restaurants analyzed, Yangp'yŏng Tofu and The Wiener's Circle, employ similar impolite strategies in order to flout the norms of service industry politeness. We identified four of the same strategies in both videos: (1) use taboo words, (2) use inappropriate identity markers, (3) flout service industry routines, and (4) condescend, scorn, ridicule (Culpeper 1996). The Wiener's Circle featured two additional strategies: (1) put the other's indebtedness on record and (2) invade the other's space. In both restaurants, the majority of swearwords were used propositionally to refer to the hearer, thus rendering them the most likely to cause offense (Jay and Janschewitz 2008, 270). The impoliteness in both restaurants is performed multimodally through nonverbal features including the withholding of gaze (Yangp'yŏng Tofu) and the middle finger gesture (Wiener's Circle).

Despite the similarities between the videos, we observed differences in how the impoliteness was interpreted by participants and viewers. Halmŏni was evaluated positively by the immediate participants, whereas Heechul's reaction to Morris was more ambivalent. In contrast to this, the Korean viewer comments were notably more critical of Halmŏni than they were of Morris. They were more likely to interpret Halmŏni's swearing as genuinely rude, whereas Morris's swearing was perceived as being funny and as representing a less-developed and weaker former of abuse. The analysis of the viewer comments confirms previous claims that language users experience higher emotional intensity for insults in their native language (Dewaele 2010; Harris et al. 2003) and that non-natives perceive English swearwords in a light-hearted way (Fägersten 2017; Jaffe 2017).

We also see important culture-specific factors that determine the different perceptions of Halmŏni and Morris. Specifically, the interaction at Yangp'yŏng Tofu and perceptions of it rely on the kinship-based trope that the restaurant owner is a fictive "grandmother" to the customers. She is referred to ubiquitously as "Halmŏni"; in fact, we could not locate her actual name in any of the materials. Agha (2015, 402) notes that kinship terms are used in non-kin is known to evoke the metaphor of kinship in order for language users to "inhabit kin-like relationships with persons or groups" (Agha 2015, 402). The way that Halmŏni is positioned as a grandmother relies on a culture-specific mode of sociality in Korea, whereby social interactions tend to be organized around fictive family structures (Harkness's 2015, 495). Hur (2016) dubs this phenomenon *kajok-hwakchangsŏng* "family expansionism," which is defined as a tendency for Korean people to understand all social structures as having the same roles as family relations. In the video, Halmŏni's use of swearing is positioned as an index of her "grandmother" identity and therefore interpreted as warm and intimate. Her position as the "grandmother" is verified via the deferential behavior that Trickid-z and other participants perform toward her. However, for many of the viewers, the insulting language is perceived as incongruous with her status as a grandmother, which becomes a crucial factor in the negative comments aimed at her. In these comments, viewers evoke comparisons between Halmŏni's coarse behavior and the more refined behavior of their own grandmothers, thus displaying blurring between consanguineous family relationships and fictional ones. This confirms Hur's (2016, 243) observation that in Korea an elderly woman is identified as everyone's own grandmother.

Although The Wiener's Circle is described in the Korean media as *miguk-p'an yokchaengi halmŏni siktang* (the American swearing granny restaurant), the analysis shows that interactions in this restaurant do not follow the grandmother trope, and are not perceived in these terms by the viewers. Rather than showing deferential behavior toward Morris and other serving staff, customers frequently reciprocate the impoliteness (see Helm 2017). Heechul appears to be aware of this in the way that he calls Morris an *asshole* and criticizes the food. In addition, although viewer comments do refer to Morris as *halmŏni*, they never criticize her behavior as being unbecoming to her status, nor do they compare her behavior to that of actual non-fictive grandmothers. Rather than family-based tropes, the use of swearing at The Wiener's Circle plugs into the use of swearwords during the ritualized impoliteness that occurs within groups of friends, which has been referred in previous studies on various English-speaking contexts with terms such as "banter" (Leech 1983), "teasing" (see Haugh 2010) "taking the piss/mickey" (Goddard 2009) and "jocular mockery" (Haugh 2010). The use of swearing in these two restaurants is thus mediated via quite different modes of sociality: The Korean restaurant relies on a kin-based social structure, whereas the American restaurant does not.

One thing that the two restaurants share, however, is that the use of swearing in both contexts is somewhat subversive. Price (2010) notes that The Wiener's Circle features "a black staff catering to a predominantly white clientele," meaning that the restaurant is a venue where African Americans are able to insult their White American customers. It also appears that most of the serving staff are female. At Yangp'yŏng Tofu (and other swearing granny restaurants in Korea), the swearing is performed by working-class grandmothers. Although senior citizens are afforded respect in Korea due to their status as *noin* (Yoon 2004), they have also become an impoverished and disempowered section of society. Recent years have witnessed an increase in elderly poverty due to the erosion of traditional Confucian family structures. Younger Koreans are increasingly reluctant or unable to financially support their elders, while the government has been slow to improve the low level of financial support that they provide to the elderly (see Lee 2014 and Park Hong-jae's chapter in this collection). As noted by Heechul himself in the comments at the end of the video, the image of the grandmother is connected with someone who is physically weak and who needs to be looked after. The use of rude language by these service staff thus confirms Jaffe's (2017, 90) observation that swearing has the potential to challenge or subvert authority and dominant linguistic and social ideologies. However, at the same time that the swearing subverts authority, it also somewhat confirms the existence of the dominant order. It is precisely because the staff are perceived as socially and physically non-threatening that their use of impolite language can be more readily forgiven. And their use of crude language also works to index and thereby replicate their lowly social positions as people who lack refinement and education.

In the extant literature on Korean linguistic (im)politeness, being polite has been assumed to be an important aspect of Korean sociality. Kim (2018) points out that Korea has a long history of being recognized internationally as a polite nation, including the historic use of the epithet

Tongbang yeŭi chi kuk (The Nation of Propriety in the East) for referring to Korea. In this paper, we have seen that impoliteness also plays an important role in Korea-specific forms of sociality, including in materials produced by YouTube content creators. We thus follow Harkness (2015) in seeing impolite language (and other forms of slang) as being "an emergent linguistic emblem of South Korean society," which represents the subversive language of those challenging the more widely accepted norms of social interaction in modern Korea. This alternative linguistic emblem is now emerging on the global stage with the increasing representation of Korean swearing, impoliteness, and slang on YouTube channels featuring cross-cultural content and aimed at both Korean and overseas audiences. This emergence of slang as a linguistic emblem of Korea is underlined by the recent emergence of the term K-slang (in other words, "Korean slang") on websites and online tutorials teaching casual and impolite Korean expressions. The coining of the term K-slang elevates slang to the same level as other nouns that appear with the "K" prefix (notably K-pop, but also K-drama, K-food, and so forth) which are marketed internationally as commodified emblems of Korean culture. Going forward, more research will be needed into the cultural specificity of Korean impoliteness and the importance of swearing and slang as symbols of Korean culture.

Notes

1. Åmål is the name of a small Swedish town.
2. The full title of the video is 방송 80 번탄 베테랑 욕쟁이할머니를 만난 외국인 반응, 국내 1 호 드럼통 철판 두루치기 삼겹살 먹방 with 카슨, 마리아, 트리키즈. The link is: https://www.youtube.com/watch?v=x4A07SsvgQM.
3. The full title of the video is "The Famous cursing grandmother in the US" The link is: https://www.youtube.com/watch?v=NP7xAQB3dHI.
4. Bottom-up coding involves starting with the data and identifying patterns occurring in it via an inductive process, and then assigning labels to them. This contrasts with top-down coding where the researcher starts with pre-defined labels, and then applies them to the data.

References

Agha, Asif. 2015. "Chronotopic Formulations and Kinship Behaviors in Social History." *Anthropological Quarterly* 88 (2): 401–415.

Blitvich, Pilar Garcés-Conejos. 2009. "Impoliteness and identity in the American news media: The 'Culture Wars.'" *Journal of Politeness Research* 5 (2): 273–303.

Blitvich, Pilar Garcés-Conejos, Patricia Bou-Franch, and Nuria Lorenzo-Dus. 2013. "Identity and Impoliteness: The Expert in the Talent Show *Idol*." *Journal of Politeness Research* 9 (1): 97–121.

Bousfield, Derek. 2007. "Beginnings, Middles and Ends: A Biopsy of the Dynamics of Impolite Exchanges." *Journal of Pragmatics* 39 (12): 2185–2216.

Brown, Lucien. 2013. "'Mind Your Own Esteemed Business': Sarcastic Honorifics Use and Impoliteness in Korean TV Dramas." *Journal of Politeness Research* 9 (2): 159–186.

Brown, Lucien. 2015. "Honorifics and Politeness." In *The Handbook of Korean Linguistics*, edited by Lucien Brown and Jaehoon Yeon, 303–319. Malden, MA: Wiley-Blackwell.

Brown, Lucien, and Bodo Winter. 2019. "Multimodal Indexicality in Korean: 'Doing Deference' and 'Performing Intimacy' Through Nonverbal Behaviour." *Journal of Politeness Research* 15 (1): 25–54.

Brown, Lucien, Bodo Winter, Kaori Idemaru, and Sven Grawunder. 2014. "Phonetics and Politeness: Perceiving Korean Honorific and Non-Honorific Speech Through Phonetic Cues." *Journal of Pragmatics* 66: 45–60.

Brown, Penelope, and Stephen Levinson. 1987. *Politeness: Some Universals in Language Usage*. Cambridge: Cambridge University Press.

Culpeper, Jonathan. 1996. "Towards an Anatomy of Impoliteness." *Journal of Pragmatics* 25(3): 349–367.

Culpeper, Jonathan. 2005. "Impoliteness and Entertainment in the Television Quiz Show: *The Weakest Link*." *Journal of Politeness Research* 1 (1): 35–72.

Culpeper, Jonathan, and Michael Haugh. 2014. *Pragmatics and the English Language*. Basingstoke: Palgrave Macmillan.

Culpeper, Jonathan, Derek Bousfield, and Anne Wichmann. 2003. "Impoliteness Revisited: With Special Reference to Dynamic and Prosodic Aspects." *Journal of Pragmatics* 35 (10–11): 1545–1579.

Dewaele, Jean-Marc. 2010. *Emotions in Multiple Languages*. Basingstoke: Springer.

Dunn, Cynthia Dickel. 2013. "Speaking Politely, Kindly, and Beautifully: Ideologies of Politeness in Japanese Business Etiquette Training." *Multilingua* 32 (2): 225–245.

Eelen, Gino. 2001. *A Critique of Politeness Theories*. Manchester: St Jerome Publishing.

Fägersten, Kristy Beers. 2017. "FUCK CANCER, Fucking Åmål, Aldrig fucka upp." In *Advances in Swearing Research. New Languages and New Contexts*, edited by Nuria Lorenzo-Dus and Pilar Garcés-Conejos Blitvich, 65–86. Basingstoke: Palgrave Macmillan.

Fägersten, Kristy Beers, and Karyn Stapleton. 2017. "Introduction." In *Advances in Swearing Research: New Languages and New Contexts*, edited by Kristy Beers Fägersten and Karyn Stapleton, 1–15. Amsterdam: John Benjamins.

Goddard, Cliff. 2009. "Not Taking Yourself Too Seriously in Australian English: Semantic Explications, Cultural Scripts, Corpus Evidence." *Intercultural Pragmatics* 6 (1): 29–53.

Harkness, Nicholas. 2015. "Basic Kinship Terms: Christian Relations, Chronotopic Formulations, and a Korean Confrontation of Language." *Anthropological Quarterly* 88 (2): 305–336.

Harris, Catherine L., Ayse Ayçíçeği, and Jean Berko Gleason. 2003. "Taboo Words and Reprimands Elicit Greater Autonomic Reactivity in a First Language than in a Second Language." *Applied Psycholinguistics* 24 (4): 561–579.

Haugh, Michael. 2010. "Jocular Mockery and Face in Anglo-Australian Interactions." *Journal of Pragmatics* 42 (8): 2106–2119.

Haugh, Michael, and Lara Weinglass. 2020. "'The Great Australian Pastime': Pragmatic and Semantic Perspectives on Taking the Piss." In *Studies in Ethnopragmatics, Cultural Semantics, and Intercultural Communication*, edited by Kerry Mullan, Bert Peeters, and Lauren Sadow, 95–117. Singapore: Springer.

Helm, Eliza. 2017. "What It's Like to Work at The Wiener's Circle, Chicago's Most Foul-Mouthed Restaurant." Last modified July 19. https://www.thrillist.com/lifestyle/chicago/the-wiener-circle-chicago-hot-dog-stand.

Hur, Taekyun. 2016. *Ŏtchŏda Han'gugin* [A Korean by Chance]. Joongang Books.

Jaffe, Alexandra. 2017. "Fuck in French." In *Advances in Swearing Research: New Languages and New Contexts*, edited by Kristy Beers Fägersten and Karyn Stapleton, 87–106. Amsterdam: John Benjamins.

Jay, Timothy, and Kristin Janschewitz. 2008. "The Pragmatics of Swearing." *Journal of Politeness Research* 4 (2): 267–288.

Kádár, Daniel, and Yuling Pan. 2011. "Politeness in China." In *Politeness in East Asia*, edited by Daniel Kádár and Sara Mills, 125–146. Cambridge: Cambridge University Press.

Kádár, Dániel, and Michael Haugh 2013. *Understanding Politeness*. Cambridge: Cambridge University Press.

Kádár, Dániel, Michael Haugh, and Wei-Lin Melody Chang. 2013. "Aggression and Perceived National Face Threats in Mainland Chinese and Taiwanese CMC Discussion Boards." *Multilingua* 32 (3): 343–372.

Kim, Eunseon. 2018. "Language and politeness in the 'Nation of Propriety in the East': A history of linguistic ideologies of Korean honorification." PhD diss., University of British Columbia.

Kim HeeSook. 2003. "Hyŏndaehan'gugŏ hoch'ingŏŭi yŏksŏl: 2ch'a sahoe nae nŭrŏnanŭn ch'injogŏ sayong" [The Paradox of Address Term Usage in Modern Korean: The Increase of Kinship Term Usage in Secondary Society]. *Sahoeŏnŏhak* [The Sociolinguistic Journal of Korea] 11 (1): 55–93.

Kim Sang Yoon. 2002. "Yoksŏl-ŭi t'ŭkchil-e kwanhan yŏn'gu" [A Study on the Characteristics of Abuse in Korean]. *Hwabŏb yŏn'gu* [Discourse Analysis] 4: 271–290.

Kim, Sun Hee Ok, and Donna Starks. 2008. "The Role of Emotions in L1 Attrition: The Case of Korean-English Late Bilinguals in New Zealand." *International Journal of Bilingualism* 12 (4): 303–319.

Lakoff, Robin. 1977. "What You Can Do with Words: Politeness, Pragmatics and Performatives." In *Proceedings of the Texas Conference on Performatives, Presuppositions, and Implicatures*, edited by Andy Rogers, 79–106. Arlington, TX: Center of Applied Linguistics.

Lee, Iksop, and S. Robert Ramsey. 2000. *The Korean Language*. Albany, NY: SUNY Press.

Lee, Jiyoon, and Lucien Brown. Forthcoming. "Honorifics in the Marketplace: A Multimodal Indexical Analysis." *Korean Linguistics*.

Lee, Keunyoung. 2020. "Impoliteness, Identity and Power in Korea: Discourse Analysis and Perception Study of Impoliteness." PhD diss., University of Oregon.

Lee, Sun Jae. 2014. "Poverty Amongst the Elderly in South Korea: The Perception, Prevalence, and Causes and Solutions." *International Journal of Social Science and Humanity* 4 (3): 242.

Leech, Geoffrey. 1977. "Language and Tact." Linguistic Agency University of Trier (L.A.U.T), A/46.

Leech, Geoffrey.1983. *Principles of Pragmatics*. London: Longman.

Leech, Geoffrey. 1999. "The Distribution and Function of Vocatives in American and British English Conversation." In *Out of Corpora: Studies in Honour of Stig Johansson*, edited by Hilde Hasselgård and Signe Oksefjell, 107–120. Amsterdam: Rodopi.

Locher, Miriam, and Richard Watts. 2008. "Relational Work and Impoliteness: Negotiating Norms of Linguistic Behaviour." In *Impoliteness in Language: Studies on Its Interplay with Power in Theory and Practice*, edited by Derek Bousfield and Miriam Locher, 77–99. Berlin: Mouton de Gruyter.

Lorenzo-Dus, Nuria. 2009. "'You're Barking Mad, I'm Out': Impoliteness and Broadcast Talk." *Journal of Politeness Research* 5 (2): 159–187.

Lorenzo-Dus, Nuria, Patricia Bou-Franch, and Pilar Garcés-Conejos Blitvich. 2013. "Impoliteness in US/UK Talent Shows: A Diachronic Study of Evolution of a Genre." In *Real Talk: Reality Television and Discourse Analysis in Action*, edited by Nuria Lorenzo-Dus and Pilar Garcés-Conejos Blitvich, 199–217. Basingstoke: Palgrave Macmillan.

Okano, Emi, and Lucien Brown. 2018. "Did Becky Really Need to Apologize? Intercultural Evaluations of Politeness." *East Asian Pragmatics* 3 (2): 151–178.

Price, Catherine. 2010. *101 Places Not to See Before You Die*. Harper Collins.

Ringbom, Håkan. 2001. "Developing Literacy Can and Should Be Fun: But Only Sometimes Is." In *Reflections on Multiliterate Lives*, edited by Diane Belcher and Ulla Connor, 60–66. Clevedon: Multilingual Matters.

Shin, Gi-Wook, and Rennie J. Moon. 2017. "South Korea After Impeachment." *Journal of Democracy* 28 (4): 117–131.

Wessel, Jennifer, and Dirk Steiner. 2015. "Surface Acting in Service: A Two-Context Examination of Customer Power and Politeness." *Human Relations* 68 (5): 709–730.

White, Rob. 2002. "Indigenous Young Australians, Criminal Justice and Offensive Language." *Journal of Youth Studies* 5: 21–34.

Yeon, Jaehoon, and Lucien Brown. 2019. *Korean: A Comprehensive Grammar—Second Edition*. London: Routledge.

Yon Woo-Sang. 2015. "Saik'odŭramaesŏ yogŭi ŭimiwa yŏk'al" [The meaning and role of swearing in psychodrama]. *Han'guksaik'odŭramahak'oeji* [Korean Journal of Psychodrama] 18 (1): 1–14.

Yoon, Kyung-Joo. 2004. "Not Just Words: Korean Social Models and the Use of Honorifics." *Intercultural Pragmatics* 1 (2): 189–210.

PART IV

Society and Space

INTRODUCTION

Andrew David Jackson

The final part of the book deals with two different areas connected to changes resulting from North and South Korea's global interactions. Three of the chapters address the social transformations resulting from Korean contact with the wider East Asian region and beyond. There are two areas of interest in particular; first, the transformation of South Korean society in the wake of Kim Young Sam's promulgation of his *segyehwa* policy. Second, the long-term transitions that occurred within the North Korean sphere of influence resulting from global developments.

South Korea's *segyehwa* drive saw the country commit to a central principle underlying globalization, namely the free movement of people across national borders. As a result of this commitment, South Korea witnessed significant demographic and social changes from the 1990s onwards. In 1990, only 0.1% of the population was made up of foreign citizens, but by 2019 this number had risen to 5%, or 2.5 million people (Gorbunova 2020, 174). While this may not sound much compared to more multicultural societies in Australia, North America, or Western Europe, these figures represent a significant demographic change in Korean terms.[1] Traditionally, the Koreans liked to differentiate their population from regional neighbors by characterizing themselves as a "single nation, bound together by clearly demarcated geographical boundaries" that shared a long history of relative linguistic and social homogeneity (Chang

2009, 35). In addition, South Korea had a relatively long experience as a country that exported large numbers of people escaping poverty and political repression by seeking opportunities abroad. In the 1960s and 1970s, many South Koreans sought work in Middle East construction, West German hospitals and mines, and South American agriculture. In the 1980s, many South Koreans sought better lives in North America, leading to significant diasporic communities in cities like Vancouver and Los Angeles. In addition, many orphaned Korean children were adopted into families in Scandinavian countries and elsewhere in Western nations. These extremely diverse groups joined the already significant Korean communities in China, Central Asia, Russia, and Japan, many of which had been dislocated by the disruption of the colonial period, to form the Korean diaspora.

By the 1990s, however, South Korea had transformed from a labor exporting to a labor *importing* country (Gorbunova 2020, 174), as workers from China and Southeast Asia came to work in South Korea's large manufacturing, agricultural, and fishing sectors, taking the jobs that Korean nationals had begun to shun. Joining many of these lower-paid foreign nationals were members of the Korean diaspora who started to return to South Korea by taking advantage of preferential immigration legislation introduced in 1999. These rule changes were adopted as a strategy to attract resource-rich, well-educated, multi-lingual, and talented overseas Koreans into the local labor market (Gorbunova 2020, 173).

As well as the immigration of foreign workers and the return of overseas Koreans, other factors also caused significant demographic changes in South Korea. One important transformation has been the international marriage phenomenon, which saw an influx of women from China, Vietnam, the Philippines, Russia, and Uzbekistan arriving in South Korea to marry local men, often working in occupations seen as undesirable by South Korean women, such as farming. Between 1990 and 2005, around 160,000 foreign women married South Korean men, and such arrangements accounted for approximately 40 percent of all marriages in rural areas (Lee 2008, 107–111). From the early 2000s onwards, education has also been a major reason for resettlement abroad for many Koreans, leading to a curious transnational family phenomenon. Many wealthy families have begun educating their children abroad to provide them with advantages in a fiercely competitive society. It is widely perceived that Koreans with vital foreign language skills (especially in English) and prestigious foreign qualifications will later excel in the job market (Park 2009). To facilitate this process, fathers remain in South Korea to continue earning while mothers stay with their children attending schools abroad. By 2020, there were roughly half a million South Korean transnational families (Gorbunova 2020, 175). Finally, an unprecedented number of South Koreans have traveled, experiencing life abroad since restrictions on overseas trips were removed in January 1989. During the 1961–1979 military dictatorship, there were age restrictions on travel, and only citizens over the age of thirty were eligible for passports. Generally, only those involved in business, government, or academia were permitted to receive passports, while travel visas from the Korean government required a significant deposit, limiting overseas travel (Son 2014). The dictatorship was keen to restrict South Korean contact with North Koreans overseas and prevent the contamination of foreign ideas about democracy and human rights from entering the country. With travel restrictions removed, many South Koreans, young and old, began spending time traveling, studying, and living outside the Peninsula. The net result of these developments was a South Korean society, which in terms of demographics, attitudes, and outlook was significantly different from the pre-*segyehwa* era.

The DPRK, on the other hand, throughout its seventy-year history, has shared significant cultural and economic ties to a minority, migrant community, not within its North Korean state borders but beyond it. Vital political and financial support for the DPRK came from the pro-North Korean communities residing in Japan. A sizeable Korean diaspora has lived in Japan for several decades, many of whom had either emigrated during the colonial period or were forcibly mobilized into labor in the service of the Japanese imperial economy following Japan's invasion of Manchuria (Lankov 2013, 23). In the early 1950s, there were an estimated 700,000 Koreans in Japan (Lankov 2013, 23). Following Japan's surrender and the widespread unrest and uncertainty that accompanied the division of the Korean Peninsula, many Koreans decided to remain in Japan rather than return to an unsettled homeland. Splits emerged within the community between pro-South and pro-North Korean groups, mirroring the divided Peninsula. Many within the Korean diaspora in Japan claimed allegiance to the North rather than the South despite having no familial or geographical connections to the northern part of the Peninsula. This was the period of economic growth in the DPRK, and for many in the Japanese community, the communist North must have looked a safer bet than the stagnant South under the corrupt and dictatorial leadership of Syngman Rhee. Many Korean emigrants in Asia could still remember Japanese colonial rule in this period, and communism (at least the Stalinist version of it) may well have looked a more attractive ideology than the capitalist model represented by ongoing or former colonial European and American powers. In addition, the primary pro-North Korean group Chongryon (Chosen Soren) was more effective at organizing, recruiting, and mobilizing its supporters than its pro-ROK counterpart (Lankov 2013, 23).

From the late 1950s onwards, pro-North activists succeeded in persuading a significant proportion of Japanese Koreans to "return" to the DPRK, even though most of them had never set foot in the place. Many went off to an uncertain fate, discriminated against yet simultaneously privileged because of the goods they brought back with them and because of the remittances dispatched to them from relatives in Japan (Lankov 2013, 24). Generally, however, many returnees were gravely disappointed by the deprivation and repression they faced in the North when they got there. Korean-Japanese were regarded with suspicion by the authorities and their neighbors and were often relegated to menial professions. However, in yet another shift, in economic terms, the fortunes of the Korean-Japanese communities changed for the better in the DPRK following the 1990s famine, when their economic connections to the Japanese archipelago served to support many. Overall, the mass migration greatly damaged the reputation of organizations like Chongryon among the Japanese Korean community (Ishikawa 2017). Chongryon membership has dwindled since the great migration, but many of those who have retained their pro-Pyongyang allegiance live in separate communities and attend North Korean schools. Koreans on the Japanese Archipelago provide valuable economic and political support for Pyongyang. They now form a central part of North Korea's contacts to the world beyond the Peninsula.

The chapters that follow investigate some important cultural outcomes of the demographic changes brought about by greater globalization in South Korea. One vital transformation initiated by the increasing internationalization of society has been the adoption of the idea of "multiculturalism" (or *tamunhwa*) in South Korea, which was made a cornerstone of the policy of President Roh Moo-hyun's administration. Andreas Schirmer analyzes the considerable literature that has appeared on South Korean multiculturalism over the past ten years. Schirmer concludes that since the beginning of the new millennium, official discourses over what constitutes the Korean nation have shifted significantly due to the increasing diversification of South Korean society. He finds contradictory and occasionally surprising understandings of multiculturalism among different actors in society that vary according to diverse agendas, and argues that multiculturalism should not always be taken as the antithesis to nationalism that it is assumed to be.

Hong-Jae Park's chapter shifts its focus to another challenging social and demographic phenomenon facing South Korea, its rapidly aging population. As mentioned in Maliangkay's chapter on music preservation, providing for the elderly represents a particularly complex problem for the government in the context of a low birth rate. Park examines problematic issues relating to the human rights of elderly people in the context of the rapid transformation of South Korean society. Park argues tensions have emerged within state and personal care provision for the elderly as South Korea is increasingly caught between two forces pulling in opposite directions—traditional beliefs based on Confucianism and modernizing forces based on the notion of a welfare state. On the one hand, the state attempts to provide care for the elderly with an eye on international human rights standards. On the other hand, policymakers also take into account traditional Confucian thought, which reveres the elderly. Generations of Koreans are torn between customary practices and more recent political, economic, and social developments. While many Koreans still invest in their children's education, many children choose not to support their parents into old age. The result is ineffective provision for the elderly and high rates of severe poverty in a country where older people are supposed to be culturally privileged.

The final essays in this collection shift their attention to the DPRK. One chapter examines some of the cross-border interactions with the DPRK. Min Hye Cho's work deals with the educational system of the Chongryon community in Japan, particularly the development of English education over a period of socio and geopolitical change within a pro-Pyongyang community. The final area of exploration for this book, space, is found in the last chapter, and it is perhaps the most curious of all topics examined in the collection. The bizarre and obscure case of the North Korean fishing industry almost merits a section of its own since it deals with commerce, international agreements, and environmental sustainability—topics that put it at odds with the social-cultural bent of other chapters. Yet it also deals with the DPRK's interactions with the most global of spaces—the commons—those fragile, environmental resources made for everyone on earth to share. It also treats a topic that has entered the public imagination thanks to increased media interest since the second decade of the new millennium in the North Korean ghost ship phenomenon. From 2011 onwards, dozens of North Korean fishing boats have washed up on Japanese shores, either abandoned or with human remains onboard (Urbina 2020). These boats are thought to be part of North Korea's "dark fleets"—illegal fishing vessels operating outside international agreements and legitimate operations implemented to maintain a sustainable industry. Robert Winstanley-Chester's essay investigates the fascinating story behind the appearance of these "ghost ships" and contextualizes this phenomenon within historical attempts by Pyongyang to engage in fishing. Winstanley-Chesters argues that we see significant continuity in the DPRK's historical dealings with Cold War-era socialist allies and the present post-socialist period.

Note

1. Dong-Hoon Seol, for example, notes that in 2007 the foreign population of Spain was five times higher than that of South Korea as a percentage of the total population (2010, 595).

References

Chang Yun-shik. 2009. "Introduction: Korea in the Process of Globalization." In *Korea Confronts Globalization*, edited by Chang Yun-shik, Seok Hyun-ho, and Donald Baker, 1–39. New York: Routledge.

Gorbunova, Ekaterina. 2020. "Korean Diaspora in the South Korean Media Discourse: Changing Narrative." *Diaspora Studies* 13 (2): 170–188.

Ishikawa, Masaji. 2017 [2000]. *A River in Darkness: One Man's Escape from North Korea*. Seattle: Amazon Crossing.

Lankov, Andrei. 2013. *The Real North Korea: Life and Politics in the Failed Stalinist Utopia*. Oxford: Oxford University Press.

Lee, Hye-Kyung. 2008. "International Marriage and the State in South Korea: Focusing on Governmental Policy." *Citizenship Studies* 12 (1): 107–123.

Park, Joseph Sung-Yul. 2009. *The Local Construction of a Global Language: Ideologies of English in South Korea*. Berlin: Mouton de Gruyter.

Seol, Dong-Hoon. 2010. "Which Multiculturalism? Discourse of the Incorporation of Immigrants into Korean Society." *Korea Observer* 41 (4): 593–614.

Son Min-ho. 2014. "After Travel Rules Relaxed, Koreans Took to the Skies." *JoongAng Daily*. January 14. http://koreajoongangdaily.joins.com/news/article/article.aspx?aid=2983445. Accessed March 27, 2020.

Urbina, Ian. 2020. "The Origin of North Korea's 'Ghost Boats.'" *BBC News*, September 10. https://www.bbc.com/future/article/20200909-the-origin-of-north-koreas-ghost-boats. Accessed September 3, 2021.

CHAPTER 10

Korean "Multicultural Literature" and Discourses About Koreanness

Andreas Schirmer

Tamunhwa munhak (multicultural literature) is a term coined to describe a broadly defined genre in Korean fiction and poetry that has emerged over the last two decades. The texts gathered under this label are not only defined by their subject matter but also by a common goal: they can be understood as attempts by fiction writers to contribute to a more inclusive society by inducing readers to feel empathy for those who have been excluded by virtue of their foreignness. Often, these texts focus on exposing the shameless exploitation of foreign workers (labor migrants) and the plight of foreign brides (marriage migrants)—cases of massive xenophobic discrimination that look all the more appalling when contrasted with Koreans' immense adoration for white Westerners. Some *tamunhwa munhak* novels have an additional focus: contesting the infamous *tanil minjok sinhwa* (myth of the homogenous nation), in other

A. Schirmer (✉)
Palacký University Olomouc, Olomouc, Czechia
e-mail: andreas.schirmer@upol.cz

© The Author(s), under exclusive license to Springer Nature Switzerland AG 2022
A. D. Jackson (ed.), *The Two Koreas and their Global Engagements*,
https://doi.org/10.1007/978-3-030-90761-7_10

words, the "myth of monoethnic and monocultural Korea" (Lie 2015, vii).

Koreanness is usually conceived of as being constituted from either "archetypes," "DNA," "software," or a bundle of "codes"—or (alternatively) constructed as a set of skills, beliefs, and habits. However, what the struggling characters in these novels are most haunted by are not any presumed essential attributes of the *homo coreanicus* but troubles stemming from outward appearance. A society "wrapped up in surfaces," a "republic of plastic surgery" (*sŏnghyŏng susul ŭi konghwaguk*), South Korea proves unforgiving not only toward the "permanent underclass" of the "unlovely" (Park 2015) but most of all unforgiving of those whose appearance marks them as outsiders in the most literal sense: the lowly underclass from abroad.

Dissecting the motif of "problematic appearance" that dominates *tamunhwa munhak*, this chapter dwells specifically on examples of resistance to or subversion of ascribed identity that are to be found in *tamunhwa munhak*. In these texts, fraud, deception, and camouflage are used to construct and take on an identity of one's choosing—or at least one that allows a better life. While such identity construction is portrayed as mere escapist denial, or even as leading to total debacle and disaster, these novels and short stories nonetheless voice powerful interventions into public discourse.

Everybody Is "Born with Mixed Blood"

An-na is an ordinary Korean woman, but when sleeping she could be taken by an outsider for Chinese, Japanese, Southeast Asian, Mongolian, American Indian, and so on. Such thoughts occur to the narrator of Son Hong-kyu's *The Muslim Butcher* (Son 2016 [2010]) when looking at an elderly resident of his local neighborhood. The novel is one of the foremost examples of *tamunhwa munhak*, and is centered on an orphaned Korean teenager adopted by a former Turkish soldier still stranded in Seoul decades after the Korean War. If it is impossible to ascribe a single identity to An-na, then this one person's face becomes the face of humanity. The usual distinctions between various ethnicities become, at least for the time of sleep, meaningless:

> Her sleeping face was peculiar. She looked like a typical Korean woman but then it would be credible if someone said that she was of Chinese, Japanese,

Vietnamese, or Indonesian descent. She could have been a Hispanic, a mulatto, or a Native American with some black blood thrown in. In the end, I was confused about who she was, whose blood she inherited, and it began to dawn on me that people were born with mixed blood. It was the same with Uncle Hassan and Uncle Amos. They had spent so many years in Korea that despite their stubborn personalities, they'd been tamed by the place. Some recognized them as foreign on sight, but others didn't have a clue about their foreign origins. Some people, even after they were told that the duo was from Turkey and Greece, insisted that they had to be Korean. They offered what they called evidence, saying that the two men resembled so-and-so they knew and that so-and-so they knew was doubtlessly Korean, and therefore (…). (Son 2016, 121)

Such insights are also reflected in a game that the teenager plays. He collects "ambiguous" faces, cutting photographs out of newspapers and magazines:

I opened my scrapbook and quizzed Agent about the nationality of a face I was pointing to. That face had dark skin, prominent cheekbones, a round and upturned short nose, and thick lips. Agent let slip a smile and said, "Isn't he African?" He said that he couldn't say which country the guy was from because there were so many newly independent countries over there. He listed African countries he knew – Kenya, Ghana, Nigeria, the Republic of South Africa, Ethiopia – and said that he was sure the guy was from one of them. But the person in question was Korean. "If this guy is Korean, I bet he's a mongrel," he said. I proved that the owner of that particular face was a pure-blood Korean. "You see his face here in this picture? He's with his parents and siblings. They are all alike, aren't they?" Agent shrugged and said, "Our country is tiny but look how many weird-looking people we have out there!" (Son 2016, 164–165)

The conclusion that everybody is "born with mixed blood" (Son 2016, 121) is, of course, not simply an apodictical claim, but a dialectical contradiction of or antithesis to the belief that Koreans form a *"tanil minjok"*: an undiluted, singular people or, even, "race."

To anticipate my subsequent argument: What weighs on the minds of the main characters in many of these novels—insofar as it makes them stand out and thus makes them a target—is not any conflict with the spiritual essence of Koreanness, nor any inability to conform with purported common, collective features of Korean personality. Rather, the problem concerns something that is, by contrast, much simpler: namely, "appearance."

Multiculturalism and Koreanness

One of the most salient changes in South Korea during the last two decades is epitomized by this pervasive buzzword *tamunhwa* (multi-culture or multiculturalism). For South Koreans, globalization entailed an unprecedented increase in possibilities for experiencing the foreign, both at home and abroad. Foreigners living in Korea are now highly visible in Korean media, all the more so since increasing numbers of them are able to communicate their lived experience in fluent Korean. Hybrid identities based on "mixed blood" have also come more into the spotlight (thanks in part to a number of celebrities bearing such mixed identities), complicating the long-cherished concept of a single-race or pure-blood nation in which everyone shares a supposedly similar basic mindset. Moreover, popular awareness of Koreans in the diaspora has grown continuously, and attention is also increasingly drawn to *t'albukcha* (refugees from North Korea), their struggles to adapt in South Korea making evident the precariousness of claiming a Korean identity based on common ethnicity (mandating future reunification), as well as to the transnational experience.

For all these reasons, those notions and concepts of Koreanness that developed most vigorously between the 1960s and 1990s, a period that was dominated by a nationalist agenda, now seem outdated.[1] At least, the established stereotypes deployed to define the *homo coreanicus* (Chin 2007) have lost much credibility and are regularly called into question. At the same time, the obstinate persistence of some longstanding clichés of identity (such as the commonplace that much of Korean behavior is ruled by *chŏng*, that is, a feeling of affection or mutual attachment said to underpin social bonds between Koreans) shows that they still cannot be dismissed outright.

In the common discourse about what it is that makes Koreans ultimately Korean (and thus unique), the standard approach is to describe Koreanness as a specific set of "archetypes" (*wŏnhyŏng*) (Kim 1995) or "codes" (Kang 2006), an "ethos" (Yoon and Williams 2015), or as a software or blueprint, claiming, for example, the ideal of the *sŏnbi* (the Confucian scholar) as what defines Koreans' "DNA"—metaphorically, of course, not in the sense of a genetic heritage (see Han 2014). Or we find *chŏng* presented as the ruling principle of many aspects of Korean behavior: why do Koreans not serve an individual plate of food for each person? Because if they can share food, they can show each other their *ttattŭthan chŏng* (warm heart).[2] Why do they drink out of all measure and gamble until they have lost their house? Because their fighting spirit and tenacity does not allow them to let go.[3]

Other attempts to define Koreanness revolve not around a basic program that governs Korean culture and behavior, but around more tangible phenomena: concrete cultural skills and knowledge such as proverbs, songs, dances, games, and recipes (see Prébin 2008). This constitutes either the basic knowledge that any Korean would know by heart, or a special set and branch of knowledge that is nevertheless considered to epitomize Koreanness (such as knowing how to produce Korean-style pottery).

Backgrounds

Since the turn of the new millennium, official discourse on what constitutes or ought to constitute the nation has almost completely reversed: from the myth of homogeneous monoethnic purity to the ideals of multiethnic and multicultural harmony (Suh 2015). In the mid-1990s, grassroots networks to assist migrant workers began to emerge, and the plight of these foreigners started to become a matter of public concern. A sit-in protest by Nepali "industrial trainees" (as they were euphemistically named) in front of the Myŏngdong Cathedral in Seoul in 1995 had a powerful impact, arousing the shocked public "with anger, shame, and sympathy" (Jun 2016, 674). Around the mid-2000s, the Roh Moo-hyun administration officially began to use the term "multiculturalism" in relation to national policy. In 2006, a governmental "Plan for Promoting the Social Integration of Migrant Women, Biracial People, and Immigrants" was announced.

Multiculturalism, however, reached well beyond a state policy agenda. Many actors played a role here: government, media, academia, civil society, the cultural industries, and so on. Multiculturalism became "a renewed nation-building project" (Ahn 2018). The conservative administrations that followed the progressive presidency of Roh Moo-hyun embraced multiculturalism as a fundamental state policy. It may seem highly contradictory, taking "multiculturalism" at face value, that this should be promoted by conservatives. However, according to a common criticism, the conservative policy here was not about ethical values but about cheap labor, re-boosting the Korean economy by recruiting dispensable foreign workers who are only allowed temporary residency.

The other main focus of multiculturalism policy—female marriage migrants—can also be explained as congenial to a conservative agenda: the assimilation of female marriage migrants and their biracial children offered a solution to major issues (especially in conservative eyes): the aging population, low birth rate, and lack of care workers. It has often been pointed out that the multicultural policy mostly targeted (at the expense of other possible areas) the union of a Korean man with a female marriage migrant, plus support for subsequent childbirth and childcare, and the cultural assimilation of spouse and offspring.

As of 2019, more than 2.5 million foreign nationals were residing in South Korea under various visa schemes, accounting for 4.9% of the entire population.[4] (Of course, thousands of undocumented foreign laborers living and working without a valid visa are left out of this total). More than a quarter of these are migrant workers brought in mostly from China and Southeast Asian countries to take up jobs that are shunned by more educated South Korean workers. The majority are in manufacturing, but there has been a noticeable rise in the agricultural and fishery sectors, which have been struggling with chronic labor shortages.

In 2019, out of every 100 births, around six came from a *tamunhwa* family, with one parent being a foreigner; in new marriages, around ten out of 100 included a foreigner.[5] In 2020, four percent of all primary school children were from *tamunhwa* families.[6]

Multicultural Literature

The policy of fostering "multicultural education" since the middle of the last decade was concomitant with the appearance of what became identified as *tamunhwa munhak* (multicultural literature). Under this category are subsumed texts depicting the lives of foreign workers, migrant marriage women, second-generation children of "multicultural families," Koreans living abroad in the Korean diaspora, and North Korean defectors. One PhD dissertation (Ch'oe 2014), two monographs (Yi Mi-rim 2014; Yi 2015), and reams of academic articles have been concerned with proposing typologies of this genre of fiction. The wealth of academic discussion has even warranted a "meta-analysis" (Kang and Yi 2018).[7]

While *tamunhwa munhak* in the narrow sense was written mostly in the second half of the noughties, there are *avant-la-lettre* examples of literary representations of foreigners in Korea from the 1950s onwards, many of which contain representations of Black American soldiers stationed in Korea or their "mixed-race" Amerasian offspring. However, these narratives tend not to deal with issues pertaining to identity struggles; rather, they use the presence of foreigners as a device for covering issues concerning the Korean characters, or even to construct the "mixed" as just a deviation from the normal "full-blood" (Ahn 2018, 39).

What remains peculiar (although this situation will likely change in the near future) is that while many first-person narrators are foreigners, the authors, in all cases, are Korean—and not "multicultural" Korean.[8] Apparently, "the design and implementation of Korean multiculturalism do not offer a space for the immigrants to speak for themselves" (Suh 2015, 38) and the question is, of course, whether a full-fledged "multicultural literature" will not indeed require authors who are migrants or have a migrant background. This objection, however, must be put into perspective: fiction usually implies that an author takes on an identity, a subjectivity, which is not his or her own, and that he or she empathizes with imagined individuals according to his or her fantasy. Can't a man write a story in which he takes on the narrative role of a woman or vice versa? In the end, it does not seem reasonable to argue against *tamunhwa munhak* on the grounds that it is written by Korean authors. And there is no doubt that the future will bring authors of Korean literature whose identity is truly multicultural, hybrid, and transnational, so that their perspective can at last stand in the spotlight. We should also not forget that it is quite probable some *tamunhwa munhak* exists that has not seen the light of day: texts submitted for prizes but rejected, texts written for the drawer out of a low tolerance for frustration, and so on.

THE QUESTION OF IDENTITY AS A QUESTION OF PURITY?

The assumption of clear-cut, homogeneous cultures can only bring about a naïve multiculturalism that has very narrow confines:

> Without the ability to accept that what is now called Korean culture may simply be an outcome of ongoing compromises, competitions, negotiations, and contradictions between different cultures, you end up with the

rigid notion that cultures always have to be defined according to their respective boundaries and closures. (Han 2003, 28)

The brilliant short story "Arpan" by Park Hyoung-su (2014 [2011]) delves into this topic in an intriguing way. The Korean protagonist of the story studies the language and culture of the Waka, a fictitious minority tribe on Thailand's northern border. The Waka boast precisely one writer, the eponymous Arpan. Arpan is a true literary genius, and the protagonist ends up plagiarizing Arpan's stories (instead of translating them), publishing them under his own name in Korean and thus scoring huge success. But instead of simply showing an act of plagiarism, of intellectual theft, the story challenges established notions of originality. The protagonist justifies his act in a lengthy diatribe of which the following excerpt is the most telling part:

> But what do you suppose happens when we insist on cultural purity? The culture disappears. (...) Culture has always been mixed. Do you know what it takes for a single culture to live forever? It has to absorb another culture, or be absorbed into a larger culture. (Park Hyoung-su 2014, 71)

As much as this seems a cynical defense of a cowardly act of stealing, the protagonist eventually finds out, to his genuine surprise, that he was in fact just as much "used" as the writer whose work he exploited. He realizes, as the author explains in his afterword, that the Waka "spread their culture to the rest of the world by inducing a foreigner to commit plagiarism" (Park Hyoung-su 2014, 103). Justifying himself in front of Arpan, the protagonist points to a song being sung in the background. Now popular in Korea, he explains, with Korean lyrics, this song was imported from Japan a few years ago. But there, it was known as a British children's song. The British had learned this song as a Dutch peasants' song, but ultimately the rhythm could be traced back to the Guangdong province of China (Park Hyoung-su 2014, 63).

The reader realizes that all this is a sophisticated questioning of the concept of purity and the notion that it is necessary to preserve distinct cultures, arguing for a different take on contact with the foreign. In a very puzzling way, this also implies an unconventional assessment of supposedly weaker positions: the Waka are actually spreading their culture using the far more powerful culture of Korea (and clearly Koreans themselves are not on top of the global hierarchy, and the reader might infer that this fact could make them inclined to avail themselves of similar methods of dissemination in turn). The questioning of cultural purity—in this case, by showing how adaptation, incorporation, and even theft from other cultures (or, indeed, the manipulation of others so that they steal) can in fact be a means for cultural survival—aligns this story with the concerns of *The Muslim Butcher*: There is no purity, everything is mixed.

OUTWARD APPEARANCE VERSUS INNER ESSENCE?

The significance of outward appearance is indeed a far-reaching and hotly-contested topic in modern South Korea. "Republic of plastic surgery" or "kingdom of plastic surgery" are national nicknames for Korea, and more than a few Koreans even take pride in this dubious global fame. There are few countries in which it is so accepted that a person designs their outward appearance. Beyond the explanation that women's willingness to change their bodies reflects their submission to male control and power (Kim 2009), there are also strands of traditional thought that can be seen as grounding the willingness to change one's looks—and this despite solemn Confucian teachings prescribing that one should honor with respect the body bequeathed by one's parents. The said strands of traditional thought hold that one's fate and fortune are carved in one's physiognomic features. This belief or pseudoscience, which enjoys a considerable following in Korea even today, is in fact not so far-fetched because it can rely on a circular effect: if many people assume that facial features reveal personality traits, then such features will have a socially-determinative effect on how people are treated and thus how well they fare. Consequently, making one's face more auspicious according to the beliefs of physiognomy (*kwansang*, that is: "see the shape," in the end "face reading"), for instance, through "physiognomic surgery" (*kwansang susul*), is an obvious option. This phenomenon is often noted as very peculiar in the West:

> Men and women of all ages are increasingly undergoing plastic surgery so that a new nose with a straight bridge (…), a (…) protruding forehead, or sufficient cheekbones will bring wealth and the drive to take charge of their lives. (Su Hyun Lee 2006)

The South Korean obsession with looks is the topic of a wide range of academic research. However, there seems to be less awareness of how much this issue permeates Korean literature as well. For example, Park Min-gyu explores it in his remarkable novel *Pavane for a Dead Princess* (Park 2014), which has been described as an "attack upon the beauty-fetish that reigns over popular culture, detailing the relationship between a man with *matinee idol* good looks and 'the ugliest woman of the century.'"[9] The links made between looks and class are salient here: Park Min-gyu's novel shows, as one reviewer has succinctly put it, "the unfairness of a society wrapped up in surfaces, in which the unlovely are confined to a kind of permanent underclass, at least until they go under the knife" (Park 2015).

If outward appearance decides a person's fate—success or failure, acceptance or rejection—it stands to reason that there are those who will resist their apparent destiny. When an identity that is ascribed on the basis of outward appearance leads to hardships or social rejection, it is no wonder that we find bold constructions of self-determined, self-chosen identities (appealing to the logic that everyone is the architect of their own fortune). And if pride in one's identity is impossible, then fraud, deception, and camouflage can take place, as the unlovely strive for a better life. We see this in a pioneering example of multicultural literature, and still to this day one of the genre's most popular texts, Kim Jae-young's story "K'okkiri" (The Elephant), first published in 2004:

> Khun is wearing Levi's jeans and a Nike jacket. I know they are imitations bought for cheap at Dongdaemun Market, but you can barely tell. He has defined facial features, and his hair is dyed blonde. He was a fair-skinned Arere, one of the Nepali tribes of Aryan descent, and could almost pass for an American. That's probably why he dyed his hair in the first place. (Kim Jae-young 2014, 33)

Later, Khun loses a finger, rendering futile everything he had done to change his appearance: "There is no need to dye his hair anymore. No one's going to believe that an American came to Korea to have his fingers cut off in a press" (Kim Jae-young 2014, 37). But he teaches the young and naïve protagonist a compelling lesson about the links between appearance and appreciation. According to him, the solution to evading discrimination is not to mimic the Koreans but rather to look like a white American,[10] in what is veritably a form of overcompensation:

I remember what he told me (...): "Don't be fooled. Koreans may say they're uncomfortable with foreigners because they're a homogenous nation, and that that's why migrant workers are treated the way they are. Shoot, they're not like that to Americans," he sneered. "Polite doesn't cut it. Koreans would get on their hands and knees for Americans. If your face was a bit whiter, you'd look American ...." (Kim Jae-young 2014, 37)

Mindful of this teaching, the protagonist starts applying laundry bleach in an attempt to whiten his face, an endeavor for which his father beats him. There is another story in the corpus of *tamunhwa munhak* where skin is bleached[11] out of the (futile) desire to accomplish chameleon-like deception and camouflage—the telling title of this story by Jeon Sungtae (Chŏn Sŏng-t'ae) is "Imitation" or, rather, "Imitayshun" (the English word is simply transcribed into Hangul). At its center is a Korean who is constantly teased because of his un-Korean looks.

Intriguingly, the difficulty in categorizing him is reminiscent of that of the sleeping An-na in *The Muslim Butcher* (see above):

Wherever he went, people called him Yankee (...). But no one could quite put their finger on what race he looked like. Some said Middle Eastern; others, South American. In the summer, when his face tanned, some people asked if he was from Southeast Asia. His was a multinational face, but one thing was for sure: he did not look like an ohrijinal [sic!] Korean. (Jeon 2009, 180)

The troubled protagonist creates his own theory, that he is perhaps one of the descendants of Hamel's crew of shipwrecked Dutch sailors. The point where he really embraces the idea that he is "mixed blood" is reached in a history class at high school:

The teacher was explaining that Koreans were an ethnically homogenous people who used the same language and all looked alike, when one of the students looked at Gary and said, "What about him?" The classroom erupted into a sea of laughter. (Jeon 2009, 181–182)

Initially, reacting to the situation, the teacher scolds Gary, assuming that his atypical looks are the result of treatment:

Look at this kid – bleaches and curls his hair. Think you are too good for us? (Jeon 2009, 182)

In the end, however, having received a "self-reflective" essay—a typical pedagogical punishment in Korea; we do not learn the content, but apparently the protagonist presented as fact his theory that he is racially mixed—the elderly teacher consoles the black sheep:

> Why didn't you just say you're mixed blood? Kids like you have to try harder, do your best. Show more pride in your country than everyone else. Race isn't in your blood. It's right there, in your heart. Our people have always been generous. Behave yourself, and we'll take care of you. We've been invaded 449 times, so tons of half-breeds must've been born. We took in other people's runts, and now we're one big melting pot. (...) So cheer up, kid. (Jeon 2009, 182)

This seemingly complete change of message from the teacher reflects a strand of thinking that is, in fact, even older than the "one race" myth, and obviously interchangeable so long as it serves the same purpose. In Korean history, after all, inclusion was not granted on the basis of ethnicity, but rather on that of successful cultural assimilation:

> Koreans were ready to agree that birth itself did not condemn a person to uncivilized status. Civilization was attainable to those who chose to change and make the necessary effort (...). A Jurchen (Yeojin) chief or a Japanese pirate could become a civilized Korean by discarding his old ways to adopt a Korean way of life and cultivate himself. It may have taken time, but was not impossible. Therefore, discrimination was theoretically based on one's intention to assimilate or not, and not on place of birth or ethnic origin. (Han 2007, 16)

Arguably, this approach resurfaces today, when "Koreanness is (...) in the process of being reconstituted as relatively inclusive and heterogeneous, ready to serve the interests of the South Korean state and capital" (Lee 2017, 157).

Now, while the elderly teacher seems to suddenly embrace multiculturalism, having very shortly before propagated the myth of the homogenous nation, these ostensibly competing views can prove to be two sides of the same coin. The apparently generous and welcoming message that "race isn't in your blood" can actually imply a notion that is, under certain circumstances, not generous at all: that belonging to the nation depends on allegiance to the agenda of the state (that is, the government), and thus on a willingness to contribute to inward stability by refraining from critique.

Probably, this thinking also nursed a specific recent form of "South Korean nationalism" (Campbell 2011). Emma Louise Gordon Campbell quotes the example of one student she interviewed "who stated that they would (…) much prefer a foreigner who loved Korea to be part of the South Korean nation than an ethnic-Korean who was ambivalent toward South Korea" (2011, 247). We can see here how "inclusion" and "exclusion" can be intertwined in a more complicated way than usually acknowledged:

> The emergence of this new nationalism has exposed a fissure between the generations in South Korea where older South Koreans still hold onto an ethnic concept of nation. Young people, in contrast, are quite willing to embrace non-ethnic Koreans as South Korean and to exclude those ethnic Koreans whom they consider (…) not properly qualified for South Korean national identity — in other words not globalised, cosmopolitan, enlightened or modern. (Campbell 2011, 247)

In view of this, we can understand the seemingly paradoxical fact that despite the xenophobic anti-immigration agenda usually being a matter of right-wing populism, many right-leaning Korean politicians have pushed the message of multiculturalism. After all, "many advocates of multiculturalism in Korea are nationalists who regard multiculturalism as a survival strategy for the nation-state" (Han 2007, 11); they consider the openness to foreign workers as part of the "state's human resource management that involves the construction of citizen-subjects commensurable with neoliberal norms" (Yuk 2014, 272).

In recent years, on the other hand, "a specific version of South Korean progressive xenophobia" (Kang 2020, 94) has become visible, rendering "opposition to multiculturalism compatible with progressive politics" (Kang 2020, 103). Historically, the Korean left-wing did not find much fault with the concept of ethnic homogeneity, and this has an inherent logic as well, because this concept lends itself to egalitarian ideas. Within this logic, the inflow of migrant labor is primarily seen as a factor that puts downward pressure on wages and undermines working conditions. While being "critical of global capitalism and of the flexibilization of labor that sustains it" (Jun 2019, 399), this rejection of multiculturalism bears the risk of turning against foreign workers and marriage migrants as "scapegoats for South Korea's neoliberalism" (Kang 2020, 103).

This way, (Korean) "anti-multiculturalism" (*pan-tamunhwa*), which wants "to safeguard the privilege of being Korean in a situation in which this appears to be the only privilege available for the majority of the population vis-à-vis migrants" (Jun 2019, 392), can be seen as a backlash against the "precarity caused by state-driven neoliberalism" (Kang 2020, 87). In investigating online xenophobia, Jiyeon Kang has studied how Korean netizens

> attacked the particular South Korean logic of multiculturalism as a part of this neoliberal scheme. In a 2014 Bullpen post, a contributor asked why the conservative Saenuri Party embraced multiculturalism, "which would typically align with progressive parties." The twenty-one responses to this post predominantly characterized then-President Park Geun-hye's version of multiculturalism as a disguise for a global market policy that enabled corporations to bring in foreign workers and suppress strong domestic labor unions. (Kang 2020, 96)

On the other hand, if we look at the right-wing as well as the neoliberal partisanship for multiculturalism the ostensible tolerance (towards foreigners) can give the impression of being only the paradoxical by-product of a deeper-lying ideological intolerance vis-à-vis those "fellow" Koreans who demand better income distribution, more welfare and social solidarity, but less cut-throat competition.[12]

Teaching Koreanness?

Teaching Korean Studies means, to a certain extent, teaching students about concepts of Koreanness. Boudewijn Walraven has described the task poignantly as follows:

> What we cannot teach our students is the secret formula of true Koreanness ("one part of *han*, one part of *mot*, add plenty of kimch'i, cover with some 5,000-year-old soy sauce, and mix well"), but we should teach them the cultural grammar of Korean culture (…), in the hope that they themselves will be able to enter into the debates of Korean society and will not have to rely on fixed stereotypes and tired academic commonplaces. For example, we should teach them the terms in which Koreans themselves discuss what Koreanness consists of, (…) rather than perfunctorily

dismiss certain Korean concepts of self-identity as *ahistorical* or *academically unsound*, strive to make our students understand what the rationale is behind these views. (Walraven 1999, 13)

In other words, busying oneself academically with constructions and definitions of Koreanness does not entail any affirmation of their validity, but simply follows a very basic requirement of the anthropologist: to learn about others' self-interpretations. However, adopting concepts of Koreanness as an academic topic of study might possess the same difficulties as, for example, exploring "superstitions." There is a popular conception of science according to which its primary concern would be demonstrating the fallaciousness of superstitious claims. For its part, humanist research in the field of Folkloristics or Religious Studies, for example, finds sufficient value in examining such beliefs insofar as they are observable, concrete, and significant social, anthropological, and psychological phenomena. *Mutatis mutandis*, all concepts of Koreanness may be fundamentally fallacious, but they are nevertheless a reality in their own right and merit study on this basis.

Another very valid objection against Koreanness discourses maintains that any concept of Korean culture, as a mere essentialist construct, inevitably ignores the coexistence of various "sets" of Korean culture(s), let alone the conflicts within them: "Cultural variations in Korea can be much more profound than unity" (Yi 2003, 66). Dialectically this leads to the recognition that "multiculturalism," or at least the concept thereof that we often find promoted, is in fact not the clear antithesis to nationalism that it is commonly taken to be. After all, the proclaimed acknowledgment of plurality often does not consider the plurality "within" the various assumed units. In his insightful "Archaeology of the Ethnically Homogeneous Nation-State and Multiculturalism in Korea," Han Kyung-Koo has rightly admonished that "many advocates of multiculturalism in Korea are not prepared to see the diversity within a culture, nor are they prepared to recognize an individual except as a member of a clear and distinct, homogenous cultural or ethnic group" (Han 2007, 28). The inability to overcome essentialist paradigms is often behind those "well-meaning attempts to respect difference" that "actually trap people from minority cultures in the 'authentic' representations of those cultures that have come to be expected of them" (La Shure 2018, 177).

In order to overcome such constraints, it is clear that the concept of the homogenous cultural or ethnic group needs to be questioned;

but if so, the problem should, of course, not simply be shifted further down, to essentialist definitions of antagonistic regional characters (most archetypically, for Korea: Honam, the South-West, and Yŏngnam, the South-East).

The Migrant Worker as a *Déjà Vu*: A Potential for Identification

In seeking to engender empathy for the plight of foreign workers in Korea, the texts of multicultural literature frequently find their source material in the horrendous cases of abuse and exploitation that have marked the treatment of foreign migrants in South Korea. Pak Pŏm-sin (Park Bum-shin), for instance, was motivated to start writing *Namaste* (Pak 2005), one of the foremost pieces of *tamunhwa munhak*, by the dismay triggered in him by a migrant worker's suicide, committed in protest at imminent deportation: Chiran Tharaka from Sri Lanka, who had come to Korea in 1996, jumped in front of a subway train on November 12, 2003, and the distressing images of him standing on the platform, with the train approaching, deeply shocked the Korean public. Amnesty International, among others, has continuously reported on abhorrent working conditions and constant accidents suffered by labor migrants in Korea. Despite considerable public awareness and numerous initiatives to improve conditions, we nevertheless encounter, over the years, an astounding repetition of similar headlines:

- About half of migrant workers fall victim to industrial accidents within the first year of their arrival (*Hankyoreh*, October 29, 2002 [quoted in Lee 2010, 200])
- South Korea Must End the "Rampant Abuse" of Migrant Farm Workers, Says Amnesty (*Time*, October 20, 2014)
- Migrant workers treated like "slaves" in South Korea's agricultural industry (AP Migration, May 29, 2015)
- 5800 migrant workers killed in South Korea in a decade (*The Standard*, August 10, 2018)
- Another Workers Dies at a Shipyard, Just 6 Days after Accident at Hyundai Heavy Industries (*Kyunghyang Sinmun*, September 27, 2019).

This situation might, at first glance, seem almost paradoxical because of Korea's own history as a source country for a migrant workforce. Indeed, one would, on this basis, expect greater sensitivity: "Our ancestors immigrated to the United States, Germany, and other countries in the world. *The frog forgets about the time when it was just a polliwog.* How can they treat people from other countries in such a way now that the economy is a little better?" So remarks a labor union activist in 2008 to EuyRyung Jun (2016, 669), obviously referring to the Korean proverb *kaeguri olch'aengi sijŏl morŭnda.*

But in fact, such reasoning does not factor in the history of labor in Korea itself. That is to say, this invocation of a collective historical subject ("our ancestors") appeals to a fiction, inventing a unity which, in reality, did not exist. On the contrary, the history of Korea is inextricable from the exploitation of Koreans by other Koreans. Pointedly, EuyRyung Jun—with reference to a 2002 study by Yu Myŏng-gi that referred to foreign workers as "our yet-incomplete future" (Yu 2002)—maintains that the shameful reality of South Korea's past is reincarnated in the contemporary reality of foreign workers' plight:

> Those things of the 1960s and the 1970s (e.g., brutal labor exploitation, women factory workers' slums) that Koreans would like to think have disappeared, revive and reanimate themselves in the figure of the foreign worker and his or her present misery. In this context, it is the remnants of Korea's "undeveloped era" (or what Yu calls the "premodern") and/or the failure or the incompleteness of its development manifested through the plight of the foreign worker that operate as the very source of Korea's shame. (Jun 2016, 681)

Thus, the plight of the foreign worker mirrors that of Korean workers in the past, but also holds a magnifying glass to the ongoing plight of precarious labor in general: in other words, the many (be it Korean or foreign) day workers and "informal" workers that "slip through the cracks of labor regulations" (Yi and Chun 2020, 123).

While Chiran Tharaka's suicide constituted a direct and immediate inducement for the writer Pak Pŏm-sin, he revealed another, more fundamental or broader rationale behind his novel *Namaste*:

> I also remembered the time I moved to Seoul with no plan in mind—only the determination to make a better life for myself. (…) Back then, I, too, was a migrant worker. Filled with fear and dread, I had often longed to go

back to my hometown. (...) how terrified he must have been. In a country where the people looked and sounded different from him, he must have been far more frightened then I. (Park 2011, 47)

In other words, as with the declaration that "all are mixed blood" (see above), there is an empathy-inducing identification to be found in the slogan "we are all migrants." This leads us to the potential of attributions of Korean working class identity to serve as an incentive to identify with migrants.

A "refugee consciousness" is, according to Kim Wŏn-u's novel *Mosŏri esŏ ŭi insaeng tokpŏp* (*The art of reading life from the margins*), the collective unconscious that defines Korean society (Kim 2008), given that so many abandoned their hometowns and wandered through the country, be it as a consequence of the Korean War, be it because of the extremes of Korea's high-speed condensed development. If this is so, it would offer itself as a basis (along the lines of the logic of the frog and the polliwog invoked above) for a greater understanding of migrants' struggles. This understanding is at times strikingly absent, as has been demonstrated, for instance, in the case of the 500 Yemeni refugees on Cheju Island, where a seemingly unlikely alliance of xenophobic groups and women's rights groups staged a protest against their presence.

In the ingenious story "Headlock" (Hedŭrok'ŭ) by Park Min-gyu (2005, 243–270), a Korean student in Oklahoma becomes the victim of a humiliating attack by non other than the wrestler Hulk Hogan, and afterward tries to resolve this trauma by terrorizing those weaker than himself: Latinos, South Asians, and others. Back in Korea, with a good job and a family, he is appointed to a post in Indonesia, where he begins to subject his employees to the headlock treatment, mostly by agreement and with compensation, but occasionally to quell the workers' demands.

This is not one of those alternative stories of a Korean becoming a patronizing and benevolent settler in an underdeveloped country,[13] but only an average story of a Korean enjoying quasi-colonial privilege and passing on discrimination (by the hegemonic USA) to those who rank lower in the global hierarchy, according to a kiss-up-kick-down principle.

A Literature of Engagement and Resistance

Tamunhwa munhak is almost per definitionem an engaged literature of political commitment. It is worth considering this against the backdrop of the "worker-intellectual alliance" (Lee 2005) and generally the history and role of *littérature engagée* in South Korea:

> Political engagement of writers is not uncommon practice in other countries, but decades of military dictatorship in Korea created a special pact between readers and writers: a desire to tell "the truth" and an expectation to hear the "real story," even in the form of fictional novels and lyrical poetry. Literary works provided a channel for the unofficial 'true' story/history. (Lee 2006, 2)

It may be true that in the early 2000s, "the rearticulation of the *minjung* subject" in works of Korean literature sometimes resorted to taking "place outside of South Korea's borders" (Hughes 2008, 115). But at the same time, we can see (albeit in altered ways) some rearticulation of this "*minjung* subject" (representing "the masses," in the sense of the oppressed ordinary people) in the *tamunhwa munhak* of the 2000s, in the sense of a partisanship for an emancipatory struggle against oppression and alienation. Accordingly, Chris Hanscom has argued persuasively that "migrant labor fiction" generated a return to "a sense of the real" in Korean literature.

> If the 1990s and early 2000s were characterized by what critic Hwang Chongyŏn [Hwang 2007] called a "postmodern turn," marked by unreliable narrators who no longer speak for all Koreans, the supersession of a literature of political commitment by fiction focused on the minutiae of everyday life, and the disappearance of national culture into the uncertainty of individual identity (5–6), then we could say that a sense of the real had perhaps returned in migrant labor fiction. (Hanscom 2019, 12)

Perhaps *tamunhwa munhak*, from its full emergence in the noughties, paved the way for a general revival of a literature in the 2010s that is concerned with social issues, imbalances, and "flaws of the system," as one of the sharpest representatives of this new wave, Chang Kang-myoung (Chang Kang-myŏng), sums it up:

> Back when Korea was under military dictatorship literature was at the vanguard of resistance, of democracy and social reform. We had what we now call resistance literature. That was a big part of Korean literature up to the 1980s, until we became a democratic society. Since then we've had introspective novels that are deeply personal but from the 2010s onwards

I feel like Korean readers and young readers in particular are ready to read about society again. There are so many things about Korean society today that you look at and think, that's not right. Starting with gender inequality, or the economy how come anybody starting a new business fails, how come there are no jobs, what's the story there? And nobody knows the answer. You wish that somebody would write about that, to read about the pain you're going through from a slightly different angle, maybe read about what other people are going through, too. There are a lot of writers working that angle now, not just me. (Chang 2018)

Chang Kang-myoung has provided one of the most prominent examples of this new type of resistance literature, one that gives a voice to the widespread South Korean desire to leave the "Hell Joseon": *Because I hate Korea* (Chang 2015). The portmanteau "t'alcho"—combining "t'al," escape, and "(Chosŏn)" for today's Korea (the latter having, in this view, become untenable just like the fallen dynasty that ruled for more than 500 years until the country's downfall and loss of independence)—was coined to label this pervasive willingness to emigrate out of frustration over conditions in South Korea. *T'alcho* is thus associated with disgust at elitist meritocratic conceitedness that engenders so many social ills as, among others, the prevailing contempt for manual labor: "in contrast to Korea, Australian blue-collar workers and manual laborers are not treated as 'losers'" (Epstein 2018, 4).

Mirror of Reality?

However, we might feel prompted to question the value of *tamunhwa munhak* if its purpose were merely to confirm things that we already know from sources outside of literature. Treating literature as a mirror, taking fiction as representative of non-fictional circumstances, can seem very precarious. The objection is effortlessly raised: why not look directly at reality? Why go the roundabout way, taking a detour via literature? Fiction always distorts fact, novels are not concerned with what really happened, and the charge that poets are liars was already discussed in ancient Greece. So why not use more reliable sources?

But there are classic counterarguments. First, there is no clear lens anyway. Be it a newspaper report, be it a personal interview with a living witness: narration, and thus some core element of "fiction," is everywhere. Nowhere can we find direct access to reality. There is always mediation and brokering. Thus, literary representation of social circumstances can become a source of valid "authoritative knowledge" even for sociologists.[14] Second, literature always becomes a reality in its own right. It produces a discourse that, once published, is inextricably part of the world, a material fact like any other. Charles Dickens' novels, for example, exist as a body of work that has become a very powerful historical reality in its own right, because these books have influenced people and their actions. Hence, fiction is not merely about imagination, exiled in some "cloud cuckoo land," but is often an active participant among other forces that shape private lives as well as whole societies.

In a similar vein, *tamunhwa munhak*, displays a capacity to act, via the creation of empathy, upon a challenge and shape the society in which it is produced. In this light, *tamunhwa munhak* deserves attention not only because of what it depicts, but even more so because we can regard this fiction as a response, shedding light on ongoing discussions and offering interventions in public discourses around thorny questions: "In its unreserved critique of the appalling labor exploitation, racist policies, and practices of South Korean authorities and employers, and the xenophobic discrimination by the mainstream population, the novel as a whole is a major intervention that attempts to educate the South Korean public" (Lee 2010, 217).

Indeed, if we visualize "multiculturalism" in the center of a semantical association web generated from hits in online searches, the word "education" would be very close to the center (see Kim 2010). The function of *tamunhwa munhak* can thus be described as a "novel education," just as movies of the analogous genre could be labeled "film education" (Chung 2018, 137). Such "new enlightenment" (Chung 2018, 136) or even "healing" (Im 2018)—*hilling* having become a tellingly common word in South Korean, with "Konglish"-specific semantic shades and usage—is a key purpose of many of these texts. This makes them, by their very nature, a form of politically-engaged literature that aims at transforming social conditions for the better.

Forging Bonds

One of the most remarkable features of *tamunhwa munhak* is the representation of emotional bonds between otherwise weak or victimized foreigners and Koreans who are lacking in love, company, communication, or simply in human contact.

The stumbling, staggering Sikh who sensitively prompts a married Korean woman to talk about her innermost troubles is a source of astonishment for her prejudiced Korean husband in Kim Yŏn-su's imaginative short story "Happy New Year to Everyone" (*Modu ege pok teon saehae*; Kim 2014 [2007]). The Korean midget and hunchback cabaret clown marries a beautiful Vietnamese woman to produce a son who is the protagonist of Kim Ryŏ-ryŏng's immensely popular novel *Wandŭgi* (Kim 2008), later made into the successful movie *Punch*, where the mother is instead a Filipina. The socially degraded and economically devalued Korean man falls in love with the struggling foreign worker in "Homecoming" [*T'oegŭn*] by Ch'ŏn Myŏng-gwan (Cheon 2015 [2014]). The juvenile homeless Korean girl befriends the destitute migrant from Pakistan in "Dust Star" [*Mŏnji pyŏl*] by Yi Kyŏng (Lee 2014 [2011]). Likewise, in "Brown Tears" (*Kalsaek nunmul pangul*) by Kang Yŏng-suk (Kang 2008 [2004]) the Korean protagonist has a breakthrough in her English conversation class thanks to her exchanges with a neighbor, a Sri Lankan woman, in the house where she lives.

Instead of being troubled by "identity," the individuals in the center of these novels form emotional bonds that are based on their ability to connect in a way that does not rely on linguistic proficiency. Tellingly, the Sikh with his almost ridiculously limited language is communicatively very efficient, because he and the protagonist's wife agree on using each other's language (that is, the Sikh speaks in Korean, the wife in English), forcing on them similar handicaps that make them aware of how much they can compensate by way of mutual empathy and the serious ambition to guess well at each other's intended meaning. Ultimately, such bonding with foreigners can bring about a self-determined identity, as when the orphan raised by a Turk concludes: "My adoptive father's blood is flowing in my body" (Son 2016, 1).[15]

Conclusion

Shock at exotic appearance is often central when it comes to the literary description of Korean encounters with foreigners, as in this encounter with a migrant worker from the Punjab, a Sikh:

> Looking upon the kind of face that could sprout such a beard as prodigious as his: reaching out to shake a hand so damp with sweat: these things were all firsts to me. (Kim Yeon-su 2014, 11)

While language barriers and conflicting customs would be expected to constitute the problem, instead, we find that if problems arise, it is rather outward appearance that is in the foreground of what troubles *tamunhwa munhak*'s protagonists. And we have seen that the solution sought by these troubled protagonists is not an adaption to any presumed Korean phenotype, but rather an "overcompensation" in terms of a "solution on a higher level": a mimicry of what could be taken as American looks. Likewise, if there is a language problem, it is also quite often solved by overcompensation as a switch to English often turns the tables, empowering the foreigner who is usually more fluent—or otherwise enabling a talk from the heart to happen.

The concept of "Koreanness" is the peculiarly absent factor in *tamunhwa munhak*. Remarkably, it has been argued that the Korean language itself starts to become decoupled from any (postulated) essence of Koreanness. Lee Jin-kyung maintains that what used to be considered specifically Korean has wandered semantically and thereby become applicable to the new foreign migrants in Korea—once again forming a relation between excluded foreigners and those Koreans who themselves remain not included or only on the margins:

> This multiethnicization of "Koreanness" is illustrated by a deracialization of language, by which I mean the decoupling of Koreanness from certain concepts and expressions that have been intensely and exclusively associated with Korean identity. (…) The subtitle of a Korean book of photography on migrant workers, *Borderless Workers*, is "The Record of Tragic Bitterness of Foreign Workers and Korean Chinese." This use of "t'onghan" (tragic bitterness)—previously associated with ethnonational tragedies, such as the Japanese colonization of Korea, national division, or the Korean War—to describe the plight of non-ethnic Koreans disrupts the close linkage between the Korean language and the Korean race. (Lee 2017, 157)

A quasi-parallel case of the value of the English language in South Korea—which has indeed, in some ways and aspects, reached the point of an "English or perish" predicament (Lee et al. 2010)—is the high value of a Western appearance. In other words, just as speaking English is a more secure way to earn respect than speaking Korean, camouflage pays off even more when it means taking on Western looks.

Notes

1. For a short introduction to historical Koreanness discourses see Han (2003). For a critique of one of the most popular promoters of concepts of Koreanness, Ch'oe Chun-sik, see Yi (2003).
2. This example is taken from the very popular textbook *Saenghwal sok Han'guk munhwa 77* [77 (chapters on) Korean culture in real life] (Yi et al. 2011, 33).
3. This is the gist of one of the chapters of *Korea Unmasked*, the volume on Korea in the popular series *Mŏn nara iut nara* (Far away country, neighboring country) by Rhie Won-bok (Yi Wŏn-bok).
4. Official numbers published by the South Korean Ministry of Justice, as of 2019: 2,524,656 residents of foreign origin; total population: 51,849,861 (https://www.moj.go.kr/moj/2412/subview.do).
5. Numbers available from Statistics Korea, e-Nara Chip'yo (https://www.index.go.kr).
6. According to the KESS Korean Educational Statistics Service (https://kess.kedi.re.kr).
7. It must be noted here in passing that the *tamunhwa munhak* phenomenon is paralleled by the appearance of migrants or "multicultural" characters on the Korean screen (cf. Chung 2018).
8. The issue of Korean authors speaking for the experience of foreign migrants in literature is reminiscent of the occasionally debated issue of foreigners being played by Koreans in Korean movies.
9. This is how the publisher of the English translation summarizes the theme of this novel in the promotion of the book.
10. Indeed, it has often been noted that Korean beauty standards gravitate towards an "Americanized beauty" (Bisell and Chung 2009). It is contested, however, whether these beauty standards can indeed be called Americanized or Westernized, whether they are just globalized without any true country of origin, or whether there are other layers here that need consideration. According to Holliday and Elfving-Hwang, "the Western body (…) was mobilized in defiance of Japanese standards of beauty – as anti-colonial discourse" (2012, 69).
11. For broader context, we should consider here the "extreme popularity of the 'BB' ('blemish blocker') cream, which is used to

smooth and whiten the skin" (Holliday and Elfving-Hwang 2012, 76) in South Korea.

12. As a side note, there is one film that connects two main motifs that have surfaced here: *Pangga! Pangga!* (*He's on Duty*, Yuk Sang-hyo), a black comedy from 2010. Like in "Imitayshun," we encounter a Korean who is disadvantaged due to what are perceived to be his untypical looks. Unemployed, he resorts to camouflage, disguising himself as a foreigner from Bhutan, which allows him to finally land a job, albeit one that is of the "3D" kind (that is, dirty, dangerous and demeaning).

13. "Middle-class businessmen have also made advances into various Southeast Asian locations (...). In something of a contradistinction to the triumphalism accorded the multinational corporations and their mythic success, the media often portray these overseas small-to-medium-sized businesses in the tradition of pied-noir colonial settlers, all-sacrificing pioneers in the hinterland, educating the natives while selectively participating in their local culture and ultimately becoming patriotic expatriates" (Lee 2017, 159).

14. Using literature to teach sociology is not new, but has achieved prominence thanks to the seminal article "The Fiction of Development: Literary Representation as a Source of Authoritative Knowledge" (Lewis et al. 2008), in which the authors argue that "there may be a case for widening the scope of the development knowledge base conventionally considered to be 'valid'" (199). The authors highlight the importance of narrative and storytelling in social science, as well as the significance of fiction as a means of exploring and expressing human experience and understanding of the world. The basic idea that literature represents an important source for studying the conditions of a time is, of course, much older, not to say trivial.

15. This is both the first and (with the addition of the word "still") last sentence (on page 179) of the novel.

References

Ahn, Ji-Hyun. 2013. "Global Migration and the Racial Project in Transition: Institutionalizing Racial Difference Through Multiculturalism Discourse in South Korea." *Journal of Multicultural Discourses* 8 (1): 29–47.

Ahn, Ji-Hyun. 2018. *Mixed-Race Politics and Neoliberal Multiculturalism in South Korean Media*. London: Palgrave Macmillan.

Bissell, Kim L., and Jee Young Chung. 2009. "Americanized Beauty? Predictors of Perceived Attractiveness from US and South Korean Participants Based on Media Exposure, Ethnicity, and Socio-Cultural Attitudes Toward Ideal Beauty." *Asian Journal of Communication* 19 (2): 227–247.

Campbell, Emma Louise Gordon. 2011: "Uri nara, Our Nation: Unification, Identity and the Emergence of a New Nationalism amongst South Korean Young People." PhD diss., Australian National University.

Chang, Kang-myoung (Chang Kang-myŏng). 2015. *Han'guk i sirŏsŏ* [Because I hate Korea]. Seoul: Minŭmsa.

Chang, Kang-myoung (Chang Kang-myŏng). 2018. "On the Flaws of the System: Interview with Chang Kang-myoung." *Korean Literature Now* 42 [Web Exclusive] (https://koreanliteraturenow.com/interviews/chang-kang-myoung-web-exclusive-flaws-system-interview-chang-kang-myoung).

Cheon, Myeong-kwan (Ch'ŏn Myŏng-gwan). 2015 [2014]. *T'oegŭn / Homecoming*. Translated by Jeon Miseli. Seoul: Asia Publishers.

Chin, Chung-gwŏn. 2007. *Homo k'oreanik'usŭ / Homo-Coreanicus*. Seoul: Ungjin Chisik Hausŭ.

Ch'oe, Nam-gŏn. 2014. "2000-nyŏndae han'guk tamunhwa sosŏl yŏn'gu: Ijumin chaehyŏn yangsang kwa munhakchŏk chihyangsŏng ŭl chungsim ŭro" [(Parallel title:) "A Study on the Korean Multicultural Novels of the 2000s: With Focus on Immigrant Re-enactment Aspect and Literary Direction"]. PhD diss., Hankuk University of Foreign Studies.

Choo, Hae Yeon. 2016. *Decentering Citizenship: Gender, Labor, and Migrant Rights in South Korea*. Stanford: Stanford University Press.

Chung, Hye Seung. 2018. "Multiculturalism as 'New Enlightenment': The Myth of Hypergamy and Social Integration in *Punch*." *Journal of Korean Studies* 23 (1): 135–152.

Epstein, Stephen J. 2018. "Introduction" [to Chang Kang-Myoung: "Because I Hate Korea." Translated by Stephen J. Epstein and Mi Young Kim]. *Asia-Pacific Journal: Japan Focus* 16/11 (4): 1–4.

Han, Kyung-Koo. 2003. "The Anthropology of the Discourse on the Koreanness of Koreans." *Korea Journal* 43 (1): 5–31.

Han, Kyung-Koo. 2007. "The Archaeology of the Ethnically Homogeneous Nation-State and Multiculturalism in Korea." *Korea Journal* 47 (4): 8–31.

Han, Young-woo (Han Yŏng-u). 2014. *An Intellectual History of Seonbi in Korea: Korean Cultural DNA / Han'guk sŏnbi chisŏngsa: Han'gugin ŭi munhwajŏk DNA*. P'aju: Jisik-sanup.

Hanscom, Christopher L. 2019. "The Return of the Real in South Korean Fiction." *Acta Koreana* 22 (1): 1–16.

Holliday, Ruth, and Joanna Elfving-Hwang. 2012. "Gender, Globalization and Aesthetic Surgery in South Korea." *Body & Society* 18 (2): 58–81.

Hughes, Theodore. 2008. "'North Koreans' and Other Virtual Subjects: Kim Yeong-ha, Hwang Seok-yeong, and National Division in the Age of Posthumanism." *The Review of Korean Studies* 11 (1): 99–117.

Hwang, Chongyŏn. 2007. "A Postmodern Turn in Korean Literature." *Korea Journal* 47 (1): 5–7. [Hwang, Chongyŏn. 2010. "A Postnational Turn in Contemporary Korean Literature." *World Literature Today* 84 (1): 50–52.]

Im, Chi-yŏn (Im Ji-Yeon). 2018. "Konggam kaenyŏm ŭi hwakchang kwa tamunhwajŏk konggam sŏsa: *Isŭllam Chŏngyukchŏm* chungsim ŭro [(Parallel title:) The expansion of empathy and multicultural healing community – Focusing on 'Islamic butcher shop']. *Munhak ch'iryo yŏn'gu / Journal of Literary Therapy* 47: 225–254.

Jeon, Sungtae (Chŏn Sŏng-t'ae). 2009. "Imitayshun" [Imitation]. In: Jeon Sungtae, *Wolves*. Translated by Sora Kim-Russell. Buffalo, NY: White Pine Press.

Jun, EuyRyung. 2016. "'The Frog That Has Forgotten Its Past': Advocating for Migrant Workers in South Korea." *positions: asia critique* 24 (3): 669–692.

Jun, EuyRyung. 2019. "'Voices of Ordinary Citizens': *Ban damunhwa* and Its Neoliberal Affect of Anti-Immigration in South Korea." *Critical Asian Studies* 51 (3): 386–402.

Kang, Chin-gu, and Yi Ki-Sŏng. 2018. "Han'guk munhak ŭi tamunhwa tamnon e taehan met'a punsŏk (Meta-Analysis)" [(Parallel title:) A Meta-Analysis of Multicultural Discourse in Korean Literature]. *Uri munhak yŏn'gu* 59: 7–28.

Kang, Chun-man. 2006. *Han'gugin kodŭ* [The Code of the Koreans]. Seoul: Inmul kwa sasangsa.

Kang, Jiyeon. 2020. "Reconciling Progressivism and Xenophobia through Scapegoating: Anti-Multiculturalism in South Korea's Online Forums." *Critical Asian Studies* 52 (1): 87–108.

Kang, Yŏng-suk. 2004. "Kalsaek nunmul pangul" [Brown Tear Drops]. *Munhak kwa sahoe* 17 (4): 1517–1535.

Kang, Young-sook (Kang Yŏng-suk). 2008. "Brown Tears." In *New Writing from Korea 1*, translated by Teresa Lee, 132–151. Seoul: Literature Translation Institute of Korea.

Kim, Eun-Shil. 2009. "The Politics of the Body in Contemporary Korea." *Korea Journal* 49 (3): 5–14.

Kim, Jae-young (Kim Chaeyŏng). 2014. *The Elephant / K'okkiri*. Translated by Jeon Seung-hee. Asia Publishers 2014 (Bi-lingual Edition Modern Korean Literature 49).

Kim, Mi-yŏng. 2010. "Tamunhwa sahoe wa sosŏl kyoyuk ŭi han pangbŏp" [A Study on a Method for Multicultural Society and Novel Education]. *Han'guk ŏnŏ munhwa* 42: 79–102.

Kim, Ryŏ-ryŏng (Kim Ryeo-ryeong). 2008. *Wandŭgi* [Wandŭk]. P'aju: Ch'angbi.

Kim, Wŏn-u. 2008. *Mosŏri esŏ ŭi insaeng tokpŏp* [The Art of Reading Life from the Margins]. Seoul: Kang.

Kim, Yeon-su (Kim Yŏn-su). 2014 [2007]. *Happy New Year to Everyone: To Raymond Carver / Modu ege pok toen saehae: Reimŏndŭ K'abŏ ege*. Translated by Maya West. Seoul: Asia.

Kim, Yong-un. 1995. *Wŏnhyŏng ŭi yuhok: Wŏnhyŏng sagwan ŭro minjok kwa munhwa ŭi simch'ŭng ŭl ingnŭnda* [The Temptations of Archetype: Reading the Depths of Nation and Culture Through an Archetypal View of History]. Seoul: Hangilsa.

La Shure, Charles [Na, Su-ho]. 2018. "Tamunhwa sahoe esŏŭi chŏngch'esŏng kwa kubi munhak" [Identity and Folklore Studies in a Multicultural Society). *Kubi munhak yŏn'gu* 49: 145–177.

Lee, Ji-Eun. 2006. *A New Pedigree: Women and Women's Reading in Korea, 1896–1934*. PhD diss., Harvard University.

Lee, Jin-kyung. 2010. *Service Economies: Militarism, Sex Work, and Migrant Labor in South Korea*. Minneapolis: University of Minnesota Press.

Lee, Jin-kyung. 2017. "Immigrant Subempire, Migrant Labor Activism, and Multiculturalism in Contemporary South Korea." In *The Routledge Handbook of Korean Culture and Society*, edited by Youna Kim, 149–161. London and New York: Routledge.

Lee, Jong-hwa, Min Wha Han, and R. McKerrow. 2010 [2011]. "English or Perish: How Contemporary South Korea Received, Accommodated, and Internalized English and American Modernity." *Language and Intercultural Communication* 10: 337–357.

Lee, Kyung (Yi Kyŏng). 2014 [2011]. *Dust Star / Mŏnji pyŏl*. Translated by Jeon Miseli. Seoul: Asia.

Lee, Namhee. 2005. "Representing the Worker: The Worker-Intellectual Alliance of the 1980s in South Korea." *The Journal of Asian Studies* 64 (4): 911–937.

Lee, Su Hyun. 2006. "For Love and Money, Koreans Turn to Facial Tucks." *New York Times*, May 14.

Lewis, David, Dennis Rodgers, and Michael Woolcock. 2008. "The Fiction of Development: Literary Representation as a Source of Authoritative Knowledge." *Journal of Developmental Studies* 44 (2): 198–216.

Lie, John, ed. 2015. *Multiethnic Korea? Multiculturalism, Migration, and Peoplehood Diversity in Contemporary South Korea*. Berkeley, CA: Institute of East Asian Studies, University of California.

Lim, Timothy. 2010. "Rethinking Belongingness in Korea: Transnational Migration, 'Migrant Marriages' and the Politics of Multiculturalism." *Pacific Affairs* 83 (1): 51–71.

Pak, Pŏm-sin (Park, Bum-shin). 2005. *Namasŭt'e* [Namaste]. Seoul: Han'gyŏre Sinmunsa.
Park, Bum-shin (Pak, Pŏm-sin). 2011. "Is Korea Ready to Become a Multicultural Society?" In *The Globalizing World and the Human Community: Proceedings of the 3rd Seoul International Forum for Literature*, edited by Kim Uchang, 46–51. Seoul: Seoul Selection.
Park, Ed. 2015. "Sorry Not Sorry. Reading Dalkey Archive Press's Library of Korean Literature." *New Yorker*, October 12.
Park, Hyoung-su (Pak Hyŏng-sŏ). 2014. *Arŭp'an / Arpan*. Translated by Sora Kim-Russell. Seoul: Asia.
Park, Min-gyu (Pak, Min-gyu). 2005. *K'asŭt'era* [Castella]. P'aju: Munhak Tongnae.
Park, Min-gyu (Pak Min-gyu). 2014. *Pavane for a Dead Princess*. Translated by Amber Hyun Jung Kim. Dallas: Dalkey Archive Press.
Prébin, Elise. 2008. Three-Week Re-Education to Koreanness. *European Journal of East Asian Studies* 7 (2): 323–355.
Rhie, Won-bok (Yi Wŏn-bok). 2005. *Korea Unmasked: In Search of the Country, the Society and the People*. P'aju: Gimm-Young International.
Son, Hong-gyu. 2010. *Isŭllam chŏngyukchŏm* [Islam Meat Shop]. Seoul: Munhak kwa Chisŏngsa.
Son, Hong-kyu (Son Hong-gyu). 2016. *The Muslim Butcher*. Translated by Yu Young-nan. Portland, ME: Mervin Asia.
Suh, Jung-won. 2015. "Korean Identity Constructions in Relation to Racialized Differences." PhD diss., University of Illinois.
Walraven, Boudewijn. 1999. "P'ansori and Park Soo Keun." *Korea Foundation Newsletter* 8 (5): 12–13.
Yi, Hae-yŏng, Kim Ŭn-yŏng, and Sin Kyŏng-sŏn. 2011. *Saenghwal sok Han'guk munhwa 77*. Seoul: Han'gŭl P'ak'ŭ.
Yi, Jeong Duk. 2003. "What Is Korean Culture Anyway? A Critical Review." *Korea Journal* 43 (1): 58–82.
Yi, Kyŏng-jae. 2013. "2000 nyŏndae tamunhwa sosŏl yŏn'gu: Han'gugin kwa ijumin ŭi kwan'gye yangsang ŭl chungsim ŭro" [A Study of Multicultural Fiction of the 2000s: On Aspects of the Relationship Between Koreans and Migrants]. *Han'guk hyŏndae munhak yŏn'gu* 40: 249–287.
Yi, Kyŏng-jae. 2015. *Tamunhwa sidae ŭi han'guk sosŏl ilkki* [(Parallel title:) "Reading Korean Novels in the Age of Multiculture"]. Seoul: Somyŏng.
Yi, Mi-rim. 2014. *21-segi Han'guk sosŏl ŭi tamunhwa wa ibangindŭl* [(Parallel title:) "Multiculture and Strangers of the 21st Century Korean Modern Novels"]. Seoul: P'urŭn Sasang 2014.
Yi, Mi-rim. 2016. "Tamunhwa sŏsa kujo wa munhakchŏk t'ŭkching" (A Study on the Multicultural Narrative Structures and Literary Characteristics). *Hyŏndae sosŏl yŏn'gu / The Journal of Korean Fiction Research* 61: 137–167.

Yi, Sohoon, and Jennifer Chun. 2020. "Building Worker Power for Day Laborers in South Korea's Construction Industry." *International Journal of Comparative Sociology* 61 (2–3): 122–140.

Yoon, Keumsil Kim, and Bruce Williams. 2015. *Two Lenses on the Korean Ethos: Key Cultural Concepts and their Appearance in Cinema.* Jefferson, NC: McFarland.

Yu, Myŏng-gi. 2002. "Oegugin nodongja, ajik miwansŏngin uri ŭi mirae" (Foreign Worker, Our Yet-Incomplete Future). *Tangdae Pip'yŏng* 18: 12–35.

Yuk, Joowon. 2014. "Talking Culture, Silencing 'Race,' Enriching the Nation: The Politics of Multiculturalism in South Korea." PhD diss., University of Warwick.

CHAPTER 11

Realizing *"Filiality Rights"*: The Role of Filial Piety in Localizing Human Rights in the Contemporary Korean Context

Hong-Jae Park

The Republic of Korea (henceforth *South Korea* or *Korea*) represents a unique location for human rights practice and theory, given its East Asian cultural heritage, the impact of rapid industrialization and modernization, and its combination of different religious traditions (see Beer 1991). In turn, the nation's modern identity has been shaped by its intense democratization movement in the 1980s, where human rights ideals played a crucial role in achieving political, social, and economic development (Cho 2010). Issues associated with human rights have continued to emerge from grassroots activities and diverse communities, as well as through the influence of foreign governments and international institutions. There have been significant achievements in the implementation of human rights over the last few decades of transformation, although

H.-J. Park (✉)
Western Sydney University, Penrith, NSW, Australia
e-mail: h.park@westernsydney.edu.au

© The Author(s), under exclusive license to Springer Nature Switzerland AG 2022
A. D. Jackson (ed.), *The Two Koreas and their Global Engagements*, https://doi.org/10.1007/978-3-030-90761-7_11

289

some aspects of universal principles are still controversial and underdeveloped at present. This Korean experience provides an important arena for developing human rights theories and practices, both locally and globally.

Arguably, the modern idea of human rights emerged from the European Enlightenment and so has, inevitably, been influenced mainly by the narratives of Western modernity. The Western ideas of human rights have significantly contributed to the recognition and respect of people's dignity and well-being, as well as promoting equality and fairness in society. Recently, however, human rights have been increasingly contested, and the earlier consensus around human rights ideals seems to no longer hold in many areas (see Arnold 2013). This does not mean that human rights have ceased to be important; on the contrary, they are as important as ever due to widening gaps in inequality and injustice. Contextual factors have an impact on constructing the human ideal—the ideal of a human who has rights, and building up individuals' morals and expectations about their natural rights (see Fagan 2011). They also affect the definitions of "rights" and "obligations" relative to the relationships of individuals, families, communities, and states. In this sense, it is to be understood that human rights in South Korea have been introduced, defined and ultimately, achieved in its wider cultural and social context. Like many other countries around the world, South Korea has a family-oriented culture in which people are likely to be committed to and dependent on their families, having stronger identification and solidarity with their family members than other social relationships. For many people, the family, as a basic social, financial and cultural unit, provides an ongoing source of their beliefs, values, and practices, and the volume and tightness of connections with family and kinship members tend to determine how their social identity, role, and status are shaped and accepted in the community and the wider society. People's interests and needs, as well as their well-being and happiness, are also likely to be affected by, or perceived with, the quality of kinship and family relationships. This family-oriented tradition is closely associated with the complex nexus of Korean religions, consisting mainly of local Shamanism, Buddhism, Confucianism, and latterly, Christianity. All these religious beliefs have served, regardless of their origin and popularity, as the bedrock of Korean familism focusing on harmonizing individuals with their immediate and extended families. Such Korean familism, as a type of collectivist culture (Schwartz 1990), has been enduring, in line with valuing the tradition of *filial piety* that emphasizes a set of family duties and obligations toward one's parents, older relatives, and ancestors (de Bary 1998; Sung 2007). Not only does the concept of filial piety refer to the expression of care, support and respect for one's parents (living ones), but it also encompasses the veneration of ancestors and the psychological and emotional connection with those who have died (Park 2020). Although many aspects of filial piety descend from the Chinese Confucian philosophy, this enduring tradition has distinctively evolved to constitute a major component of family-centered ideas and practices in Korean culture.

As filial piety has been a core element of traditional Korean history, so too, are human rights in the nation's modern identity. These two principles, human rights, and filial piety, are the main features representative of the Korean transformation that occurred during its modernization and democratization processes. The interaction between local and foreign cultures has been relentless in driving political, social, and economic adjustments to promote human rights and the evolution of relevant legal and administrative systems. The traditional culture of filial piety has struggled to retain its power in determining what social values and norms would prevail, while Western culture has continued to infuse many aspects of human rights into the nation's modernization process and the formation of its modern identity. Compatibility between filial piety (more generally, Korean familism) and human rights (particularly, equality between gender and/or generations) is highly controversial (see Choi and Woo 2018; de Bary 1998); the nation has still fought to ensure that both principles are necessary to sustain fully functional families and to concurrently promote individuals' freedoms and rights.

The purpose of this chapter is to provide a critical discussion on the relationship between filial piety and human rights as experienced in the transformation period of South Korea. To achieve its aim, the chapter critically explores the issue of poverty among the elderly in a society in which higher income inequality among older people has grown within the interwoven fabric of the filial piety tradition and human rights ideas. The discussion focuses on how the tradition of filial piety has affected the establishment of economic, social, and cultural rights, particularly for older people living in poverty. For this, the chapter will start with a brief outline of South Korea's human rights experience, and review the tradition of filial piety in contemporary times. A critical analysis of the issue of poverty among older people will be discussed with reference to the welfare and dignity of those poor and disadvantaged parents. Then, the essay will develop a discussion about the impact of filial piety on the localization of human rights and will conclude by outlining the notion of filiality rights as a means for advancing Korean human rights more globally.

RESEARCH QUESTIONS AND METHODS

As indicated earlier, this work focuses on specific research questions: "How has the tradition of filial piety played a role in localizing the principles of human rights related to the welfare and dignity of older people?"; and "What are the implications of filial piety for the future development of human rights in modern Korean society?" These questions are formulated based on the belief that the core principles of filial piety have had a mixed impact on the implementation of certain types of human rights, and vice versa, in contemporary Korean society. The questions are not intended to add to any debate on the age-old controversy about "universalism and cultural relativism" in human rights (for example, Mullender 2003). Rather, this chapter makes the point that there is much to admire and respect in the Korean tradition of filial piety and what it is able to achieve in the human rights area.

The study employed documentary research to capture major issues related to the research questions. It was conducted as the qualitative arm of an integrated project on "Studies on Filial Piety in Modern Korea" and comprised ethnographic, cross-cultural, and sociological inquiries. A total number of 171 abstracts of scholarly journal articles on filial piety, published from the 1950s up to the present, were collated into a bibliographic portfolio on a webpage. Evidence was drawn from a critical documentary review of these peer-reviewed articles (written in the Korean language) to elicit deeper insights on the phenomenon of filial piety throughout the transformation period of Korea. Among the archived literature, there was no specific article that aimed to discuss filial piety from a human rights perspective, but most were useful for understanding the complexity of the relationship between two factors (filial piety and human rights), in different social and historical contexts. Documents were also collected from media and news media to capture ideas and insights from a public media perspective, and these were coupled with the examination of community and government publications available both online and offline in South Korea.

Built upon this documentary resource, a case analysis of senior poverty was conducted to examine a real-life contemporary issue associated with both filial piety and human rights. The data collected were published articles (including news articles and debate articles) both in South Korea and overseas. To add weight to the documentary analysis on the issue of poverty, the author carried out informal visits to two churches whose volunteers gave out 500 Korean Won coins (equivalent to approximately US45 cents) to older people who lined up to receive this pocket money and a free lunch meal. Such cash allowances are regularly offered by several churches and cathedrals in Seoul, the capital city of South Korea, to those elders suffering from extreme poverty and dependent upon charitable handouts. To obtain a real sense of what was going on and what was needed at a grassroots level, the author also met with two church volunteers and three elderly people waiting in line. In addition, the analysis in this paper was enhanced by adding insights from consultation with two experts in the human rights sector in South Korea. Conversations with these scholars were particularly beneficial for assessing the validity of documentary data as well as the successful implementation of the research methods used for this study.

The Localization of Human Rights in South Korea

The basic principles of human rights are not new concepts, nor are they foreign ideologies in Korean culture. From ancient times onwards, people in the Korean Peninsula have accumulated ideas and had debates about "rights inherent to all human beings." Several philosophers, politicians, religious leaders, and literary figures pursued an underlying moral consensus that might be valid for all human beings and any just society (Han 1995). Under the rules of premodern kingdoms or empires, however, the achievement of such humanistic ideas was rarely accomplished, and a significant proportion of the population had to live their lives without the full enjoyment of those natural rights. The nation's history illustrates numerous cases where the inherent rights of ordinary or lower-class people were abused and exploited by a relatively smaller population of privileged individuals, groups, and authorities (see for example, Jackson 2019).

The global version of human rights, expressed in the Universal Declaration of Human Rights in 1948, became gradually localized in most arenas of Korean society after liberation from Japanese colonialism in the middle of the twentieth century. The nation has established its civil, judicial, and democratic apparatuses with a significant volume of economic, food, and military aid from international communities. The Constitution of the Republic of Korea, promulgated on July 17, 1948 and subsequently amended until October 27, 1987 (9th amendment), continues to proclaim that the state ought to guarantee people's freedom and rights, as well as equal opportunities in all sectors. That is, the Constitution makes clear that the government has obligations to promote and protect the human rights and fundamental freedoms of individuals and groups. The Constitution also states that the government should strive to establish a welfare state by implementing policies and interventions for all citizens, particularly for children, people with disabilities, and older people. At least in a constitutional sense, therefore, all people in Korea (literally, not limited to South Koreans) are entitled to a reasonable standard of living and other related rights, regardless of their age, gender, family arrangements, or other social categories.

In reality, however, such constitutional guarantees have been often corrupted and politicized, and there continues to be a distance between human rights ideals and their implementation in multiple sectors (Lee 1993). Certain freedoms and rights of citizens were significantly curtailed in the context of the military tension between South and North Korea. For example, civil and political rights were restricted by strong political and military leadership under the name of national security (see Lim 1998). In the wake of North Korea's threats, freedom of speech and association were strategically ignored or restricted to retain the nation's capitalist-oriented economy and strong solidarity among citizens and communities. This security-first ideological approach led to the nation's extreme reaction to the political activities or speeches, mainly led by "progressives" or "leftists" who were often thought to be in favor of the North Korean regime or Marxist communism. The question of how to balance individual rights and national security was an unsolved dilemma, while the nation's modernization process over the last few decades has continued to pay attention to international human rights conventions and regulations.

The human rights consciousness of people in South Korea has rapidly grown during the nation's democratic period, particularly since the 1980s. Through two major milestones, the "April 19 Revolution" in 1960 and "May 18 Kwangju Democratization Movement" in 1980, people have become more aware of the importance of democracy for a fair and righteous country than ever before. This awareness nurtured the seed of the "June Democracy Movement of 1987" and further democratic transformations since then (see Cho 2002). A number of civil activists, including labor unions, student groups, and academics strived to have an impact on the legislation and policies that affected them and/or the marginalized in society (Chang 2015). Although there were different attitudes toward democratic progress, both conservative and progressive Korean thinking has gradually accepted the principles of human rights, especially including the right to participate in associations and the prohibition of torture and unlawful detention (Baik 2013). This notable achievement in the "first-generation" (of civil and political) rights reflects, not only increased pressure on the government's commitment and intervention, but also an increase in people's morals and expectations about private freedom and human dignity, as well as equality and social justice.

Compared with civil and political rights, a set of economic, social, and cultural rights has been largely ignored, and local ideas about welfare rights (such as a right to a pension and minimum levels of material security, or freedom from severe poverty) have been under-developed in South Korea. Many people, including those needing the basic necessities of life, have been forced to tolerate potential breaches of those welfare rights over the last few decades (Lee 1993). Despite the nation's remarkable economic growth between the 1970s and 1990s, a high level of inequality persists relative to people's wealth and socio-economic status. Poverty still remains an everyday reality for a significant proportion of its population, particularly for older people (World Bank 2016). The nation's family-oriented paradigm has affected a range of legislation and guidelines fundamental to the well-being of individuals, and consequently, its implementation of economic, social, and cultural rights has been limited in terms of both amount and depth. Such structural problems prevent those less-advantaged people from having access to essential social services and economic opportunities. Recently, the Korean government and academics have tried to implement more Western systems and policies originating and developed in so-called "advanced welfare states," but the actual *effect* and *effectiveness* of implanting such foreign structures and programs on the nation's family-centered culture remain uncertain in many areas (see Kim 2018).

Overall, the localization of human rights in South Korea has been primarily led by emphasizing civil and political rights and individual freedoms, while the importance of welfare-related rights was largely ignored or under-valued. The democratization movements that occurred in the context of ideological tension stood up against successive military regimes and aimed to achieve mainly first-generation rights, including the freedom of speech and association (Cho 2002). The provision of social welfare to protect people's economic, social and cultural rights has not been established well, whereas the nation's filial tradition continues and partially compensates for the shortfalls in government social care and services. Under these circumstances, the government's focus on economic growth has benefited mainly a privileged minority, such as the Chaebol (family-controlled economic conglomerates), and led to widening gaps between social classes and other socio-cultural groups (see Kalinowski 2009). This experience of inequality indicates, in turn, that, while there have been significant achievements in human rights development in the country, some aspects of equality and human dignity for the vulnerable population sectors still remain disputed domestically and internationally.

Transformation of Filial Piety in Contemporary Korean Society

In Korean family-oriented culture, children have universal and inherent duties and obligations (to respect and support their parents and elders), whereas the responsibilities of parents and older relatives for their descendants are also recognized as unquestionable human traits in a civilized society. Throughout the nation's history, parents' sacrifices for children prevail; so does children's dedication to their parents and ancestors. It is the filial piety tradition that characterizes the Korean version of familism, which can be defined as "the strong normative feelings of loyalty, dedication, reciprocity, and attachment of family members to their family and familial relationships" (Sayegh and Knight 2011, 3) in the nation's wider historical and cultural context. For both older and younger generations, filial piety serves as a drive, or a long-lasting emotion that continues to bind people together in a mutual support network offering commitment and compassion and serving a broad spectrum of needs and interests (further, human rights). Numerous stories about those children who expressed extraordinary filial piety have been embodied into written and verbal literature, arts, and rituals in every chapter of Korean history. For example, *The Tale of Sim Ch'ŏng* (Simch'ŏgga), written about the eighteenth century, illustrates a touching story of a 15-year-old girl who fell overboard and drowned in the sea to pay for offerings to a local god to help her father recover from blindness (Yoon 2014). Such stories about filial children constantly reflect the deep-rooted assumption that adult children have moral and practical obligations to respect (literally, *obey*) their parents, to support them when their parents are in need and unable to fend for themselves, and then honor and remember them after they have died.

Filial piety, as an essential aspect of Korean familism, serves as the core principle that facilitates intergenerational solidarity and reciprocity, including care, love, respect, and support for, not only one's parents, grandparents, and ancestors, but also one's children, grandchildren, and younger generations. This traditional principle, on the one hand, provides children with relatively straightforward guidelines about how they treat their parents and other elders, as well as ancestors, throughout their lives from childhood to adulthood. On the other hand, the filial piety tradition offers fertile ground for parents' commitments to rearing and supporting their children and offspring, regardless of reward (through economic or material gains) from their children immediately or later. In this vein, filial piety exists as a historical assumption that people have parents who provide unconditional care and love until they become independent, and, in turn, they are expected to repay or respond to what they have received from those providers and givers. To realize this, there has been a range of forms of integrational cooperation and solidarity, including physical assistance, emotional and psychological support, and even spiritual sharing. Monetary and non-monetary exchanges between older people and adult children are prevalent (Oxford Institute of Ageing 2007), and such communal reciprocity is believed to promote psychological well-being of both generations positively (Lee et al. 2014; Ju et al. 2016). For many families, a two-way flow of financial and non-financial aid provision between generations has served as a safety net for each generation, prior to the government's implementation of social welfare services, throughout the nation's modernization period.

The acknowledgment of continuing relationships across life and death is another essential part of the filial piety tradition in the wider cultural and religious context of Korean familism. The extended scope of filial piety includes practicing "respect and care for ancestors," known as "ancestor worship" in many indigenous cultures around the world. The tradition of ancestor worship (more precisely "ancestor reverence or veneration") originated from ancient Shamanism, and has continued to evolve in realizing a spiritual connection with the dead, ancestors, and loved ones who have died. In contemporary times, continuing bonds between the dead and the living are expressed as a non- or less-religious aspect of ancestral worship, whereas the superstitious nature of this tradition has significantly diminished (Bae 2004; Janelli and Janelli 1982; Lee 1984). Modernized rites or rituals for ancestor remembrance, such as *chesa* or *ch'arye* (in Korean), are commonly observed by the majority of Korean families on special days, including death anniversaries, Lunar New Year's Day, and other traditional holidays (Gallup Korea 2014). Such filial piety toward ancestors also involves a range of activities, including grave visits, keeping family genealogy records, and kinship conferences, and has contributed to sustaining Korean family-centered culture for many generations (Park 2017).

Korean familism, based on filial piety, has evolved tremendously in the latest period of its transformation due mainly to changes in family formation, size, and patterns, as well as the population structure (Park 2013). Some filial traditions, including co-residence among three generations (grandparents, parents, children) and family care for aged parents, have eroded as people's attitudes and behavior toward filial obligations, particularly related normative concerns, have changed in modern Korea (Chee 2000; Ch'oe and Chang 2010; Park and Kim 2016). For example, national data show that the commitment of adult children to family caregiving has decreased from about 90% to under 40% between 1998 and 2014 (Kim 2016). Modern filial piety is also believed to have many faults as its origin relates to the establishment of premodern family relationships between younger and older generations (including ancestors). The patriarchal nature of traditional filial piety has made it a major target for criticism concerning gender equality, religious freedom, and the filial rights movement (human rights of children and young people against parents) (see Kim 2007; Park 2013). An increased social awareness of "non-traditional families," such as sole-member families, non-married couples, and civil partnerships (if any), is also helping to devalue or diminish the traditions of filial piety and ancestor veneration. The nation's current dominant left-wing political popularity also contributes to escalating negative perceptions toward the entire concept of filial piety which is seen by progressive critics as a tool to solidify a conservative ideological enclave. Under these circumstances, the future of filial piety is uncertain while its religious, political, and economic impacts are still particularly significant for those older generations whose attitudes, beliefs, and values are deeply affected by Korean familism, particularly the filial piety tradition.

POVERTY AMONG THE ELDERLY: A CASE WHERE FILIAL PIETY CONFOUNDS HUMAN RIGHTS

Despite growing criticism, South Korea has continued to sustain the tradition of filial piety that is woven into the basic social fabric (Park 2015). As a result, ideally, older people ought to be supported by their children, emotionally, financially, and physically, and thus, be able to live a good, full quality of life in an inclusive and respectful environment. Ironically, however, a significant proportion of older people in South Korea experience poverty and economic hardship without adequate support from family or wider society (McCurry 2017; Novak 2015; Yoon 2016).

Data collected by the Organisation of Economic Co-operation and Development (OECD 2020) reveal that nearly half of older people in South Korea were in poverty (defined as earning 50% or less of median household income) in 2018—the highest level among the 34 OECD countries. This does not mean explicitly that the majority of Korean seniors live in absolute poverty, but it does indicate that they are relatively poorer than other age groups and the Korean income gap between generations is far wider than those of other comparable countries. The following graph (Fig. 11.1) directly contrasts this widening gap in the poverty rate in Korea, showing the largest gap between people aged over

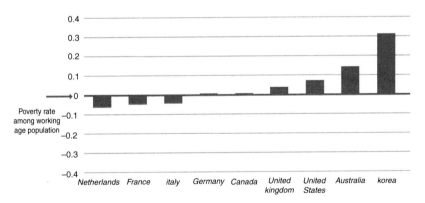

Fig. 11.1 The gap in poverty rate (between 18–65-year-olds and 66-year-olds or over; figure by author) (Source of information: OECD Social and Welfare Statistics [Income distribution]: Poverty rate [2018])

65 and those aged 18 to 65 years (working age) among OECD countries in 2018.

The causes of poverty among the elderly in South Korea are complex and varied, depending on personal and family situations, as well as socio-economic circumstances. The risk factors for this age-specific issue are known to include the lack of both employment opportunities for older people and social assistance for those needing public help (Lee 2014). On the one hand, older people are likely to be out of employment in order to allow their younger counterparts to enter the workforce. They are often forced to retire, even before reaching their retirement age (around 60 or 65), as the nation has experienced increased competition in the workforce due to its internal and external economic challenges. On the other hand, the lack of social welfare security contributes to the poverty and economic hardship of older people because they do not receive enough government support during their retirement. While the nation's population continues to age, social welfare, particularly income security, has not increased in line with economic growth and living costs in South Korea (Yoon 2013). The nation's spending on its welfare budget for its older population is ranked second-to-last among OECD members and, as a result, the current pension system seems to leave many older people to fend for themselves with very minimal support (for instance, approximately US$270 per month of the basic pension in 2018) from the public sector.

More critically, the nation's family-centered culture has played a role in creating senior poverty in two ways (Kim and Cook 2011). First, with the emphasis on the prosperity and harmony of the family over individual life, people are likely to spend their income and assets on the education, marriage, or housing of their children, rather than on their own retirement plans and investment. Many people are unable to put aside enough savings for later in life because they spend too much on their children's education and other needs. Such parental commitment and practice often force them to face serious financial shortages when they become older and unemployed. A national survey showed that, after highly expensive educational expenditure, Korean parents spent an average of 130 million won (US$110,000) on their children's marriages, including expenses for the newlyweds, wedding ceremonies, and parental gifts for in-laws, as well as housing support (such as the lump sum bond for the married couple's lease) (Yoon and Cho 2016). It was estimated that parents' average spending on their children's marriage could be equivalent to more than half of the retirement funds they need for later in their lives. There are also cases where older people voluntarily hand over their assets and savings to their own children in advance, thus putting themselves into the lowest-income bracket, so that they will be eligible for means-tested pension and subsidies for long-term care in the future.

Second, the filial piety tradition also generates an assumption that older people will be supported and cared for by their own children and grandchildren as they have been successful in rearing them and maintaining a functioning family. It is commonly assumed that private allowances (pocket money), offered by children regularly or occasionally, are the main financial sources for many older people in the context of intergenerational exchanges. This anecdotal assumption about filial traditions has been underpinned in a range of social interventions for older people, and is often used as an excuse for the state's lack of support for those seniors needing social welfare assistance. An example is the National Basic Living Security Act which aims to "ensure the minimum level of living for the needy individuals and help them support themselves by furnishing them with the required assistance" (National Law Information Center 2018). The provisions in this law are supposed to enable those people in the lowest-income bracket to be eligible for "livelihood benefits" that are a form of monetary payment for daily commodities such as food, clothing, and energy bills. According to this welfare law, however, if older adults (aged 65 or over) have an "obligatory provider" who is "a lineal blood relative of the first degree and his/her spouse," then they are not eligible for this basic provision of a social safety net. In other words, welfare payments are not available for those low- or no-income older people, if they have a child *regardless of whether the child can or cannot support his/her parents*. The consequences of this "unreasonable" exclusion are significant for those older people in poverty, as well as for the whole community.

Overall, the high poverty levels within the elderly population in South Korea are likely to stem from a vicious cycle of fewer economic opportunities, limited social support, and low savings and incomes for retirement. While parents are still expected to spend an unsustainable amount of money for their children, some of them are unlikely to receive adequate support from their offspring when they themselves are in need. Senior poverty, in this vein, is an issue associated with the structural inequality and cultural dissolution embedded in contemporary Korean society. Nevertheless, senior poverty exists in a blind spot of social welfare and justice, and adversely affects the well-being and dignity of the older persons marginalized economically and socially. This age-specific problem also provides fertile ground for increased levels of senior suicide and health problems, reduced life expectancy, and the prevalence of social isolation and loneliness among older people (see Park et al. 2009, 2016). The universal nature of human rights in this area justifies the idea that older people in poverty deserve the state's support and social care services, regardless of whether they have offspring to support them or not. Action to tackle poverty-related problems remains the state's responsibility, beyond relying on family duties, to promote the dignity and well-being of older people in an inclusive and just environment.

Discussion

The Impact of Filial Piety on the Localization of Human Rights in South Korea

The case of senior poverty in South Korea indicates that the mindset of filial piety has adversely affected the state's intervention in promoting human rights, particularly for older people relative to their welfare needs and rights. The tradition of filial piety is likely to reinforce an ancient assumption that older people ought to rely on family support and care in their later lives. It has been culturally constructed that the family is the main resource of aged parents' well-being and happiness, so it is the last resort and safety-net support in later life. This long-lasting and taken-for-granted feature of filial piety tends to create a situation where the basic needs and rights of those older people in poverty are neglected under the cloak of the filial piety paradigm. In addition, the nation has placed an economic growth focus above its social policies and interventions, coupled with extreme caution about national security against the North Korean communist regime (Baik 2013). This macro-political situation has allowed the state and local authorities to pay less attention to individuals' welfare needs and rights, particularly for older people who are *assumed* to receive adequate support from their own family members.

It is equally worthwhile noting that the principle of filial piety has also had a positive impact on the development of human rights in contemporary Korean society. In other words, through its family-centered approach, the nation has been partially successful in localizing many aspects of human rights in its modernization process. The principles of filial piety and ancestor reverence have helped people cooperate with each other in harmony to fulfill their own and family's needs and rights, collectively pursuing their welfare and happiness. More specifically, since the end of the Korean War in the 1950s, the state's goal was to lift people out of poverty, not with well-established social welfare, but by encouraging people's aspirations in education, jobs, income, and economic success. It was mainly the family (solidarity among family members) that enabled people to take advantage of the opportunities available to them, such as more accessible tertiary education, tenure employment, and increased personal wealth. Through these opportunities, people achieved better education and higher incomes, and, thus, developed their awareness and understanding about the influence of human rights ideas and Western civilization. Some aspects of human rights, particularly welfare rights, were alternatively provided through voluntary family duties and responsibilities, which effectively paved an avenue for the significant improvement of the first-generation of human rights, such as political freedom, during the nation's modernization and democratization.

The impact of filial piety values on human rights is proven by the fact that Korean laws include a number of provisions that aim to sustain and promote the Confucian ideology of filial piety. A pro-family culture has been deeply engraved into the Korean constitution, and there is a range of legal reinforcements (including general tax deductions) for families supporting aged parents (see Kim 2015). For example, Section 224 of the *Code of Criminal Procedure* (which has been in place since 1954), prohibits children from filing a criminal complaint against their parents while parents can do so against their children or grandchildren. In 2011, the Constitutional Court (Case No: 2008Hun-Ba56) endorsed that this limitation on lineal descendants is a "rational and well-grounded discrimination … based on our historical ideology of *Hyo* [filial piety] or the Confucian tradition of filial duty," and, therefore, does not breach the right to equality (Constitutional Court of Korea 2011). The *Korean Civil Act* (1958, last amended in 2007) also continues to encourage adult children to attend to their duty to support their parents who are unable to fend for themselves with their own financial resources or labor (Article 974). More recently, the *Korean Act on the Encouragement and Support of Filial Piety 2007* was passed to promote the practice of filial duties and responsibilities within family units, the community, and in wider society (Park 2015).

The Implications of Filial Piety for Developing Korean Human Rights

Then, do the principles of filial piety and ancestor veneration have any implications for human rights practice in response to the rapid changes and challenges in modern Korean society? What aspects of filial piety are compatible with human rights, particularly welfare-related rights? How could filial piety (Korean familism) be effectively used to tackle existing prevalent human rights issues, such as senior poverty, ageist attitudes or discrimination against older adults, and social isolation and exclusion? The potential implications of filial piety for developing Korean human rights are profound.

Basically, the nature of filial piety inherently, encompasses *all* human beings regardless of our gender, ethnicity, religion, or social class. Just as all human beings are supposed to be born free and equal in dignity and rights, we are given certain statuses and roles related to filial piety when we are born. The logic for this argument is that all human beings have parents somewhere; most of us receive care and support from them, share life developments and events with them, look after them when they are aged or in need, and remember them after their death (see Park 2017). This life-long relationship between child and parent, mainly based on biological connection, occurs naturally with the birth of a human being, and is likely to grow and remain continuous through the practice of a wider range of expressions of love and filial piety, valuing the dignity and rights of parents and fulfilling their basic needs. Even if some people do not have such meaningful relationships with their parents, this does not mean that those people's interests regarding filial piety have to be denied or excluded. Rather, they equally deserve to have their fundamental relationship healed and rehabilitated in a restorative sense of harmony and reciprocity between generations.

This universal aspect of filial piety can be seen as an integrated form of "natural rights" and "natural obligations" which are indivisible and unavoidable for both givers (mainly children) and receivers (mainly parents) in nature, regardless of beliefs, religions or laws. It can be argued, therefore, that the nature of filial piety, as a universal value, is compatible with that of human rights, at least, in some ways. In other words, fundamental aspects of filial piety are universal, interrelated, and interdependent, comprising both obligations and rights in its nature and practice. More specifically, filial piety provides the right to know who our parents and ascendants (as our parents' parents, parents, and so on) are, to rely on them in our early life-stages, and to express our filial love and affection. It is a right to care for and support our parents materially, emotionally, and physically when they are in need. It is also a right to remember and respect them after their death in an appropriate cultural and spiritual context. As filial piety is an expression of concern for parents' dignity and welfare, it also forms a basic type of second-generation rights which are important for people's economic, social and cultural lives.

These types of rights can be identified, defined and conceptualized as *"filiality rights"*—the rights to filial piety and ancestor veneration; here, the term *filiality* is used as an overarching notion, incorporating all manner of concepts involving people's positive behaviors, perceptions and attitudes toward parents, older relatives, and ancestors. The unique nature of filiality rights, compared with traditional human rights concepts, lies in its emphasis on the universal and inherent relationship between child and parent. These filiality rights are *outward-looking* rights in human relationships, distinct from those based on individuals per se, while their nature is closely related to the concept of third-generation rights (group and collective rights). Solidarity is the key component of these reciprocal bonds between generations. The cooperative nature of filial piety is likely to contrast the individual freedoms and liberties people take for granted, with an integrated concept of human rights—both being entitled to human rights and having to respect those of others. If the concept of filiality rights could be accepted as a type of human right, states would be assumed to have obligations and duties to respect, protect and fulfill those natural and collective rights in a formal, structural and systematic way. This further means that states ought to take positive action to facilitate the enjoyment of filiality rights, and at the same time, prevent interference with, or curtailment of, entitlements to these basic rights. The idea of filiality rights, evident in the Korean experience of filial piety, can contribute to tackling existing, prevalent human rights issues, such as senior poverty, ageism against senior citizens, elder abuse, and social isolation. It would also be useful for tuning the extreme spectrum of individualized human rights and related ego-centric or ethnocentric ideologies.

Research Limitations

The discussion in this paper has been limited to an aspect of the connection between filial piety and human rights, based on a critical analysis of poverty among older people in South Korea. The senior poverty case, per se, is an extremely complex issue associated with, not only filial piety, but also personal, economic, educational, social, and technological issues. Given such limitations, the focus of this paper is on pursuing a more plausible explanation for the phenomenon, rather than generalizing the findings and interpretations of the data collected and analyzed. In addition, there are no reliable quantitative data available to elaborate the relationship between the level of human rights and that of filial piety, and thus, the discussion of this study is inherently restricted in terms of its empirical approach to supporting the presented ideas and arguments.

Concluding Comments

South Korea represents an important location for human rights discourse globally, given its East Asian cultural heritage, the mix of local and foreign religious traditions, the impact of rapid industrialization and modernization, and the experience of the Democracy Movement in which human rights ideals played an important role. From this unique experience, a particular Korean perspective on human rights is emerging, and this can make a significant contribution to understanding human rights at the global level.

Overall, the localizing of human rights in South Korea has been an ongoing and controversial issue in the nation's democratic transformation period since the 1950s. As in many other countries around the world, challenges associated with universal rights are significant and complex in this nation. Its political, economic, religious, cultural, and social systems are all interwoven in creating, and responding to, the issue of human rights among diverse demographic and socio-economic groups. As can be seen in the case of poverty among the elderly, the filial piety tradition has played a role in the nation's implementation of human rights particularly for older people living in poverty. It is argued that the welfare-related rights of older people are likely to remain within the filial piety mindset on family and kin levels, while there is a lack of attention to them on a wider societal level. This is partially because the family is persistently considered as the most important social safety net for aged parents in a context where Korean family-oriented practices are deeply entrenched. Built on this analysis, the paper proposes that the tradition of filial piety has had a mixed impact, both positive and negative, on the settlement of human rights in modern Korean society. This analysis also proposes a potential area of *filiality rights* based on the notion that all human beings have an inherent, universal right to express filial piety to their parents (and ancestors) regardless of background or relationships. The influence of filial piety on human rights is a major feature that will determine whether Korea continues to keep struggling with Western ideas of human rights, or if it will see an important and unique location for human rights practice and theory in the coming years.

References

Arnold, Rainer. 2013. "Reflections on the Universality of Human Rights." In *The Universalism of Human Rights*, edited by Rainer Arnold, 1–12. Springer Netherlands.

Bae, Choon Sup. 2004. "Ancestor Worship in Korea and Africa: Social Function or Religious Phenomenon?" *Verbum et Ecclesia* 25 (2): 338–356.

Baik, Tae-Ung. 2013. "Stabilizing Democracy and Human Rights Systems in South Korea." *The University of Hawaii Law Review* 35 (2):877–907.

Beer, Lawrence W. 1991. "Comparative Perspectives on Human Rights in Korea." In *Human Rights in Korea: Historical and Policy Perspectives*, edited by William Shaw, 265–282. Harvard University Asia Center.

Chang, Paul Y. 2015. *Protest Dialectics: State Repression and South Korea's Democracy Movement, 1970–1979*. Stanford University Press.

Chee, Yeon Kyung. 2000. "Elder Care in Korea: The Future Is Now." *Ageing International* 26 (1–2): 25–37.

Cho, Hyo-Je. 2002. "Human Rights in Korea at the Crossroads: A Critical Overview." *Korea Journal* 42 (1): 204–227.

Cho, Hyo-Je. 2010. "Two Concepts of Human Rights in Contemporary Korea." *Development and Society* 39 (2): 301–27. https://doi.org/10.21588/dns.2010.39.2.006.

Ch'oe, Sŏng-Jae, and In-hyŏp Chang. 2010. *Koryŏnghwa sahoeŭi noin pokchihak* [Social Welfare for Older Persons in Aging Society]. Seoul National University Press.

Choi, Eunjung, and Jongseok Woo. 2018. "Confucian Legacies and the Meaning of Democracy in South Korea: A Cultural Interpretation." *Korea Observer* 49 (3): 493–515. https://doi.org/10.29152/KOIKS.2018.49.3.493.

Constitutional Court of Korea. 2011. *Case on Prohibition of Filing a Complaint Against Lineal Ascendants* (Case No: 2008Hun-Ba56). http://search.ccourt.go.kr/ths/ep/selectThsEp0101List.do.

de Bary, Wm. Theodore. 1998. *Asian Values and Human Rights: A Confucian Communitarian Perspective*. Harvard University Press.

Fagan, Andrew. 2011. "Philosophical Foundations of Human Rights." In *Handbook of Human Rights*, edited by Thomas Cushman, 9–22. Routledge.
Gallup Korea. 2014. 2014 *nyŏn han'gukinŭi sŏlp'unggyŏng* [The Sŏl (Lunar New Year's Day) Landscape for Koreans in 2014] [Unpublished report]. Seoul, Korea: Gallup Korea.
Han, Sang-Bum. 1995. Human Rights (in Korean), In Encyclopedia of Korean Culture (Academy of Korean Studies). http://encykorea.aks.ac.kr/.
Jackson, Andrew D. 2019. "The Punishments of the 1728 Musin Rebellion Leaders." *Korean Studies* 43, 120–144, August 2018.
Janelli, Roger, and Dawnhee Janelli. 1982. *Ancestor Worship and Korean Society*. Stanford University Press.
Ju, Yeong Jun, Kyu-Tae Han, Tae-Hoon Lee, Woorim Kim, Juyeong Kim, and Eun-Cheol Park. 2016. "Does Relationship Satisfaction and Financial Aid from Offspring Influence the Quality of Life of Older Parents? A Longitudinal Study Based on Findings from the Korean Longitudinal Study of Aging, 2006-2012." *Health and Quality of Life Outcomes* 14: 1–8. https://doi.org/10.1186/s12955-016-0509-4.
Kalinowski, Thomas. 2009. "The Politics of Market Reforms: Korea's Path from Chaebol Republic to Market Democracy and Back." *Contemporary Politics* 15 (3): 287–304. https://doi.org/10.1080/13569770903118770.
Kim, Erin Hye-Won, and Philip J. Cook. 2011. "The Continuing Importance of Children in Relieving Elder Poverty: Evidence from Korea." *Ageing & Society* 31 (6): 953–976. https://doi.org/10.1017/S0144686X10001030.
Kim, Hee-Kang. 2018. "A caring welfare state in South Korea: Challenges and prospects." *International Journal of Care and Caring* 2(3):333–48. doi:https://doi.org/10.1332/239788218X15347573010033
Kim, Marie Seong-Hak. (2015). "Confucianism That Confounds: Constitutional Jurisprudence on Filial Piety in Korea." In *Confucianism, Law and Democracy in Contemporary Korea*, edited by Sungmoon Kim, 57–80. Rowman & Littlefield International.
Kim, Seseoria. 2007. "The Meaning of "Filial Piety" and Ethics of Care in the Korean Family." *The Review of Korean Studies* 10 (3): 9–34.
Kim, Yugyeong. 2016. "The Family Support and Policy Implications on Support Environment Changes" [in Korean]. *Health and Social Welfare Forum* 235: 62–79.
Lee, Hyo Jung, Jiyoung Lyu, Chae Man Lee, and Jeffrey A. Burr. 2014. "Intergenerational Financial Exchange and the Psychological Well-Being of Older Adults in the Republic of Korea." *Aging & Mental Health* 18 (1): 30–39. https://doi.org/10.1080/13607863.2013.784955.
Lee, Kwang Kyu. 1984. "The Concept of Ancestors and Ancestor Worship in Korea." *Asian Folklore Studies* 43 (2): 199–214.

Lee, Suk Tae. 1993. "South Korea: Implementation and Application of Human Rights Covenants." *Michigan Journal of International Law* 14: 705–738.

Lee, Sun Jae. 2014. "Poverty Amongst the Elderly in South Korea: The Perception, Prevalence, and Causes and Solutions." *International Journal of Social Sciences and Humanity* 4 (3): 242–245. https://doi.org/10.7763/IJSSH.2014.V4.355.

Lim, Timothy C. 1998. "Power, Capitalism, and the Authoritarian State in South Korea." *Journal of Contemporary Asia* 28 (4): 457–483. https://doi.org/10.1080/00472339880000251.

McCurry, Justin. 2017. "South Korea's Inequality Paradox: Long Life, Good Health and Poverty." *The Guardian*, August 2. https://www.theguardian.com

Mullender, Richard. 2003. "Human rights: Universalism and Cultural Relativism." *Critical Review of International Social and Political Philosophy* 6 (3): 70–103. https://doi.org/10.1080/1369823032000233564.

National Law Information Center. 2018. *National Basic Living Security Act*. http://www.law.go.kr/.

Novak, Kathy. 2015. "Forgotten: South Korea's Elderly Struggle to Get by." *CNN*, October 23. https://edition.cnn.com/

OECD (Organisation of Economic Co-operation and Development). 2020. *Poverty Rate (Indicator)*. Accessed December 27, 2020. https://data.oecd.org/inequality/poverty-rate.htm

Oxford Institute of Ageing. 2007. *The Third Annual HSBC Future of Retirement Study*. HSBC (Hong Kong Shanghai Banking Corporation).

Park, Bo Hyun, Minsoo Jung, and Tae Jin Lee. 2009. "Associations of Income and Wealth with Health Status in the Korean Elderly." *Journal of Preventive Medicine and Public Health* 42 (5): 275–282. https://doi.org/10.3961/jpmph.2009.42.5.275.

Park, Hong-Jae. 2015. "Legislating for Filial Piety: An Indirect Approach to Promoting Family Support and Responsibility for Older People in Korea." *Journal of Aging & Social Policy* 27: 280–293. https://doi.org/10.1080/08959420.2015.1024536

Park, Hong-Jae. 2017. "Lessons from Filial Piety: Do We Need "Memorial Social Work" for the Dead and Their Families?" *Qualitative Social Work Practice* 16: 367–375. https://doi.org/10.1177/1473325015616289

Park, Hong-Jae. 2020. "Lessons from Filial Piety: A Social-life-span Approach to Building the Connection that Survives Death." *Death Studies* 44 (1): 25–30. https://doi.org/10.1080/07481187.2018.1516703

Park, Hong-Jae, and Chang Gi Kim. 2016. "Bystander Attitudes toward Parents? The Perceived Meaning of Filial Piety among Koreans in Australia, New Zealand and Korea." *Australasian Journal on Ageing* 35 (2): E25–29. https://doi.org/10.1111/ajag.12223.

Park, Jong-Il, Jong-Chul Yang, Changsu Han, Tae Won Park, and Sang-Keun Chung. 2016. "Suicidal Ideation among Korean Elderly: Risk factors and Population Attributable Fractions." *Psychiatry: Interpersonal and Biological Processes* 79 (3): 262–281. https://doi.org/10.1080/00332747.2016.1175837.

Park, Keong-Suk. 2013. "Consecrating or Desecrating Filial Piety? Korean Elder Care and the Politics of Family." *Development and Society* 42 (2): 287–308. https://doi.org/10.21588/DNS.2013.42.2.007.

Sayegh, Philip, and Bob G. Knight. 2011. "The Effects of Familism and Cultural Justification on the Mental and Physical Health of Family Caregivers." *The Journals of Gerontology. Series B, Psychological Sciences and Social Sciences* 66 (1): 3–14. https://doi.org/10.1093/geronb/gbq061.

Schwartz, Shalom H. 1990. "Individualism-Collectivism: Critique and Proposed Refinements." *Journal of Cross-Cultural Psychology* 21 (2): 139–157. https://doi.org/10.1177/0022022190212001

Sung, Kyu-Taik. 2007. *Respect and Care for the Elderly: The East Asian Way*. University Press of America.

World Bank. 2016. *Live Long and Prosper: Aging in East Asia and Pacific*. World Bank.

Yoon, Hyun-Sook. 2013. "Korea: Balancing Economic Growth and Social Protection for Older Adults." *The Gerontologist* 53 (3): 361–368. https://doi.org/10.1093/geront/gnt018.

Yoon, In Sun. 2014. "The Narrative Structure of the Unconsciousness in The Story of Sim Cheong." *Technology and Health Care* 22 (3): 443–451. https://doi.org/10.3233/THC-140802.

Yoon, Min-sik. 2016. "Elderly Poverty Increases in Korea." *The Korea Herald*, January 13. http://www.koreaherald.com/

Yoon, Sungeun, and Myungki Cho. 2016. *Chanyŏŭi kyŏlhon, pumoŭi nohu* [Children's Marriage, Parents' Old Age]. Samsung Life Retirement Research Center.

CHAPTER 12

Natural Consequences for Koreans in Japan: The Fluid Nature of the Identity Formation of Chongryon Koreans

Min Hye Cho

I first encountered real-life accounts of the lives of Koreans in Japan during a conference in 2018, voiced by their younger generations who had studied these issues. As an immigrant to Australia myself, while my decision to leave Korea in no way equates to the experiences of the ethnic Korean poet Zhan'g Zhon'g, I was particularly impressed by the way Zhan'g accurately described Korean minority groups' feelings about living outside Korea in his poem "Zainichi Saram Mal"[1] (The language of the Zainichi[2] people). Zhan'g writes: "Japanese, yet not Japanese ... Korean, yet not Korean ... The bastard child/Of Japanese/Of Korean." Zhan'g expresses the confusion of being caught between two identities, of being unable to fully integrate himself into either Korean or Japanese society. The formation of identity is inextricably linked to a set of beliefs, values,

M. H. Cho (✉)
BNU-HKBU United International College, Zhuhai, China
e-mail: minhyecho@uic.edu.cn

© The Author(s), under exclusive license to Springer Nature Switzerland AG 2022
A. D. Jackson (ed.), *The Two Koreas and their Global Engagements*, https://doi.org/10.1007/978-3-030-90761-7_12

and ideas that are intrinsic to an individual and which determines his or her membership within a given group. Zhan'g's Chosŏn nationality[3] (where nationality is defined as being officially part of an ethnic minority that forms part of a political nation) reflects the many nationalities and identities of overseas Korean diasporas.

Korean minority groups often struggle to adapt to their host societies where they face various conflicts in regards to their identity. In the case of Japan, Koreans there have experienced difficulties that largely derive from discrimination against them. Meanwhile, the ideological division among different Korean communities (based on allegiance to North or South Korea) has posed another challenge for them in terms of expressing their sense of belonging. In Japan, Chongryon Koreans (Ch'ongnyŏn, 總聯)[4] seek to embrace their Korean identity by affiliating themselves with North Korea, while struggling against Japanese societal discrimination. In contrast, another longstanding Korean organization, Mindan (民団),[5] is pro-South Korea. This division of political hegemony between Chongryon and Mindan reflects the division of the Korean Peninsula at the 38th parallel (Suzuki 2012, 55).

Chongryon's schools, known as Chosŏnhakkyo (朝鮮学校),[6] were established in 1946 and follow teaching curricula that are independent of the Japanese education system. Younger generations of Chongryon Koreans have been educated in this school system, where in order to promote a Korean ethnic identity, most lessons are delivered in Korean to students who speak Japanese as their first language. This study looks at Chosŏnhakkyo secondary English as a Foreign Language (EFL) textbooks to explore the way Chongryon Koreans' identity has changed over time. It is during secondary schooling that students become conscious of their own language and are therefore more influenced by new ways of using it (Halliday 2007, 62). This research therefore focuses on secondary EFL textbooks in order to explore the dominant ideas Chongryon students are taught about their identity.

Textbooks reveal the association between socio-cultural, political, and economic issues (Apple 1999, 170). Textbook developers and writers are inclined to integrate their beliefs, especially in the case of ethnic minority producers, whose unique socio-cultural and political environment would inspire discussion on the interest of promoting a given ideology. Textbooks also work to identify the present collective identity and the ideologies of the dominant group (Lee 2000). Identity change can occur in two different ways: the identity element is either changed by the social actors themselves by participating in the process of change, or the social actors accept the imposition of new elements of identity (Norris 2011, 235). Which one is the case for Chongryon Koreans? The presentation of identity via the EFL textbooks reveals that the textbook producer is attempting to enforce a change in identity without providing Chongryon readers with any options to explore the matter for themselves.

Chosŏnhakkyo education has remained independent from the Japanese government thanks to North Korea's direct sponsorship of Chongryon educational programs. This essentially means that for Chongryon Koreans, their unique learning environment has influenced the identity of all the Chongryon members because of their need to adapt to this environment. Chongryon Korean identity is therefore worthy of investigation, as the community's culture and education provide a unique insight into their situation. While scholars such as Song (2011) and Lee (2017) have investigated the relationship between political ideologies and identity formation as reflected in recent Chongryon Korean language textbooks, little serious attention has been given to the community's foreign language textbooks. It is therefore important to analyze how Chongryon EFL textbooks' treatment of English language education has shifted over time, and how these changes reflect a Chongryon community that continues to negotiate its identity within Japan while maintaining strong attachments to North Korea.

Understanding Chongryon Koreans' identity is vital as it enables us to understand the community better, thereby establishing a better rapport with Chongryon Koreans after decades of conflict. By considering different periods, this research will explore the influence of these textbooks on Chongryon Korean identity formation, as expressed through official Chongryon EFL teaching texts published between 1968 and 1974, and in 1994 and 2014. Each new edition of text coincides with different leadership eras in North Korea. The updating of textbook contents every twenty years reveals significant changes in Chongryon's belief systems.

The Lives of Koreans in Japan

During the colonial era (1910–1945), the Japanese government forcibly relocated a large number of Koreans to Japan. These first-generation immigrants were mobilized by the Japanese authorities to solve Japan's shortage of manual laborers. Approximately 990,000 male and female

Koreans were also relocated to serve in the Japanese Army during World War II (Chapman 2006, 90). Despite the compulsory nature of these relocations, around 650,000 of the 2.4 million Koreans remaining in Japan at the end of the war decided to remain there, because Japan provided their only source of income (Ryang 2000, 33). Another reason for remaining in Japan was the chaotic state of the Korean Peninsula, due to the conflict between the two mutually antagonistic ideologies of communism and capitalism (Ha 2015, 3). Meanwhile, restrictions imposed upon the amount of money and property Koreans could take back to the Peninsula (¥1,000[7] and 250 pounds [about 133 kg]) made people uncertain as to whether they would have the means to restart their new lives in Korea (Cho and Lee 2019, 179). The numbers of Koreans living in Japan have grown significantly over the past hundred years, and third, fourth, and fifth-generation Koreans now make up a large part of the Korean communities in Japan.

When Koreans were taken to Japan in order to boost the Japanese labor force, they were offered Japanese citizenship. However, later, one consequence of the 1952 San Francisco Peace Treaty was that this citizenship and the rights that came with it became annulled. With fewer legal rights, Koreans were subjected to greater levels of discrimination in education and employment and no longer qualified for social benefits. In response, they sought ways to create safe communities for themselves. After forming many different organizations to support and protect themselves in Japan, the pro-North Korean Chongryon was established in Japan in 1955. Its goals included the construction of a stable Korean community within Japan, and the majority (about 98%) of these Koreans living in Japan as part of the Chongryon community had, in fact, originally come from the southern provinces of the Korean Peninsula (Ryang 1997, 2).

While South Korea was heavily influenced and dominated by the US government, North Korea was ruled by Kim Il Sung. Having experienced lives governed by foreign nations (firstly Japan in the colonial period, and then the US in the postwar period), many Koreans living in Japan felt that life under Kim Il Sung would lead to a unified Korea under a Korean ruler. The US Government's intervention in the Korean War had left many Koreans believing that foreign influence was the cause of Korea's division (Jin 1999). Consequently, Koreans in Japan felt that Kim Il Sung could provide better protection and security for them than any foreign nation, and this became an important historical belief among Japan's Korean community (Cho 2019). Kim Il Sung's support was a clear demonstration of North Korea's interest in this new organization, and Kim Il Sung himself was keen to depict North Korea as Chongryon Koreans' homeland despite their South Korean origins (Cho 2020, 167).

The alliance between Chongryon Koreans and North Korea was demonstrated further during the process of Korean repatriation from Japan to North Korea. Roughly 93,000 Koreans were repatriated to North Korea between 1959 and by the early 1980s (Bell 2018, 5). The main reasons for this mass migration were the discrimination Koreans experienced in Japan and the financial support that the Koreans received from North Korea when they were experiencing significant economic hardship in Japan. The Japanese media encouraged this repatriation, knowing that the Koreans were imposing a large financial burden on the Japanese government (Jin 1999, 598–601).

The number of migrants decreased after the 1965 Normalization Treaty which allowed Koreans in Japan to retain South Korean nationality, and also because many younger generation Koreans chose to become Japanese citizens. Their desire to integrate into Japanese society resulted in an increased rate of naturalization, which in turn enabled Koreans to gain better education and equal employment opportunities, although some Koreans opposed naturalization and saw naturalized Koreans as "traitors" to the Korean diaspora in Japan (Suzuki 2012, 52). Numerous Japanese policies encouraged this view of naturalized Koreans as "traitors." For example, the Japanese government demanded that naturalized citizens take Japanese names, thereby encouraging Koreans to forgo their Korean identity. In response to Japan's assimilationist policies, Chongryon educated the younger Korean generations by encouraging them to retain their ethnic Korean identity while still providing these students with opportunities to integrate themselves into Japanese society.

Over the years since its inception, Chongryon influence over Koreans living in Japan has to some extent faded. When Chongryon was established in 1955, 75 percent of Koreans in Japan held Chongryon membership, but by 1995 that figure had dropped to 26 percent. Since the implementation of the Normalization Treaty in 1965, the Chongryon organization has experienced a decline in membership while Mindan has grown. Estimates show that around 500,000 people are registered with Mindan whereas only 30–40,000 people are registered with Chongryon (Kim 2019, 70). This steady decrease results from a number of factors. One is that knowledge of the hard lives experienced by those who went back to live in North Korea negatively affected Chongryon's public image, while news about North Korea's illegal activities, including the kidnapping of Japanese citizens, has further tarnished Chongryon's reputation.

EFL Education under Chongryon's Management

While there have been many studies on education at Chosŏnhakkyo in general, little attention has been paid to the learning content of language education in general, and EFL in particular. As the first researcher on EFL education at Chosŏnhakkyo, I would therefore like to share primary resources that were directly collated from the Chongryon community. My earlier studies (2019, 2020) show that EFL was included in school subjects in some secondary Chosŏnhakkyo (mainly institutions located in Tokyo) in 1946, the purpose being to educate younger generations to identify themselves as Korean in the hope that they would return home to the Korean Peninsula, which remained undivided at the time. As there were no official textbooks, it was left to teachers to identify and use simple teaching materials, supplemented later by textbooks that were supplied by the Soviet Union. This remained the case until the first EFL textbooks were published by the official Chongryon publishing company Hagusobang (学友書房;) in 1965.

The use of the Soviet Union's textbooks created gaps in areas of learning and reduced student achievement. For example, the structure of relative clauses in Russian is the same as in English, so there was no explanation provided in the books, whereas the Korean language has no relative clause form. This meant that students were not provided with adequate explanations for some foreign grammatical issues, which resulted in Chongryon deciding to publish their own EFL textbooks. Additionally, Chosŏn University in Tokyo[8] began to provide foreign language courses at its School of Education in 1966, which resulted in the foundation of the School of Foreign Languages in 1974.

Students were taught English to provide them with skills that would improve their standard of living if they were to repatriate to North Korea. It was believed that North Korea would valorize Chongryon Koreans more highly if they knew English. In 1959, when Chongryon Korean repatriation began, parents had begun to develop more interest in EFL education, assuming that speaking English would benefit their children's futures in North Korea (as foreign language ability would improve one's marketability in the workforce). Some parents asked Chosŏnhakkyo to teach their children English, on the assumption that English was an important language in North Korea. However, at that time, Chongryon Koreans' attitudes toward English was contradictory. During the 1960s, Chongryon students had the option to study either English or Russian—and, interestingly, the top-ranking students predominantly chose Russian. This choice was made in line with Chongryon Koreans' belief that English was the language of Korea's enemy, America.

During the early 1980s, Chongryon began to stress English education and the use of EFL as English grew in importance as an international language in an increasingly globalized world. This meant that Chongryon students' attitudes toward learning English changed markedly over the years, and Chongryon members later regarded the language as a useful skill that could provide them with future advantages. In 1983, Chongryon members decided that they should change the content of their textbooks in order to better suit their students' situations, such as providing the necessary English skills for students to attempt the entrance examinations for Japanese universities. The EFL textbooks were edited to match the grammatical syllabus provided by the Japanese government's education policy.

Throughout the textbook revision process—which has occurred nearly every ten years since 1965—the aims and the themes have shifted from glorifying North Korea and its leadership to aspects pertaining to students' real lives, such as school life, culture, foreign languages, the environment, global interaction and the life of Koreans in Japan. The most recent revision of EFL textbooks for junior high school students occurred in 2014, and these changes were designed to improve students' opportunities in a competitive Japanese job market. In order to increase the numbers of highly skilled workers, a greater need for English education was recognized, and EFL textbooks were partly revised to improve communication skills. Moreover, Chosŏnhakkyo have begun to teach English to Grade 5 and 6 primary students since 2017, using their own materials, which include speaking and listening-focused textbooks.

The revision process of the Chongryon EFL textbooks reflects Chongryon's changing interest in English—from using English as a tool to promote North Korean ideology to using English as a communicative device in a global economy. This change in attitude signifies Chongryon Koreans' diminishing belief that their future lies in North Korea and their increasing hope to improve their integration into Japanese society.

Textbooks and the Identities of Korean Minorities

Among critical theorists (such as Apple [1999], De Castell [1990], Luke [1995], Shardakova & Pavlenko [2004]), it is agreed that textbooks are not neutral in their choice of grammar and lexical forms. Instead, it is commonly accepted that textbooks present a sanctioned version of knowledge in any given area. As such, readers are encouraged to become a homogeneous interpretive community. Textbooks have been described by scholars such as De Castell, A. Luke, and C. Luke (1989), Bernstein (1996), Stray (1994), and Lee (2000) as "ideological message systems" designed to transmit and reproduce society's dominant values and beliefs. Moreover, Lee (2011, 47) has argued that language "conveys ideas, cultures and ideologies," and that textbooks contain the embedded interests of the dominant classes and their ruling ideologies and cultural values. Due to textbooks' crucial role in the classroom, the publication and distribution of textbooks are influenced by the ruling class.

When it comes to publishing textbooks containing perspectives on politics, culture, or the economy, the choice of what these textbooks contain and what is taught in schools is made by a dominant class that holds cultural, economic, and political power. Publishers have to meet the demands of consumers, guide authors to write what the target market wants, and meet government educational requirements (Cho 2019, 40).

According to Chapman's research into Zainichi Korean residents (2004, 42), identity is determined by numerous variables which encourage individuals to seek membership of a specific group or community. In a study by Lee (2017), Chongryon's 2015 Korean language textbooks used in primary schools display a strong attachment to North Korea. The texts indicated that Chongryon members identify themselves as North Koreans, and students were encouraged to remain loyal to the Chongryon organization and to volunteer to serve North Korea. As Chapman (2004, 42) has outlined, Zainichi identity location has shifted from a diasporic attachment to their homeland to regarding Japan as a permanent home, which hints at a level of complexity in the identity of the minority group. It is claimed that Chongryon Koreans have two identities—an "official" identity, which demonstrates their alignment with North Korea (due to North Korea's material support), and an affective identity that highlights the longing for North Korea as a historical homeland. Overall, the duality of this transnational imagining reflects the relationship between Chongryon Koreans and North Korea (Bell 2019, 37).

A comparison with the Korean ethnic minority group in the People's Republic of China (PRC, known as the Chosŏnjok) is relevant to this study, since this community expresses its ideology in a similar fashion to Chongryon Koreans. According to Cho (2007), geography textbooks use charts, maps, and illustrations of Beijing to represent Chosŏnjok national identity as Chinese. At the same time, Korean terminology is commonly used in expressions for "our school" and "our country" to construct a national identity that sets them apart from other ethnic minorities in China. Images and texts suggest conflicting views but when combined, create a unique dual identity for the minority group. Korean language textbooks produced during the early 1950s were also used to encourage primary school Chosŏnjok students to become patriotic communists. In particular, the textbooks had students focus on their identity as valuable citizens of the PRC (Lee 2014).

Kang's study of the Chosŏnjok (2008, 115–116) suggested that the national identity of the Korean minority in the PRC should be understood as a process of political identity-formation. The Korean minority's view of itself has changed from an ethnically centered to a nationality-centered dual identity. The significance of such a change demonstrates the impact of political interactions within ethnic population groups. In the case of Chongryon, the Korean minority group has adopted an identity influenced by both their political stance and their awareness of a heritage and political lineage that has been passed down from generation to generation.

Approaches

This study examines eleven EFL textbooks that were published between 1968 and 1974, and in 1994 and 2014, and which were designed for students between Grades 1 and 3 in junior high schools (students aged between thirteen and fifteen).[9] The significance of editions published in these periods is that they were used at a time of major change in the North Korean leadership, with overall control transferring from Kim Il Sung to his son Kim Jong Il and then to his grandson, Kim Jong Un. Since the 1990s, the leadership has attempted to open up North Korean society in different ways: Kim Jong Il played the nuclear card as a way to engage with the West (principally America) while Kim Jong Un has also tried to open up North Korean society by making friendlier gestures toward the US. Given this fluctuating geopolitical context, it is valuable to compare three textbooks from different time periods in which Chongryon Korean beliefs and ideals were also shifting. All the textbook materials were obtained from Hagusobang, except for the 1974 Grade 1 textbook and the 1968 Grade 3 textbook, which were acquired from the Korean National Library in South Korea and the Institute of Developing Economies of the Japanese External Trade Organization (IDE-JETRO) respectively.

I selected and investigated texts from lessons with specifically Korean content (such as language and culture) because I felt this would best demonstrate the development of Chongryon Korean identity. Due to the large quantity of material involved, I chose texts that reflected the focus of this study by considering the titles of the lessons, reading the textual content, and looking at the images. A lesson's title represents the establishment of power through language (Mooney 2015, 15–17), since it summarizes the writer's ideas. However, it is important to note that the title of a lesson does not necessarily match with the lesson content. Consequently, a textual analysis must be conducted in order to reveal the true embedded learning content. This study examines the content of each selected lesson in depth and categorizes each lesson into major themes based on its main reading passage.

Underlying their ethnic identity as Koreans in Japan, the group expresses a nostalgic longing for a North Korean homeland that lies beyond any sense of physical and temporal existence. The concept of North Korea for Chongryon Koreans is predominantly associated with an idealized concept rather than a physical reality (Bell 2019, 38). The concept of identity can also be applied to research areas such as language education. Lee (2011, 47) suggests that language education is a complex social practice that reaches beyond the instruction of phonology, morphology, and syntax. In particular, language carries ideas, cultures, and ideologies that are both embedded in and related to the language, meaning that language affects different areas of the social and cultural lives of people. Therefore, language education must be examined both at a linguistic level and at a broader social and political level.

This study will examine how textual representations in textbooks reflect political and ideological changes within the Chongryon community. To do this, the study will critically apply a lexico-grammatical analysis (focusing on vocabulary and grammar items) and an intertextual analysis on selected texts in Chongryon's EFL textbooks published between

1968–1974, and in 1994 and 2014. By analyzing selected texts critically according to their political, social, and cultural contexts, this chapter will demonstrate there to be a fluidity within Chongryon Koreans' perceptions of their own identity. The selected texts, which are italicized in this paper, contain some unintentional grammatical errors and misspellings, which are ignored in this investigation.

ANALYSES AND INTERPRETATIONS OF IDENTITY CHANGES WITHIN SELECTED TEXTS

I. Chongryon Koreans' First Identity Formation Expressed in Publications between 1968 and 1974: Being North Korean and Showing a Desire to Return to their Homeland, North Korea

After the end of the Korean War (1953), while US troops were operating in South Korea, Kim Il Sung amassed absolute power in the North and spread his Juche ideology into all aspects of life. Education systems in North Korea were used to promote Juche ideology, and this also spread to the Chongryon system of Chosŏnhakkyo.[10] It was during the 1960s and 1970s that Chongryon Koreans were most heavily influenced by North Korean ideology and most strongly tied to North Korea. As a result, in publications between 1968 and 1974, Chongryons are portrayed as being devoted to North Korea, rather than to the community of Koreans living in Japan. Hence, there are few lessons on Koreans' everyday lives in Japan.

43 of the 61 lessons focused on the four main themes, such as "Glorifying North Korea as a desirable homeland," "Our father, Kim Il Sung, as a true leader of the homeland," "Anti-Americanism and negative interpretations of South Korea," and "Conflict between being Chongryon Korean and residing in Japan." This illustrates how strongly Chongryon Koreans were tied to North Korea and how they were educated to identify themselves as North Koreans. This is further demonstrated by the following excerpts.

Lesson 1: The birthday of Marshal[11] Kim Il Sung (Grade 2)

1. Today is the fifteenth of April.
2. It is the birthday of Marshal Kim Il Sung.
3. We are his sons and daughters.
4. We are growing up under the warm care of Marshal Kim Il Sung.

5. *We are very happy.*

(Excerpt 1)

Excerpt 1 is taken from the first lesson of the Grade 2 textbook and discusses "the birthday of Marshal Kim Il Sung." The repetition of the pronoun "we" (Lines 3, 4 and 5), used at the beginning of these sentences, evokes a tone of solidarity (Fitzgibbon 2013). The phrase "We are his sons and daughters" (Line 3) presents Kim Il Sung as a father to the Chongryon students as well as the North Korean state. In Korean, the noun "father" [abŏji] can also be used to address one's uncle. For example, the term "k'ŭn-abŏji" (big father) refers to the older brother of one's father, whereas "chagun-abŏji" (small father) refers to the younger brother of one's father. The word "father" is used predominantly between blood relatives. As such, the writer makes it known to students that their relationship to Kim Il Sung is comparable to that with their own biological fathers. Consequently, students were encouraged to show loyalty to Kim Il Sung in the same way as a son would to his biological father. This familial relationship is encouraged by the speaker addressing the "sons and daughters" of Kim Il Sung celebrate the Marshal's birthday.

Lesson 24: What a beautiful place Mangyongdae is! (Grade 1)

1. ... *a picture of Mangyongdae.*
2. *Mangyongdae is the birthplace of Marshal Kim Il Sung, the respected and beloved Leader.*
3. *Mangyongdae is a very beautiful place.*
4. *What a beautiful place Mangyongdae is!*
5. *Beautiful flowers ...*
6. *... sky is blue.*
7. *... cloud is white.*
8. *... river Taedong-gang flows gently.*
9. *... How clear the sky is!*
10. *How wide the River Taedong-gang is!*
11. *... Korean people love Mangyongdae.*
12. *Many people of the world visit Mangyongdae.*

(Excerpt 2)

North Koreans are taught that Kim Il Sung's birthplace and childhood home is Mangyongdae. In Excerpt 2, Line 2 describes Marshal Kim Il Sung as "the respected and beloved Leader." Use of the past participle forms as adjectives create an implied passive sentence that depicts Kim Il Sung as the receiver of a given action. Potential actors (those who respect Kim Il Sung) are omitted, so the definition of the actor is unclear. The adjective "beautiful" (Lines 3, 4, and 5) is repeated three times to describe Mangyongdae. The adverb "very" (Line 3) and the exclamatory sentence (Line 4) emphasize Mangyongdae's beauty. Exclamatory sentences (ending with an exclamation mark "!") offer statements as declarative sentences that are not open to contradiction. However, they also convey a more energetic tone that denotes excitement or intense emotion in the same way as exclamatory sentences are used in advertisements.

The text describes Mangyongdae, where the "sky is blue" (Line 6), "cloud is white" [sic] (Line 7), and "the river Taedong-gang flows gently" (Line 8). The text helps students to imagine the beauty of Mangyongdae, since the photograph can display only a limited color spectrum. The combination of texts and images encouraged students to see Mangyongdae as an idyllic location. Through its use of exclamatory sentences, the text acts like an advertisement, promoting the value of Mangyongdae and encouraging viewers to study hard to gain an opportunity to go there.

Lines 11 and 12 express Mangyongdae's popularity among Koreans and the rest of the world. However, the writer has presented only subjective and one-sided statements that are not evidence-based. Instead, the statements in Lines 11 and 12 express the writer's beliefs. The statement addresses "the Korean people" and does not specify which Korean group—North Koreans, South Koreans, or both. Furthermore, the phrase "many people of the world" is a very general statement that gives no information about who visits Mangyongdae—the determiner "many" generalizes the statement by outlining a large number without being specific.

II. Chongryon Koreans' Second Identity Formation as Expressed in 1994 Publications: Being North Koreans Prepared to Reside Permanently in Japan

In the three textbooks investigated, the majority of lessons were dedicated to exploring four themes; "Ethnic Koreans and Chosŏnhakkyo schools," "School activities, and the proactive maintenance of an ethnic community," "The exploration of foreign countries and cultures," and

"Nature and well-being, advocating a harmonious lifestyle." These themes present Chongryon Korean lives in Japan and express an interest in foreign cultures, which is very different to the emphasis of the 1968–1974 textbooks. This reflects an acceptance by Chongryon Koreans of their status as permanent residents in Japan rather than evoking their desire to return to North Korea. Notably, thirteen out of the 36 lessons presented focus on ethnic Korean communities and Chosŏnhakkyo, reflecting the desire of the textbook producer to educate younger generations of Chongryon to retain their Korean identity. This shift reflects a loss of control and leadership by the North Korean state, as Chongryon Koreans, influenced by their educational experiences in Japan, began to move away from seeing North Korea as their homeland and showing unquestioning loyalty to Pyongyang.

Lesson 9: You speak Korean (Grade 1)
1. *I have a nice picture ...*
2. *It's a picture of Pyongyang ...*
3. *Pyongyang is a beautiful city.*
4. *I like it very much.*

(Excerpt 3)

Excerpt 3 exposes readers to North Korean ideas. Specifically, the speaker discusses his "nice picture ... of Pyongyang." Here, the character likes his picture of the North Korean city "very much." Adjectives are used to evoke a favorable image of North Korea by describing the picture as "nice" and Pyongyang as "beautiful." The speaker presents the idea that "Pyongyang is a beautiful city." The speaker does not seek to force readers to agree through exclamatory sentences, nor does he provide any rational justification for why Pyongyang is "beautiful" (Line 3). Unlike the previous examples from earlier years, the speaker expresses his statement as an opinion rather than a fact, and readers are encouraged to develop their own conclusions about Pyongyang. As such, the speaker demonstrates confidence in his belief, which in turn provides assurance to readers that the speaker's opinion is valid.

5. *Yong Ho: I have some stamps from Korea. These are for you, Ted*
6. *Ted: Kamsahamnida*
7. *Yong Ho: Oh, do you speak Korean?*

8. *Ted: I don't. Only a little*
9. *Yong Ho: Do you know "hello" in Korean?*
10. *Ted: Yes, ... Annyonghaseyo, right?*
11. *Yong Ho: That's right*
(Excerpt 4)

Later in the Lesson 9 passage, a dialog is introduced. Ted, a foreigner, can speak "a little" Korean. The dialog begins with Yong Ho giving stamps "from Korea" to Ted. Given that North Korea's capital, Pyongyang, was mentioned earlier in Excerpt 4, readers can assume that the stamps are from North Korea. The exclamation "Oh" (Line 7) expressed Yong Ho's surprise that Ted spoke enough Korean to say "Kamsahamnida" (thank you). In Lines 6 to 10, Ted speaks some Korean, and this depiction of foreigners learning Korean is aimed to encourage Chongryon students to continue their Korean education and to be proud of their linguistic heritage.

Pyongyang was introduced in Excerpt 3, setting up the context for the dialog in Excerpt 4, positioning the mention of "stamps." Consequently, the writer is encouraging readers to maintain a positive perspective of North Korea, while also introducing readers to different topics of conversation, such as foreigners speaking Korean. Yong Ho holds dominant power as Ted seeks his approval with the interrogative phrase "right?" which is followed by Yong Ho's response, "that's right." According to Heritage (2009), turn-taking procedures presuppose the recognition of more than one participant. The marker "right?" creates an opening for the opposite participant to reply with the intention of either agreeing with the previous statement or clarifying it further. Consequently, the Chongryon student appears knowledgeable in Korean and supportive of North Korean ideology. Therefore, Yong Ho is depicted as the ideal Chongryon student.

Lesson 3: Learning the Korean language (Grade 3)

1. *My Japanese friend Yumiko has studied Korean for a month*
2. *She thinks that learning Korean is not so difficult as learning English*
3. *"Korean is similar to Japanese in some ways*
4. *You can learn it without much difficulty," ...*
5. *Yumiko: ... The word orders in Korean and Japanese are almost the same*

(Excerpt 5)

In Excerpt 5, Mi Sun introduces her Japanese friend, Yumiko, who "has studied Korean for a month" to a Singaporean student named Cindy. The excerpt discusses the Korean language's impact in foreign countries by introducing Korean, Japanese, and Singaporean characters. Line 1 presents the relationship between Yumiko and the speaker, who addresses Yumiko as "my Japanese friend." Referring to Yumiko as Japanese implies that the speaker is not Japanese. The discussion is about "learning Korean," thereby eliciting readers' beliefs that the speaker is Korean. The writer describes the relationship between the Japanese and Korean languages as "being similar" (Line 3), and the result is that Yumiko "thinks that learning Korean is not so difficult as learning English" (Line 2). The phrase "not so…as" creates a comparison between Korean and English, thereby highlighting the close relationship between Japanese and Korean. Consequently, the excerpt argues that Korean can be learned "without much difficulty." Yumiko provides some explanation, stating that it is easy because of the languages' similar "word orders" (Line 5).

Consequently, readers are motivated to learn Korean by the understanding that acquiring the skill is easily attainable. The directive speech in Lines 3 and 4 causes the information provided by Yumiko to hold greater authority, resulting in readers better assimilating the message. The text's modality is increased as a result.

> 6. *Yumiko:* I'm also interested in Korean culture. I've just read a book about it
> 7. *Cindy:* Is Korean culture quite different from Japanese culture?
> 8. *Yumiko:* … two cultures are similar in some ways, but… big differences, too…
> 9. *Yumiko:* Both Japanese and Koreans use chopsticks when they eat rice
>   But Koreans use spoons as well
> 10. *Mi Sun:* … Japanese often bring the bowl up to their mouths
>   But that's bad manners in Korea…

(Excerpt 6)

The dialog in Excerpt 5 continues on to Excerpt 6. Yumiko expresses interest in learning Korean language and culture, particularly table manners. While Yumiko discusses the similarities and differences between Korean and Japanese culture, Cindy prompts her further. Yumiko's knowledge comes from "read[ing] a book about [Korean culture]" (Line 6). Yumiko explains that Japanese and Korean culture are "similar in some ways, but there are big differences" (Line 8). The examples of Japan and

Korea's similarities and differences include "both use[ing] chopsticks," but only Koreans "use[ing] spoons as well" (Line 9). Korean culture is compared to Japanese culture throughout Excerpt 6, and readers learn about the unique characteristics of both countries. In general, neither culture is presented as superior, although the producer does contradict this to some extent. While the lesson advocates the acceptance of cultural differences, there was still some contradiction. Cindy and Yumiko appear interested in Korean culture, but Mi Sun warns her that some of Japan's eating customs are considered "bad manners" in Korea (Line 10), implying that Korean culture is more polite than Japanese culture. Consequently, the producer is subtly encouraging readers to regard Korean culture as superior.

III. Chongryon Koreans' Third Identity Formation as Expressed in 2014 Publications: Being Ethnic Koreans (ambiguous between North and South) Living in Japan

The latest edition of the 2014 publication contains four major themes; "Chongryon Korean ethnic schools," "Chosŏnhakkyo, School activities, proactive improvement of an ethnic community's image," "Local and global cultures, development of cultural knowledge," and "Travel overseas, improvement in standard of living." Such major themes omit significant references to North Korea or Kim Il Sung, in marked contrast to the earlier publications. North Korean ideology is no longer explicitly expressed in the textbooks, despite Chongryon's enduring allegiance. In part, this connection is maintained because many Chongryon members repatriated to North Korea, with financial support provided by the family members of the repatriates.

Kim Jong Un, the new North Korean leader, has advocated improvements in educational content and teaching methods so that North Korean schools can provide an education that is relevant to the "Knowledge and Economy" era. As such, Chosŏnhakkyo began to view EFL education as essential for preparing students for modern society (Jang 2017).[12] The 2014 EFL textbooks therefore present areas of learning that are more practical for students in comparison to previous textbooks. More content is still devoted to Korean culture than to foreign cultures. This may be because while younger Chongryon Korean generations appear less interested in their Korean identity, older generations still have a strong desire to educate their children about Korean culture.

However, their viewpoint on Korean culture mirrors a change in their growing desire to identify themselves as neither North nor South Korean, but simply as ethnic Koreans residing in Japan.

Lesson 4: Korean Schools in Japan (Grade 2)

1. Su Chol: ... I'll go to Korean University when I graduate from high school.
2. Salma: good. you speak Korean at school, don't you?
3. Su Chol: ... Korean is our national language.
4. Salma: ... when did Koreans come to Japan?
5. Yong Sil: our great-grandparents came over to Japan before 1945. Then Korea was under Japanese Rule.
6. Su Chol: ... After 1945 they built schools for their children ...
7. John: Those schools are an important part of your history.

(Excerpt 7)

In Excerpt 7, the writer depicts Chongryon students who uphold their Korean identity in a positive manner. Su Chol states that he will "go to Korean University when [he] graduate[s] from high school" (Line 1). Su Chol represents the ideal Chongryon student, who wishes to maintain his connection to the Chongryon organization while being culturally open-minded. Ng Tseung-Wong and Verkuyten (2015) claim that it is difficult to encourage people to take pride in their own culture while being open-minded about other cultures. However, the text encourages Chongryon students to maintain their Korean ethnic identity. The repetition of "Korea" and "Korean" emphasizes the main topic of the conversation, which is "Korean Schools in Japan." As such, despite conversations about language and cultural diversity, the main focus of the discussion is Korean identity. "Korean is our national language" shows Su Chol as a representative member of the Chongryon community, although the pronoun "our" and the adjective "national" creates ambiguity regarding which Korea the speaker is referring to (Line 3).

While the use of foreign characters provides diversity in representation, each character serves a purpose. Salma, who is African, inquires about Korean schools, allowing Su Chol and Yong Sil, who are both Chongryon Koreans, to teach readers about Chongryon's history. John, an Australian, conveys the writer's message about the importance of Chongryon schools and university from an objective viewpoint.

Lesson 6: The Harvest Festivals (Grade 3)
1. *Chusok is an important festival Koreans celebrate...*
2. *Chusok is the harvest moon festival ...*
3. *... traditional games Koreans play on Chusok.*
4. *Sireum, Hwal-sogi, Nol-twigi and Kanggangsuwollae ...*
5. *Chusok is the time to give thanks to the ancestors...*
6. *... they hold chesa early in the morning, and they visit their family graves.*
7. *They offer their ancestors new rice and other special food.*
8. *Songpyun is a traditional rice cake prepared for Chusok.*

(Excerpt 8)

In Excerpt 8, the cultural tradition of the Harvest Festival is explored. The biggest festival celebrated in Korea is known as Chusok (Ch'usŏk), which is commonly referred to as a "harvest moon festival" that is celebrated "in the fall." Chusok can also be translated as "Korean Thanksgiving." Within the excerpt, the writer includes Romanized Korean words, such as Chusok, Sireum (ssirŭm),[13] and Songpyun (songp'yŏn).[14] The Korean nouns are provided as there is no direct English translation. The use of these Korean words also demonstrates the writer's interest in introducing aspects of Korean culture to expose readers to their Korean heritage. A general introduction of Chusok is given to readers (Lines 1 and 2), which is followed by a description of traditional activities and foods that Korean people enjoy during Chusok (Lines 3 to 8). In particular, Chesa[15] is described to provide meaning to readers about an aspect of Korean culture that is less well-known in other cultures (Lines 5 to 7). Today, Koreans in Japan continue to perform Chesa, with variations among different families on what they perform, when and how many times (Cho 2019).

Throughout Excerpt 8, the writer uses the present simple tense, such as "Chusok is the harvest moon festival." The present simple tense portrays the information presented by the writer as categorical truths. Therefore, Chongryon readers learn to accept the facts provided about Korean culture as the truth. By introducing traditional Korean activities in an English environment, Chongryon students learn to converse in English by relying on their Korean culture, thereby helping students to view themselves as unique and able to share Chongryon Korean culture with non-Koreans.

Consequently, the writer is educating Chongryon students to appreciate their Korean culture and to find a practical use for it when communicating with foreigners, thereby encouraging students to adopt a global perspective. However, the pronoun "they," when addressing Koreans who celebrate Chusok, reveals a separation between Koreans and Chongryon Koreans. The pronoun "they" being exclusive, is used to refer to participants outside the speaker's circle, while the inclusive and collective pronoun "we" is used to refer to the speaker and his peers (Fitzgibbon 2013). Considering that the readers of the textbook are Chongryon students, this separation stresses the belief that Chongryon Koreans do not necessarily regard themselves as Koreans. While Chongryon Koreans share their roots with Korea, the belief that Chongryon Koreans have developed their own unique identity, independent from Korea, is presented in the 2014 textbook.

Conclusion

Textual analysis reveals significant changes in the Chongryon Koreans' views of their sense of belonging over time. However, beyond the EFL texts, Chongryon's identity changes must be further understood in the context of different political climates, social environments, and generational shifts within the organization.

Textual examination first shows that between 1968 and 1974, Chongryon students learned to view North Korea as their homeland and to accept its leader, Kim Il Sung as a father figure, which encouraged them to identify as North Koreans. Excerpt 1 refers to Chongryon students as the sons and daughters of Kim Il Sung, and the excerpt focuses on glorifying North Korea and Kim Il Sung, leading readers to disregard South Korea, which ironically was the country of origin for most Chongryon Koreans.

Secondly, the analysis of 1994 texts reveals Chongryon's acceptance of their existence in Japan, and their interest in educating younger generations to maintain their North Korean ethnic identity. For example, in Excerpt 3, the favorable description of their North Korean homeland demonstrates Chongryon's interest in preserving their North Korean identity. Most notably, the curriculum highlighted the value of Korean language and culture, as seen in Excerpts 4, 5, and 6. It appears that

Chosŏnhakkyo played a crucial role in preserving Korean identity, partly by controlling teaching materials in order to educate younger generations of Koreans in accordance with specific Chongryon values and ideologies. This change in focus implies a greater concern for the actual conditions of Chongryon Koreans in Japan over the idealization of North Korea and Kim Il Sung.

Thirdly, the 2014 texts—unlike the earlier publications—express no obvious political ideology. Any discussion about Korea remains ambiguous, for example in Excerpt 7, where the speaker does not specify whether he is referring to North or South Korea. Instead, the writer in Excerpt 8 describes Korea as if it were a foreign country. The Chongryon organization has been obliged to respond to their changing environment by adjusting their educational strategies in order to maintain their significance and value as a minority group whose influence might otherwise risk dying out.

In conclusion, this study outlines significant changes in Chongryon Koreans' identity by comparing textbook representations of North Korea that signify Chongryon's own changing attitudes and interests. Despite their South Korean origins, Chongryon Koreans identified themselves initially as North Koreans, then as North Koreans living in Japan, and most recently, as Koreans who are part of Japanese society.

For further research, a comparison between Korean language textbooks and EFL textbooks could be made, to verify these conclusions about Chongryon Koreans' changes in outlook.

Acknowledgements I would like to express my special thanks to the staff at Hagusobang; Mr. Ryang Nam In, Ms. Kim Kyong Suk, and Ms. Moon Mi Ja; Ms. Jang Malryo at Chosŏnhakkyo in Yokohama; Mr. Kang Sŏng Bok at Chosŏn University in Tokyo for their invaluable support. Their help in providing primary resource material in the form of Chongryon EFL textbooks has made this research project possible. As publishers of Chongryon's EFL textbooks and as Chongryon Koreans themselves, they have helped contribute to my research through their sharing of life stories, experiences, values, and ideas.

Notes

1. Introduced at the Conference on Zainichi and Korean Diaspora, titled "Zainichi Koreans in the 21st Century: Assimilation, Re-ethnicisation, Education and Next Generation" hosted by the University of Auckland on December 1–2, 2018.
2. This term applies to Koreans who were forcibly brought to Japan during the colonial period, and their descendants who were only meant to remain in Japan temporarily. The label is used by the Japanese state and society (Suzuki 2012, 52).
3. Also known as "Chosen-seki," this is an alternative nationality assigned to ethnic Koreans living in Japan who have neither Japanese nor South Korean citizenship (Komai 1995).
4. This term is also applied to individuals of Korean ancestry who support North Korean ideologies. It is sometimes spelled "Chongryun" or "Ch'ongnyŏn" and "Soren" in Japanese. This study follows the spelling used by the Chongryon organization. The English translation is "The General Association of Korean Residents."
5. This organization is a Korean Residents Union in Japan that was established in 1946 and has ties to South Korea.
6. Also known as "Minjokhakkyo" meaning "Korean ethnic schools in Japan."
7. The equivalent value would have been no more than a few cartons of cigarettes in Korea during that time (Motani 2002, 228).
8. Founded in Tokyo, Japan in 1956 by Chongryon, it is called the "Korea University in Tokyo" in English, to distinguish it from the Korea University in Seoul.
9. These school years are equivalent to Year 7, 8 and 9 in some countries such as Australia and England.
10. Juche is the dominant nationalistic ideology of the DPRK; for more on this system of thought, see Winstanley-Chesters' discussion in this volume.
11. The English word "Marshal" is "Wonsu" in Korean, meaning a leader of a country.
12. Malryo Jang is an English teacher at a secondary Chosŏnhakkyo located in Yokohama, and was granted a Master of Philosophy in Linguistics at Kim Il Sung University, North Korea, in 2017.

Due to restricted public access, the thesis was sent via email on 8 December 2017 in order to maintain privacy.
13. This term is also spelled "Ssireum." It is a traditional Korean form of wrestling, practiced since the fourth century.
14. This term is also spelled "Songp'yŏn." It is a traditional Korean rice cake made of rice powder for the Korean thanksgiving festival.
15. This term is also spelled "Jesa." Performing Chesa is a form of memorial to the ancestors of the participants.

REFERENCES

Apple, Michael. 1999. *Power, Meaning, and Identity: Essays in Critical Educational Studies*. New York: P. Lang.
Bell, Markus. 2018. "Patriotic Revolutionaries and Imperial Sympathizers: Identity and Selfhood of Korean-Japanese Migrants from Japan to North Korea." *Cross-Currents: East Asian History and Culture Review* 7(2): 237–265. https://doi.org/10.1353/ach.2018.0008.
Bell, Markus. 2019. "Reimagining the Homeland: Zainichi Koreans' Transnational Longing for North Korea." *The Asia Pacific Journal of Anthropology* 20 (1): 22–41. https://doi.org/10.1080/14442213.2018.1548642.
Bernstein, Basil. 1996. "Pedagogy, Symbolic Control and Identity: Theory, Research, Critique." London: Taylor & Francis.
Chapman, David. 2004. "The Third Way and Beyond: Zainichi Korean Identity and the Politics of Belonging." *Japanese Studies* 24 (1): 29–44. https://doi.org/10.1080/1037139041000168469 7.
Chapman, David. 2006. "Discourses of Multicultural Coexistence (tabunka kyōsei) and the 'Old-comer' Korean Residents of Japan." *Asian Ethnicity* 7 (1): 89–102. https://doi.org/10.1080/14631360500498593.
Cho, Min Hye, and Dong Bae Lee. 2019. "Critical Analysis of Chongryon XE 'Chongryon' Secondary English Textbooks Published between 1968 and 1974." *The Review of Korean Studies* 22 (2): 177–204. https://doi.org/10.25024/review.2019.22.2.008.
Cho, Min Hye. 2019. *"A Comparative Study of the Construction of Culture and Ideology Seen in Secondary English Textbooks Published by Chongryon during the 1970s, 1990s and the Present Day."* PhD diss.: The University of Queensland.
Cho, Min Hye. 2020. "Joseonhakgyo, Learning under North Korean leadership: Transitioning from 1970 to Present." *International Journal of Korean Unification Studies* 29 (1): 161–188. https://doi.org/10.33728/ijkus.2020.29.1.007.

Cho, Young Mi. 2007. *"The National Identity in Geography Textbooks of Korean-Chinese."* MA diss.: Seoul National University.
De Castell, Suzanne. 1990. "Teaching the Textbook: Teacher/Text Authority and the Problem of Interpretation." *Lingusitics and Education*, 2: 75–90.
De Castell, Suzanne., Luke, Allan. and Luke, Carmen. 1989. *Language, Authority and Criticism: Readings on the School Textbook*. East Sussex: The Falmer Press.
Fitzgibbon, Linda. 2013. *"Ideologies and Power Relations in a Global Commercial English Language Textbook used in South Korean Universities: A Critical Image Analysis and a Critical Discourse Analysis."* PhD diss.: The University of Queensland.
Ha, Kyung Hee. 2015. *"Between Ethnic Minority and Diaspora: Zainichi Koreans in the Era of Global War on Terror."* Ph.D diss.: University of California, San Diego.
Halliday, Michael Alexander Kirkwood. 2007. "Some Thoughts on Language in the Middle School Years" *Language and Education* 9: 49–62.https://doi.org/10.5040/9781474211895.
Heritage, John. 2009. "Conversation Analysis as Social Theory." In *The New Blackwell Companion to Social Theory*, edited by Turner Bryan, 300–320, West Sussex: Blackwell Publishing Ltd.
Jin, Huigwan. 1999. *The Study on Relations of Chongryon and North Korea, The Institute for Peace Affairs*. Seoul: Kyobo Book Center.
Kang, Jin Woong. 2008. "The Dual National Identity of the Korean Minority in China: The Politics of Nation and Race and the Imagination of Ethnicity." *Studies in Ethnicity and Nationalism* 8 (1): 101–119. https://doi.org/10.1111/j.1754-9469.2008.00005.
Kim, Han Jo. 2019. *Zainichi Koreans whom we Disregarded*. Seoul: Foxbook Press.
Komai, Hiroshi. 1995. *Migrant workers in Japan*. London: Routledge.
Lee, Dong Bae. 2000. *"The Ideological Construction of Culture in Korean Language Textbooks: A Historical Discourse Analysis."* Ph.D diss.: The University of Queensland.
Lee, Dong Bae. 2014. "The Critical Analysis of Korean Language Textbooks for Primary Dchools in China- Chosunjok (ethnic Korean) under Mao's Rule in the early 1950s." *Journal of Cheongram Korean Language Education* 49: 165–194.
Lee, Dong Bae. 2017. "Chongryon Identity as Represented in Chongryeon Korean Language Textbooks." *Institute for Humanities and Social Sciences* 18 (2): 247–266. https://doi.org/10.15818/ihss.2017.18.2.247.
Lee, Incho. 2011. "Teaching how to Discriminate: Globalization, Prejudice, and Textbooks." *Teacher Education Quarterly* 38 (1): 47–63.

Luke, Allan. 1995. "Text and Discourse in Education: An Introduction to Critical Discourse Analysis." *Review of Research in Education* 21: 3–28.
Mooney, Annabelle. 2015. "What is Language?" In *Language, Society and Power: An Introduction*, edited by Mooney Annabelle and Betsy Evans, 1–19, Oxon: Routledge.
Motani, Yoko. 2002. "Towards a More Just Educational Policy for Minorities in Japan: The Case of Korean Ethnic Schools." *Comparative Education* 38 (2): 225–237. https://doi.org/10.1080/03050060220140593.
Ng Tseung-Wong, Cariline and Verkuyten, Maykel. 2015. "Multiculturalism, Mauritian style: Cultural Diversity, Belonging, and a Secular State." *American Behavioral Scientist* 59(6): 679–701.https://doi.org/10.1177/000276421456649
Norris, Sigrid. 2011. *Identity in (Inter) Action: Introducing Multimodal (Inter) Action Analysis*. Berlin: De Gruyter Mouton. https://doi.org/10.1515/9781934078280.
Ryang, Sonia. 1997. *North Koreans in Japan: Language, Ideology, and Identity*. Colorado and Oxford: Westview Press.
Ryang, Sonia. 2000. "The North Korean Homeland of Koreans in Japan." In *Koreans in Japan: Critical voices from the Margin*, ed. Sonia Ryang, 32–54. London: Routledge.
Shardakova, Marya, and Aneta Pavlenko. 2004. "Identity Options in Russian Textbooks." *Journal of Language, Identity and Education* 3 (1): 25–46.
Song, Jae Mok. 2011. "Curricular Changes of Chongryon Korean Schools in Japan: Focused on Korean Textbooks." *Journal of Korean Language Education* 22 (1): 145–178.
Stray, Chris. 1994. "Paradigms Regained: Towards a Historical Sociology of the Textbook." *Journal of Curriculum Studies* 26 (1): 1–29. https://doi.org/10.1080/0022027940260101.
Suzuki, Kazuko. 2012. "The State, Race, and Immigrant Adaptation: A Comparative Analysis of the Korean Diaspora in Japan and the United States." *Regions and Cohesion* 2 (1): 49–74. https://doi.org/10.3167/reco.2012.020103.

CHAPTER 13

North Korea All at Sea: Aspiration, Subterfuge, and Engagement in a Global Commons, 2020, Dark Fleets and Empty Streets

Robert Winstanley-Chesters

2020 has been a year when many of the drivers of globalization appeared to go into reverse or halt uncomfortably, as that most global of forces, a worldwide pandemic of Covid19 ravaged international travel and connections through which intercontinental trade and travel have become so normalized in recent decades. As the airport lounges emptied and the stratospheric sinews that stretch across the planet became ever thinner and more tenuous, it was if we had returned, apart from the ever-present and very global virus, to the world of our grandparents and great-grandparents where nations such as Australia and South Korea,

R. Winstanley-Chesters (✉)
University of Leeds, Leeds, England
e-mail: R.Winstanley-Chesters@leeds.ac.uk

University of Edinburgh, Edinburgh, Scotland

© The Author(s), under exclusive license to Springer Nature Switzerland AG 2022
A. D. Jackson (ed.), *The Two Koreas and their Global Engagements*,
https://doi.org/10.1007/978-3-030-90761-7_13

337

from Europe at least were very, very distant, very much over there or down there, half known about and seldom visited. Just as these more familiar and practically useful products of globalization receded, so alongside the virus, and perhaps because of the disconnection brought by this extraordinary year, other seemingly uncontrolled globalizing energies began to disturb and dismay popular and political media. A particularly widely spread academic article published in July 2020 raised the issue of Chinese "dark fleets" of fishing boats (Park et al. 2020), which had come to dominate many of the fishing grounds once important to North Korea (North Korean boats perhaps displaced or reduced due to Covid19 related epidemic restrictions which saw most of its fleet restricted to port). Later in the year, the "dark fleets" were reported just outside the Exclusive Economic Zone of the Galapagos Islands (sovereign to Ecuador), and further reports suggested that they had created ecological pressure on waters off West Africa (displacing, of course, the very public fleets from European Union nations which had previously exploited these same waters). Such masses of fishing boats are of course, dark in many ways in global discourse. Dark in the literal sense, that they are generally invisible to the normal monitoring technologies, which are so important to contemporary global fishing (they switch their AIS [Automatic Identification System] transponders off or do not have them fitted in the first place). But Dark also in the conceptual sense that they are in some way regarded as nefarious and evil in intent, another long arm of the autocratic People's Republic of China (PRC) with which it shamelessly and brutally seeks to strip resources without limit from the global commons.

The Chinese global fishing fleets of 2020 perhaps are highly obvious given their size, and perhaps provocative given their avoidance of the regularized monitoring systems so prevalent across the globe, but they are not really unique in their ecological impact. Industrial fishing since the 1950s has seen something of a developmental and technological arms race across the planet that has stripped the oceans of life and abundance, fishing down trophic levels and exploiting species such as krill that would never previously been considered worth catching, and radically altering the topography of the deep sea, transforming sea floors across the planet into flat, featureless deserts, marked by the drag lines of trawler gear. The PRC is late to this enterprise, as fleets from the European Union, from the United States, from Japan, and from the former Soviet Union and Warsaw Pact nations prior to 1992, have ranged across the globe over previous decades. They are perhaps brazen in their efforts, which resemble a form of poaching on the high seas, but interestingly have displaced the previous fleets of concern regionally, namely those North Korean "ghost ships" which began to appear after 2012 (Winstanley-Chesters 2020). These forlorn, old fashioned, and decrepit boats which washed up hundreds of times on the coasts of northern Japan and the Russian Federation, sometimes with cargoes of deceased North Koreans were themselves the offspring of poaching fleets in the West Sea/Sea of Japan exploiting the rare rainbow squid populations on and around the Yamato Bank and competing uncomfortably with far more technologically advanced Japanese squid boats. These North Korean fleets were once almost as visible in the media as the Chinese from 2020, and aside from the impact of the occasional dead crew members on the Japanese and Russian coast, were almost as impactful when it comes to poaching and illicit extraction from the commons. There was huge concern about North Korea's monetization of potential maritime resources and what that might have meant for the support given to its military capacity and capability, as well as the breaking of the sanctions regime designed to restrict and constrain Pyongyang. There was also some concern that North Korean institutional pressure on non-fishing coastal communities given the other pressures on its economy and government, was pushing people who weren't actually fishermen to sea, endangering them and leading to those unfortunate situations which resulted in some boats becoming "ghost ships." The Russian Federation in particular was most upset by North Korean fleets impacting on the delicate conservational balance of the shores of Primorsky when it comes to Pacific Salmon returning to spawn in its far eastern rivers.

This chapter takes a longer view of Russian/North Korea maritime interactions, seeing recent unexpected engagements between unwanted fleets under Pyongyang's nominal control and the Russian Coastguard as but one instance in a complicated international history of connection at sea between these two countries. However, the chapter also takes a longer view of internationalization and globalization when it comes to fishing or watery matters. Whereas globalization is generally considered a product of the WTO and GATT agendas, post-Cold War deregulation, financialization, and neo-liberal ideologies, when it comes to the extraction of value from under the waves and the exchange of products from the sea, global interactions have long been the reality for many participants. Extending a nation's fishing capabilities and capacities across the globe was essentially an invention of the first couple of decades of the twentieth century, but which was injected with a new sense of urgency and radicalization after the end of the Second World War. In the Pacific, the late 1940s and 1950s were an era of technological development and international competition in what was considered a global commons by the United States, Japan, and other postwar allies, and the Soviet Union and other Warsaw Pact nations. After 1960 nations sought to claim sovereignty once again over waters closer to them, a trend which eventually led to the development of 200 mile EEZ's (Exclusive Economic Zone's), but this did not reverse the pressure and urgency on countries participant in global fishing efforts. This chapter therefore recounts just a little of that quite different narrative of globalization and internationalization before alighting on its temporal, geographic, and subject focus.

NORTH KOREA ALL AT SEA: ASPIRATION, SUBTERFUGE, AND ENGAGEMENT IN A GLOBAL COMMONS

North Korea is one of the most political spaces on the globe. Its historical narratives are equally driven by political ideology and have been reconstructed anew throughout the last seven decades. North Korea's politics often generates intense geopolitical response and feedback, and political ecosystems and industries are generated around its containment, restriction, and hypothecated eventual destruction. Since the collapse of the world communist bloc and the fracture of the Cold War status quo North Korea as a nation and its citizens have been forced to adopt many new strategies to underpin their own survival, including attempting greater levels of mobility through migration, developing practical elements of enterprise and exchange, many of which make environmental connection or impact on local or regional ecosystems. New patterns of social and economic organization at both formal and informal levels and at intersections with nature and environment have emerged with accompanying frameworks of practice and interaction.

North Korean histories are therefore interactions with these frameworks and complex relations between a politics of possession and dispossession. In contemporary political and media culture, Pyongyang's rule is marked by a repertoire of dispossession; the dispossession of material goods, of intellectual mores, of freedom and liberty themselves. Absence or lack is certainly a key feature of North Korean history, through war, colonial occupation, and the frozen conflicts of the Cold War and the Post-Cold War (North Korea is one of those few places where the Cold War continued past 1992 in such an acute and concrete fashion), its citizens lack peace and security. However, they also lack material possessions, stores of value, and stores of calories. In a manner familiar to South Koreans for much of the twentieth century, North Koreans have been dispossessed by politics, history, and nature. Even in the acts of development and production North Korea and North Koreans experience dispossession. This is of course historically common to much of the globe dominated by capital and capitalism, surplus value extraction, the co-option and appropriation of property, nature, and abstract goods. However, in North Korea this appropriation has been more dramatic in form and has historically been much more significant. Ostensibly the work of my research addresses the historical geographies of fishing, a developmental sector directly focused on the appropriation of commons. While engaging with a waterscape once thought infinite, fishing and fishermen have been busy in the twentieth and twenty-first century manufacturing the collapse of a global ecosystem through appropriation and dispossession. This collapse impacts on North Korea absolutely, but the nation has not itself been excluded from this history, often seeking desperately to be a dispossessor and appropriator itself. This chapter will encounter this in the institutional relationships between the Soviet Union and North Korea. North Korea certainly sought to dispossess resources belonging to the Soviet Union as much as in return the Soviet Union attempted to co-opt North Korean institutional and research organizations into its wider framework of socialist solidarities and fraternity, as well as to prevent North Korea from taking more than or too much of the fishing commons in its sphere of influence and waters in the Pacific. In spite of these connectivities born of the world socialist or communist system, both sides were determined to maintain their own security.

This chapter recounts some of the practices of subterfuge North Korea utilized in order to negate the security practices of the Soviet Union and to gain advantage in fishing and other matters. Fishing practices are not rooted in North Korea or the Soviet Union's contemporary ideological frameworks, but in the presuppositions, presumptions, and predilections of modernism and colonialism. Fishing technologies and science which now scours the seas for the last vestiges of maritime life were born in the Japanese Empire and the Cold War military-industrial complex of the United States, in the research centers designed to bring forth total power on behalf of the modern capitalist (Finley 2011). As committed to socialism or communism as the Soviet Union was, its fishing technologies and strategies were similarly sourced from these extractive imperatives and predicated on the fishing science of Maximum Sustainable Yield and other statistical sleights of hand. Whether Japanese, American, or Soviet, all fishing institutions of this period were focused on an inexhaustible maritime commons and never-ending growth in catches. North Korea in this sense is a bit player in a highly destructive historical, economic, technological enterprise already underway.

North Korean fishing histories are thus not unique or exceptional, *sui generis* in space and place. While much media, academic and popular narrative asserts that North Korea is a place out of time, history and space, it is as connected to the themes of global development and politics as anywhere else, as riven by future crises and struggles as any other territory. Its fishing histories therefore have much in common with others in neighboring nations, who have been subjected to similar attempts at and processes of dispossession. Small South Korean fishing communities have been dispossessed by the exploitative modes of capital and debt bondage represented by the *Kaekchu* middlemen at the same time as the larger industrial complex of that nation's fisheries was busy engaging in the global dispossession and despoliation of the deep sea that was the trawling revolution. Chinese communities focused on fishing and sea products were dispossessed by European adventurism in the nineteenth century and are now crowded out by both the appropriation of space and place by speculative urbanism and rampant vulture and venture capital and by the environmental disaster generated by both global and local developmental agendas.

Conceptualizing Global and International Efforts at Sea Post-1945

A full history of globalization at sea would of course extend back, particularly when it comes to the waters of the Pacific, to Japan's efforts to develop a modern and technologically advanced maritime economy following the Meiji Restoration of 1868 and the defeat of the Russian Empire in 1905. Tokyo used its status as an early adopter of industrial and military technology, dominant regional position following 1905, and the annexation of Korea in 1907/1910 to develop practices and technologies of deep-sea fishing and canning. It eventually inherited in 1919, at the behest of the League of Nations, Germany's Southwest Pacific territories, which it then used to further develop its offshore capacities and oceanic reach, putting it within touching distance of Samoa and the United States' sphere of influence. This chapter is not such a full history, and starts in 1945 after the defeat of Japan, but at the start of the period in which the United States as the victor was thrown into a complicated symbiotic relationship with its former foe in order to contain the developing communist bloc and its allies.

Harry Truman (President between 1945 and 1953), responsible for the unwinding of America's war effort, and setting the course for future American interests in the Pacific, is renowned for the difficult decisions made across the former field of conflict. Koreans were astonished in 1945 when the United States Military Government in Korea, for example, decided to utilize much of the Japanese imperial government personnel and infrastructure on the Peninsula, rather than build up local Korean capabilities, essentially because the United States was concerned about the influence of communist agitators, and felt the Japanese had been effective administrators (Seth 2016, 93). Similarly, within two years of dropping two atomic bombs, American policy became more supportive of Tokyo, influenced by the fear of communist success in Asia and requiring a functional and useful ally in the area to serve as a bulwark and a base for American force projection against both communist China and the Soviet Union in the future (Cha 2000). Truman it seems was profoundly concerned with extending the maritime sovereignty of the United States across the Pacific, not simply to support its military and diplomatic capacities, but with globalizing intent, also to create opportunities for American business (Cowhey 1993). Truman and the Supreme Commander of Allied Powers (SCAP) (which occupied and governed Japan until 1952), were also concerned that Japan should not be too expensive and costly to occupy and that it should be capable of servicing its own food supply and other material needs (Johnson 2000). Thus, while American restrictions on Japanese fishing boats were quite severe in the initial months following the surrender, by the end of 1945, SCAP gave Japanese boats opportunities to fish further offshore (SCAP 1946, 88). Within eighteen months, SCAP was infuriating former war allies in Australia and New Zealand by allowing the Japanese whaling fleet to travel to access its former whaling grounds in the Antarctic (SCAP 1946, 68). Carmel Finley describes extraordinary policy shifts relating to tuna fishing and resource control in the Pacific, which had long been hugely important to the Californian fishing industry (Finley 2017). Former Japanese colonies such as those next to American Samoa and Guam became vitally important to the global supply chain for maritime products in the Pacific, but rather than exclusively as sites of enterprise for American companies, these were declared duty free areas and this included Japanese companies (Finley 2017, 69). Thus Japanese-owned tuna fishers were allowed to land catches in American Samoa and trans-ship their product to the American mainland free of tax or import charges. This act, resembling later trends of the globalizing, offshoring, and outsourcing of manufacturing industries, put mainland American tuna canneries and other businesses at a distinct disadvantage, and this aspect of the United States fishing industry followed its predecessor, the sardine canning industry into decline and eventual extinction (Finley 2017, 74). However, the policy served greater American aims by reducing the cost of fish products in the American food industry, securing notions of maritime sovereignty and control over the Pacific for the United States, underpinning the economic functionality and future of American colonial territories such as Samoa, and finally, integrating Japanese business and enterprise as well as wider diplomatic interests into the post-1945 status quo.

Such policies produced a flexible developmental landscape which as well as being underpinned and funded by this new globalizing, geopolitical reality found itself energized and enabled by developing scientific and statistical models derived in part from the work of fisheries scientists such as Johan Hjört and Michael Graham on the other side of the world (Finley 2011). Graham's "optimum catch" had developed following what Hjört and others referred to as the "second great fishing experiment," namely the European war of 1939–1945. While Hjört would not live long after the end of the war, Graham, now a vital figure in the infrastructure of fishing and maritime research, and other scientists such as H.R. Hulme continued working on a statistically minded and empirical approach which might counter the practices of overfishing, damaging to both fishers and fish populations alike (Smith 1994, 296). Graham's young protégé's Raymond Beverton and Sidney Holt ensconced at the United Kingdom Ministry of Agriculture, Fisheries, and Food, Lowestoft Fisheries Laboratory in the United Kingdom developed the theories of population dynamics as they pertained to fish which would go on to underpin globalized fishing (Smith 1994, 310). These theories, first published in the journal *Nature* as "Population Studies in Fisheries Biology" in 1947, took into account both fluctuations in population across the planet, fishing effort projected onto or at them, and the carrying capacity of the environment itself to articulate what has been described as the "steady state yield." This calculation was a twin of the analysis which produced an abstract notion of "optimal yield" which could be applied internationally (Smith 1994, 312).

President Truman's declarations of September 28, 1945 extending the United States claims over the sea bed and rights to fisheries in waters contiguous to it, made a dramatic impact on the geopolitics of the Pacific, however, they also provided the opportunity for this geopolitics to become further enmeshed in science and to begin reconfiguring statistical methodologies for international political goals. Just as Hjört and Graham drove forward the development of the scientific basis behind fisheries research and were heavily involved in the creation and foundation of new institutions and places of empiricism, the United States was home to an academic who would become central to the research and management framework befitting the new needs of the expansionist nation (Finley 2011, 55). Wilbert M. Chapman, a scientist from Washington State who had extensive experience of working within the state and federal fishing agencies, was tasked after 1945 with building the practical institutions on the ground in the United States' new Pacific mandates and new semi-colonies. Chapman was appointed to the State Department in Washington DC as an undersecretary for fisheries policy (Finley 2011, 57). Within the State Department, Chapman was a tireless organizer of the realities of US focus on the ocean, and very much at the behest of the close nexus between state power and business interest, as Carmel Finley recounts (Finley 2011, 88). He was known for his energy directed at two principle elements of United States policy toward the global oceans, firstly the creation for multi-national agencies to manage fishery and maritime resources, but which essentially placed scientific principle second behind geopolitical needs (Finley 2011, 88). Secondly, he was famous for the rationale that lay behind the activity which the United States would apply in, on, and under the high seas (Finley 2011, 88).

On January 16, 1949, via a State Department Bulletin, Chapman articulated how the fishing was to be undertaken in this new geopolitical and business world, including a graphic curve known as the Maximum Sustainable Yield curve in the document (Finley 2011, 94). While the curve looked, and still looks classically scientific, there were absolutely no statistics given and no references listed in the bulletin (Finley 2011, 94). In fact, the mathematical formulae which underpinned the curve were not made accessible for another five years, however, the curve was essentially used as a scientific fact by the United States from the moment it was released. Contrary to the science and approach that the Europeans and the Japanese had been seeking, Chapman was articulating an extremely utilitarian view of fisheries and the seas in which methodologies derived from industrial management were applied to the sea. Fish and the other living things in the sea are, as crops in a field, products to be harvested. Just as one would not leave wheat grown in a field to fail and rot, so to leave any more fish than were strictly necessary in the sea was to waste them (Finley 2011, 94). Chapman's concept included an assumption that fish populations would as Graham, Holt, Beverton, and others had ascertained, fluctuate and fall, but that they would at some point recover and return to a useful or functional level (Finley 2011, 95). Maximum Sustainable Yield held to the strange tautology that young fish are helped by the capture of old and large fish and the reduction in a population's food requirements, because that leaves more food and resources for the young fish (Finley 2011, 96). This is strictly counter to earlier analysis done of Sockeye Salmon populations in the Pacific, which suggested that removing the large and old fish from a population or impacting on their ability to create more generations of young fish, means that there will in the future simply be fewer fish of any size around (Finley 2011, 96). One of the fundamental problems of modern global fishing has been that fish are simply not allowed or left to get old or large, so notions of what is a large fish or what is an old fish begin to change, and fishermen themselves begin to misread and misremember species potential for growth and length (Stokstad 2007).

Maximum Sustainable Yield held that it was the impact of fishing and human effort according to Chapman's model that would stabilize populations; not going to sea or vigorously harvesting them would even result in less efficient, smaller, less useful stocks (Finley 2011, 95). While the United States demarcated its own maritime territories, the policy of the State Department with Chapman at the helm was to internationalize everything else, to the extent that local governments could only exert control over coastal waters—international waters were free game for the practices and policies of Maximum Sustainable Yield, no matter where they were in the world (Finley 2011, 96). The United States even pushed the idea in the face of considerable pressures from Latin American countries reacting against increased American tuna fishing and whaling in the oceanic commons. By 1955, the United Nations was so concerned about these global ructions that it held the International Technical Conference on the Conservation of the Living Resources of the Sea (Finley 2011, 134). At this conference, Chapman and his scientific colleague Schaefer, who had attempted to better theorize Maximum Sustainable Yield essentially defeated the arguments of the Europeans such as Graham and Holt, by appealing to the industrial and economic interests of their own countries (Finley 2011, 146). Disregarding aspects of the theory which might make overfishing worse or reduce catches, the Americans succeeded (supported unexpectedly throughout the conference by the Soviet Union, which was looking out for its own deep-sea interests across the globe), in maintaining the deep sea as a commons, though allowing for offshore economic zones, and in placing the concept of Maximum Sustainable Yield at the heart of the conference's conclusions, which were to form the basses for international law of the sea (Finley 2011, 148).

This would be the law of the global maritime commons for decades, and would involve not just the United States and the Soviet Union, but allied nations of the Warsaw Pact such as the People's Republic of Poland and the German Democratic Republic (East Germany) whose ships could be found across the world's oceans, and of course South Korea, which after the technological and developmental efforts of the Park Chung-hee government became something of a global fishing power. This was the law and the waters of course with which North Korea sought to engage. In the next section, the reader will encounter more of the wider history of North Korean fishing efforts, which are as is natural, colored by its own unusual ideological predilections. When it comes to the science behind the ideology and aspiration, however, as much as it sought to counter and negate the United States and its allies when it comes to Pyongyang's sense of what scientifically driven, developmentally modern fishing looked like, it was certainly not fishing "in our own style." Fishing under the Great and Dear Leaders was as rooted in conceptions of Maximum Sustainable Yield, optimum catch, and surplus populations as that which occurred under any capitalist nation, and its fishing strategies over the decades demonstrate this.

POLITICAL FISHING HISTORIES OF NORTH KOREA

Just as this chapter does not aim to give a comprehensive historical account of the development of fishing globally or in the Pacific, it will not go extensively or at length into the history of North Korean fishing.[2] It will not surprise the reader to hear the suggestion that fishing for North Korea was deeply connected both to the various periods of its political and ideological development, and as a developmental sector essentially aimed at a resource of the commons and therefore for the most part free, vital to its developmental strategies. It must be said categorically any efforts focused on the construction of a coherent periodization of North Korean fishing and fishing practices can only be termed political fishing histories. In North Korea, all aspects of life, development, social practice, invention, and governmentality are imbued and enmeshed with politics and ideology, there is virtually no escape from this for North Koreans living in North Korea and in this historical process, for the fishing sector this is also the case.

Fishing was vital to Kim Il Sung's ambitions from very early on in North Korea's history, in part to both build a new economy and to deconstruct Japanese efforts to Japanize Korean fisheries during the colonial era (Kim Il Sung 1948, 304). Fishing development was delayed by the chaos and destruction of the Korean War, but soon after the war institutional focus returned to the sector, in close relation to North Korea's close ally in its early years and technical supporter even in more complicated diplomatic times. Kim Il Sung even remarked on North Korean-Soviet interactions in 1957: "We invited Soviet scientists who were engaged on maritime research in the Far East. They came to our country under an agreement reached when our Government delegation visited Moscow last year." (Kim Il Sung 1957, 96) While the Soviet Union may have influenced North Korea's initial efforts on the seas and some of its first efforts at planning extractive goals, Stalin's death in 1953 drove a geopolitical turn toward Maoism and the People's Republic of China (Prybyla 1964). The implications of this for the wider strategies in North Korea's development have been also noted by analysts from the period (Kuark 1963). The Chollima movement, North Korea's developmental movement and response to Maoist urgency would generate statements on fishing such as; "We must intensify ideological education among the fishery officials and eradicate mysticism, empiricism and all other outdated ideas so that they will improve the fishing method zealously with the attitude of masters," (Kim Il Sung 1960, 38) and "Fish culture is a not a difficult job. A little effort and everyone will be able to," (Kim Il Sung 1960, 39), suggest that in these acute, urgent times it was not a time for fishing "experts."

North Korea more generally quickly attempted to avoid the collapse of the Great Leap Forward and the famine period following it in the PRC, reconnecting more fully with partners in the Soviet Union, while exploring further afield for new contacts in non-aligned nations. In the fishing sector, North Korea's strategy focused on reconfiguring its goal setting and institutional structures in a more coherent manner, especially focusing on technical capacity and technologies (Kim Il Sung 1968, 261). Notions of catch and capacity were, as said in the previous section, and as relayed by Soviet scientists and technicians to North Korea, rooted in and predicated on notions of Maximum Sustainable Yield and optimum catch, as much as was the case in the United States. Fish were there to be harvested, not conserved, and framed by Juche and other aspects of North Korean ideology, since man is the master of all things, a nation's aspiration must be to gather and extract as many fish as possible.[3]

Aside from the theoretical construction of what scientifically driven or modern fishing was, North Korea has always been as hampered by technical aspects as the sea. The size, tonnage, and capabilities of fishing boats and other fishing technology for North Korea have always been problematic. Pyongyang has always found it hard to manage the development of larger or more complicated boats, as well as the infrastructure required to produce such boats. For many years, North Korea sought to obtain these from the Soviet Union and other fishing nations of the Warsaw Pact, but in the late 1960s, this too became problematic: "The 450-ton trawler we are now producing has many shortcomings. [For example,] it can be used for fishing only in the Black Sea or the Baltic Sea… [and] it cannot be used in the Pacific Ocean where the waves are moderate (Kim Il Sung 1968, 55)." By the early 1970s, North Korea was engaged in reconfiguring its institutional framework and trying to carefully manage a few centers of maritime industrial excellence—for example, the Ryukdae (Ryuktae) Shipyard in the Komdok Island area near Sinpo city, South Hamgyong. This shipyard was to serve as such a center for the industry in the East Sea (Kim Il Sung 1968, 57). The primary site for this renewal of North Korea's fishing fleet and accompanying infrastructure was located at Chongjin's (Ch'ŏngjin) historically important port, where apart from Ryukdae's efforts to build mid-range ships of some 600–1,000 tons, North Korea sought to construct much larger vessels of between 3,000 and 10,000 tons (Kim Il Sung 1968, 57). From the perspective of 2018, it is possible to say that in fact North Korea never managed to reach these heights of boat and infrastructure production. Even in contemporary times of the Great Fish Hauls as announced in 2015's New Year's Address, fishing boats and processing technology are still a huge problem for North Korea.

Internationalizing North Korean Fishing Aspirations: Interactions in Soviet Institutional Archives and Memory

While it is possible for external readers to get a sense of the periodization of North Korean fishing efforts from its own publications, it has been to this point nigh on impossible to get a coherent sense of the reality of North Korea's historiography or the aspirations within it for development and success in the sector. FAO (Food and Agriculture Organization of the United Nations) fisheries statistics are notoriously complicated and troublesome, methodologies being reconfigured every few years anyway (FAO 1972). When it comes to North Korea, the FAO received one set of statistics in 1957 which were so outlandish that from that point 'til now the organization simply estimated and extrapolated the nation's statistics. Looking elsewhere to the statistics of the various commissions which manage the pelagic and anadromous fishing stocks of the Pacific, such as the North Pacific Fisheries Commission (NPFC), North Korean boats make no appearance, not even as illegal fishers (Taiwanese boats being the prime concern of the authorities of Japan, the United States and Canada). Thus while boats from the Soviet Union, the German Democratic Republic, and the People's Republic of Poland are all included within the documents by the NPFC, Pyongyang's boats are nowhere to be found (NPFC 1972). Fish for North Korea was important, lively matter, but perhaps Pyongyang was not successful at all in connecting with their vibrancy. This chapter, however, recounts a rare instance (in English,) of encounter with the fisheries archives of the Soviet Union, which most certainly has a place for North Korea's international efforts at sea within their historical narrative.

The author's interest in Soviet archives was first piqued a couple of years ago when North Korea's *Rodong Sinmun* reported on the meeting of the Joint Fisheries Commission of the Russian Federation and North Korea. A reading of past North Korean media reports suggested this commission had met for many years, but its publications and minutes were never publicly available and certainly not made available by North Korea. North Korea and the Soviet Union in fact set up the predecessor to the currently constituted Commission in the late 1960s following some twenty years of attempts at engagement on Moscow's part. This author had in fact never seen any of the reports issued by these committees, however recent visits to the Russian State Archive of the Economy have allowed access to all of the committees' previous reports and the documents that surround them. These certainly give an external, Soviet perspective on North Korea's fishing history and especially its success or otherwise in Moscow's institutional eyes.

Interestingly Soviet efforts toward conservation and the management of fisheries stocks were, counter to the imperatives of communist rationalism and international notions of Maximum Sustainable Yield not simply designed to extract resources from the sea at this time, so cannot be classified as seeking to dispossess the great treasury or commons of the ocean. The Soviet Union it seems had been very concerned to support North Korea's own efforts to develop its capabilities and capacities, perhaps to mitigate the cost of the various loans, credits and exchanges offered to Pyongyang by Moscow following the Korean War and to support relations between the two during the difficult politics following the death of Stalin and North Korea's dalliance with Beijing. Reports from the Ministry of Fisheries and VNIRO (Russian Research Institute of Fisheries and Oceanography) suggest that the Soviet Union had sought to connect with North Korean fisheries throughout most of the 1960s, especially to engage in researcher swaps and exchanges on each other's boats and ships (Joint Soviet-North Korean Fisheries Commission 1970a, 3). But contrary to Kim Il Sung's assertions in previous decades, they had never happened. Vladivostok's branch of VNIRO and the Russian Academy of Sciences Fisheries Section especially were concerned to develop joint projects in the Sea of Okhotsk, knowing that North Korea sought snow and other crabs for their value and for local markets and that stocks had declined within its territorial waters (Joint Soviet-North Korean Fisheries Commission 1970e, 2). There were, it seems, also a number of instances of illegal and dangerous fishing practices by North Korean boats in or near Soviet declared or territorial waters. After much negotiation and many false starts, North Korea and the Soviet Union signed a protocol on September 5, 1969 which established the joint Soviet-North Korea Fisheries Commission (Joint Soviet-North Korean Fisheries Commission 1970e, 1). The first meeting of the commission was delayed by Pyongyang's preparations for a Workers Party of Korea Congress (the 5th, eventually held in November 1970), but was held between February 26, and March 10, 1970 (Joint Soviet-North Korean Fisheries Commission 1970e, 4).

Soviet reports on the commission's meetings give a fairly thorough if frustrated view of what sounds like a complicated and difficult series of exchanges. North Korea's representatives are described as intransigent, setting the agenda ended up taking an entire day and that the Koreans were extremely reluctant to discuss the procedure (Joint Soviet-North Korean Fisheries Commission 1970e, 5). The Soviet Union on the other hand had wanted to discuss the granular details of fish stocks and the North Koreans perception of their own stocks and the framework of management and administrative principles governing joint exercises whereas the North Koreans were determined to discuss potential joint collaboration and interactions as soon as possible (Joint Soviet-North Korean Fisheries Commission 1970e, 6). The Soviet Union it seemed already had a careful and complicated network of restrictions and management around Kamchatka, the Sea of Okhotsk, and Sakhalin and even joint agreements on stock capacity with Japan (with whom, even in spite of very difficult relations given the post-war status quo on Sakhalin and the Kuriles, the Soviet Union had a joint fisheries commission), which North Korea was keen to avoid being constrained by (Joint Soviet-North Korean Fisheries Commission 1970e, 8). After much discussion the North Korean side agreed to abide by the wider restrictions on salmon fishing across the western Pacific which the Soviet Union subscribed to in collaboration with the Japanese (also quite possibly to avoid complicating relations with the United States and Canada on the subject of fishing for migratory species in the Pacific), as well as restrictions on crab fishing around Kamchatka, trawling the mid sea on the west coast of Kamchatka and herring fishing in the Gulf of Shelikov between mid-April and mid-July (herring fry season) (Joint Soviet-North Korean Fisheries Commission 1970e, 8). In exchange, the Soviet Union allowed Pyongyang to access the inshore waters of the Commander Islands, fish for flatfish around Kamchatka and Sakhalin, and access the herring fisheries of the Soviet area of the Bering Sea (Joint Soviet-North Korean Fisheries Commission 1970e, 8).

In exchange for these supplementary rights North Korea supplied the Soviet side with the details of its fleet and catch. According to the Korean side, its fishing fleet in 1969 had been some 35 boats, half medium-sized trawlers, and some purse seine boats[4] (Joint Soviet-North Korean Fisheries Commission 1970e, 7). North Korea also claimed to have four mother ships and four transport ships (having even bought two mother ships from the Netherlands) and had plans to two large trawlers with refrigeration capacity (Joint Soviet-North Korean Fisheries Commission 1970e, 7). These boats had caught in 1969, according to the North

Korean fishing experts, some 11000 tons of flatfish and 25000 tons of herring in the Sea of Okhotsk. In the Sea of Japan, North Korea claimed to have caught 1000 tons of pink salmon, 400000 tons of Pollack, up to 60000 tons of squid, and 15000 tons of crab (both hairy crab and snow crab) (Joint Soviet-North Korean Fisheries Commission 1970e, 7). The Soviet side thought these figures an understatement and that North Korea, in spite of its consent to restrictions sought to exploit Pacific salmon resources as much as possible and to exploit the highly endangered fur seal populations on Tyuleny Island off Sakhalin (Joint Soviet-North Korean Fisheries Commission 1970e, 7).

Despite their own concerns and lack of trust in the North Koreans, the Soviet Union in the joint commissions sought to negotiate joint research collaborations between fishing experts of both countries in 1970. While this seemed very difficult to set up in 1970 owing to the demands of the forthcoming Workers Party Congress on North Korea's scientific bureaucracy, the commission managed to come to an arrangement (Joint Soviet-North Korean Fisheries Commission 1970e, 4). Many complex challenges were overcome when it came to matters of responsibility and lines of control and even the issue raised by the North Koreans, that Soviet ships in the Pacific were subject to mandatory boarding rights in certain areas by foreign powers, and Pyongyang was absolutely keen to avoid any circumstance where hostile or unfriendly agencies might have access to North Korean workers and operatives on board Soviet ships far from its control. These joint exercises were to begin in late September 1970, the culmination of many years of effort on the part of the bureaucrats, diplomats, and scientists from the various Soviet institutions (Soviet Union Ministry of Fisheries Archive 1970a).

These efforts were to be severely challenged on September 28, 1970 when a highly urgent telegram found its way onto many desks across the Soviet Union. In the week that research cooperation efforts were supposed to begin on ships of both the USSR and North Korea, the telegram reported that a North Korean purse seine boat with its identifying marks illegally disguised had attempted to set its own nets across and above the nets of the Soviet Union's chief research ship, damaging them and the Soviet boat's floats beyond repair (Soviet Union Ministry of Fisheries Archive 1970b). Responses to the initial telegram revealed that this was not an isolated incident and that in fact, North Korean boats had been repeatedly disguising their identification marks and using incorrect or impossible to decipher marks on their nets and floats in the Sea of Okhotsk (Soviet Union Ministry of Fisheries Archive 1970c). Further telegrams from "Far East Fish" the "Fishing Cooperative of Kamchatka" reported near collisions and other dangerous interactions between North Korean boats and tugboats, an ocean-going barge, the Dagystanka, and a fishing trawler, the Kammeniy. Unsurprisingly interactions between the research institutions of the Soviet Union and North Korea which had been very carefully organized and negotiated earlier in the year were for the moment curtailed while authorities in Moscow reconsidered how to approach and engage a partner like Pyongyang (Soviet Union Ministry of Fisheries Archive 1970c).

While activities at sea were restricted in 1970, the Soviet Union decided to allow North Korean researchers to engage on land with the Ministry of Fisheries institutions near Vladivostok in Nakhodka. North Korean researchers were in the Soviet Union between December 15, 1970 and January 16, 1971 for what was a fact-finding mission for the Koreans and an exercise in epistemological training from the Soviets—according to the accounts it was an extremely difficult month (Soviet Union Ministry of Fisheries Archive 1971). The events of the previous year, which the Soviet institutions had essentially put down to some form of industrial sabotage, coupled with the complication of the discussions surrounding the joint research efforts had soured the mood between the two nations. The Soviet side considered the reasons for some of the more difficult moments in the discussions, such as North Korea's lack of willingness to allow any reciprocity in contract arrangement and complex negotiation over the legal framework and responsibilities for any of that nation's citizens on Soviet boats as exposing its institutions to moral hazard (Soviet Union Ministry of Fisheries Archive 1970d, 4). It appeared that there was a high-security risk in engagements with North Korean institutions and that under the guise of interest in fishing, Pyongyang could send intelligence operatives and engage primarily in industrial espionage on Soviet infrastructure and factories in the far east, but also to extract knowledge not available to it on fishing stocks and fishing areas in the Sea of Okhotsk and in the wider Pacific.

The exchange in 1970/1971 certainly did not begin in the most comfortable manner. In order to avoid issues of subterfuge, espionage, and security threat, the Soviet Union stipulated that none of the researchers or technicians sent by North Korea should have visited the area before or been involved in the institutions on the Soviet side in the past. Certainly none should have security or intelligence backgrounds, and essentially, all should have fishing and fishing research experience. Of course, North Korea claimed that none of its researchers had ever been in the Soviet Union before and all were trained and experienced fishing experts, but Soviet intelligence soon reported that one had been to college in the USSR and two had worked in their consulate in Vladivostok—a fourth member of the Korean team it was decided actually had nothing to do with the fishing industry and knew nothing about fishing at all (Soviet Union Ministry of Fisheries Archive 1970d, 6). The Ministry of Fisheries efforts to entertain the North Koreans continued to be combined with a concern for security and the obvious dangers of their potential efforts at subterfuge and espionage, concern which only grew when the Koreans appeared to be fairly consumed by the technological aspects of their visit to the extent that when they demanded the blueprints and layouts for the machinery in the various canning and preparation facilities they visited, the Soviet side actually restricted access (Soviet Union Ministry of Fisheries Archive 1970d, 2). Eventually, a reasonable negotiation of the problems was done by the Soviet side, with extensive reports in the documents of the North Koreans being refused visits to irrelevant infrastructure and careful management of their visits to technical or research institutions, so that they could not extract data or spend too long with technology that was delicate when it came to security matters. Of course, the documents also report a number of moments of push back from the North Koreans and frequent returns to their hotel rooms after difficult moments with their hosts, to review material at length or to communicate with North Korea (Soviet Union Ministry of Fisheries Archive 1971). Finally, in scenes familiar to watchers of North Korea in the present, the researchers, aside from their focus on machinery and technology, were fascinated by shopping opportunities in the fishing towns they visited—The Soviet Union's Ministry of Fishing even sent the North Koreans back to their own country with an extensive supply of Soviet crab, caviar, shrimp, and herring (Hong 1995).

These moments of complicated engagement between North Korea and the Soviet Union at sea in the 1970s are not the end of the story. Reports from the very end of the Soviet Union in 1989 and 1990 suggest that North Korea never gave up trying to extract value from the commons of its territorial waters, recording that Pyongyang had engaged in efforts during research exercises in the late 1980s to breach Soviet information security in Nakhodka and Vladivostok (Soviet Union Ministry of Fisheries Archive 1991, 3). North Korea had also developed an elaborate ruse by buying small trawlers from Japan and crewing them with Japanese fishermen who were instructed to insist that they were working on behalf of Japanese companies and to fish illegally in Soviet waters of Sakhalin and Kamchatka (Soviet Union Ministry of Fisheries Archive 1991, 4). When this was discovered, the Soviet Union fined North Korea millions of US dollars for such an extreme breach of protocol and restricted any further collaborative efforts (Soviet Union Ministry of Fisheries Archive 1991, 6). Whatever its own lack of capability, North Korea placed a huge value on attractive and valuable maritime species such as Snow Crab and Pollack and was willing to engage in all manner of behavior to get them with whatever resources it had to hand. Fish and fishing technologies it seems have always been hugely important to North Korea's institutional and developmental mind. The Soviet Union on the other hand, was extremely patient and determined to bring Pyongyang into its institutional fold when it came to fishing, perhaps because of the challenges presented by illegal North Korean fishing in its waters, perhaps to reduce the concerns of other nation's focused on the Pacific, perhaps even because of the residual sense of socialist fraternity between the two nations. Even North Korea's absurd acts of sabotage to long-negotiated and organized joint projects, a technique, behavior, and practice familiar to those attempting to engage Pyongyang in institutional development internationally throughout its history, and acts of espionage and subterfuge did not completely stop Soviet interest. Moscow's institutions were instead required to develop new strategies and levels of surveillance and security when working with North Korean boats and institutions. While North Korea is repeatedly dispossessed by circumstance and geopolitical positionality, it appears that Pyongyang was certainly not beneath or beyond dispossessing the commons or an ally when it came to fishing stocks and resources in the 1970s.

From Small Fry in the Western Pacific to Ghost Ships

North Korea as the reader of this chapter may know, was never to reach the heights of global fishing extraction managed by the Soviet Union during its existence. The Soviet Union and perhaps unlikely partners such as the Polish People's Republic and the German Democratic Republic would join the United States, Japan, South Korea, and Canada in the 1970s and 1980s as global fishing powers, the ships of these nations were found across the seas of the earth and at their farthest reaches. North Korea, in spite of efforts made in the 1970s as recounted by this chapter and later in its history would never be a great success. However, that has never stopped it aspiring to such success as seen in 2015's New Year's Address from Kim Jong Un, and in following years, which features seas (and mountains) of gold as a developmental imperative (Kim Jong Un 2015). As much as Kim Il Sung wanted, desired, and demanded it, North Korean fishing success on a global scale has never happened. The institutional redesign, scientific focus, and technological jump required by North Korea's fishing strategy in the late 1960s and 1970s produced very little. North Korean fishing boats seldom top 1000 tons, whereas South Korea's are in the tens of thousands.

While there is a relative wealth of information about North Korea's unwanted interactions with the Soviet Union at sea in the archives of Moscow's institutions, there is little elsewhere. Had North Korea even illicitly made efforts in the deeper waters of the Pacific, and taken its place among those global fishing nations, its presence would have been recorded. In order to ascertain the optimum population of different fishing ecologies, as well as to map the spreads of fish types and their migrations across the ocean, Japan, the United States, and Canada (sometimes joined by the Soviet Union), spent several decades through the auspices of the North Pacific Fisheries Commission (NPFC) and later the North Pacific Anadromous Fisheries Commission (NPAFC), engaged in labor and resource-intensive scientific expeditions. Over the years, careful sampling along lines of longitude in the middle of the Pacific would reveal, through studying the gut bacteria and parasites of salmon and other migratory (anadromous), fish, exactly which rivers these fish called home or returned to. Thus a salmon could be claimed as a Japanese salmon, a Canadian salmon, or an American salmon (even a Soviet salmon) (Finley 2011). As these, mainly Japanese research boats, plied their meticulous and slow furrows across the water, their crews took note of what other boats and vessels traveled nearby or alongside, either legally or illicitly. The reports of the NPFC, would have reported North Korean interlopers and poachers in the open ocean south of the Aleutian islands, if there were any. What unknown or illegal boats there were almost invariably turned out to be Taiwanese fishermen sailing anonymously or under an assumed flag, and not once in the detailed records of the NPFC or NPAFC were North Korean boats sighted (Winstanley-Chesters 2020).

But North Korea could not resist attempting at least to make good its more recent claims to fishing capability and a place in the global maritime enterprise, and so it seems sought to develop its tuna fishing capacity. However, doing so did not exactly generate the "great fish hauls" of Kim Jong Un's aspiration. When North Korea finally successfully joined the West and Central Pacific Fisheries Commission (WCPFC), (an organization set up to manage the tuna and migratory fish in the waters around the Federated Republic of Micronesia, Vanuatu, Nauru and the other island archipelago nations of this area of the Pacific), in 2014 after many years of trying and diplomatic push and pull, its first membership of such an organization it was required to submit useful and legitimate data on its fishing efforts in the area (West and Central Pacific Fisheries Commission 2014a). Extraordinarily, this North Korea did, providing what to this date are the only reasonable and functional statistics on its fishing efforts and catch size in the wider Pacific area since its submission to the Soviet Joint Commission in the 1970s. These statistics reveal the minuscule scale of North Korea's contemporary fishing capabilities and effort in the area, comprising only two small purse seine boats and one long line boat, collecting in total a sum of some 368 tons of tuna in 2014 (West and Central Pacific Fisheries Commission 2014b).

Ultimately Pyongyang's efforts in the deep sea have been so small as to scarcely register against the extractive and accumulative ambitions of the great nations of the ocean. In the evidential terms necessary for conventional historical narratives, North Korea is normally entirely opaque and corroboration of events is almost impossible. However, access to the Soviet archives has certainly challenged this frequently used truism for this author and has provided the evidence for this revealing chapter. Intriguingly while the amount of fish extracted by Korea is small globally, the impact of its fishing efforts and their impact on both its own population and regional ecologies has been much greater. In recent years its Ghost Ships and unexpected fleets have plagued the Japanese coastline and caused maritime legal issues for the Russian Federation. In 2020 however, the global pandemic of SARS Cov2, kept North Korean boats at home, just as China's "dark fleets" traversed the world's oceans extracting infinitely more fish and other maritime resources than Pyongyang's efforts ever could. While North Korea's subterfuge and unwanted and unexpected fishing efforts in the Sea of Okhotsk in the 1970s were troublesome to the Soviet Union and threatened scare fish populations and delicate ecologies, this contemporary global maritime threat endangers global ecosystems at an entirely different level.

NOTES

1. The author recommends both his previous book connected to the subject (Winstanley-Chesters 2020) and the work of Carmel Finley (2011, 2017), if the reader requires one.
2. This author has already published a fairly comprehensive account of the strategies, processes, ideologies and themes of North Korea's approach to the sector (Winstanley-Chesters 2016).
3. Juche (or Juché, Chuch'e as it is often spelt), is perhaps the ideological form North Korea is most famous for. Claimed to be the unique idea of Kim Il Sung, it is an unsystematic melange of autocratic aspiration, metaphysical nationalism and a transcendental sense of collectivization. It has been frequently analyzed, and very heatedly debated as a concept for decades by scholars. Perhaps the most helpful if contradictory works on the subject and its analysis for the initiated are by Park (2002) and Myers (2010).
4. Purse seine fishing is a technique of fishing that uses a net which has at its base a set of rings of concentric sizes. Through these rings runs a fishing line, known as the purse line, which when pulled upwards draws all the rings close together and prevents fish from escaping the bottom of the net. This technique is particularly used against fish species that school together, such as herring and mackerel. It is also heavily regulated as a technique because of its efficiency and the fact that an entire local population can be caught at once in the net.

REFERENCES

Cha, Victor. 2000. "Abandonment, Entrapment, and Neoclassical Realism in Asia: The United States, Japan, and Korea." *International Studies Quarterly* 44 (2): 261–291.
Cowhey, Peter. 1993. "Domestic Institutions and the Credibility of International Commitment: Japan and the United States." *International Organization* 47 (2): 299–326.
FAO. 1972. *"Fisheries Statistics Yearbook."* Geneva: United Nations.

Finley, Carmel. 2011. *All the Fish in the Sea: Maximum Sustainable Yield and the Failure of Fisheries Management*. Chicago, IL: Chicago University Press.
Finley, Carmel. 2017. *All the Boats in the Ocean: How Government Subsides led to Global Overfishing*. Chicago, IL: Chicago University Press.
Hong, Seung-yong. 1995. "Marine Policy in the Republic of Korea." *Marine Policy* 19 (2): 97–113.
Johnson, Chalmers. 2000. *Blowback: The Costs and Consequences of American Empire*. London: Macmillan.
Kim Il Sung. 1948. "On Developing the Fishing Industry on a New Basis." *Works*, Vol. 4, Pyongyang: Foreign Languages Publishing House.
Kim Il Sung. 1957. "On the Development of the Fishing Industry." *Works*, Vol. 11, Pyongyang: Foreign Languages Publishing House.
Kim Il Sung. 1960. "On the Tasks of the Party Organizations in South Pyongan Province." *Works*, Vol. 14, Pyongyang: Foreign Languages Publishing House.
Kim Il Sung. 1968. "For Bringing About Rapid Progress in the Fishing Industry." *Works*, Vol. 22, Pyongyang: Foreign Languages Publishing House.
Kim Jong Un. 'New Year's Address, 2015', *Rodong Sinmun*, January 1, 2015.
Kuark, Yoon. 1963. "North Korea's Agricultural Development during the Post-War Period." *The China Quarterly* 14 (2): 82–93.
Myers, Brian Reynolds. 2010. *The Cleanest Race: How North Koreans See Themselves and Why it Matters*. New York: Melville House.
North Pacific Fisheries Commission. 1972. *"Annual Report 1972."* San Francisco: NPFC.
Park, Han S. 2002. *North Korea: The Politics of Unconventional Wisdom*. Boulder, CO: Lynne Reinner.
Park, Jaeyoon, Jungsam Lee, Katherine Seto, Timothy Hochberg, Brian A. Wong, Nathan A. Miller, Kenji Takasaki et al. 2020. "Illuminating dark fishing fleets in North Korea." *Science Advances* 6(30): eabb1197.
Prybyla, Jan. 1964. "Soviet and Chinese. Economic Competition within the Communist World." *Soviet Studies* 15(4): 464–473.
Seth, Michael. 2016. *A Concise History of Modern Korea: From the Late Nineteenth Century to the Present*. Lanham, MD: Rowman & Littlefield.
Smith, Tim. 1994. *Scaling Fisheries: The Science of Measuring the Effects of Fishing, 1855–1955*. Cambridge: Cambridge University Press.
Soviet Union Ministry of Fisheries Archive. 1970a. "The Soviet Union delegation's account of work on session of Joint Soviet – North Korean Fisheries Commission." Russian State Archive of the Economy, Fondy, 8202-20-2323.
Soviet Union Ministry of Fisheries Archive. 1970b. "Urgent Telegram from USSR Ministry of Communications 'Urgent Moscow harbour to Ishkov Dal'ryba (FarEastFish) to Starzinskiy,'" September 28. Russian State Archive of the Economy, Fondy, 8202-20-2323.

Soviet Union Ministry of Fisheries Archive. 1970c. "Letter to D. Gafin from Volkov A.A," September 28. Russian State Archive of the Economy, Fondy, 8202-20-2323.
Soviet Union Ministry of Fisheries Archive. 1970d. "A list of violations committed by DPRK boats fishing in the Sea of Okhotsk regarding the Regulations for Preventing Collisions at Sea and the fisheries regulations." October. Russian State Archive of the Economy, Fondy, 8202-20-2323.
Soviet Union Ministry of Fisheries Archive. 1970e. "The Soviet Union delegation's account of work on session of Joint Soviet – North Korean Fisheries Commission." Russian State Archive of the Economy, Fondy, 8202-20-2323.
Soviet Union Ministry of Fisheries Archive. 1971. "A report on the work with Korean delegation during a period of 15 December 1970 until 16 January 1971." 29 January. Russian State Archive of the Economy, Fondy, 8202-22-468.
Soviet Union Ministry of Fisheries Archive. 1991. "Report on the activities of the [Overseas] Office of the USSR Ministry of fisheries in the DPRK during 1990." January 28, p. 3. Russian State Archive of the Economy, Fondy, 8202-23-1869.
Stokstad, Erik. 2007. "The Incredible Shrinking Cod," *Science*, January 31, 2008. Accessed 27 April, 2019. https://www.sciencemag.org/news/2007/01/incredible-shrinking-cod.
Supreme Commander for the Allied Powers. 1946. *Summation of Non-Military Activities in Japan and Korea*, No 9, June, 1946, Tokyo: Supreme Commander for the Allied Powers Japan.
Western and Central Fisheries Commission, *Report on admission of North Korea*, August, 2014. Marianas Islands: Phonpei.
Western and Central Fisheries Commission, *Report on admission of North Korea*, *Letter from Ri Hyok, North Korean Minister of Fisheries*, August 5 2014. Marianas Islands: Phonpei.
Winstanley-Chesters, Robert. 2016. "Politics and Pollack: maritime development paradigms under the Kims." In *Change and Continuity in North Korean Politics*, edited by Winstanley-Chesters, R., Cathcart, A., and Green, C., London: Routledge.
Winstanley-Chesters, Robert. 2020. "Ghost Ships as Spectral Geography: An Introduction to North Korean Necro-Mobilities." *International Journal of Diaspora and Cultural Criticism* 10 (2): 149–183.

Index

A
The Admiral: Roaring Currents
   film, 30, 39
ancestor worship, 297
anti-multiculturalism, 272
April 19 Revolution, 294
Arirang, 17, 18, 152, 153
Arpan
   multicultural literature, 266
Asian Financial Crisis, 6, 123
Assassination, 30, 31, 44–48, 54

B
B.A.P.
   Band, 174
Big Bang
   Band, 171, 175
black markets, 11
Block B
   Band, 172, 180
BTS
   Band, 167, 175, 179, 180

C
Chaebol, 37–39, 45, 52, 296
ch'angguk
   form of music, 126–128
changmadang. *See* black markets;
   marketization
Chinese characters
   case for and against teaching them, 209
   Hantcha, 184, 193–195, 197–199, 208–210, 212, 215
Chongryon, 256, 257, 311–325, 327–332
   definition, 312
Chosŏnhakkyo, 312, 313, 316, 321
Chun Doo Hwan, 7, 60, 61, 64, 66, 70, 72, 74, 78
   embezzlement charges, 61
Chu Si-gyŏng, 183, 191
cinema
   South Korean domestic cinema, 7
CJ Entertainment, 38
Comfort Women, 32, 44, 45, 50–52, 151, 200

CPC
  Cultural Properties Committee, 144, 146, 147, 150
Crossroads of Youth
  flim, 123
Cultural Heritage Protection Act, 144, 145

D
dark fleets
  (China), 338, 358
Daudet, Alphonse, 189
demographic changes, 253
diaspora
  Korean diaspora, 23, 188, 199, 254, 255, 262, 264
Ditto
  film, 124
DPRK
  as autarkic, 13
Dreamcatcher
  Band, 169, 171

E
EFL textbooks, 312, 313, 316, 317, 319, 320, 327, 331

F
famine
  in the DPRK, 11, 84–86, 90–92, 102, 106, 107, 348
father figure
  in DPRK film, 105, 106, 126, 130. *See also* Socialist Realism
filiality rights, 307
filial piety, 291–293, 296–299, 301–306

G
G-Dragon
  Singer, 171, 176
ghost ships
  in the DPRK, 339
globalization, 1–5, 9, 13, 22, 23, 31, 114, 119, 121, 136, 152, 195, 200, 204, 212, 214, 253, 256, 262, 337, 339, 342
  definition, 1
Grand National Party, 68, 77

H
Hagusobang
  Chongryon Publisher, 316, 320
hallyu
  Korean Wave, 6, 19, 21, 162
Halmŏni
  proprietor of granny restaurant, 230, 233–239, 244–246
Hangul, 50, 183, 185, 191, 194, 198, 201–204, 208–210, 216, 219, 221
Hantcha. *See* Chinese characters
Han Yong-un, 189–191, 211
"Headlock"
  multicultural literature, 276
Hell Joseon, 278
Hinomaru
  Japanese flag, 40, 46, 48, 51
historical film
  definition, 64
"Homecoming"
  multicultural literature, 280
Human Rights
  Universal Declaration of Human Rights, 293
human rights, 62, 87, 255, 257, 289–296, 298, 302–306
Hunmin chŏng'ŭm, 193
Hyo. *See* filial piety

INDEX 365

I
I Can Speak
film, 42, 44, 48, 50–55
Impolite language
in Korean, 228
impoliteness, 184, 185, 225–227,
229, 232, 233, 236, 237, 239,
240, 242, 243, 245, 246, 248
impoliteness strategies
Culpeper, 232, 233, 239
Im Su-gyŏng, 16
Inoki, Antonio, 17
(Kanji Inoki), 17
intentional fallacy, 89
intermediality, 167
definition, 166
ironic reading
approach to DPRK literature, 90

K
kapchil, 224
karate, 152
Kim Dae Jung, 7, 9, 41, 95
Kim Il Sung, 11, 13, 15, 85, 89, 94,
106, 107, 314, 319, 321, 322,
327, 330–332, 348, 349, 351,
357, 359
Kim Jong Un, 12, 319, 327, 357,
358
Kim Young Sam, 5, 7
KOFIC
Korean Film Council, 6–8
Korean War, 19, 23, 39, 65, 71, 118,
122, 143, 200, 260, 276, 281,
303, 321, 348, 351
Korean wave. *See hallyu*
Koryŏmal, 207
K-pop, 19, 22, 114, 115, 154,
162–164, 166, 176, 178, 248
K-slang, 248
kugak

traditional national music, 119,
120, 128, 154, 155
Kuleshov effect, 72
Kwangju Uprising, 33, 60, 61, 64, 67
details of the massacre, 60
Kyokujitsu-ki. *See* Rising Sun

L
loanword
from Japanese, 191

M
Mangyongdae, 323
maritime commons, 342, 347
marketization, 12, 32, 86, 87, 102,
106
Maximum Sustainable Yield
(fishing), 342, 345–347, 349, 351
May 18, 60, 61, 67, 73, 74, 77, 79,
216, 294
meta-authorial
approach to DPRK literature, 89,
90
migrant worker, 274
minjung, 127, 277
The Mother
Gorky novel, 89
Muhammad Ali, 17
multiculturalism, 262, 263
multicultural literature, 259, 264,
265, 268, 274
The Muslim Butcher
multicultural literature, 260, 267,
269
My Way
film, 41, 65

N
Namaste
multicultural literature, 274, 275

neologism, 204
  in Korean, 192, 195, 205, 206
N-generation
  definition, 206
NICP
  National Intangible Cultural Property, 144, 146–148, 150
1988 Olympic Games, 14, 93
Normalization Treaty
  with Japan (1965), 315
North Pacific Fisheries Commission (NPFC), 350

O
Obalt'an
  flim, 123

P
panmal
  lower level language, 224, 229, 233, 234
p'ansori, 114, 115, 118–120, 126, 128–134, 136, 137, 148
  definition, 113
Park Chung Hee, 36, 37, 39, 51, 60, 143, 347
Park Geun-hye, 32, 35–39, 42, 44, 45, 48, 51, 52, 57, 272
Pavane for a Dead Princess
  multicultural literature, 268
Peppermint Candy
  film, 61
A Petal, 61, 62, 64, 77, 78
physiognomy, 267
PIFF
  Pyongyang International Film Festival, 101
ponmyŏng
  Christian name, 212
poverty
  amongst the elderly, 299

R
Reader-recognisant Meta-Authorial Reading
  approach to DPRK literature, 91
Rising Sun
  Flag, 42

S
Sadae chuŭi
  definition, 195
sanctions
  (against the DPRK), 4, 12, 339
The Schoolgirl's Diary
  DPRK film, 83, 85, 88, 94, 97, 103–108
segyehwa, 3, 21, 23, 113, 253
  significance of term, 6
Sejong, 193, 197–199
Shin Sang-ok
  ROK/DPRK film director, 19, 20, 95, 103
Shinzo, Abe, 45, 51
Shiri
  significance of, 29
The Silenced
  film, 44
Snow Melts in Spring
  DPRK film, 93, 94
Socialist Realism, 89, 106, 108
Sopyonje, 113–115, 117–120, 123, 125, 126, 131–137
  famous long take sequence, 137
Soviet Union, 2, 15, 19, 85, 316, 338, 340, 341, 343, 347–358
Spirits' Homecoming
  film, 45, 51, 54
Super Junior
  Band, 168, 171, 180
swearing granny restaurants, 184, 224, 225, 229, 244, 247
Swear words, 227
Syngman Rhee, 256

T
taekwondo, 152
t'alchum
  mask-dance drama, 127
Tamunhwa munhak. See multicultural literature
tanil minjok, 259, 261
A Taxi Driver, 61, 62, 64, 66, 77
13th World Festival of Youth and Students, 15, 17
Time travel film, 124
Tongbang yeŭi chi kuk
  The Nation of Propriety in the East, 248
The Tooth and The Nail film, 47, 51, 54
T.O.P.
  Band, 167
  Band member, 175
transnational families
  in Korea, 254

Truman, Harry, 343, 345
26 Years
  film, 33, 59, 63–68, 70, 72–74, 77, 78
2009: Lost Memories
  film, 125

U
UNESCO, 141, 143, 151–153, 155, 156

Y
Yi Myŏng-bak, 68
Yokchaengi halmŏni ŭmshikchŏm. See swearing granny restaurants

Z
Zany Bros, 166, 168, 177, 178

Printed in the United States
by Baker & Taylor Publisher Services